Roman Catholicism in America

Columbia Contemporary American Religion Series

The United States is the birthplace of religious pluralism, and the spiritual landscape of contemporary America is as varied and complex as that of any country in the world. The books in this new series, written by leading scholars for students and general readers alike, fall into two categories: some of these well-crafted, thought-provoking portraits of the country's major religious groups describe and explain particular religious practices and rituals, beliefs, and major challenges facing a given community today. Others explore current themes and topics in American religion that cut across denominational lines. The texts are supplemented with carefully selected photographs and artwork, annotated bibliographies, concise profiles of important individuals, and chronologies of major events.

—

Islam in America
JANE I. SMITH

Roman Catholicism in America
CHESTER GILLIS

ROMAN CATHOLICISM

in America

Chester Gillis

COLUMBIA UNIVERSITY PRESS

NEW YORK

COLUMBIA UNIVERSITY PRESS
Publishers Since 1893
New York, Chichester, West Sussex
Copyright © 1999 Columbia University Press

Library of Congress Cataloging-in-Publication Data
Gillis, Chester, 1951–
  Roman Catholicism in America / Chester Gillis.
      p.   cm. — (Columbia contemporary American religion series)
  Includes bibliographical references and index.
  ISBN 0-231-10870-2 (hardcover). —ISBN 0-231-10871-0 (pbk.)
  1. Catholic Church—United States—History. 2. United States—
  Church history. I. Title. II. Series.
BX1406.2.G45   1999
282'.73—dc21
                                                                    99-17945
                                                                       CIP

Casebound editions of Columbia University Press books are printed
on permanent and durable acid-free paper.
Printed in the United States of America
c 10 9 8 7 6 5 4 3
p 10 9 8 7 6 5 4 3 2 1

For Marie Varley Gillis

and

in memory of

Lauren Jeanne Gillis

1975–1997

"In Every Living Thing Is the Spirit to Be Free"

CONTENTS

ACKNOWLEDGMENTS

While I was writing this book, my wife and I had friends in for dinner. One of them, Diana Lawrence, picked up a copy of the incomplete manuscript next to the computer in my office. When she emerged half an hour later, Diana, a Catholic, said she could identify herself and many friends in the text. That simple event convinced me that others would likely recognize themselves as well. And that hopefully, non-Catholics who read the book will also be able to identify what distinguishes Catholics from others, religious and secular, in America today.

The challenge to fit American Catholicism between the covers of a single volume required much capable assistance. I thank James Warren, my editor at Columbia University Press, who conceived the Columbia Contemporary American Religion series and who ably guided this book from conception to completion; the Landegger Foundation in New York for the generous research grant.

At Notre Dame: the Cushwa Center for the Study of American Catholicism at the University of Notre Dame for the research and travel grant; John Haas and Barbara Lockwood for their hospitality; and American Catholic Church historian Scott Appleby for his insightful comments on a draft of the text; the staff of the University of Notre Dame Archives, who assist every researcher competently and courteously.

In Washington, D.C.: Members of my department at Georgetown University, John Haught, Otto Hentz, S.J., Elizabeth McKeown, Vincent Miller, Theresa Sanders, and James Walsh, S.J., for their careful reading and helpful comments on various drafts of the manuscript; Marilyn G. Dunphy, for her valuable suggestions from her perspective as a laywoman; Page Salazar, the book buyer for the Freer and Sackler Galleries of the Smithsonian Institution, who not only reviewed the manuscript, but expanded and improved it considerably; feminist theologian Mary Hunt offered suggestions that sharpened my focus on a number of points.

Jay Dolan, historian from the University of Notre Dame, carefully read the manuscript and offered suggestions for improvement and in his work provided me with a model for how to relate history to a wide audience. Sister Mary Fisher went through the text line by line to improve the style and writing and offered useful additions as well. Ross Hess, Theology Department student research assistant, spent time and expertise tracking down sources, documents, and references and helped me keep my sense of humor during the process. Another student, Alexander Timchak, carefully proofread the manuscript. Sean Corry, from Georgetown's Academic Computer Center, performed delicate surgery to retrieve files on a badly damaged disk containing three chapters of the manuscript, and Chris Davis, student-assistant in the Theology Department, skillfully created tables and graphs. My thanks also go to the staff of Woodstock Theological Library, who not only helped me find things but permitted a significant portion of their collection on American Catholicism to lay on the floor of my office for the past year.

My wife, Marie, and my daughter, Alison, supported my efforts and tolerated my absence during the long days that such a project inevitably renders.

Roman Catholicism in America

INTRODUCTION

The picture of Pope John Paul II at Camden Yards baseball park in Baltimore is on the cover of this book because it represents a good deal about Roman Catholicism in America. In October 1995, tens of thousands of people came to Camden Yards for a celebration of the Eucharist because the pope was presiding. No one represents the institution of *Roman* Catholicism more than the pope. This may have been a celebration of the American church, but the pope, who is the bishop of Rome, is also the hierarchical head of the church all over the world. The American church is under the guidance of Rome. The celebration took place in Baltimore, the founding diocese of the American church with roots going back to John Carroll, the first bishop in America.

The mass was celebrated in Oriole Park at Camden Yards, at the time a brand new stadium intentionally built to resemble an old one, like Fenway Park in Boston, with the city as a backdrop and a warehouse over the right field wall. It is a state-of-the-art facility with an air of nostalgia.

This is not unlike the church in America, a part of the richest and most technologically advanced society, but holding on to a tradition that ties it to antiquity. The mass in Camden Yards was one of the highlights of the pope's visit to America in October 1995. But, as with a baseball game, even an important one like a playoff or part of a world series, people came in droves to watch, but they returned the next day to their lives, and routines, little changed after the event. American Catholics seem to enjoy the pageantry of the papacy and are charmed by the personality of the pope. Yet the majority fail to agree with him on issues such as birth control, clerical celibacy, women's place in the church, capital punishment, and nuclear arms.

This book deals with Catholic identity and community in America—from without and within. How would a stranger to Catholicism identify a Catholic: by his/her beliefs, religious practices, ethics, politics, economic status, education, profession, family life, or social circle? Judging by externals, it is often difficult to distinguish a contemporary Catholic from a non-Catholic. In the first half of the twentieth century it was possible to recognize American Catholics by their immigrant status, their public and unique religious practices (for example, abstinence from meat on Fridays—a practice some American bishops proposed reviving in 1997), and their loyalty to the Vatican, in Rome. But even the most articulate and informed Catholics do not find it easy to define what it means to be a Catholic in America today. Many disagree with Vatican teachings on birth control, premarital sex, homosexuality, and assisted suicide; on church disciplines such as mandatory celibacy for priests and the exclusion of women from the priesthood; or theological positions such as the mediation of a priest for the reconciliation of sin; and on church regulations such as those governing divorce and inter-communion.

Yet there remain significant differences that distinguish Catholics from other religions and Protestant Christianity in the United States. Celibate clergy, the religious leadership of the pope, the celebration of seven sacraments coupled with a spirituality that sees the world itself as sacramental, and being part of the largest denomination in the world, are aspects of their faith that set them apart. Catholics also have a distinct history within America. Until fairly recently they have been outsiders politically and culturally in America, often distrusted and ghettoized by mainstream Protestant America. Their church is hierarchical with the highest echelons of power situated in Rome. Their religious beliefs are steeped in a tradition carefully articulated over a period of almost two thousand years. They operate a school system second in size only to the public system, educating and inculturating their own and increasingly educating also a non-Catholic population in urban centers. They created a subculture in America that included professional associations, recreational opportunities, schools, neighborhoods and investment clubs as well as spiritual activities. They have constituted a clearly identifiable group that in the past forty years has been increasingly assimilated into larger cultural patterns.

Although written in a different era, that is, after the changes instituted by the Second Vatican Council (the 1962 to 1965 meeting of the bishops of the world with the pope to set a direction for the future of Catholicism), this book echoes the observation of Jaroslav Pelikan, in his 1959 book, *The Riddle of Roman Catholicism*, that "many Americans are poorly informed about the Roman church."[1] Roman Catholicism is mysterious, particularly for Protestants; and Pelikan attempted to explain the Roman church to them, although his work was informative for Catholics as well.

Today, the religious landscape in America boasts greater diversity than it did in 1959. Muslims, Hindus, Buddhists, Sikhs, Jains, and New-Age practitioners as well as other religious groups, constitute a significant and growing presence in America. This work is a portrait of the largest denomination in the United States. It describes the history of the church and the character of the community of Catholics today. I explore the worship, practices, beliefs and structures of Catholicism found universally within the church and given particular expression in America.

The book explores the interplay between the universal and the particular: Roman Catholicism is a world religion, but its expression in America is a national and often local one that deviates in various ways and to various degrees from the formal and universal conception and expression of Catholicism. I also survey the myriad challenges that confront the contemporary church. Not the least of these challenges is the complex relationship between Roman Catholicism as it is articulated in doctrines, dogmas, councils, papal encyclicals, and pastoral letters from the bishops, and Catholicism that is lived by persons in the pews or even those who do not frequent the pews but still consider themselves Catholics, so-called "nominal" or "cultural" Catholics.

A preliminary word of caution: there is no definitive portrait of Roman Catholicism in America. What the Catholic historian Jay Dolan wrote in 1984 is more apparent now than then: "A new Catholicism has come to life during the past two decades, and one of its most striking features is pluralism,"[2] that is, its diversity in beliefs, practices, and practitioners. Contemporary Catholicism in America shows the face of every person: the successful business executive, the newly arrived immigrant from Latin America or Southeast Asia, the senator, the university president, the auto worker, the artist, the janitor, the national journalist, the store clerk, the partner in a law firm, the supreme court justice. Socially and politically, contemporary Catholics are more diverse and less identifiable than their predecessors. There is also an increased pluralism of belief among them religiously. And while they may not look to the church for answers to all of their questions, the culture of Catholicism is deeply embedded within them. They present their children in the church for baptism; they know the "Hail Mary" by

heart; they understand what it means to develop a personal and a social conscience; they check "Catholic" on forms that ask their religion.

The church in the United States is pluralistic because it is embedded in
the most diverse and pluralistic society in history and because there is simply no singular experience of Catholicism. Roman Catholicism represents a
long and complex history beginning with the life of Jesus and developing
into a community that continues into the third millennium. It is a living
body—of people, of doctrines, of interpretations, of actions. Those who
argue that the church should adhere to an unchanged and unchanging tradition, have only to review the tradition to know how much the church has
changed. Those who insist that the church is free to be and profess anything
desired by its contemporary community also need to examine tradition to
learn that the church's continuity is predicated on the preservation of tradition. Any tradition that is ongoing is also forever changing. The changes
are often slow and subtle yet when examined historically, they are pronounced. It is the static notion of tradition that gives rise to radical difference between contemporary embodiments of the church and historical ones.
Unfortunately many Catholics view change and tradition in opposition,
when in reality tradition itself changes.

Eugene Kennedy, a psychologist who studies American Catholics,
describes two cultures of Catholics:[3] "Culture One Catholics" identify with
the traditional institutional structures of the church; "Culture Two
Catholics," though less inclined to follow institutional directives to the letter, still consider themselves Catholic. These two cultures coexist, sometimes harmoniously, sometimes not. Both types are living in America, wor-
shiping side by side, some sending their children to the same parochial
schools. Culture One Catholics listen to the Vatican and attempt to comply
with the pope's directives. Culture Two Catholics filter out, ignore, or resist
Vatican teachings with which they disagree. Often they claim that the teachings do not reflect an adequate grasp of the realities of contemporary life,
or more specifically, of American life or of the Catholic tradition and the
gospel message. However, Culture Two Catholics are not the same as "cultural" (or nominal) Catholics. "Cultural" Catholics have an occasional and
distant relationship with the church. They are baptized, have been married
in the church, and intend to be buried from the church; but they are otherwise unobservant and uninterested. They know vaguely that the church is
changing, but they cannot say how. They know a few basic prayers and rituals but understand little about the history, theology, or practice of the
church. Culture Two Catholics look to the church spiritually and emotion-

ally as a source of meaning, a foundation of tradition, and a teacher of religious and moral values. They are, however, indifferent to the intricacies of institutional Catholicism constructed by the pope and the bishops. Kennedy argues that Culture One is passing away. This book testifies, on the contrary, that it remains alive and well in America although it does not represent the majority of Catholics.

Some contemporary authors write about a "crisis" in American Catholicism. They interpret the tensions between the Vatican and the American laity as a foreshadowing of schism. But church history teaches us that no pope has led the church without tensions, and that no pope's reign lasts forever. In recent times the shift from Pius XII to John XXIII had dramatic consequences for the church; the later pope opened the church to the modern world by convening the Second Vatican Council in Rome at which the world's bishops promulgated documents that changed the ways in which Catholicism was practiced, such as using English instead of Latin for the liturgy in America. It is true that there are many American Catholics who assess John Paul II as intransigent and controlling. It is also true that there are American Catholics who think that he has not gone far enough to enforce orthodoxy and assert authority. Either way, there is no denying that American Catholicism at the end of the twentieth century is a church marked by diversity and difference. Catholics differ with one another about authority, abortion, issues of sex and gender, social and ethical concerns, and even spirituality. They differ with the Vatican on the same issues and the more central issues of identity and control: who is the church and who should be making the rules? Fifty years ago these were not questions. Catholics thought of the church as the hierarchy and ceded virtually all authority to administer the church to the pope, bishops, and priests, in that order. The laity were the footsoldiers in the army of Christ. The inspiration, they believed, came from God, but the orders came from the church's elite, those blessed with the sacrament reserved for them alone, the ordained. Those twice ordained, the bishops, were doubly revered.

A second theme, in addition to the interplay between universality and particularity, is the role of authority—what constitutes it, who exercises it, and do Catholics acknowledge it? Is personal experience more authoritative than papal power? Is a Marian apparition more compelling than a sacrament? Is celibacy a holier state than marriage? In what ways is the American Catholic Church independent of Rome and in what ways bound by Rome's authority? Discerning who has authority and what is authoritative for American Catholics reveals an often underlying and sometimes explicit

tension for individual Catholics and the American church as a whole—a
tension between a hierarchical and a horizontal view of church, between
different forms of spirituality, between conservatives and liberals, between
the loyalists and the loyal opposition. As the American church embraces the
twenty-first century, it is less than homogeneous in the beliefs and practices
of its members, yet this body of God's people in great variety continues to
call itself Catholic.

This book is a *portrait* of the church in America. As with any complex
subject, the portrait one creates captures certain dimensions and highlights,
but leaves other features in the shadows. It is by definition a selective enterprise. No one observer can adequately capture the complexity and depth of
Catholicism as it is appropriated by any national community. Thus I have
made choices concerning inclusion and exclusion, description and analysis,
highlights and background. Other choices were possible and would have no
doubt resulted in a different portrait. Gilbert Stuart's Washington, a Grant
Wood portrait, or Edward Hopper's self-portrait are particular interpretations of their subject. So too is this book. Even a photograph requires selection and interpretation if it is to convey not merely image but meaning.

Roman Catholicism in America is written for the general reader as well as
for students. Any chapter, indeed any section of any chapter, could easily be
the subject of a scholarly monograph. But this book is written to paint the
landscape within which American Catholics live, or as much of it as this
limited written "canvas" can hold. American historians, sociologists, and
theologians have published scores of perceptive books and articles on various aspects of American Catholicism. This book takes a broad view of a
large and complex subject. It is, in the end, an introduction. My hope is that
ordinary Catholics and non-Catholics, students and educators may find it
helpful to situate Catholicism on the religious map of America. Read in
conjunction with the other volumes in the Columbia Contemporary American Religion series, this work should give its readers a portrait of the diversity of American religious life—a diversity that is much greater today than
at any previous time in the history of America.

American Catholics are painfully aware that they belong to a church
that faces enormous challenges. They live in an era in which the Vatican and
America sometimes interpret the world differently, and for many in their
community spiritual development does not mean obedience to Rome's
directives. They wonder if the next generation will be as religious as past
generations or the present generation. They are part of a church that
esteems tradition, yet they live in a society that often values the present over

the past. Their church is divided over gender issues, authority, and future direction. It is an institution that yearns to see the face of God but sometimes hesitates to look in the eyes of its own; a church bent but not broken.

The eloquent words of the Jesuit theologian Walter Burghardt's baptism homily on the occasion of welcoming baby Sonia Marie into the church go far in capturing just why it is that people continue to call themselves Catholic, to worship, to believe, to belong:

> Sonia Marie, before we welcome you through symbol and ritual in to this paradoxical people, this community of contradictions, let me make an uncommonly honest confession. In the course of half a century (and more), I have seen more Catholic corruption than most Catholics read of. I have tasted it. I have been reasonably corrupt myself. And yet I joy in this Church, this living, throbbing, sinning people of God; I love it with a crucifying passion. Why? For all the Catholic hate, I experience here a community of *love*. For all the institutional idiocy, I find here a tradition of *reason*. For all the individual repressions, I breathe here an air of *freedom*. For all the fear of sex, I discover here the redemption of my *body*. In an age so inhuman, I touch here the tears of *compassion* In a world so grim and humorless, I share here rich *joy* and earthly *laughter*. In the midst of death, I hear here an incomparable stress on *life*. For all the apparent absence of God, I sense here the presence of *Christ*.[4]

CHAPTER ONE

Who Are American Catholics?

The American church is sometimes criticized by the media, by outsiders, and by Catholics themselves. Yet for all of the controversies that swirl around this ancient institution, 60 million people find a spiritual home within it. The National Basilica of the Immaculate Conception in Washington, D.C., is filled to capacity at three o'clock on a Saturday afternoon in May with married couples of all ages celebrating their wedding anniversaries by renewing their wedding vows. At Holy Cross parish in Batavia, Illinois, Father Stephen St. Jules and a team of volunteers lead a teenage retreat called a "Lock-in" in which the retreatants literally lock themselves in the parish hall for a weekend of talks, prayer, skits, fun, music, confession, and Eucharist, much of which is prepared and presented by the teenagers themselves. In a poor neighborhood in St. Louis, Catholic volunteers stand side-by-side with people of other religions, cooking and serving meals for the homeless in a soup kitchen. After mass in a parish in New York City, a Right to Life group gathers signatures to send Congress urging them to pass a partial-birth abortion restriction. At Gethsemane Monastery in Kentucky a handful of Catholics visit the monastery for a retreat during which they join the monks in chapel for prayer in the middle of the night. In a nursing home in Idaho, shut-ins attend mass in the nursing home all-purpose room. In a hospital in Las Vegas, Father Gerard McNulty of the Veteran's Administration administers the sacrament of the sick to a patient weakened by cancer. In Myrtle Beach, South Carolina, at ten o'clock on a Sunday morning tour buses park next to St. Andrew's Church as people dressed in vacation-wear stream into the church for mass. At the Motherhouse of the Racine Dominicans in Wisconsin, "retired" sisters in their 80s and 90s knit, crochet, and sew clothes for the poor—their arthritic fingers fashioning colorful garments, in an attempt to bring beauty to the lives of the homeless and disenfranchised. Keeping the sisters in touch with modernity, Sisters Therese Rotarius and Mary Fisher teach computer skills to community members. On Saturday afternoon at five o'clock, theologian David Tracy celebrates Eucharist with the community at Calvert House, the Catholic student center at the University of Chicago. In the U.S. penitentiary at Lompoc, California, Father Michael Kirkness, a federal prison chaplain, counsels an inmate. In Burlington, Vermont, the Knights of Columbus host a communion beakfast. None of these events will be noted in the media, but they are part of the everyday realities of Catholicism in America.

A Community that Worships

In the still of an early April night, as spring crowds out winter and darkness overcomes the dying light of day, several hundred people gather outside the entrance to Saint Rose of Lima Catholic Church in Gaithersburg, Maryland. A small fire struggles against the wind in a charcoal grill. A few people distribute candles to the crowd. Cars pass by in the background. It is eight o'clock, and it is already dark. The Easter Vigil is about to begin. The murmur and shuffling subside as the presider, a priest, Father Robert Duggan, dressed in a plain white robe covered by a cream-colored outer vestment and stole with gold embroidered threads enhancing their simple beauty, begins the ceremony with the words:

> Dear friends in Christ, on this most holy night, when Our Lord Jesus Christ passed from death to life, the church invites her children throughout the world to come together in vigil and prayer. This is the passover of the Lord: if we honor the memory of his death and resurrection by hearing his word and celebrating his mysteries, then we may be confident that we shall share his victory over death and live with him for ever in God.

The priest, assisted by another white-robed man, a deacon, Rev. Mr. James McCann, blesses the new fire. The deacon holds a thick white candle about three feet long while the priest inscribes a cross on it and places the first letter of the Greek alphabet (alpha) above the cross and the last letter

Sister Mary Fisher (standing) helps Sister Mary Ann Pohl master the intricacies of computer work.

(omega) below it, symbolizing that Christ is the beginning and the end of all creation. He also places numeral figures of the current year in the arms of the cross, and five grains of incense symbolizing the five wounds of Christ. Then the priest lights the candle from the fire.

    The congregation funnels into the church, which is shrouded in darkness. When they are situated in their places, the deacon, preceded by the priest and several altar servers (girls and boys, men and women), raises the lighted candle high and chants "Light of Christ," to which the people sing in response "Thanks be to God." Then the deacon lowers the candle while two of the servers light their small candles from the large one. They, in turn, light the candles of the other servers, who begin to light the candles of each person standing at the ends of the rows. The procession continues to the middle of the church where the deacon raises the Paschal Candle a second time and repeats the chant, to which the people respond again in simple song. As the procession advances to the altar, the entire church is aglow in soft candlelight. A third time the ritual elevation of the candle is repeated, and when the congregation has responded, the deacon goes to a holder prominently placed in the sanctuary, and gently places in it the candle, which he circles, swinging a censer that releases the smoke of incense rising in reverence to the Paschal Candle.

Then the deacon, or in some parishes a designated member of the congregation, stands at the lectern (technically, an ambo) in the sanctuary and sings the Easter proclamation that recalls the meaning of this sacred night. After this dramatic exultation, the people assume their seats, extinguish their candles, and listen to the history of salvation as recounted in nine Bible readings proclaimed by members of the community.

The readings begin with the first book of the Bible, Genesis, that recounts the story of creation. The readings move through several other Old Testament accounts of God's interaction with humanity ranging from Abraham's near sacrifice of his son Isaac, through to the parting of the Red Sea, to the salvation offered in the Messiah. Communal responses follow each Old Testament reading. Then readers proclaim from a letter of Paul and one of the gospels in the New Testament.

This is the richest ceremony in the church's liturgical calendar. The Easter Vigil is a special celebration that often brings the most active Catholics in the parish together on the Saturday night before Easter. Many Catholics, however, have never attended the Easter Vigil. Routinely, they will go to mass on Sunday morning, or at the regular Saturday evening mass that fulfills Sunday mass obligation. In most parishes on any given Sunday, many masses are offered to accommodate the varying schedules of the parishioners.

The priest's invitation to prayer at the beginning of the ceremony and his introduction to the readings reveal many of the essentials of the Catholic faith. He addresses the assembled community as "friends in Christ." It is because of their common bond in Christ that they are together. They believe that Jesus Christ is God's own Son, and that his message is God's word for humanity. Because they are baptized Christians, they are no longer strangers, but are related to one another as children of God—brothers and sisters of Christ and one another. By virtue of their baptism and membership in the church, they are also "children" of the church, a part of a world community as well as this local community of Catholics. When the priest invites the people to listen to the "word of God," he is speaking about the scriptures. These are texts from the Bible, which the Catholic Church believes are God's revelation to humankind of who God is for us, how God has interacted with us, and what God expects of us and what we can confidently expect of God. The ceremony recalls how God has saved his people throughout history. Christianity is an historical religion; not only by virtue of its own two-millennia history, but also because Catholic Christians believe that God has acted in human history to lead people to God and to their eternal salvation. A central belief for Catholic Christians is that God sent Christ who by his death on the cross and resurrection from the dead saved humanity from sin. Thus, he is the "Redeemer."

The ceremony, interwoven with symbols, continues with the rite of initiation into formal membership in the church, the sacrament of baptism. Normally the church baptizes infants and young children; however, on this occasion adults receive baptism as well as children. In many American parishes, the Easter Vigil is the culmination of a months-long process of preparation for adults to become Roman Catholic Christians. Called "The Rite of Christian Initiation for Adults" (RCIA), this program prepares non-Christian candidates for baptism, and baptized persons who are joining Roman Catholicism for membership in (called "full communion with") the church. Often led by Directors of Religious Education in parishes, this rite within a rite merits careful description. Roman Catholic practice recognizes seven sacraments, the first and most important of which is baptism. Baptism was practiced before the formation of the church, as attested in the New Testament as in the event of Jesus's baptism by John the Baptist in the Jordan River. The central symbol is water; for Catholics, who believe in original sin, water symbolizes the cleansing from sin. Original sin can be explained in various ways. Earlier in this century often popularly characterized as a stain on the soul, it is not a physical mark but the human condition of moral imperfection that every person is heir to at birth. We inherit that which our forebears give us. The theologian Monika Hellwig reminds us that the "human community in which we are rooted . . . is out of focus and estranged from its end and purpose in God."[1]

Baptism is a public initiation into the Roman Catholic Church; thus it is fitting that the community should be present to recognize, welcome, and encourage its new members. The priest blesses the water of the baptismal font (in this case a pool of water into which the newly baptized will be immersed), asking God to welcome those "reborn" in this sacrament as God's own children. Calling upon the assistance of those faithful and holy ones who have lived an exemplary Christian life before us, the cantor sings a litany of the saints, praying for the intercession of well known saints like Mary the mother of Jesus, Michael the Archangel, and Joseph, as well as saints known to the local community because of ethnic connections or the namesake of the local church community, and also the saints after whom the baptized are named (if indeed they are named after saints). Traditionally Catholics received only saints' names. Today the tradition is not adhered to strictly, although it remains the preferred mode of the institutional church. The other symbolic elements used in baptism are oil and light (represented by a small baptismal candle lighted from the larger Paschal Candle). The oil, called chrism, is used to consecrate the person as a follower of Christ. The local bishop blesses the oil at the liturgy called the Chrism Mass celebrated three days earlier on Holy Thursday. The candle represents the light of Christ.

During the rite of baptism, the priest questions the candidates as to their intentions, motives, and commitment (a ritualized, symbolic questioning which represents the more-detailed, personal interviews that had been conducted earlier). The priest asks the candidates, along with the assembled community, to reject sin, to believe in Christ, and to follow the beliefs and practices of the church. The priest immerses (in other parishes pours water over the heads of) the candidates, baptizing them while saying the Trinitarian formula: "I baptize you in the name of the Father, and of the Son, and of the Holy Spirit."

There are three sacraments of initiation: Baptism, Confirmation, and Eucharist. Normally the bishop confers Confirmation annually in the parish in a separate ceremony and children receive their first communion (Eucharist) at another special liturgy, but at the Easter Vigil the priest may confirm the newly baptized and they will receive their first Eucharist later in this elaborate ceremony.

The ritual continues with prayers for the church and the world, songs and the celebration of the Eucharist during which the priest consecrates bread and wine into the Body and Blood of Christ. Members of the congregation receive the Eucharist under the forms of bread and wine distributed by the priest, deacon, and several lay members of the congregation designated Eucharistic ministers. The Easter Vigil as described above and celebrated in a parish church is one way in which Catholics worship, but it is not the only way.

The Feast of Our Lady of Guadalupe

The Sanchez family of Anaheim, California gets up at four o'clock on the morning of December 12. Today they celebrate the feast of Our Lady of

Guadalupe at their parish church, Saint Boniface. The church schedules the major liturgy of the day for 5 A.M. Getting up in the dark and leaving so early is part of the sacrifice that makes this day special. The 7 P.M. mass that night, for those who simply cannot make the pre-dawn celebration, will not even be full. The day before a group of volunteers began decorating the church—a project the mass-goers will complete by bringing flowers and large candles in glass holders and placing them in the sanctuary before the large framed painting of Our Lady of Guadalupe.

The Sanchez family drives the short distance to the church. Those near-by walk. A sizable crowd is already waiting outside the church at 4:45 A.M. At five o'clock the church doors open and the crowd of men, women, and children from infants to school age, streams in and quickly fills all the pews. Those too far back in the line end up standing along the walls, exceeding the 1,100 seat capacity.

Many of the children are dressed like Juan Diego, pencil-drawn mustaches on the boys in imitation of the favored young Mexican boy to whom the Blessed Virgin appeared at Tepeyac, Mexico, in 1531. Everything must be done reverently and joyfully, but also quickly because the faithful must go to work as usual.

The mass begins when the mariachis band, attired in smart black outfits with silver-buttoned jackets, strikes up the spirited music for the processional song "Las Mañanitas" (The Lovely Morning) to greet the dawn. The sound of their violins, bass, and trumpets fills the entire church and brings the sleepy crowd to life. Three priests and a permanent deacon process into the sanctuary. The pastor, Monsignor Wilbur Davis, understands the significance of this day. The parish of 4,700 registered households has many ethnic celebrations during the liturgical year for its English-, Spanish-, and Vietnamese-speaking members. Father Wil, as the people call him, worked with the Maryknoll Missionaries for five years in Chile. He enjoys the Latin culture and loves the people. Today, in Spanish, he leads the community in prayer honoring the Blessed Virgin Mary. But the people make the celebration. Father Wil, wearing a colorful serape in place of a chasuble, invites the children to join the priests, and they quickly fill the floor of the sanctuary. Members of the congregation proclaim the scriptures. Mexican teenage girls in white dresses with different-colored sashes around their waists, dance while bringing the gifts of bread and wine to the altar during the offertory of the mass. The mariachis band plays lively but reverent music and everyone sings. The liturgy reminds the Sanchez family of their homeland, but their lives, religious and secular, are now securely rooted in California.

After mass families wait their turn to take pictures of each other in front of the now flower- and candle-laden picture of the Virgin. Today, the picture is set up in the main sanctuary of the church but nearby, in the converted baptistery, is a special chapel dedicated to Our Lady where people come daily from 6 A.M. to 10 P.M. to place lighted candles and pray in front of the many representations of Mary, which include one each from Mexico, Cuba, Bolivia, and other Latin American countries. This church is never locked during the day and the chapel has worshipers all the time. Hurriedly, the Guadalupe crowd retreats to the parish hall to continue the celebration with a Mexican breakfast of menudo (soup), pan dulce (sweet rolls), and hot chocolate.

A Liturgy and a Protest

On another night, a different group is also celebrating a liturgy, but this celebration differs dramatically from the formality of the Easter Vigil and the ethnic flavor of the feast of Our Lady of Guadalupe. It constitutes at the same time a prayer and a protest. In a living room in Denver, Colorado, a group of women gathers, as they regularly have since 1990, around a table draped with a linen cloth, decorated with fresh flowers and displaying a crystal goblet to be used as a chalice for their celebration of the Eucharist. They read, discuss, and interpret the scriptures they have chosen for the ceremony. They pray for themselves and for others, bless and break bread, share it and the one cup of wine after they "consecrate" them with either the words of the mass "this is my body, this is my blood" or similar words indicating that they participate in this meal in memory of Jesus who broke bread and shared a cup with his disciples at the Last Supper.

Many of these women do not consider themselves radicals and in many respects they are indistinguishable from other Catholics. At other times, they go to church to participate in masses presided over by ordained males. However, in addition to their ordinary participation in the Eucharist celebrated in church, they meet regularly, often in homes, to conduct Eucharistic liturgies by themselves, without an ordained priest as a presider. They find the patriarchy in the church oppressive, unjust, and insensitive. What began for many as a gesture of protest against this patriarchy, evolved into a spiritually sustaining and liberating regular practice.

They are part of a larger movement, called WomenEucharist, that exists in groups all over the United States as well as other countries. The movement includes nuns and other lay pastoral leaders.[2] After one such celebration, one woman, Sheila Durkin Dierks of Boulder, Colorado, who hosted the liturgy in her home, reflected: "What in the name of God were we doing? The church's official position is that we were breaking the law, but the wisest people I knew were joining me. If you're told that you always have to pray with a male priest and then do it for yourself, it's revolutionary. We discovered our power to pray and found other women who, in secret, had found it too."[3] In certain dioceses, if their participation became known, women who work in the church suffered repercussions, losing their positions. In other dioceses they have been left alone, with church officials rationalizing that according to canon law these "liturgies" do not constitute Eucharist since that requires that an ordained person preside and none of these women hold that qualification.

Types of Catholics

The heart of the church in America is the parish. This is the place where people gather regularly to worship, where they come to be known by name, where they find a sense of identity and belonging. There are variations of the parish where people worship together on college campuses, in hospitals, monasteries, convents, military bases, and chapels designed to serve a variety of communities. But the parish constitutes one community that is part of the local diocese and the universal church.[4]

> The parish is the central structure through which Catholics experience, nurture, and act out their faith. It is a community of a particular people living in a particular society as part of an international church. . . . It is a vehicle for both experiencing the faith and for motivating Catholics to relate to the broader community and to shape it according to Gospel [Jesus' teaching] values.[5]

Many Catholics do not have regular contact with a local parish, which most likely means that they do not participate fully in the life of the church. Recent statistics indicate that one third of Americans who identify themselves as Catholics, approximately 20 million Catholics, do not belong to parishes. So clearly, these Catholics who remain uncommitted to a specific parish can also skew statistical results when attempting to ascertain the views of faithful Catholics on a number of issues, since studies indicate that

Number of Parishes, 1945–1997

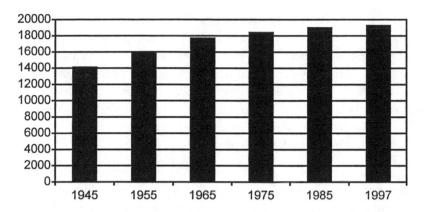

"Catholics without parishes have very different social characteristics and quite different orientations towards faith and morals."[6] Church leaders question whether this group should be included in national statistical surveys that measure behaviors and attitudes of Catholics.

The contemporary church includes a variety of Catholics who might be characterized under five categories or types.

1. *By the Rules Catholics*: The first type attends mass weekly, listens to and obeys the teachings of the church as articulated by the pope and bishops, and while they may have questions about some aspects of church life and teaching, give the benefit of the doubt to church authorities, cooperate with the mission of the church, and look to the church for direction. These are loyal Catholics whose dedication may be attributed to any number of factors, among which are complete agreement with the institutional church; fear that disagreement will have far-reaching consequences spiritually (may not go to heaven) or socially (unwelcome in family or circle of friends); or (less likely but possible) an inability to think for oneself. The numbers of this type of Catholic have declined in the post-Vatican II era, although the church continues to count on them to support even unpopular positions.

2. *Bend and Break the Rules Catholics*: The second type also attends mass weekly, but on certain issues chooses to follow their conscience instead of church teachings or practices. This type represents the good Catholic who identifies with the church, participates regularly, but disagrees with some practices or beliefs. These Catholics practice birth control, or believe in capital punishment, or think that abortion is permissible under certain circum-

stances, but go to mass and communion regularly. They represent the largest segment of churchgoing Catholics.

3. *Ignore the Rules Catholics*: The third type attends church irregularly, perhaps once a month, chooses which teachings and practices to follow, and ignores those that either do not seem to make sense or appear inconvenient. These Catholics are weary of church teachings and practices that seem to them backward, but they do not leave the church. Instead they operate within, yet independent of, the church. They appreciate the ritual the church provides, the sense of community, and the spiritual dimension, but they do not allow the church to dominate their moral or spiritual life.

4. *Rules Don't Pertain to Me Catholics*: The fourth type attends church on Easter and Christmas and perhaps a few other select times such as Ash Wednesday, weddings, and funerals. Sometimes derisively called "Christmas and Easter" Catholics, this group has existed in America (and elsewhere) for as long as the church. They clearly claim Catholicism, but have little formal contact with the Catholic community and do not look to the church to guide their lives on a regular basis. If there is a crisis, such as a death in the family, they turn to the church for assistance, but generally they live their lives unaware, uninterested, or unaffected by the activities and teachings of the church.

5. *Don't Know the Rules Catholics*: The fifth type are baptized Catholics who have abandoned all forms of Catholic religious practice. This group is ill-informed about recent church teachings and practices and uninterested in what the church says or how it functions. They are for all intents and purposes non-Catholic. Only their baptism identifies them as Catholic. They may seek to be married in the church, want their children baptized, and hope to be buried from the church, but aside from these chronological life markers, they have little or nothing to do with Catholicism.

This typology is not completely new since the church always has been home to "active" Catholics and "lapsed" Catholics. What is different is the decline in the number of type 1 Catholics, and the growth in types 2 and 3. Types 1, 4, and 5 have been present in significant numbers among American Catholics since colonial times. Type 5 Catholics, those who as infants were brought to the church for baptism by their parents, but were not raised with religious beliefs or habits as an essential or even an occasional part of their development, most often end up Catholic in name only. They may be married in the church or buried from it, but otherwise they remain disconnected. Some sociologists, and not a few bishops, think that their participation in statistical surveys about Catholics skews the results. Bishops complain that these nonparticipants in Catholic life should not identify themselves as Catholic, and sociologists sometimes have trouble identifying them. But since many insist on calling themselves Catholic, some argue that survey percentages should be adjusted to reflect the fact that they are de facto non-Catholics (even if de jure Catholics because of their baptism).

The church has always included type 2 and type 3 Catholics in its membership. However, the proportions of these types has grown significantly since Vatican II while the number of type 1 Catholics has shrunk. Data to support this observation comes first of all from statistics on church attendance, perhaps the first criterion for a type 1 Catholic. If estimates for attendance reveal that between 29 and 44 percent of Catholics (depending upon whose statistics one uses) attend mass on Sundays, significantly below the numbers before Vatican II. Additional data comes from surveys conducted regionally and nationally.[7]

Sociologists confirm that polarization exists among Catholics, but it is limited to a few areas, namely church leadership, priesthood, and moral teachings. These areas receive significant attention in the press, surveys, and in books like this one. For the most part, American Catholics identify with the central doctrinal claims of the church.

Different Generations of Catholics

Some sociologists have identified three distinct communities of Catholics according to a chronology defined by the Second Vatican Council.[8] Pre-Vatican II Catholics, born from 1910 through the 1930s, reached adulthood well before Vatican II. Vatican II Catholics are the baby-boomers born in the 1940s and '50s. This group has a mix of pre-Vatican II religious upbringing in a highly structured and dogmatic church, combined with the tumultuous experience of the changes initiated by Vatican II, as well as the social experience of the 1960s in America. The third group is the post-Vatican II Catholics who were born at the time of, or since, Vatican II. They have only a post-Vatican II experience of the church, although they have no doubt heard anecdotes or read about the pre-Vatican II church and have been taught about the events and significance of the era of the Second Vatican Council. At the beginning of the twenty-first century, pre-Vatican II Catholics are an aging but important resource because they bear the imprint of time and experience, both valuable resources if the Catholic community is to learn from its history. Vatican II Catholics, now middle-aged or approaching retirement, form the most powerful constituency by most measures from economic to political.

However, it is the post-Vatican II generations of late baby-boomers, Generation Xers, and the Millennium Generation, who are the future of Catholicism in America. And this group is quite different from its predecessors. Two distinct constituencies compose this community. The first group includes those who are descendants of the first great wave of European immigration. They are a generation of increasingly college or graduate-school educated young people. The second group, largely comprising Hispanic and Asian immigrants who came to the United States in the latter half of the twentieth century, are those working to establish themselves economically and become inculturated into American society without completely surrendering their native cultures.

The first group of post-Vatican II Catholics, those who are third, fourth, and fifth generation Americans, are less institutionally identified than pre-Vatican II Catholics, less informed on theological and doctrinal matters, more inclined to favor individual conscience over institutional dictates, better educated but more likely to have at least part of their education outside of Catholic schools. They want democratization at all levels of the church, and have experienced greater religious pluralism in their social, professional, and personal relationships. This is a generation raised on religious education programs that stressed Christian behavior more than doctrinal beliefs. It is a generation that may know a few lines in Latin of a traditional Christmas hymn, but has known the liturgy only in English. They have seen the number of nuns, brothers, and priests decline. Some are children of former priests, brothers, and nuns who left the active ministry to marry; a generation that is aware of sexual misconduct by the clergy; a generation that, although perhaps unaware, has witnessed a decline in the number of regular churchgoers while the actual number of Catholics has increased. They are a generation that has read about the civil rights movement, the war in Vietnam, and free love, but that has grown up in the Reagan, Bush, and Clinton years. They grew up watching *MASH*, *Oprah Winfrey*, *Happy Days*, *The Simpsons*, *Cheers*, and *Seinfeld*. They have seen the salaries of professional athletes skyrocket and the prestige of the ordained ministry erode. For the most part, the church has not functioned as the center of their social and cultural life. Professor of Religious Studies and campus minister at DePaul University, Robert Ludwig confirms this observation: "A growing percentage of young people who were baptized Catholics as infants have experienced no meaningful socialization in the church or its traditions—gone are the days of twelve to sixteen years of exclusively Catholic education. They have little ownership and tend not to participate, particularly as leaders, in the organizations and activities of groups tied directly to the church."[9] This is confirmed by the authors of *The Search for Common Ground*, an ambitious sociological survey of Catholics conducted in the middle 1990s that indicated "new networks satisfy many social needs which parishes used to meet."[10]

Post-Vatican II Catholics also include recent immigrants who have found hope in the church. Those who came to America uneducated and unable to communicate in the common language of the country were welcomed by many parishes whose members offered them assistance. Some parishes are returning to the habits of the early nineteenth century when macro cities first developed. At that time cities, and the Catholic population, were small enough so that one Catholic church could serve the entire Catholic community. Particular ethnic neighborhoods had not yet taken shape, and the demand for ethnic parishes had not yet been made. Priests said masses in several languages to accommodate immigrants spread out throughout the city. In New York City around 1800, St. Peter's Church offered masses in English, French, and German on Sunday.[11] Similarly today, at St. Boniface Church in the diocese of Orange in Southern California, masses are celebrated in Vietnamese, Spanish, and English, accommodating an ethnically mixed population of recent immigrants from Mexico, Latin America, and Vietnam, as well as a rooted Anglo population. On any given Sunday, mass is celebrated in 47 different languages in the archdiocese of Los Angeles.

This second wave of immigrants differs, facing circumstances that distinguish it from the first wave. Those of Hispanic descent are Catholics, but their form of Catholicism is different from that of the Germans, Poles, Irish, and Italians who immigrated a century or more ago. Hispanic Catholics, although generally united by a more-or-less common language, do not have identical cultures. Catholicism is a deeply ingrained part of the Hispanic way of life, which is imbued with Catholic symbols and traditions. For some Hispanics, however, one of those traditions is not weekly attendance at mass. Certain religious days like Good Friday, with its reenactment of Christ's passion and death, are observed with great fervor, while others like the Easter celebration of his resurrection are less compelling. Depending upon the country of origin, the Hispanic immigrant carries the celebration of various feast days important in the native land over into his or her religious experience in America.

Many Asian immigrants have not come from Catholic countries as did the first wave of immigrants or the current Spanish-speaking immigrants. Most of these people are converts to Catholicism. While Christianity has flourished in Vietnam and the Philippines for many generations, many immigrants from Cambodia and Laos, for example, come from Buddhist traditions. Not only are American society and culture different, American *religion* is as well. Catholic Christianity represents a different world view for them.

A Changing Church Steeped in Tradition

For all of its traditions, this is a changing church. Some of the changes are welcomed by the church hierarchy; some are feared. Some of the changes have been initiated from within; many are beyond the control of the church. The majority of post-Vatican II Catholics do not relate to the church in the same ways that their grandparents or parents do. This is not to claim that the church is unimportant in their lives. It is to claim that they understand and relate to the church differently.

For example, the church has holy days of obligation, special feast days on which Catholics are bound by church law to attend mass. A sampling of post-Vatican II Catholics would reveal that, if asked, most could not name these holy days and give their dates, and the majority of them do not observe the days religiously. For example, a 1995 survey indicated that 57 percent of Catholics thought that it was possible to be a good Catholic without going weekly to mass.[12] The same survey, the results of which are reported in *The Search for Common Ground*, found that 72 percent of pre-Vatican II Catholics claim to go to mass weekly, but only 44 percent of post-Vatican II Catholics say they go weekly and the real numbers are probably closer to 33 percent attending.[13]

Even many pre-Vatican II Catholics have a changed relationship with the church, as exemplified by the obituary of one Catholic woman who died in Florida in 1996. The obituary gives the usual data about her birthplace, husband, and children, as well as listing the Catholic schools in which she received her education. In a previous era one line of the notice would have shocked the Catholic community. "Her ashes will be scattered in Marco Bay, which she loved dearly, and a memorial Mass will be celebrated at Saint Benedict Catholic Church . . . at a later date."[14] For decades, the church has

permitted cremation but has requested that the ashes be interred in consecrated ground, in other words, in a Catholic cemetery. Families are ignoring
tradition and law by creating their own private rituals.

Although one in seven Americans born into a Catholic family have left
the church,[15] surveys conducted in 1987 and 1993 indicate that most
Catholics would never do so.[16] However, this does not automatically translate into obedience to church authorities or agreement with church doctrine
and policy. In a previous era, when the church exerted greater control over
its members via the pulpit and the confessional, some may have feared the
church's power more. Today, many members of the church are "selective
Catholics," (sometimes derisively called "cafeteria Catholics"), "who don't
feel guilty about missing Mass and are not particularly interested in what the
pope and bishops have to say. They are not angry with the church; they simply take what they like and leave the rest go."[17] Of course, there are many
Catholics, both earlier immigrants and later Hispanics, who listen to what
the bishops have to say and take it seriously.

But for "selective Catholics," this means that they want a priest to visit
their seriously ill grandparents or parents. They bring their children to religious education classes; and, when asked, they readily tell people that they
are Catholic. Yet they practice birth control, want to hasten the elimination
of social welfare programs, go to church irregularly, and think the pope is a
charismatic figure who is, however, out of touch with American Catholics.
The church is not excommunicating them, and they are not voluntarily leaving. Many are making decisions about their religious practice without consulting church authorities. For example, Marilyn Dunphy lives near the
Connecticut shore. The population of her town triples in the summer. Summer Sunday masses are crowded with tourists, and, to her mind, offer less
than the optimum spiritual experience. She decided to attend mass on
Wednesdays instead. Liturgy during the middle of the week is more prayerful than summer Sundays. In the pre-Vatican II era Catholics would not
dream of such a trade, feeling bound by church law to attend mass on Sunday under pain of sin.

The American Catholicism described above is in stark contrast to "the
intense devotionalism, the piety, the drive for personal sanctity—all coupled with deep loyalty to the church—that was so conspicuous a feature of
Catholic life in the pre-conciliar era."[18] For Roman Catholics in the United
States, the beginning of the twenty-first century is an era different from the
middle of the twentieth century. In 1958, 74 percent of U.S. Catholics

attended mass weekly; in 1984 the figure declined to 51 percent;[19] in 1996 surveys show attendance dipped as low as 33 percent. While these figures may alarm some Catholics, they are much higher than the percentages of most of the countries of the developed world. For example, church attendance for Roman Catholics in England in 1995 stood at 27 percent; in French-speaking Canada, 18 percent; in Brazil, 12 percent; and in France, 12 percent. Thus American Catholics are actually more attentive to religious practice on a regular basis than Catholics from almost any developed country in the world. In this regard Catholics reflect the general population in America, who are more likely to attend religious services than their counterparts from other Western countries.

Table 1.1
Concentration of Catholics by State

State	Catholic Pop.	State Pop.	Percent Catholic
Alabama	136,184	4,135,392	3.3
Alaska	50,016	612,083	8.2
Arizona	687,051	4,021,241	17.0
Arkansas	85,992	2,483,769	3.5
California	8,053,296	33,280,324	24.2
Colorado	549,654	3,709,590	14.8
Connecticut	1,359,910	3,270,788	41.6
Delaware	164,973	1,049,769	15.7
Dist. Columbia	440,000	2,388,506	18.4
Florida	1,982,676	14,310,296	13.8
Georgia	329,902	7,152,122	4.6
Hawaii	232,780	1,178,600	19.7
Idaho	116,500	1,163,000	10.0
Illinois	3,650,022	11,805,501	31.0
Indiana	739,084	6,499,770	11.4
Iowa	509,141	2,773,350	18.3
Kansas	383,428	2,403,171	16.0
Kentucky	357,155	3,694,498	9.7
Louisiana	1,336,072	4,316,324	31.0
Maine	220,983	1,227,927	18.0
Maryland	480,152	2,862,671	16.8
Massachusetts	2,968,041	6,020,374	49.3

Table 1.1 *(continued)*
Concentration of Catholics by State

State	Catholic Pop.	State Pop.	Percent Catholic
Michigan	2,191,854	9,455,635	23.2
Minnesota	1,226,202	4,539,922	27.0
Mississippi	108,896	2,685,188	4.0
Missouri	857,239	5,165,640	16.6
Montana	122,884	817,272	15.0
Nebraska	352,019	1,615,167	21.8
Nevada	438,260	1,671,019	26.2
New Hampshire	321,914	1,148,000	28.0
New Jersey	3,308,989	7,930,813	41.7
New Mexico	426,803	1,788,882	23.8
New York	7,309,228	18,496,487	39.5
North Carolina	235,954	7,264,913	3.2
North Dakota	165,340	643,952	25.7
Ohio	2,228,085	11,087,919	20.1
Oklahoma	144,335	3,451,439	4.1
Oregon	314,387	3,132,000	10.0
Pennsylvania	3,552,569	12,020,844	29.6
Rhode Island	637,554	1,003,000	63.6
South Carolina	109,629	3,673,000	3.0
South Dakota	160,916	711,591	22.6
Tennessee	156,523	5,069,870	3.0
Texas	4,317,171	18,669,605	23.1
Utah	81,021	1,964,000	4.1
Vermont	147,190	584,771	25.1
Virginia	494,655	6,677,180	7.4
Washington	519,130	5,452,091	9.5
West Virginia	103,678	1,793,477	5.8
Wisconsin	1,759,923	4,982,442	35.3
Wyoming	48,427	480,184	10.0
TOTALS	61,207,914	266,490,000	23.0

SOURCE: *The Official Catholic Directory, 1997.*
NOTE: Figures are of January 1, 1997. In some areas, a diocese crosses boundaries of states/territories, as in the case of the Washington, D.C., archdiocese, which includes part of Maryland.

Table 1.2

Family Incomes of U.S. Catholics

16%	$80,000 and over
23%	Between $50,000 and $79,999
29%	Between $30,000 and 49,999
22%	Between $15,000 and 29,999
11%	Below $15,000

SOURCE: Davidson et al., *Search for Common Ground*, 78.
NOTE: Figures are rounded.

Table 1.3

Jobs

12%	Executives or managers
24%	White-collar professionals (doctors, lawyers, teachers, etc.)
34%	Lower white-collar workers (sales people, technicians, administrative support personnel)
22%	Semi-skilled jobs (precision production, machine operators, service workers)
9%	Unskilled work

SOURCE: Same as table 1.2.

The Catholic Church in America, indeed all over the world, has changed more in the past thirty-five years than it had in the previous three and a half centuries. With Vatican II, the church embraced modernity and modernity has reconfigured the church. The sociologist Peter L. Berger observes:

> Until [the Second Vatican Council] the Catholic Church in America had successfully maintained a robust subculture whose inhabitants were kept relatively safe from the surrounding cognitive turbulence. Vatican II intended, in the words of John XXIII, to "open windows in the wall"; the unintended consequence of this so-called *aggiornamento* was to open an eight-lane superhighway through the center of the Catholic ghetto—everything came roaring in. The present leadership of the Catholic Church, especially the Rome headquarters, is trying hard to repair the fortifications; chances are that it is too late, at least in Western countries.[20]

Conservative and Liberal Voices

While Catholicism and Catholics' views on the church changed radically and swiftly after Vatican II, there is a segment of the Catholic population which is convinced that the reforms instituted by Vatican II have been too loosely interpreted by bishops, clergy, and laity alike. They pine for the discipline and order of the pre-Vatican II church, although they do not necessarily wish to return to some of its practices (for example, "fire-and-brimstone" preaching or the Latin Mass). Fordham University sociologist Michael Cuneo, in his investigation of right-wing Catholicism, *The Smoke of Satan*, avers that some secretly wish that Vatican II had never happened but find themselves having to defend it as a legitimate Council of the church.[21] Pronouncements from Rome, appointments of conservative bishops, and Vatican favor for traditional groups have all bolstered the spirits and the cause of these American Catholics, so that:

> Conservative Catholics claim that the tide is turning in their direction. They point to strong papal policies, new traditional bishops and firm Vatican reactions to dissent, as well as to the successes of conservative seminaries, religious orders and secular institutes, such as Opus Dei.[22]

While it is true that Pope John Paul II has tightened the reins on the church, especially with his strong protection of orthodoxy, on the whole the vast majority of American Catholics have not followed in lockstep. Bishops, theologians, clergy, religious, and laity have felt the impact of John Paul II's agenda for the church. Some have supported and even applauded it; others have negotiated it as best they can in their local situation, trying to avoid confrontation with authority but continuing to pursue an agenda consonant with their consciences though not explicitly defined by the Vatican.

The Vatican II document, "The Dogmatic Constitution on the Church," encouraged lay participation in the church urging that "every opportunity be given them [laity] that, according to their abilities and the needs of the times, they may zealously participate in the saving work of the church."[23] This positive endorsement led to greater lay participation and responsibility in the church. However, the decline in the number of active clergy and religious was equally responsible for the rise in lay participation even on the professional level. Increasingly the laity have filled positions previously occupied exclusively by clergy and sisters. While the church exerts more direct authority over these ecclesiastical professionals who work in areas as diverse as religious education, diocesan administration, and pastoral staff positions, they are not bound to the church as an institution by formal vowed obedience as priests are. The public oath required by Cardinal James Hickey of one priest at his installation as pastor in the archdiocese of Washington illustrates the kind of obedience that can be required by bishops of their priests.

> With firm faith I believe everything in God's word, written or handed down in tradition and proposed by the Church, whether in solemn judgment or in ordinary and universal magisterium, as divinely revealed and calling for faith. I also firmly accept and hold each and every thing that is proposed by the Church definitively regarding teaching on faith and morals. Moreover, I adhere with religious submission of will and intellect to the teachings which either the Roman Pontiff or the College of Bishops enunciate when they exercise the authentic magisterium even if they proclaim those teachings in an act that is not definitive.[24]

The oath requires that the priest adhere to all teachings of the church, even those that may still be debated in theological circles (such as the prohibition of women priests) but which the church historically and currently holds. In other words, the pastor should not undermine the church's teaching by publicly questioning any of its beliefs or practices. However, the fact is that, like lay persons, many priests question certain teachings of the church ranging from the prohibition of birth control to the condemnation of homosexual behavior or women's ordination. It may be naive to think that to suppress priests' discussion of such passionately debated topics will make the church's position more acceptable to Catholics in the pews.

For those who err on the side of extreme conservatism the church is also vigilant. In 1980, Cardinal Humberto Medeiros of Boston suspended an archdiocesan priest, Father John J. Keane, for opening three chapels in which he celebrated the Tridentine Latin Mass (the old [1570] rite with the priest's back to the people) which had been abrogated by the liturgical changes instituted at Vatican II. The mass may be celebrated in Latin using the new rite, but this priest defied Vatican II by going back to Trent, and gained a following doing so.

In an attempt to bring priests and people who were illicitly celebrating the Tridentine Mass back into accord with the church and not lose their allegiance entirely, Pope John Paul II issued a Papal Indult in 1984 allowing bishops to permit the celebration of the Latin Mass in their dioceses using the 1962 order, the final revision of the Latin Mass before Vatican II. Since then about half of the American dioceses have permitted such celebrations which often take place "at odd hours and at out-of-the-way churches and chapels."[25] One such celebration takes place at Sacred Heart Church in New Haven, Connecticut. Today there are some 150,000 Catholics in America who attend these masses. They have their own publication, *The Latin Mass*, edited by Roger McCaffery; and, although their membership includes only a low percentage of Catholics, they have gained followers consistently since the granting of the Indult.

The Vatican moved to curb abuses by those who were too lax about the rubrics governing the celebration of the Eucharist. The Vatican Congregation for the Sacraments and Divine Worship attempted to halt experimental liturgical practices that had been gradually introduced into the liturgy after Vatican II. Among these practices that were widespread enough to attract the Vatican's attention were: the laity reciting the Eucharistic prayer with the priest, nonbiblical texts being used in place of or in addition to scriptural texts for the Liturgy of the Word, unauthorized Eucharistic prayers, and the celebration of the Eucharist in locations other than churches without due cause.

Michael Cuneo, in *The Smoke of Satan*, describes the "Catholic underground" that represents a backlash against Vatican II reforms. He categorizes the various groups that make up this reactionary movement as conservatives, separatists, and Marianists. The conservatives wish to "save" Catholicism (and America) from its moral decline; the separatists think it is necessary to create alternative communities independent of present Catholicism in America and in Rome in order to preserve authentic tradition, corrupted since Vatican II; and the Marianists look to the Blessed Virgin to deliver messages of hope for the church via apparitions. The conservatives are the most vocal and visible group, manifesting their doctrine in the very public battle over abortion.

The differences between progressive and traditionalist ecclesiologies can be witnessed regularly in ordinary parishes. The parish is the place where Catholics practice their faith, and parishes are as diverse as the persons who lead them and the parish members. In any given diocese in America, there is a diversity of styles among the various parishes. Much of the difference is attributable to the leadership of a parish, that is, the pastor and his or her staff.[26] Some pastors invite extensive lay participation with accompanying responsibility and authority for the activity of the parish. Others

hold to a firm hierarchical structure in which the pastor determines all policies and practices.

Following the universal direction of Canon Law,[27] the American bishops have instituted directives to create parish councils comprising lay people
to help in the governance of parishes, but the authority and power of these
bodies varies greatly depending upon the local bishop and pastor.[28] Active
parish councils deal with a variety of administrative and ministerial tasks
within the parish. They usually have committees focused on liturgy and
worship, finances, education, evangelization, social justice and outreach,
physical plant maintenance, youth ministry and community building among
other special needs. In many parishes these leaders exercise significant
authority and, in consultation with the pastor and staff, identify the priorities of the parish. Major policy decisions are approved by this body making
it the place where people take responsibility for and ownership of parish
life.

Some pastors enforce all the rules of the church; others enforce them
selectively. For example, at a wedding or a funeral at which there are likely
to be non-Catholics and inactive Catholics in attendance, some priests will
distribute communion to whomever approaches the altar. Other priests will
make it a point to exclude non-Catholics and sometimes nonpracticing
Catholics from communion by informing congregations that only practicing Catholics in good standing are invited to receive communion.

The labels "conservative" and "liberal" can give the impression that all
Catholics are either one or the other. In fact, the majority of Catholics are
somewhere in the middle. Most are not interested in being tagged liberal or
conservative. They are a part of the church because it provides a spiritual
home. Part of that spirituality revolves around the sacramentality of
Catholicism: the sacraments, the stories, the metaphors, the images, the symbols, and the rituals. These disclose God to people in simple and sometimes
surprising ways. As the sociologist Andrew Greeley testifies, it is in "the
poetic, the metaphorical, the experiential dimension of the personality that
religion finds both its origin and its raw power."[29] Among Catholics who
claim membership in a parish, one third are members of a religious organization, a quarter pray more than once a day, and 90 percent pray several
times a week.[30]

Those with deeply vested interests in either a conservative or liberal
agenda receive more attention than middle-of-the-road Catholics for obvious reasons, and thus appear powerful or numerous. Each side characterizes
the other as smaller than most people imagine their numbers to be but also

influential beyond their size. For example, Mary Jo Anderson, writing in *Crisis*, states: "The Catholic Left, although unable to build a statistically significant membership, has power beyond its numbers because many members are employed by dioceses or Catholic colleges or universities."[31] Michael Walsh, in his book *Opus Dei*, reflects the same concern about the power of the right: "Opus is the doyen of the neo-conservative movements within the Catholic Church. It is the most powerful, with members in high office in governments of Catholic countries round the world, and in influential posts in the media and in business."[32] The Jesuit philosopher Bernard Lonergan observed: "There is bound to be formed a solid right that is determined to live in a world that no longer exists. There is bound to be a scattered left, captivated by now this, now that new development, exploring now this and now that new possibility."[33]

The various generations also react differently to the church. Most pre-Vatican II members are deeply wed to their Catholic identity. For them what the church teaches and what direction the American church takes matters, whether they agree or disagree with the direction. The church has been so formative in their lives that they cannot be indifferent. Many Vatican II Catholics are also vested in the church but are more likely to distance themselves from the politics of the church. For example, they want their children to be Catholic, but they do not want the Catholic Church to dominate their children's lives the way it did theirs in their youth. The church should be part of their lives, not the exclusive focus.

Post-Vatican II Catholics are the most likely to be indifferent to the direction of the church. Many so-called Generation Xers often are unaware of the internal disputes between competing ecclesiologies, and if made aware, find such disputes inconsequential. They do not set their social or personal compass in a direction dictated by the church. They are much more likely to be interested in career and recreation than in "churchy" concerns. The church may be a wonderful institution, but many of them find it either irrelevant or best kept at a safe distance. Many from this generation who participate will not allow the church to dominate their emotions or actions. Somehow they have seen or heard or sensed that this can be damaging, and besides it simply is not central to their lives. Bishop Daniel Pilarczyk of Cincinnati, speaking in 1980 about the ministry faced by seminarians, noted that many people "see[s] the faith as irrelevant, . . . the Church. . . as a refuge for the insecure and eccentric" and he feared that "the effectiveness of the Church as an institutional force in our society will continue to diminish."[34]

Music, liturgical styles, lay leadership and involvement all make for sig-

nificant variations in parish life. In one parish, liturgies will be well prepared with carefully crafted homilies; well chosen music may be led by a
professional director; numerous people will serve as lectors, Eucharistic
ministers, and ushers. In another parish, the liturgy is ill-prepared and
rushed, with little encouragement for lay participation either in the form of
ministries or communal singing. Differences in composition of the parish
community, leadership, interests, preaching, programs, worship, and organization can make one parish, even in the same diocese or city, very different from another. Some parishes have exciting programs for young people,
drawing them into the church community not only through religious education, but also by extensive programs designed to meet some of their social
needs, offer service to others, and explore the paths of spirituality. Another
parish may cater to the needs of the elderly, offering traditional prayer experiences such as novenas and recitation of the rosary as well as social events
like bus trips and activities during the day for their convenience.

To this extent, all Catholicism is local, and so, many contemporary
Catholics select a parish in the same way they would shop for a school for
their children, a health care facility, or a neighborhood. In all parts of the
world, the church is divided into geographically defined parishes. The
recent practice of American Catholics selecting their parish without regard
for this tradition has resulted in the blurring of parish boundaries in some
places.[35] Sometimes it has homogenized parish communities because the
process of self-selection means that liberals end up in one parish, conservatives in another, and charismatics in a third. The ideal of a parish is to *form*
a community from the diverse Catholic population in a defined geographical area. Add to this mix chapels designated for a specific community such
as campus ministries, hospitals, and military bases that attract people who
are not directly connected to the institution being served, and there is greater
choice for Catholics. Often these ministries become quasi-parishes when
they regularly attract churchgoers who are not affiliated with the university,
hospital, or military base.

Such self-selection by Catholics makes it difficult for bishops and pastors to control the demographics of parishes. Parishes do have some methods to hold people accountable, however. In order to be recognized and
receive the services rendered within a parish (religious education, sacramental preparation programs, marriage, etc.), Catholics are generally
required to register in the parish. Some parishes permit registration only to
those persons living within the geographical boundaries of the parish. In
practice, many parishes ignore this church regulation and will include per-

sons who are technically within another parochial area. Some dioceses have attempted to recognize and regulate this pattern either by granting permission for persons to change parishes or by establishing nonterritorial parishes or communities open to registration by all Catholics within the diocese. The diocese of Arlington, Virginia, has a nonterritorial community called "Nova"; the archdiocese of Louisville, Kentucky's nonterritorial parish is the Church of the Epiphany, founded in 1971. Called "a parish without boundaries," members refer to it also as "the church without walls," because of its clear glass walls that invite the outside in. It draws people from nearby Indiana as well as greater Louisville. On the one hand, such parishes can become havens for those disenchanted with their local parish for whatever reason. On the other hand, they create communities that tie different geographical areas together.

There are also regional differences in the church that are tied to history and post-World War II migration. Catholicism in the Northeast, where there are generally enough clergy to staff parishes, and churches are abundant and in close proximity to each other, is different from Catholicism in the plains states where one priest may be serving a church and several missions, and all are fifty to a hundred miles away from each other. This is different still from Catholicism in some areas of the South where Protestants outnumber Catholics, and being Catholic is a minority status.

These differences color people's experiences of the church. On the one hand, their experience, whatever it may be, is not normative and should not be universalized. On the other hand, their personal experiences concretely indicate the composition and practice of the local church.

The American church has changed radically in the latter half of the twentieth century. It has also fractured ideologically. Theologian Mary Jo Weaver asks:

> How did American Catholics get to the point where they needed adjectives to describe themselves? Why is it no longer enough, as it was in 1955, for someone to say that he or she is a Catholic? Why do we now, in 1995, meet Catholics who are "recovering," "communal," "cradle," "practicing," "Tridentine," "conciliar," "American," "disgruntled," "liberal," or "conservative"?[36]

Much of this has to do with American society and culture, to which Catholics contribute and by which they are affected. Americans are democratic; Catholicism is not. Americans often follow—or even set—trends. Sel-

dom has the church been accused of being trendy. Americans live in a pluralistic society that values tolerance for many views and practices, whereas
the church holds moral and dogmatic positions that do not abide tolerance
in its beliefs or practices. Americans live in an affluent, developed, and mate-
rialist country. The church promulgates the gospel mandate to identify with
the poor. Americans prize their independence. The church "takes care of"
her children. Often Americans are asked to compete and win at work. The
church asks them to form a community of forgiveness and compassion.
Americans demand reasonable answers to difficult questions from their
political leaders. The church asks them to accept some things on faith alone
or on the sole basis of the authority vested in the church.

It is no wonder that American Catholics sometimes find it difficult to
be both. What their culture espouses their church sometimes contradicts.
The Executive Director of the Association of Catholic Colleges and Universities, Monika Hellwig, a theologian who has studied Catholicism extensively, sums it up nicely:

> It is not surprising, therefore, that American Catholics . . . have begun
> to wonder why we do not see more local initiative in church policies
> and actions, why the faithful have no voice in choosing their pastors at
> the parish and diocesan level, and why questions of the orthodoxy of
> theologians are not referred to consultation by their peers. Such atti-
> tudes and questions can, of course, be seen as acts of insubordination
> to church authority in its present patterns, but it may be wiser to con-
> sider whether they might be a prophetic challenge concerning the
> nature of the church.[37]

The post-Vatican II church witnessed some division of the Catholic
community into conservatives and liberals, right and left, traditionalists and
progressives. These labels should not be confused with secular political positions with the same nomenclature, but should be understood against a background of church teaching and practice. In general, conservatives believe
all Catholics should follow the official teachings and practices of the church
as articulated by the pope and bishops. Liberals disagree with, and often
object to, a number of these teachings and practices and accord individuals
greater freedom to decide whether or not to follow them.

Tensions between progressives and traditionalists in the church are even
played out on the World Wide Web as various groups attempt to gather
"converts" to their persuasion. Some websites underscore the radical divi-

sions that are possible within Catholicism. For example, a group called "True Catholic"[38] puts this on the web:

> It is likely that most of you think that the "Catholic Church" now centered in Rome, in the Vatican, is the Catholic Church. Since 1958 (after the death of Pope Pius XII on October 9, 1958), the holders of offices there, have usurped the name of the Catholic Church from which they of their own free will departed. They left the faith, and therefore they left the Church that was founded by Christ on the apostles with Peter as its head. Their defection from the faith is something we must prove and that is the burden of much of the literature that you will find in this website. . . . The only way that one can prove this truth is to examine the teachings of the Catholic Church before bogus Council Vatican II, and then compare those earlier teachings with the ones now taught by that unfortunate and diabolical Council Vatican II.
>
> The immense truth that will strike you is that there is a great difference between the doctrines of the pre-Vatican II Catholic Church and those of the post-Vatican II "Catholic Church." Once you recognize this, you are forced to admit that they are not one and the same church.

Two well-known conservative groups who boast national and international membership are Catholics United for Faith and Opus Dei. CUF is a lay organization, founded in 1968, of some 15,000 members to oppose those who dissent from official church teachings. CUF founder H. Lyman Stebbins wrote to American bishops in 1968: "[We] believe that in this period when there is so much contumacious defiance of God-given authority, the church needs, and we owe, our unswerving support of her teaching and ruling authority."[39] Opus Dei, a lay organization founded in Spain in 1928 and now numbering 80,000 members worldwide, has a unique status in the church because in 1982 it was deemed a personal prelature by Pope John Paul II (reporting directly to the pope) and maintains loyalty strictly to the pope. This status allows it to operate independently of the local bishop, to establish seminaries and to ordain candidates to the priesthood. The organization, which counts laity and clergy (approximately 1,600 members are priests) among its membership, according to Mary Jo Weaver, "aims to promote piety among the laity by appealing to well-educated, highly disciplined, profoundly committed Catholics who, in their ordinary job, can penetrate society in ways not open to priests within the Church."[40] Its founder, Monsignor Josemaría Escrivá de Balaguer, received beatification in 1992.

The fact that the membership rolls of Opus Dei are not public concerns some Catholics who interpret the organization as "spying" on behalf of the Vatican.[41]

In contrast to these conservative voices is "Call to Action."[42] The group describes itself as

> [A]n independent organization of over 16,000 people who believe the Spirit of God is at work in the whole church, not just in its appointed leaders. We believe the entire Catholic Church has the obligation of responding to the needs of the world and taking initiative in programs of peace and justice.
>
> We believe the church should be a model of openness on all levels; theologians and Catholic institutions should be free in their search for the truth; laity and clergy should be consulted in the formulation of church doctrine and discipline, especially on human sexuality issues; priesthood should be open to married persons and to women; all people and clergy of a diocese should be consulted in the selection of their bishops.

The Call to Action group meets annually in conference to promote their liberal agenda for the church. Local chapters meet between the national gatherings, but some groups have had difficulty receiving permission to meet on church property. A 1996 directive by the diocese of Arlington, Virginia, prohibiting the local Call to Action Group from meeting on church property led to public confrontation between conservatives and Call to Action members, and required police intervention to calm the situation.

The same restrictions have plagued Dignity,[43] the organization of lesbian, gay, bisexual, and transgendered Catholics. In its statement of position and purpose Dignity says: "We believe that gay, lesbian, bisexual and transgendered persons can express their sexuality in a manner that is consonant with Christ's teaching. We believe that we can express our sexuality physically, in a unitive manner that is loving, life-giving, and life-affirming. We believe that all sexuality should be exercised in an ethically responsible and unselfish way."

In many dioceses across the country, Dignity has been denied the right to meet on church property and prohibited from conducting Eucharistic liturgies in parish churches or diocesan facilities. In Boston, in a letter sent to approximately 750 priests, bishops, and deacons of the archdiocese, Auxiliary Bishop William Murphy forbade diocesan personnel from participating in the national convention of Dignity/USA, held in Boston, July 10–13, 1997. The letter advises priests that Dignity should receive no support because "they espoused a position contrary to Catholic moral teaching supporting that [sic] moral correctness of sexual relations between two persons of the same sex in a 'faithful and loving relationship.' "

The use of the internet to make public one's cause is also a local phenomenon. In Winchester, Virginia, some of the parishioners of Sacred Heart of Jesus Church are embroiled in a battle with their pastor and bishop. This group wants the pastor removed for alleged transgressions ranging from financial improprieties to breach of the seal of confession. Their website[44] is a virtual tabloid detailing the controversy between the parties, disclosing a psychological evaluation of the pastor, citing the significant decline in enrollment in the parish school since the pastor's arrival, and posting copies of news stories from the secular press chronicling the controversy. The parishioners were not shy about their discontent; and, after receiving no satisfaction from the bishop, took their appeal all the way to Rome.

"Catholics for a Free Choice" state their mission as the desire to "Shape and advance sexual and reproductive ethics based on justice, reflect a commitment to women's well-being, and respect and affirm the moral capacity of women and men to make sound and responsible decisions about their lives." For them, the issue is not simply the liberty to elect an abortion; the issue is one of control. Who has control of a woman's body? They are unwilling to relinquish personal control to the church. As they see it, the church's position leaves them out of the decision-making process in a matter of grave personal concern. The church, however, views its position as morally appropriate and in defense of innocent human life.

In 1990, 4,500 clergy and laity, including a number of prominent theologians, placed a full page ad in the *New York Times* calling for reform in the church.[45] The letter, initiated by Call to Action, asked for justice *within* the church, and it reiterated Call to Action's agenda for the church including the ordination of women priests, a democratic process of selection of bishops, and the end of mandatory celibacy for clerics. Such public actions underscore the internal conflicts in the church.

Such dissension and splintering in the post-Vatican II church led the neoconservative Catholic Michael Novak to observe:

> The very meaning of Catholicism as a coherent people with a coherent vision has been threatened. What the barbarian invasions, centuries of

primitive village life [sic], medieval plagues and diseases, wars, revolu-
tions, heresies and schisms had failed to do, the Second Vatican Council
succeeded in doing. It set in motion both positive forces and forces that
squandered the inheritance of the church. It set aside many proven
methods and traditions. It fostered some experiments that have worked
and some that decidedly have not.[46]

In the past forty years America has witnessed the erosion of Catholic
culture that supported and defined Catholics. Contemporary suburban
neighbors do not define themselves primarily by their religion as their immigrant ancestors did. In some gentrified urban settings, condominium and
townhouse dwellers do not even know their neighbors' names, much less
their religious persuasions. Neighborhoods are more likely to group similar
economic classes than they are Catholics, Protestants, Muslims, or Jews
together. In the sprawling suburbs, most people do not notice if their neigh-
bor's garage door goes up Sunday morning. And if it does, it may be to permit someone to retrieve the Sunday paper or to drive to pick up Grandma
for brunch instead of church. This change in Catholic culture may be partially attributable to Vatican II, but it is deeper than the effects of the Council. It represents the assimilation of Catholics into the wider American culture, just as Protestants and Jews before them, and now Muslims, Hindus,
and Buddhists after them.

For a long time in America there existed a vibrant Catholic subculture
that provided security and identity for the immigrant community. This
cohesive subculture has largely disappeared in the last forty years. Churches still have committees, social events, education programs, outreach and
support groups that involve many parishioners, and some continue to rely
on bingo for income. However, these opportunities compete with children's
sports teams sponsored by the town, city, or county, not the church, with
professional demands for husbands and wives, with public school activities,
with a social life that includes friends of other or no religious persuasion,
and with the temptations of the larger culture to get ahead, consume more,
and be entertained.

Charles Morris notes this in his chronicle of the Irish influence on the
church when he identifies John F. Kennedy as "an utterly secular man, a
completely assimilated product of American, not Catholic, culture."[47]
Though Catholic, he received his education at Choate and Harvard, the
elite institutions previously reserved for Protestants. In a previous era,

Symbolic of the apex of Catholic subculture, circa 1940, candidates for sisterhood dress in wedding gowns for their profession as "Brides of Christ." UNDA

Catholics would neither have been welcomed nor felt comfortable at such institutions. So they went to Notre Dame, Georgetown, Catholic University, Fordham, or other Catholic colleges or universities where their faith would be nourished and preserved. Today, Princeton, Stanford, Yale, and Brown have as many Catholic students as they do Protestants, Jews, and others.

An Attempt to Heal the Divisions

The painful divisions evident in the church in the 1990s did not escape the notice of Cardinal Joseph Bernardin of Chicago. On August 12, 1996, as he battled with what would prove to be terminal cancer, he called for a dialogue in the American church. During a news conference to announce the formation of the "Catholic Common Ground Project," he said:

I have been troubled that an increasing polarization within the church and, at times, a mean-spiritedness have hindered the kind of dialogue that helps us address our mission and concerns. As a result, the unity of the church is threatened, the great gift of the Second Vatican Council is in danger of being seriously undermined, the faithful members of the church are weary, and our witness to government, society, and culture is compromised.

Cardinal Bernardin stood ready to act. Seven bishops and sixteen other Catholic leaders agreed to join Bernardin in overseeing the Project's initiatives headed by Bernardin's hand-picked choice, Archbishop Oscar Lipscomb of Mobile, Alabama, as chairperson of the project. The committee included theologians Elizabeth Johnson, Bryan Hehir, and Virgil Elizondo, Harvard law professor Mary Ann Glendon, Judge John T. Noonan, *Commonweal* editor Margaret O'Brien Steinfels, former governor of Pennsylvania Robert P. Casey, banking industry executive Barry F. Sullivan, and Washington AFL-CIO president John F. Sweeney among others. The Project, while considered otiose by some, drew public applause from many; and shortly after its being announced, hundreds of Catholic leaders around the country from the academic and pastoral worlds were volunteering to participate. The "Common Ground" Bernardin sought to identify or establish reflected a center that could accommodate many ways of thinking and many voices.

Sadly, Cardinal Bernardin would not live to see the fruits of his initiative. He died in Chicago on November 14, 1996. The document he wrote to initiate the project, "Called to Be Catholic: Church in a Time of Peril" called for a dialogue between conservative and liberals that might bridge differences. In a candid assessment of the American church he wrote:

It is widely admitted that the Catholic Church in the United States has entered a time of peril. Many of its leaders, both clerical and lay, feel under siege and increasingly polarized. Many of its faithful, particularly its young people, feel disenfranchised, confused about their beliefs and increasingly adrift. Many of its institutions feel uncertain of their identity and increasingly fearful about their future.[48]

The document provoked opposition from some prominent members of the hierarchy, including Cardinals Hickey of Washington and Law of

Boston, who thought that it gave too much credibility to opinion and failed to give adequate deference to the magisterium, the official teaching authority of the church. Some liberal lay people also criticized Cardinal Bernardin's proposal because they felt that it did not address directly controversial issues like women priests and that the committee lacked members who would raise these concerns. Ironically, the very document designed to invite dialogue and cooperation itself became a source of division.

Differences among members of the hierarchy are nothing new, of course. Another example of controversy among the bishops occurred when retired Archbishop John R. Quinn of San Francisco responded to the pope's invitation issued in the 1995 encyclical *Ut Unum Sint* (That They May be One)[49] "to engage with me in a patient and fraternal dialogue" about the role of the papacy in the church. Quinn, speaking at Oxford University in June 1996, delivered a lecture titled "Considering the Papacy." He called for reform of the Curia (the central administrative system of the Vatican) and greater sensitivity on the part of Rome for the voice of individual bishops and national bishops' conferences. Specifically, he argued that Vatican officials have too much say in the appointment of bishops, suppress dialogue on important issues such as women's role in the church and clerical celibacy, and overrule bishops on important matters such as the final English version of the *Catechism of the Catholic Church*. His lecture drew swift reaction from some American bishops.[50] Cardinal O'Connor of New York wrote in the July 25, 1996, edition of his diocesan paper, *Catholic New York*: "I respectfully question how many such issues are the impediments to unity that the archbishop perceives them to be." Bishop James McHugh of Camden, New Jersey, wrote in *Origins*: "He gives the impression that the Curia doesn't trust bishops or episcopal conferences, and thus is unwilling to consult them. My experience is just the reverse."[51]

Such disputes are not confined to battles among the hierarchy, which are often ignored by the laity. In Lincoln, Nebraska, Bishop Fabian Bruskewitz attempted to end the open discussion of "forbidden" topics such as women priests and the commission of gravely sinful acts such as abortion, by excommunicating members of offending groups. He named a list of the offending bodies including: Planned Parenthood, the Hemlock Society, Catholics for Free Choice, the Society of St. Pius X (followers of conservative Archbishop LeFebvre who was condemned by the Vatican), the Freemasons (and associated groups), and Call to Action. He warned these groups on March 22, 1996, in the diocesan newspaper, the *Southern Nebras-*

ka Register, that anyone still belonging after April 15 would be "absolutely forbidden to receive Holy Communion" and on May 15 he excommunicated them. Canon 1318 of the Code of Canon Law states that excommunication is to be carried out "with the greatest moderation and only for serious offenses." Many among the laity and the hierarchy thought that membership in an organization did not meet this criterion, but that the bishop operated within his authority.

The conservative magazine *Crisis* criticized Cardinal Bernardin's choices for membership on the steering committee for the Common Ground project, implying that he selected only those with moderate to liberal views that matched his own leanings. Whether or not the criticism can be considered accurate or warranted, the article highlighted an important point, stating: "In the battle for America, the Vatican may have the generals in the years to come, but the heterodox [in the view of the *Crisis* article] are fighting for terrain from the grassroots."[52] John Paul II has consciously selected doctrinally conservative bishops and has used the same criterion to elevate bishops to the rank of cardinal. At the same time, however, there exists a large body of priests and laity not fitting this description, who find themselves at odds with their bishops on a number of issues.

The priest-sociologist Andrew Greeley confirms this analysis, claiming that he does not think that the Catholic lay community is polarized one against another. In his view, the division is between laity and the hierarchy.[53] The laity has become increasingly liberal in the past twenty years while the hierarchy has become more conservative. The priesthood is divided largely between some middle-aged and older clergy who hold liberal inclinations shaped from the time of their formation and early years in the priesthood and more recent conservative clergy, who although younger, hearken back to pre-Vatican II habits of clericalism. Greeley does not deny the vocal presence of hard-line conservatives among the laity but argues that they constitute a very small minority of perhaps less than five percent. While he does not oppose the Common Ground Project, he warns that it may be misdirected. While Greeley's observation about differences between the laity and hierarchy is correct, it could be extended to disagreements between bishops themselves. The problem is sometimes with the hierarchy disputing with one another as is apparent from the reaction of Cardinals Law, O'Connor, and Hickey to Bernardin's proposal.

This, of course, is not a novelty in a church that has been largely shaped by its hierarchy and women religious, many of whom are forceful personal-

Fed Up With
Fuzzy-Wuzzy Catholicism?

Recently the so-called Catholic Common Ground Project issued a manifesto urging that dissent from Catholic truth be placed on "common ground" with Catholic truth at dialogue sessions around the country. Bernard Cardinal Law roundly criticized the manifesto, saying that "dialogue as a way to mediate between truth and dissent is...deception." We at the NEW OXFORD REVIEW heartily agree with Cardinal Law.

The Common Ground manifesto — launched, ominously, by a famous cardinal we need not name — is one of the more beguiling of the many portentous campaigns currently afoot whose intent or effect is to undermine Catholic teaching and papal authority.

Alluringly, the manifesto decries "polarization" and "acrimony" in the Church, says that those with whom one differs "deserve civility, charity, and a good-faith effort to understand their concerns," and calls for "respectful dialogue." But consider: Commonweal, whose Editor signed the manifesto, recently devoted its entire back cover to an attempt to ridicule our REVIEW. The gist of the attack was that, because of our strong loyalty to the Holy Father and the Magisterium, we're stupid "ostriches," oblivious to the charms of "liberal post-Enlightenment culture." Dripping with sarcasm, Commonweal asserted that "if the pope told Catholics they could only have sex standing on their heads every Tuesday," we'd "look forward to Tuesdays." Gads, is this "respectful dialogue"?

Readers even wrote letters to Commonweal to say that while they appreciated, even relished, the attack, they nonetheless found it to be a "cheap shot" and in "atrocious" taste.

Also consider: The liberal National Catholic Reporter, which endorsed the Common Ground manifesto, recently printed pieces calling Bishop Fabian Bruskewitz a "semi-literate incompetent" and wondering out loud "whether the church of Rome is not of Christ but of the anti-Christ." Ah yes, "charity" and "civility" and all that!

If the old journalistic attack-bears of fuzzy-minded Catholicism, after decades of fomenting doubt, division, and acrimony, now wish to pose as cuddly teddy bears, well, that's a curious tactic. We aren't falling for it, nor should you.

The Church doesn't need any Common Ground yak-sessions, for, as Cardinal Law said: "The Church already has 'common ground.' It is found in sacred Scripture and Tradition, and it is mediated to us through the authoritative and binding teaching of the Magisterium."

Yes, there's polarization — and it's lamentable. But genuine unity is found, not in dialogue between truth and error (which only legitimizes disunity!), but in fidelity to the Throne of St. Peter. As Vatican II said, the Pope is "the perpetual and visible source and foundation of...unity."

The NEW OXFORD REVIEW, a traditional Catholic monthly magazine with an international audience, is published out of notorious Berkeley, so we know fuzz-ball shams when we see them. If you're an unseduceable Catholic, subscribe today! You'll get a bang out of seeing us burst balloons.

(Please allow 2 to 8 weeks for delivery of first issue)

Advertisement for the conservative journal the New Oxford Review criticizes liberal Catholicism. REPRINTED WITH PERMISSION OF NEW OXFORD REVIEW, BERKELEY.

ities. At the end of the nineteenth century during the Americanist controversy, cardinals and bishops bitterly opposed each other's positions on the church's relationship to Rome and to American culture. Liberal ordinaries, Cardinal James Gibbons of Baltimore and Bishops John Ireland of St. Paul and John Lancaster Spalding of Peoria disagreed publicly with Bishops Michael Corrigan of New York and Bernard McQuaid of Rochester, New York. Privately, each side tried to influence the Vatican to take action against the others. There was no love lost between these men of the cloth. The direction of the American church lay at stake, and they were worldly-wise politicians who understood the meaning of influence and power. The church at the end of the century differs in many ways from the church at the beginning of the century, but internal intrigue and power struggles have not noticeably changed. In the long run, the church may be guided by the Holy Spirit, governed by canon law, and defined by dogma; but in the short run personalities, ideologies, and power influence the direction the church takes.

Continued Loyalty

For all of the difficulties of the church, many Catholics continue to react to church developments with passionate concern. When the *Detroit News* published a portrait of the church, "Catholicism at a Crossroad" on September 24, 1995, many of the letters to the editor reacting to the publication defended the church. One person wrote: "As a lifelong Catholic, I would be remiss in not responding to your latest salvo directed at the Church. The two-page diatribe made us look bad. . . . Certainly we have problems, but we're working on them." Another proffered: "Since the Church is 'alive,' it has two options: It can 'evolve' or it can 'regress' as other living things do. The Church, though, is in a perpetual process of transformation, not a popularity contest."[54]

American Catholics continue to identify with the church. While they may not "pray, pay, and obey" as they did in the 1950s, they maintain a stubborn loyalty. Their identification remains evident in peoples' commitment to the church. Different dimensions keep them connected; for some, it is ritual, particularly the celebration of Eucharist. For some, it is the commitment to values that they share with the church and which so much of the world appears to have abandoned or overlooked. They want their children to grow up with a set of values, and the church is a good place to find them. For some, their loyalty derives from an ethnic identity or a family tradition. Part of the identification as Irish-American, Polish-American, or Mexican-American is being Catholic. For some, it is the belief that the church embodies an eternal truth. For some, it is a way to salvation. For others, it represents community in a country that thrives on individualism.

When asked why they remain Catholic despite internal church conflicts, personal differences with church policies and secular forces that challenge religion, people express a variety of reasons for their commitment. Paul Wilkes, a commentator on contemporary Catholicism and the author of *The Good Enough Catholic*, cites seven reasons why Catholicism serves as a viable framework for committed Catholics' lives, the first, and most important, of which is staying close to the Eucharist.[55] Rita Hunt, an elderly woman from Rhode Island who has battled cancer successfully for over twenty years comments: "My parents gave us the gift of faith which has kept our family close and guided us through the trials of life, especially illnesses. The priest brings the Eucharist once a month which strengthens us and brings God into our hearts." Richard Rosengarten, Dean of Students at the Divinity School of the University of Chicago, responds:

> It is the tradition in which I was raised and I associate it most closely with the way to worship God. I respect other churches, have worshiped with them and learned from them, but I don't find a set of practices that speak to my heart and soul the way Roman Catholicism does. My continued association is closely related to the liturgical tradition, with less reference to authority in Rome which I take seriously, but don't always agree with. While I acknowledge the authority of Rome, I believe in the exercise of one's conscience as a Catholic. I have never let that be an impediment. Yes, I have differences with the Vatican. I believe that women should be ordained, and it appalls and distresses me that they are not, but I am fortunate to be in a pastoral situation where that pain and anguish is recognized and acknowledged.

Dennis Tamburello, a Franciscan friar who teaches at Siena College in New York, offers: "I remain in the church because I have found God here. For all of the church's faults, it has been a community that has put me in touch with the sacred, and nurtured my own spiritual pilgrimage. I look at the weakness and contradictions in my own life, and conclude that there is no other group of sinners and pilgrims with whom I'd cast my lot."

Joseph Pelletier, a therapist in the Washington, D.C., metropolitan area responds: "The reason people stay has little to do with the organization of the church and more to do with ritual and the spiritual aspects of the church. That's why I stay. I don't become involved in the politics of the church but I like celebrating the liturgy. The Catholic tradition is familiar, comfortable and a part of my personal heritage."

Even some who have abandoned the church talk about themselves as "post-Christian"[56] or "recovering Catholics," confirming that the religion they have left continues to influence their self-definition. Judy Restak Scott of Silver Spring, Maryland, is such a person.[57] She left the Catholic Church while a college student in the late 1960s. "I could not negotiate the transition from organ music to guitar," she says indicating the transformation the church underwent after Vatican II. "I just decided suddenly to quit. I have never returned. Although I do occasionally go into Catholic churches. When I do, I always light a candle and say a prayer for my mother. After all these years this simple Catholic ritual still has meaning and attraction for me." Now married with a family, she joined the Ethical Society for a while in order to provide a foundation of values for her children, but she drifted away from this organization as well. Her children are ethically sensitive and moral; she and her husband have provided a proper example to follow even if it is not an explicitly religious one.

Marjorie Fusco is a sincere and active Catholic.[58] A single mother of nine children, she is enrolled in the Program for Pastoral Formation for lay people conducted by the diocese of Rockville Centre on Long Island, New York. The program is a three-year commitment, the first two of which are spent in classes either two Wednesday nights a month or all day Saturday once a month. The third year is divided into tracts focusing on different dimensions of ministry such as small faith communities, spirituality (her choice), marriage tribunal, social justice, youth, family life, administration, as well as other tracts depending upon the skills of the person and the availability of personnel to train them. Her parish, St. Peter the Apostle, in Islip Terrace, New York, shares the cost of the program with Marjorie. When she completes the program, she will work in the area of ministry for which she trained as a volunteer in the parish.

Marjorie, who has been active in her parish for over twenty years, is a professional librarian at a local college. On her sabbatical in 1997 she took the unusual step of going to the Catholic University of Louvain in Belgium to study theology for a semester in a program sponsored by the American College in Leuven. She simply wanted to know more theology so that she could be better informed to serve in this volunteer ministry. "There is a growing desire for deeper spirituality among Catholics as well as a need for theology. The younger generation, in particular those raised on religious education programs instead of in Catholic schools, is not very well versed in Catholicism." This grandmother of six says she is part of the church because there she finds a sense of community and it sustains her faith.

Another example of commitment is the Focolare Movement. Founded in Trent, Italy, in 1943 by Chiara Lubich and approved by Pope John XXIII in 1962, it spread to various places in the world including the United States. Some laypersons who are core members of this movement pledge celibacy, live together in small communities, and observe poverty, chastity, and obedience. They embrace this life while working in positions and professions in American society. The members of the movement foster unity among religions and peoples and encourage interreligious dialogue that will promote understanding and peace between religions.

Others consider themselves "the loyal opposition" and continue to be members of the church despite their disagreements with church doctrines, policies and personalities. They dislike the hierarchical structure of the church as well as its patriarchal composition; they are disappointed with the current leadership; and they accuse the institution of being unresponsive and lacking creativity. Yet they are hesitant to change allegiances to a Protestant communion, sensing different, but equally difficult problems there. At their core they are Catholic, and even if they are conflicted about their Catholicism, they stay. They disagree; they sometimes object, but curiously they continue to identify with Catholicism.

There are those who would like to see these "malcontents" leave. They would prefer a smaller but more obedient Catholic body. If Catholicism were to shrink even as much as 50 percent, they contend, those who remain would constitute a more unified, coherent, and committed Catholic body. There is no litmus test for a genuine Catholic. Those who would construct a Procrustean bed to define what constitutes a Catholic would themselves transgress the official church's own definition that recognizes all those who are baptized Catholic as members of this extraordinary and diverse communion of saints and sinners.

CHAPTER TWO

A Brief History of Catholics in America:
Colonial Times to 1900

Until June 29, 1908, Rome considered the American church a missionary territory; that is, Catholicism had not been fully established, and the task required the assistance of foreign clergy. Its status changed when Pope Pius X signed the apostolic constitution, *Sapienti Consilio* (On the Roman Curia). Until that time the American church had been under the jurisdiction of the Congregation of the Propagation of the Faith at the Vatican, an office that oversaw developing churches in foreign lands. Today American Catholics provide more financial support for the Vatican than any other national group,[1] and on January 10, 1984, President Ronald Reagan and Pope John Paul II agreed to have the United States represented in Rome by an ambassador.[2]

American Catholics today make up 23 percent of the U.S. population. Their average family size reflects the national average. Their income and education level stands above the national average. They rank in the highest echelons of business, government, entertainment, and education. They reside in the cities, suburbs, and rural areas in every region of the country. On many counts, they are virtually indistinguishable from their Protestant neighbors. The chairman of IBM attends daily mass; the president of the United States, although Baptist, attended college at a Catholic university; and three justices on the United States Supreme Court (Kennedy, Scalia, and Thomas) are Catholic. Today Catholics may seem indistinguishable in American society, yet they are heirs to a tradition and a history that sets them apart.

Before the British Colonies

The story of Catholicism in North America begins before the English settlers descended on the Atlantic seaboard and laid the political and cultural
foundation of the United States. The Spanish and the French preceded the
colonization by the British. And unlike many of the British in the Southern
colonies who were religiously identified with the Church of England, their
predecessors from Spain and France were Roman Catholics. Puerto Rico is
the oldest diocese (established in 1511) in U.S. territory. French Huguenots
established Fort Caroline (1564) in the area of present-day Jacksonville,
Florida, only to be overrun in 1565 by Spanish explorers who settled in St.
Augustine. These explorers were accompanied by priests who established,
as best they could in such conditions, parishes for their own to worship in
and missions to convert Native Americans to Catholicism. Black slaves and
free blacks also had Spanish surnames. Beginning in 1702, attacks by the
English devastated the Spanish colonies until Florida became a British
colony in 1763.[3]

The missionaries in these early territories came, in the case of Florida,
for the most part from the Jesuit and Franciscan religious orders. They met
with limited success and succumbed to British rule with the signing of the
Treaty of Paris in 1763. This changed again when a new Paris Treaty enacted in 1783 returned Florida to Spain, under whose rule it remained until it
became a part of the United States in 1821. During this period, a noted historian of the American church, James Hennesey, observed: "Roman
Catholicism became a minority religion practiced by people considered 'for-
eigners' in the land that they had helped to build."[4]

Though unsuccessful in Florida, the Spanish missionaries did not remain
confined geographically to the southeast. Missionaries from Mexico combed
the southwest and the west in search of potential converts. The famous
Spanish missions of California are part of their legacy. They also established themselves in Texas and Louisiana. But sparse populations resulted in
the missionaries serving only natives and soldiers.

Although the Jesuits preceded them, the Franciscans established deep
roots in the southwest and California. Junípero Serra (1713–1784), who
founded nine missions, is among the best known Franciscan missionaries.
The missionaries "domesticated" the Indians, teaching them how to raise
crops and herd livestock. While the intentions of the missionaries may have
seemed noble to them, the effects of their Christianizing and "civilizing"

Missions remain part of the landscape as with the Basilica Mission in Carmel, California. ARCHIVE PHOTOS

the native population often were not. In fact, they were quite harsh, as described by James Hennesey.

A majority of California's Indians never came within the system, but those who did, once they were baptized, were not free to leave the mission. Punishment for infractions was severe. Flogging was used and misdemeanors could result in chains or the stocks. Runaways were hunted down by soldiers. Some 98,000 Indians were baptized over the mission period. The greatest number in the missions at any one time was 38,000. They lived and worked in tile-roofed adobe houses laid out in town patterns. Indians were trained as cattlemen, shepherds, carpenters, blacksmiths, masons, and weavers. Village bands and choirs were organized. Mission property was held in trust by the Franciscans, who clothed, fed, and housed the Indians. In return the Indians worked the fields and herds and learned Christian doctrine and prayers. They also felt painfully their loss of freedom.[5]

Mexican independence brought about the secularization of the missions and the decline of Catholicism in California until the gold rush of 1849 swelled the population and changed the region forever.

The other major force for Catholicism in the uncharted territories was the French missionaries who appeared concurrently with the Spanish but in different regions of the North American continent. French traders came to North America to exploit the abundant supply of furs. In doing so they regularly met resistance from the Indian population who also depended on furs for their welfare. They settled in what is present-day Canada and the northern sections of the United States. The Jesuits, Franciscans, and French priests worked among the Hurons, Mohawks, Algonquins, Iroquois and other tribes, sometimes pitting tribe against tribe in various unholy alliances that resulted in massacres of large numbers of Indians and martyrdom for the missionaries. Both priests and Indian converts suffered deeply for their commitment to Christianity. Non-Christians suffered from colonial invasion, disease, and the destruction of their culture as well. The church declared some of the missionaries saints (for example, the Jesuit Isaac Jogues in 1930) by canonizing them and more recently recognized some Indians for their strong testimony to the faith (for instance, in 1980, the church declared the young Mohawk woman Kateri Tekakwitha, "Blessed").

When the Treaty of Paris was signed in 1763, France abandoned its possessions in North America. Settlers and soldiers pushed the Indians west across the Mississippi and the few remaining French posts came under British control. The northern sections and their native populations then became the spoils and the responsibility of the British.

Different conditions prevailed in the southern section of the expanding territory. France and Spain colonized the South. Prior to the Louisiana Purchase of 1803, Pope Pius VI created the diocese of Louisiana and the Floridas in 1793 with its hub at New Orleans, a location with a large French Creole population. The pope appointed a Cuban bishop to oversee the region, which was transferred to American hands in 1805 when John Carroll was named administrator.

Like California, the New Mexico region represented the missionary territory of the Franciscans. One of the problems in this area, as in other regions (except where Jesuits were prominent), remained the reluctance of the missionaries to learn the native languages required to proselytize effectively among the Indians. Jay Dolan, an historian of American Catholicism comments: "Although New Mexico offers the most extreme example of the friars' failure to learn the native languages, the situation was not much better elsewhere. The regulations of the order required the Franciscans to learn these languages, but they were not uniformly enforced; the result was that with few exceptions the Franciscan missionaries were unable to speak the language of the people."[6] The conviction that the Indians had no religion underlay the efforts of the missionaries, especially the earliest among them, who considered the Indians in essence "pagans." Contemporary studies of native American religion prove otherwise, but the early missionaries to North America saw religion through Christian lenses that, much like those of their later Protestant counterparts, filtered out all other expressions of religion as illegitimate. This insensitivity made their conversion work all the more difficult because converted Indians often continued to hold native beliefs and maintain indigenous practices alongside their Christianity. Even today in the "Catholic" pueblos of New Mexico, the Indians attend Sunday mass, then gather outside in "kivas" where they celebrate ancient rites of homage to the gods their ancestors worshiped.

The Colonies

While the founding of the British colonies in North America was tied to concerns about religion, most of the colonies quickly established a set of laws and regulations regarding religious worship and practice. Most of the early settlers who came to New England shores from Britain sought, in part, to escape the domination of the English church which still bore the imprint, in doctrine and liturgy, of the Catholic tradition despite its separate status since the days of Henry VIII. They wanted freedom to establish a "Kingdom of God" on earth without the vestiges of popery.

European Christianity had been wracked by the Reformation that created Protestantism, and England felt further effects by the separation of English Catholicism from Rome by Henry VIII. Henry's eventual successor, Elizabeth I, confirmed the separation when she declared herself the head of the English church. However, some English Christians thought the reforms had not gone far enough and wanted to "purify" the church of all traces of Roman Catholicism. These "Puritans" left England for an uncertain future first to the Netherlands, then to North America. In the meantime, particularly during the reign of Elizabeth I (1558–1603), the small community of Roman Catholics in England underwent persecution.

One could escape this persecution by emigrating to America. On March 5, 1634, a group of Catholic noblemen accompanied by Jesuits and workers, some of whom were Protestants, arrived in Maryland aboard the *Ark* and the *Dove*. On their second stop they founded St. Mary's City as the first capital of Maryland. Through the efforts of his father, George Calvert, a successful public servant in England, Cecil Calvert was granted a charter from the crown to found a new colony north of Virginia. Calvert, the second Lord Baltimore (his deceased father having been the first), was, like his father, a convert to Catholicism. Historians note that his interests in founding Maryland were likely more economic than religious, but his commitment to freedom of religion made Maryland a safe haven for Catholics. Calvert's idea meant not so much to establish Catholicism as the religion of the new colony, but to allow people to practice either Protestantism or Catholicism without interference from the governing body.

The early years of Maryland proved to be unstable ones. Events in England dictated the course of the colony. After Charles I was executed in 1649 as a result of civil war in England, Cromwell's Puritan supporters attacked Maryland. "For almost two years Maryland was in a state of chaos; its population dwindled; the government ceased to function; and Jesuit priests and Catholic leaders were led off to England in chains."[7] In 1658 Calvert regained control until the Maryland uprising in 1689 that resulted in the deposing of the third Lord Baltimore (Charles Calvert) and the appointment of a British governor. The Maryland Assembly that had passed legislation to protect religious freedom in 1639, and enacted the "Act Concerning Religion" in 1649 guaranteeing religious rights, reversed itself in 1692, and the very condition that the Calverts had fought to prevent happened— a state religion (Anglicanism) became established. From that time until the founding of the republic, Catholics no longer enjoyed the privilege of protection in Maryland.

Some of the other colonies had already demonstrated their anti-Catholic prejudice through legislation that treated Catholics either punitively or acknowledged the king as the proper religious head. Catholics eschewed life in these colonies, fleeing from them whenever possible. Catholics were not the only subjects of religious bigotry, however. Quakers escaped to Pennsylvania, and Roger Williams founded Rhode Island in 1636 as a haven for Baptists and other dissenters from Puritan orthodoxy. Prejudice continued after the original colonies had become states. Nine of the original thirteen colonies established some form of Protestantism as the state religion. The settlers left England behind but not their post-Reformation prejudice against the "Romanists."[8]

Many of the Maryland Catholics descended from noble families. They had servants and owned slaves. They were further sustained by their social status, combined with the leadership of the Calverts, the first family of Catholics in Maryland; furthermore, legislation allowed them to practice their religion for a time in private without interference from the governing bodies. Still, by 1676 they accounted for only approximately 1,800—a mere 9 percent in a population of 20,000 Maryland colonists. By 1708 their number had grown to 3,000, still only 10 percent of the population. "By no means all were wealthy planters, and those who were also did the work of traders, businessmen, and financiers. They attended Mass with small farmers who worked their own fields or lived as tenants on larger estates. Some plied the trades—such as blacksmithing and carpentry—of a rural economy. There were boatmen, oystermen, and sailors on ships which regularly traded along the Atlantic coast."[9]

Indentured servants and Catholic black slaves served many of the Catholic landed gentry in Maryland. By 1784, there numbered at least 3,000 Catholic slaves. In 1785, John Carroll, in a letter to Rome, wrote: "The Catholic population in Maryland is about 15,800. Of this number nine thousand are adult freemen, that is, above twelve years of age; about three thousand are children, and the same number are slaves of all ages, come from Africa, who are called 'Negroes' because of their color. In Pennsylvania there are at least seven thousand but very few Africans."[10]

The Jesuits proved the most influential clerical presence. From the time of their arrival on the *Ark* and the *Dove*, their numbers varied depending upon available personnel, the political climate, and high mortality rates. However, James Hennesey notes that "Between 1634 and the Revolution, over one hundred Jesuit priests, a single Jesuit scholastic (seminarian), and about thirty Jesuit brothers served in Maryland and Pennsylvania."[11] The Jesuits succeeded in their recruiting efforts as forty-one colonists entered the Society during this period, thirty-four of whom persevered to ordination and served in America and Europe. Most of the Maryland Jesuits lived on manors they helped to run and on which they maintained chapels where the local Catholic community would gather. Others were circuit riders, traveling by horseback to various locations to provide the sacraments. They pressed for special privileges such as tax exemptions and landholdings acquired from the Indians, but after a decade of dispute, lost their bid for greater autonomy.

Thus, while the colonial Catholic clergy in Maryland had the freedom to practice their religion, they had none of the special secular privileges enjoyed by their European counterparts. They did benefit materially, however, from personal bequests that left them with significant landholdings. Their work was often inhibited by adverse legislation such as the 1704 document, "An Act to prevent the Growth of Popery Within this Province," that explicitly forbids the Jesuits by name from proselytizing. Legislation in 1707 softened this by allowing for private worship.

Religious life attracted a number of women from Maryland as well. Since no convents to train them existed in America, the orders, including the Benedictines, Carmelites, and Dominicans, sent novices to Europe to complete their preparation for life in religious communities. Candidates for priesthood and religious life came from the upper classes since they received their education in Europe, which proved too expensive for the lower classes. Women who entered religious orders provided significant dowries to the church, which gave further reason that only wealthy families could afford to give up a child to the church. But the price was worth it because "Both doctrine and popular piety accorded more status to those in vows and Holy Orders than to the ordinary rank-and-file; as presumed occupants of a 'higher state of grace,' their efforts automatically assumed a legitimacy and influence that comparable efforts by the 'unconsecrated' normally could not hope to attain."[12]

The Jesuit plantations became the first parishes in America. Jay Dolan describes this transition:

> [I]n the 1760s . . . plantations began to function as parish churches. New churches were built on many of the farms; parish registers for baptism, marriage, and death appeared, detailing the performance of these rites of passage, most of which now took place at the parish church; lists of parishioners were compiled and maintained, and parish devotional societies, composed of women, were also organized. Thus, at a time when Catholics were still legally discriminated against, denied the ballot, and allowed to have only private worship services, the church was going public by building "publick meeting places of divine worship" and organizing communities. As a result, religion was becoming less domestic or private and more congregational or public. This can be seen in the congregational setting of the rites of passage, the organization of parish

devotional societies, and the maintenance of parish membership rosters. This was a significant step toward strengthening of the institutional church and a decisive move away from the more private practice of religion so commonplace in the seventeenth and early eighteenth centuries.[13]

Catholics in Maryland continued to encounter obstacles from additional taxation to restrictive oaths. However, by and large, they enjoyed greater freedom to practice their religion than did Catholics in other colonies. Their numbers grew, with the greatest concentration in St. Mary's and Charles counties in southern Maryland, swelled in part by immigrants from Ireland. Eventually they spread north to the territory of Pennsylvania where the Quakers had a policy of freedom of religion.

An internal church matter—the suppression of the Jesuit order by Pope Clement XIV in 1773—could have derailed Catholic development rather than the political and social pressures from the Protestant majority. Fortunately, the 21 Jesuits in Maryland and Pennsylvania found a capable leader in John Carroll, who would manage to keep them together and go on to become the first American bishop. Carroll came from a prominent Maryland family. His older brother, Daniel, participated in the Continental Congress and was one of two Catholics to sign the U.S. Constitution. His cousin, Charles, a wealthy landowner and industrialist, was the only Catholic to sign the Declaration of Independence.

The election of Carroll as bishop of Baltimore in May 1789 signaled a new era for American Catholicism. He came to prominence during the formation of the revolution and the fight against the British overshadowed religious differences among the colonists. Catholics "stood on the threshold of a new age, ready to build a new church which would attempt to graft the spirit of the new nation onto their colonial tradition and create something new in the history of Roman Catholicism, an American Catholic Church."[14] Carroll, although approved by Rome, was the choice of the American clergy. In line with American independence, he held the pope as a spiritual, not a temporal, authority. In order to enhance that independence he chartered a school in 1789, from which he hoped to recruit candidates for the priesthood. In 1791 Carroll began Georgetown Academy (today Georgetown University) on the banks of the Potomac, and founded St. Mary's Seminary in Baltimore, run by priests from the Society of Saint Sulpice.

These institutions gave Catholics their own niche in higher education, and Carroll hoped they would lessen the American church's reliance on

The first American bishop, John Carroll.

foreign-trained clergy. Moreover, he insisted that those who continued to come from Europe be trained well in American customs, for this constituted a church independent of the state and comprised of newly minted Americans. He "took some major steps to form a national church . . . that would be adapted to the exigencies of the rising new nation."[15] It emerged in a religiously pluralistic environment that differed from the European experience in which church and state were tied to one another. Priests regularly conducted services in English, leaving behind the Latin of continental Catholicism, and scholars translated the Bible into English as well. Elected lay trustees supervised the management of the parish. Jay Dolan, in *The American Catholic Experience*, notes:

> Thus, by 1790, a unique vision of the church was beginning to surface in the United States. This republican blueprint envisioned a national, American church which would be independent of all foreign jurisdiction and would endorse pluralism and toleration in religion; a church in

which religion was grounded in intelligibility and where a vernacular liturgy was normative; and finally a church in which the spirit of democracy permeated the government of local communities.[16]

The American Church Takes Shape

However, circumstances countered the vision of the late eighteenth century. As bishop, rather than patterning a church on American customs, Carroll looked increasingly to Europe as a model.[17] By 1800, he had abandoned the democratic electoral process by which he was chosen, and he alone recommended names of new bishops to Rome. Eventually, since Rome made the appointments, the independence of the American church ebbed away. Latin replaced English for the liturgy. Lay trusteeism survived, becoming a battleground between the clergy and laity in later years. The seminary in Baltimore did not produce enough native-born clergy; and the newly established dioceses of Boston, New York, Philadelphia, and Bardstown, Kentucky—all had foreign-born bishops.

The orders of women religious founded in America at this time experienced similar conflicts between American habits and European ones. Sometimes bishops imprudently imposed disciplines upon orders that made sense in the cities of Europe but did not readily translate to the American landscape. These orders, such as the Visitation Nuns founded at Georgetown and the Sisters of Loretto in Kentucky, had to live under rules devised in Europe involving fasting and self-denial, that in some cases were so severe that young sisters on the American frontier died.

Many of the black slaves practiced Catholicism following the religion of their slave owners. Jesuits, Vincentians, and a number of bishops owned slaves in the early part of the nineteenth century. The slaves helped provide economic stability to the nascent church in America. But Rome took a different view. In 1839 Pope Gregory XVI condemned the slave trade in the apostolic letter, *In Supremo Apostolatus Fastigio* (Condemnation of the Slave Trade) which said:

[We] . . . admonish and adjure in the Lord all believers in Christ, of whatsoever condition, that no one hereafter may dare unjustly to molest Indians, Negroes, or other men of this sort; or to spoil them of their goods; or to reduce them to slavery; or to extend help or favour to others who perpetuate such things against them; or to exercise that inhuman trade by which Negroes, as if they were not men, but mere animals, howsoever reduced to slavery, are, without any distinction, contrary to the laws of justice and humanity, bought, sold, and doomed sometimes to the most severe and exhausting labours.[18]

However, the attitude toward African Americans did not change as a result of Vatican pressure. Catholics seemed as prone to consider blacks inferior as were any other Americans, from the North or the South. Significant communities of black Catholics sprang up in New Orleans, Mobile, Savannah, St. Louis, Baltimore, and Washington, D.C. Some parishes served blacks exclusively, though securing black clergy presented a difficulty since seminaries refused admission to blacks and thereby prevented them from obtaining ordination. Other parishes that included blacks segregated them physically in back pews or the choir loft and institutionally by keeping separate parish registers for blacks and whites. Religious orders founded to minister exclusively to the African-American community eventually attracted black members. These orders, for example the Josephite Fathers and Brothers, represented another sign of the segregation within the church. In New Orleans, Henriette Delille's Community of the Holy Family, a community of black sisters established in 1842, was prohibited from wearing their religious habits in public.[19]

An Immigrant Church

By the time of John Carroll's death in 1815, comments Jay Dolan, "two schools of thought were manifest in the American Catholic community. One desired to fashion an indigenous church, an American Catholicism; the other wanted to transplant to the new nation a continental European version of Roman Catholicism."[20] That meant that the first great wave of immigrants from Europe, which numbered 33.6 million between 1820 and 1920, would face the challenge of adapting to American ways or clinging to their European roots. But these roots, while originating in Europe, represented diversity, nonetheless. Newcomers held in common their emigration to America—a melting pot that increased in population and spread West. For many, Catholicism also bonded them to each other.

The Irish who fled Ireland for America in great numbers during the potato famine in the mid-nineteenth century did not have special language needs as did other European immigrants, such as those from Germany, Italy,

Poland, or French Canada who came in the later part of the nineteenth and the beginning of the twentieth century. The Irish found themselves in conflict with the established population because they perhaps too quickly presumed that America belonged to them since they spoke English. But they were poor and for the most part unskilled. They encountered discrimination in employment ("No Irish Need Apply") and housing, and their adherence to Roman Catholicism made them unwelcome religiously as well. They also competed for unskilled jobs with the free blacks who made their way north. While the Irish encountered the hardships of discrimination, they in turn harbored racial prejudice against the African-American community.

When, toward the end of the nineteenth century, Italian immigrants came to America, many Irish immigrants, forgetful of their own initial reception, treated the Italians as unwelcome outsiders.[21] The Italians arrived accompanied by their own clergy, but the religious habits of this immigrant community differed. Men did not attend church regularly and often did not contribute financially to the support of the church. They were accustomed to the state paying the salaries of the clergy and caring for the maintenance of the church. In particular they resented "seat money" collected at the door of the church on Sunday. The established population generally treated new immigrants with indifference as historian Richard Linkh testifies: "The general public as well as the intellectual elite tended to see other differences between the two groups which often led to the conclusion that if the 'new' immigrants were not inferior, they were certainly less desirable than the 'old.' "[22]

In addition to the Irish, others—Italians, Poles, Germans, French Canadians—migrated from the north and Mexicans entered from the south. These, and immigrants from other countries who came in smaller numbers, constituted a church community that spoke many languages. As these groups settled areas of the country, they built churches where their own could worship. Many of the immigrant groups arrived accompanied by priests who could conduct services in their native languages. Thus, ethnic national parishes arose alongside, sometimes literally next door to, territorial parishes. The American church represented a mix of ethnic groups that reflected the growing pluralism of the American landscape.

Catholics constituted a minority among Christians in America at the beginning of the nineteenth century with a population of about 195,000 in 1820. By 1850, however, they had grown to become the largest Christian denomination, counting over one and a half million among their numbers. That number doubled to over three million in just ten years due to huge numbers of Catholic immigrants from Europe. Most settled in cities along the eastern seaboard. They maintained their language and many of the customs from their countries of origin. In order to meet their spiritual needs the bishops permitted ethnic parishes that functioned in the languages of the immigrants. Thus, in cities like New York, Philadelphia, and Boston, parishes serving various immigrant populations such as Germans, Poles, and Italians sometimes settled within blocks of each other. The parishioners came from different parts of Europe, spoke different languages, preferred different lines of work, but were united in their Catholicism and their desire to make it as newcomers to America. The national parish assured them of religious identity, helped them to preserve their language and traditions, and eased them into American society.

As parishes, these national churches operated differently depending upon their congregation. The German parishes had powerful lay trustees who sometimes bought land and constructed churches without consultation with the clergy. The territorial parishes, that is, those designed for everyone living within a certain area or neighborhood, were generally the preserve of the Irish who worked closely with the clergy and held them in great esteem. In his book *Catholic America*, John Cogley noted: "For years, the 'American' parish was the 'Irish' parish."[23]

But in any of these parishes there could be tensions between the people, priests, and bishop over matters of jurisdiction. Lay trustees generally had control of the purse strings in the parish, which sometimes put them at odds with the pastor or the bishop. The battle over the assignment of priests proved thornier still. In some parishes the people sought control, or at least veto power, over the assignment of priests. The bishop coveted the same control. When they disagreed, sometimes the bishop assigned a different priest who might be more sympathetic to the needs of a particular parish; at other times, when compromise did not work, the bishop threatened the people with excommunication if they did not accept his appointee. Jay Dolan comments: "Such struggles over power and authority were typically American and Catholic. In the United States, nineteenth-century Catholics, unlike their Protestant neighbors, did not go to battle over theological issues; they fought over power."[24] In the nineteenth century the American church escaped complete control by the hierarchy or clergy. In many cases the laity held the deed to parish property and buildings, giving them more of a say in the governing of the parish. As the number of clergy increased and as pastors stayed in parishes for longer tenures, lay trusteeism diminished and episcopal and clerical power increased. As noted in the first chapter, this situation demonstrated a conflict of wills and authority that is revisited today with an increasingly active and powerful laity sometimes confronted by obstinate clericalism and authoritarianism in the institutional manifestation of the church.

Meanwhile, the church in Rome attempted to solidify its power. In 1870 the First Vatican Council convened at the insistence of Pope Pius IX, and declared the pope infallible in matters of faith and morals. While Rome assumed greater powers over the cardinals and bishops, American bishops and priests consolidated their power over the laity. In 1907, an American bishop proclaimed: "The Church is not a republic or democracy, but a monarchy; . . . all her authority is from above and rests in her Hierarchy; . . . while the faithful of the laity have divinely given rights to receive all the blessed ministrations of the Church, they have absolutely no right whatever to rule and govern."[25]

Despite ongoing disputes involving lay people, priests, and bishops, for the most part the church functioned as a cohesive unit in America. One exception to this cohesive unity led to the formation of the Polish National Catholic Church, a group of Polish-speaking churches who felt dissatisfied with central authority and who chose to separate from the main body of the church. They elected one of their own, Reverend Francis Hodur, to lead them, and he served as bishop until his death in 1953. The movement attracted only a small number of Polish-speaking churches, the vast majority of which remained faithful to Rome.

Ukrainian Catholics, who adhere to the eastern rite, proved an exception to this pattern. Most Catholic immigrants arrived from western Europe and followed the Latin rite, which meant that they obeyed all of the prescriptions of Rome. Eastern-rite Catholics came from eastern Europe and recognized Rome's authority but had a different liturgical style that separated them from Latin-rite Catholics, and their priests could marry. The American bishops' desire to impose mandatory celibacy on the Ukrainian clergy led to a schism that began in 1891 in Archbishop John Ireland's archdiocese of Minneapolis. Rather than succumb to the American bishops' demands, the Ukrainians forged new alliances with the Russian Orthodox Church that would allow them to continue their liturgical customs and a married priesthood. This schism represented two different visions of the church:

One view advocated a congregational model of the church, which emphasized a democratic functioning of authority with an emphasis on local autonomy. According to this model, lay people and clergy would work together and share responsibility for the organization and government of the parish. The other view supported a hierarchical model of the church; championed by the hierarchy, this emphasized the authority of the clergy over the lay people, with the bishop exercising supreme authority over everyone, priests and lay people alike.[26]

The story of the Ukrainian Church foreshadows that of the post-Vatican II church in America. In the later part of the twentieth century, however, the divisions within the church are not ethnically based, and the issues go beyond liturgy and celibacy. Nevertheless, the foundational issues of power, authority, and autonomy remain. What kind of power does the institutional church have over Catholics, and who exercises it? These are questions that continue to be raised even as the church begins a new millennium.

Institutional authority and power were not distributed evenly among the immigrant communities. The Irish (Irish-born or Irish American) dominated the church hierarchy in America, accounting for 62 percent of the bishops at the turn of the century and still have the largest number of bishops in the American church to this day.[27] The balance of power between laity and clergy eroded as the American church produced a greater number of vocations to the priesthood from the immigrant population. The clergy's power and prestige grew as an immigrant church accorded them special status. Many Catholic families considered it an honor to have a brother, sister, or priest among their ranks. Families were large (by today's standard), so one child accepting celibacy certainly did not threaten the continuation of the family name. Besides, immigrant families were poor and ill-educated. Sending a boy off to the seminary, or a girl to the convent, meant that he or she would be well educated and cared for and end up in a highly respected profession, revered in the Catholic subculture of America.

The creation of ethnic national parishes kept the immigrant community divided—Irish Catholics, Italian Catholics, Polish Catholics and German Catholics did not interact extensively. Even though immigrant neighborhoods were ethnically diverse, ethnic national parishes permitted people to associate only with their own. In some areas of the Northeast, for example, Catholics considered an Irish boy marrying an Italian girl tantamount to a mixed marriage. Nor were the clergy well integrated. They kept to their own as well—in the parishioners they served and clerical friends with whom they associated.

For all of their internal differences, several factors united immigrant Catholics, not the least of which was their Catholic identity. Newly arrived in America, many were unskilled or semiskilled; most spoke a different language. Social, economic, political, and religious outsiders in America, their Catholicism constituted an important part of their identity and a source of solidarity. In a society dominated by Protestant money and power, immigrant Catholics found strength and solace in their religion. At the same time, they were eager to fit in. Not only did they need to prove that they had severed political ties with their homelands, but they also wanted to confirm that they were really American. This meant overcoming suspicions that their first loyalty might be to Rome, perceived by many Americans as a foreign power that could undermine Catholics' commitment to their adopted homeland. Thus, at every opportunity Catholics demonstrated their loyalty to America.

The bishops were equally anxious to demonstrate their loyalty to country. They expressed this clearly at the Third Plenary Council of Baltimore in 1884:

> We think we can claim to be acquainted with the laws, institutions, and spirit of the Catholic Church, and with the laws, institutions, and spirit of our country; and we emphatically declare that there is no antagonism between them. A Catholic finds himself at home in the United States; for the influence of his Church has constantly been exercised in behalf of individual rights and popular liberties. And the right-minded American nowhere finds himself more at home than in the Catholic Church, for nowhere else can he breathe more freely that atmosphere of Divine truth, which alone can make us free.

African-American Catholics

African Americans have been part of the Catholic constituency in America since colonial times. Well-to-do Catholic families and the Jesuits who settled in Maryland held slaves. Many of these slaves converted to the religion of their masters, in this case to Catholicism. However, just as in the colonies and later in the country, they were not treated as equals in the church. Before the Civil War, freed slaves encountered prejudice from the church hierarchy. After the Civil War, segregated parishes arose. In the antebellum period, the Catholic Church did not make much of an effort to convert the Negro population, the majority of whom were located in the South where Protestant churches dominated the religious landscape. New Orleans stands as an exception with its sizable Catholic population. Xavier University of New Orleans testifies to this. Founded in 1915 by Katherine Drexel and the Sisters of the Blessed Sacrament, it became the first Roman Catholic university for African Americans. St. Louis and Baltimore also had long-standing African-American Catholic populations.

The black Catholic population interrupted the pattern of neighborhoods dominated by European ethnicity. It had neither the numbers nor the ties to clergy and hierarchy that the ethnic communities had. For example, in mid-nineteenth century New York City Irish immigrants, themselves the subjects of exploitation, would regularly discriminate against the free blacks who competed with them for jobs. The conflict peaked in the summer of 1863 when whites rioted and attacked members of the black community.[28]

John McGreevy, a historian at Notre Dame, chronicles the movement of African Americans from the South to northern cities in *Parish Boundaries*.[29] They received a chilly reception in the church. While many Catholics fought on the side of the North in the Civil War to abolish slavery, they held deep-seated racist views nonetheless. The North supported segregation, and for a long time the church did little to resist or change this social pattern.

Tensions Between Rome and America

In the late nineteenth century Pope Leo XIII became increasingly distressed by the independence of some leaders within the American church. The church-state relationship in America differed from the one the church enjoyed in Europe where it was privileged by the state. The pope would have liked the Catholic Church in America to enjoy the same legal status as the church in most of Europe, where Catholicism was the state religion. This relationship meant government support for churches and Catholic institutions such as universities and hospitals. The American separation of church and state afforded no such relationship. Leo XIII preferred that the church be treated differently, as he expressed in his 1895 encyclical to the U.S. church, *Longinqua* (To the Bishops of the United States), which in part declared: "[The U.S. Church] would bring forth more abundant fruits if, in addition to liberty, she enjoyed the favor of the laws and the patronage of the public authority." This encyclical was one of a series in which Leo XIII decried the secularization of governments and attempted to assert his authority in Europe and America as his political influence and secular authority were eroding, even in his own backyard. If the church accommodated democracy, the pope feared that there would be those who would want to introduce democracy into the church.

Some among the American hierarchy preferred that the church be separate from the state. Cardinal James Gibbons of Baltimore and Archbishop John Ireland of St. Paul were two of the leaders of the "Americanists" as they came to be called. America was a religiously pluralistic environment, and many thought it unwise to attempt to influence the state to prefer one religion over another in its laws or customs. As the historian of American Catholicism David O'Brien wrote: "Religious freedom, separation of church and state, and religious pluralism, the three basic elements of this new religious culture, were bound to shape a new form of public Catholicism."[30]

Rome took a different view, however. On January 22, 1899, Pope Leo XIII issued *Testem Benevolentiae* (A Testament of Esteem), an encyclical directed at the American church. In it, the pope criticized those who wanted greater liberty in the American church: "There are some among you who conceive of and desire a Church in America different from that which is in the rest of the world. One in unity of doctrine as in the unity of government, such is the Catholic Church, and since God has established its center and foundation in the Chair of St. Peter, one which is rightly called Rome, for where Peter is, there is the Church." The pope held that temporal power derives from God and that the church represents God's presence in the world.

The pope was not without supporters among the American hierarchy. Archbishop Michael Corrigan of New York and Bishop Bernard McQuaid of Rochester believed that the American church should not stray far from Rome, even though McQuaid initially opposed the definition of papal infallibility introduced at Vatican I.[31] The 1899 encyclical put a stop to the disputes between Americanists and their more traditional opponents. It also allowed the Americanists to reassert their fidelity to Rome. The American church historian Gerald Fogarty claims that: "The indirect language of the letter allowed the Americanists readily to submit."[32]

And submit they did. The American hierarchy did not want to jeopardize its relationship with Rome or sacrifice the unity of the church. At the same time, however, the conditions that gave birth to Americanism did not evaporate and the church would revisit the issues raised at the turn of the twentieth century in the second half of that century after Vatican II when tensions between Rome and America increased.

A second demonstration of Rome's authority occurred shortly after the

Americanist controversy. In 1907, Leo XIII's successor, Pius X, fearing that the church's teachings were jeopardized by contemporary intellectual trends, issued the encyclical, *Pascendi Dominici Gregis* (On the Doctrine of the Modernists), warning that the church should not adopt the ways of the modern world. This warning applied particularly to Europe and America. A number of prominent European theologians like the French biblical scholar Alfred Loisy, who studied the Bible as an historical document like other historical documents, and the English theologian George Tyrell, who criticized neo-Scholasticism, increasingly appropriated modern scholarly methods in their work. Another of the offenders, in the pope's view, was the American Isaac Thomas Hecker, the founder of the Paulists, who attempted to translate Catholic teachings into distinctly American formulations.[33] Rome's authority over the American church further tightened when Pius X required priests to take an oath against modernism. The result, according to political scientist Richard Gelm, was that "Fear of Rome killed any intellectual spirit that resided in seminaries and Catholic institutions of higher learning. American Catholicism entered a dark age of conservatism, and strict obedience to Rome overshadowed free intellectual inquiry."[34]

CHAPTER THREE

A Brief History of Catholics in America: 1900 to the Second Vatican Council

The Americanist controversy and the oath against modernism involved the hierarchy and clergy of the church.[1] Catholic laity, who were mostly immigrants, were anxious to prove their loyalty to America. At the time of World War I, many Catholics had emigrated from countries which eventually became embroiled in anti-American wars. This fact, coupled with their connections to Rome, made them easy targets for anti-Catholic bigotry, and there was no shortage of that within the Protestant-dominated United States. As John Cogley noted: "Anti-Catholicism has been called America's oldest and most abiding prejudice."[2] Institutional expressions of this bigotry began with the Know-Nothings in the South before the Civil War, were manifest by the American Protective Association in the Midwest at the end of the nineteenth century, and peaked with the Ku Klux Klan in the early twentieth century. One priest who was deeply sensitive to anti-Catholic sentiment, but who did not allow the bigotry to go unanswered, was Ernest Audran of Vincennes, Indiana. In the 1890s, citing events that led to the Baltimore Council, he lamented:

> Although a century had nearly elapsed, the social condition of Catholics remained extremely precarious. Sectarian malice, which had accumulated calumnies upon calumnies, falsehoods upon falsehoods, on the doctrine, history, and practices of the Church, had so prejudiced minds against them as to keep Catholics, timid at all times, in a state of perpetual fear from insults, homicidal mobs, and popular uprisings.

It seemed as if the proud name of an American freeman, so valued by all the rest, was practically for them, a lie.

They grew rapidly. Their rapid growth was presented as a subject of alarm. They were to be found mostly in cities, yet were there in minorities. They considered it prudent to efface themselves as much as possible. Dire experience taught them the necessity. The burning of the Charlestown convent, in Massachusetts, the so-called nativist riots in Philadelphia, and New York, the Know-Nothing movement and the terrors it created everywhere, ending by the awful work of Bloody Monday, in the city of Louisville, Ky., were lessons not to be forgotten—not to be made little of.

Who would have thought it? The Civil War created a diversion which gave relief.[3]

Even the 1928 presidential nomination of Al Smith, a Catholic Democrat who was then governor of New York, did not quell anti-Catholicism in America. Smith's loss to the Quaker Herbert Hoover was due to a number of factors, but there is little doubt that his Catholicism hurt him with many constituencies in the election. Mainstream Protestants were leery of Vatican control, and post-election folklore had Smith sending a one-word telegram to the pope: "Unpack."

When Woodrow Wilson committed America to World War I, Catholics signed up for the military in droves. In 1917 James Flaherty, Supreme Knight of the Knights of Columbus, an organization for Catholic men, successfully petitioned the government to have the Knights approved as a service organization for Catholic soldiers, until then an exclusive function of the YMCA. The bishops created the National Catholic War Council (NCWC) to support the war effort in general, and Catholic troops in particular. The creation of this body under episcopal control usurped the authority of the Knights, a lay organization in existence since 1882. This was another instance of the solidification of episcopal authority over the laity, this even though prominent industrialists like Patrick Henry Callaghan of Louisville, Kentucky, himself a Knight, helped to shape the NCWC.[4]

Some bishops preferred to take their orders from Rome, and others thought the new organization interfered with their independence. However, the NCWC promoted conversation among the bishops and provided a mechanism for them to speak to the American people, Catholic and non-Catholic, with a unified voice. Or so it seemed. In 1919 the committee issued a document with a blueprint for postwar reconstruction. The document

Catholic candidate for U.S. president, Al Smith on a
visit to the University of Notre Dame. UNDA

relied on the strategies of Monsignor John A. Ryan, a moral theology professor at Catholic University, known for his support for the working person
and his liberal views on the economy and social justice.[5] It called for higher
wages and a voice for the workers in the operation of industries. Business
leaders decried it, labeling it socialism. Nonetheless, the bishops rewarded
Ryan by appointing him director of the council's Social Action Department.
Many saw the council as a chance for the church to influence national policy.

In order to achieve that ambition beyond the postwar era, in 1919 the
bishops formed the National Catholic Welfare Conference as the successor
to the NCWC. This organization and its several committees (the most powerful of which was the Administrative Committee) coordinated all dimensions of the church's work on a national level. An internal dispute among
the bishops almost prevented its creation. Conservative bishops, lead by
Cardinal William O'Connell of Boston, viewed the NCWC as the continuation of Americanism which the Vatican had suppressed at the turn of the

century. Some bishops refused to support the NCWC financially, making it difficult for the controversial organization to meet its budget. Despite these obstacles, by 1920 the NCWC established a Washington office to interact with secular national bodies responsible for American policy. Now the bishops had a mechanism in place to speak as a national body and to inject their voices into the public debate.

Cardinal Gibbons was the first chair of the organization, although his tenure was short-lived. After his death in March 1921, a debate ensued among the hierarchy as to who would replace him. The likely successor, William O'Connell of Boston, the senior American prelate, was embroiled in a controversy when it became public that his nephew, Monsignor James P. E. O'Connell, whom he had appointed at a young age to be the chancellor of the Boston archdiocese, and Cardinal O'Connell's personal chaplain, Father David J. Toomey, were each secretly married. The bishops elected Louis Walsh of Portland, Maine. Rome, however, influenced by several American prelates (including O'Connell), suppressed the NCWC in March 1922 on canonical grounds that their annual meetings could only be convened if the pope called for them. Months of negotiations with the Vatican overturned the suppression, and Pius XI endorsed the organization.

James Gibbons, the cardinal who was the ninth archbishop of Baltimore, epitomized public Catholicism. He received guidance from his mentor Archbishop Martin Spalding of Baltimore, who nurtured Gibbons in the ways of the church. Gibbons, the youngest bishop among 700 attending the First Vatican Council, exhibited extraordinary charisma and wielded immense ecclesial power. Since the archdiocese of Baltimore at that time included the national capital and the federal government, he became well known in political circles. From 1886 to 1911 Gibbons enjoyed the privileges of being the only U.S. cardinal. Sympathetic to the Americanists, Gibbons knew how to deal with Rome diplomatically and prevent further damage to the American church after the initial condemnation by Pope Leo XIII. He also ingratiated himself with political figures, leading then former President Theodore Roosevelt to say of him: "Taking your life as a whole, I think you now occupy the position of being the most respected and venerated, and useful citizen of our country."[6]

The intrigue of behind-the-scenes episcopal machinations hardly affected ordinary Catholics, who continued to look to the church for cohesion, spiritual reinforcement, and moral guidance. Charles Morris recounts an example of this piety when over a million Catholics attended the Eucharistic Congress in Chicago during a week in June 1926.[7] They came from all over America to pray, sing, worship, and bond together in a spiritual event that underscored their Catholic identity. The mystery of the Eucharist, the pomp of the prelates, and the ethnic diversity of the crowds characterized Catholic culture; and this was a chance to assert their loyalty and their uniqueness in America. It did not matter that the bishops were at odds with one another, or even that some were corrupt. These princes of the church, with their distinctive garb and public recognition, made the laity proud to be Catholic. They were happy to pray, pay, and obey.

The 1930s in America offered a stark contrast to the 1920s. The depression leveled the rich and wiped out the savings of the working class. It left a trail of social needs from New York to California. The Vatican took the lead on social ethics when Pius XI proclaimed the encyclical *Quadragesimo Anno* (On the Reconstruction of the Social Order), which commemorated and advanced the ideas of Leo XIII's 1891 encyclical *Rerum Novarum* (On Capital and Labor). These were the heart of Catholic social teaching. These encyclicals articulated a theology and a program of social justice that were championed by a group of bishops, priests, and laity. In light of the encyclicals, clergy defended the rights of the American worker and supported the formation of labor unions. The hierarchy of the American church also supported many of the reforms initiated by Franklin Delano Roosevelt in the New Deal, such as social security, minimum wage, and the National Labor Relations Act. Not all Catholics, clerical and lay, looked favorably upon this kind of activism in the church, however. Some refrained from active participation and others "avoided controversy by prudently limiting themselves to scholarly pronouncements and general statements about the wisdom of the papal encyclicals."[8]

One of the voices for social justice and fair treatment of the working person was that of Monsignor John Ryan, the architect of the 1919 "Bishops' Program of Social Reconstruction" after World War I. An advocate of the so-called "social gospel," he tied Catholic social teaching to economics and labor in America. Ryan was sometimes referred to as "The Right Reverend New Deal" because of his close personal ties with and support for FDR.

Another deeply committed to the labor movement in the 1930s and '40s was Monsignor John P. Boland from Buffalo, New York. He served as the regional chair of the National Recovery Administration, the Buffalo National Labor Relations Board, and the New York State Labor Relations Board.

In the same period Peter Maurin and Dorothy Day founded the Catholic

Worker movement, a lay initiative designed to address the needs of the poor. The endeavor eventually led to the foundation of a newspaper, a soup kitchen, and a shelter that has served as a model of social action for millions of Americans, Catholic and non-Catholic. Together, Day and Maurin attempted to put the papal encyclicals into practice, to create places where "the Works of Mercy could be practiced."[9]

Born on November 8, 1897, in Brooklyn, Day was a convert to Catholicism. Considered a saint by many contemporary Catholics, she did not always pursue holiness. Restlessness characterized her early years. She moved often, quit college after two years, worked as a journalist, changed jobs, was married and divorced, had an abortion, bore a baby out of wedlock, befriended the writer Eugene O'Neill—all before she found a spiritual home as a Catholic in 1927.

In 1932 she met Maurin, a Frenchman living in New York. Maurin was more conservative than Day in his political and ecclesial views; nevertheless they forged a lasting friendship.[10] Both staunch pacifists, they founded a paper, the *Catholic Worker*, that sold for a penny a copy and grew to a circulation of 200,000 on the eve of World War II. Their motive was not profit, it was prophecy in the classical sense of the biblical prophets who called God's people to account for their actions. They also opened hospitality houses for the poor, the first one being Day's apartment. These were simple dwellings with "little ordered regularity to things, no scheduled scrubbings and paintings, and no aseptic odors overriding the smell of bodies, long unwashed."[11] The volunteers running the house assumed the poverty of the guests so that it was difficult for an outsider to tell them apart. But the idea took hold and by World War II there were forty houses and six farms, the site of *Worker* retreats, spread around the country. Dorothy Day's identification with the poor would be matched only by Mother Teresa's later in the century. Her deep spirituality as well as her unsettled youth paralleled that of Thomas Merton, a monk twenty years her junior, who would command an international following while spending his life in a Kentucky monastery. In her later years, when some were complaining that there was no freedom in the church, she remarked: "Well, I say that we are an example of the tremendous liberty that there is in the Church . . . the layman should go ahead and quit being dependent . . . you don't need permission to perform the works of mercy."[12]

The Catholic Worker movement continues to flourish to this day with over 130 Houses of Hospitality throughout the United States. The members of the movement still embrace voluntary poverty and advocate for the poor

Catholic Worker founder Dorothy Day attends a religious service with Mrs. Coretta King supporting farmworkers. CATHOLIC NEWS SERVICE

as well as feed and clothe them. The newspaper maintains a circulation of 100,000 worldwide. Paulist Films released a full-length feature film, *Entertaining Angels*, on Dorothy Day's life in 1996 in which Moira Kelly played Dorothy and Martin Sheen played Peter Maurin. Her autobiography, *The Long Loneliness*, originally published in 1952, reached a new generation in its reissue in 1997[13] and the centenary of Day's birth focused additional attention on her life and ministry.

For much of his life Thomas Merton, arguably the most influential monk of this century, lived the quiet life of a hermit on the grounds of Our Lady of Gethsemane Trappist monastery in Kentucky. That solitude disguised a whirlwind of intensity, controversy, and contribution to the American and world church. Like Dorothy Day, he acknowledged no strong attachment to religion in his youth. Born in France in 1915, he grew up in that country, in England, and on Long Island, New York. In his early years Merton led the unfettered life of a student among intellectuals at Cambridge and Columbia universities. He fathered a child but did not marry, flirted with communism, converted to Catholicism at age 23, and joined the Trappists at age 26. Dorothy Day influenced Merton's decision to become a Catholic as one of his letters to her testifies: "If there were no *Catholic Worker* and such forms of witness, I would never have joined the Catholic Church."[14]

Early in his monastic life he published *The Seven Storey Mountain*, a best-selling autobiography. His life as a monk was never as peaceful as his surroundings. Conflicted about his relationship with the abbot, about the pull of the world despite the desire for solitude, about his genius sometimes tainted with pride, about his popularity as an author, and about his passion for justice, he led a complicated existence, far afield from the simple monastic life he initially desired. His celebrity provided a glimpse into monastic life for millions of Americans who read his books and noted his activities. He made the contemplative life more than respected; he made it attractive. Numbers increased at Gethsemane, and no doubt the presence of Merton was responsible. Merton was famous, but fame was not a welcomed commodity in the monastery. His notoriety and talent made his monastic life all the more difficult, partly due to the expectations the world now had for him, partly because, even in the monastery, the side effect of fame outside the monastery was jealousy and envy inside.

The conflicts with monastic habits and controlling authority forced him out of his passivity. Merton's biographer, Monika Furlong, contends that "He was no longer dutiful, no longer worried about being a 'good monk.' "[15] By this she does not mean that Merton abandoned the monastic ideal of aspiring to live close to God, rather that he wearied of the picayune regulations and the rote practices that numbed the mind and the spirit. If the abbot insisted on enforcing disciplines that prevented Merton from reaching greater depths of spirituality, then disobedience to authority became a permissible course of action. After all, the Sabbath was made for people, not people for the Sabbath. Merton turned his attention from the monastery to the world, involving himself in the problems of racism, war, and the environment. "This extraordinary release of energy not surprisingly felt threatening to his superiors, who somehow sensed that Merton had escaped, had passed from beyond their control."[16] The tension between authority and obedience already demonstrated between the bishops and the Vatican, the laity and clergy, and the clergy and the hierarchy found its way even into the secluded life of the monastery.

The monastery remained home for Merton, but he traveled regularly to confer with others of like mind and to participate in conferences on a variety of topics. He also changed his lifestyle, retreating to a hermitage in the

Trappist monk Thomas Merton in his work clothes on the grounds of the monastery.
CATHOLIC NEWS SERVICE

forest near the monastery. There he found the solitude that had eluded him in the larger community. Nevertheless, he frequently entertained visitors at his retreat—including long-standing friends, monks, and often well-known personalities like Daniel Berrigan from the antiwar movement. He continued to publish scholarly works, poetry, fiction, and spiritual tracts. Ironically, his life ended outside of the quiet monastic world of Kentucky. He died in an accident in Bangkok on December 10, 1968, while attending a conference of world religions.

The Baby Boomers

World War II interrupted everyone's life in some fashion or another. Although the church maintained neutrality as long as it could, after the attack on Pearl Harbor, Catholics enlisted in the military in large numbers even though there was less pressure to prove their patriotism as their numbers and influence grew. From 1940 to 1960, aided by the postwar baby boom, the Catholic population doubled. The 1950s saw the largest expansion of schools and churches since the Council of Baltimore. As the population moved to the suburbs, bishops and pastors expanded their land holdings, physical plants, and programs, delving into the pockets of Catholics to pay for them. The GI Bill paved the way to higher education for a generation of veterans, including those matriculating at Catholic colleges and universities in unprecedented numbers. Catholics continued to relish the mystery of the Latin Mass, revere the clergy and sisters, fear punishment for sin, and act in a xenophobic manner toward other Christians and non-Christians alike. Catholic culture reached its apex.

The answer to the question of whether or not a person could be a good Catholic and a good American was a resounding yes. The 1956 nomination hearings for the appointment of William J. Brennan Jr. to the Supreme Court is an example of a prominent Catholic's unhesitating willingness to support the country. When asked if he might follow the pronouncements of the pope by which he was bound as a Catholic over the requirements of his oath to uphold the Constitution, Brennan responded "[W]hat shall control me is the oath that I took to support the Constitution and laws of the United States and so act upon the cases that come before me for decision that it is that oath and that alone which governs."[17] A few years later, while running for president, John F. Kennedy would have to make a similar disclaimer during a speech to the Texas Baptist Ministerial Association reassuring his audience and all Americans that his Catholicism would not interfere with his duties.

At the same time that Catholic culture was so embedded, its foundations were stirring. Catholics were assimilating into American society, becoming wealthier, better educated, and geographically diversified. The majority were no longer immigrants. Opportunities in business, government, entertainment, education, and industry became available to Catholics in increasing numbers. They did not hold sway on the top echelons of the professions, but doors were opening that would change the economic, professional, and social status of the rising generation. Along with Georgetown, Notre Dame, Boston College, and Holy Cross, they matriculated at Harvard, Princeton, and Yale. The gap between Protestants and Catholics was narrowing though there remained a large segment of Catholic parents who viewed the traditionally elite universities as dangerous to the faith. They preferred a pastorally nurturing environment rather than prestige.

Hispanic Catholics

One immigrant population that grew but remained a minority was the Hispanic community. The church acknowledged this and attempted to address the issues relevant to this community by establishing the Bishops' Committee for the Spanish-Speaking under the inaugural direction of Archbishop Robert E. Lucey of San Antonio. At the annual bishops' meeting in November 1944, Archbishop Samuel Stritch of Chicago, who headed the American Board of Catholic Missions, appointed a committee composed of bishops from Los Angeles, Denver, Sante Fe, and San Antonio to establish "a plan for work among the Mexicans of the United States to improve their social conditions, to overcome the efforts of proselytizers, and to promote the work of the Church among them."[18]

Among the things noted by the Bishops' Committee for the Spanish-Speaking were the poverty of the community, the lack of organization, the uninformed Catholic sense, and the contempt in which they were regularly held by the dominant population. The U.S. government was complicit to some degree in creating the situation by allowing hundreds of thousands of Mexican nationals (known as Braceros) legally into the country to be agricultural workers.[19] In response to the problems faced by this migrant community, the bishops hoped to build parish centers in which to educate and inculturate them, proselytize them, encourage vocations, provide better health care, and develop leaders. The bishops approved regional centers reporting to San Antonio. Nevertheless, it was difficult for mostly English-speaking priests to reach the migrant worker population.

The Protestants were making the effort to do so, however, as noted by Archbishop Lucey in 1955. Baptist preachers organized a "Cotton Patch Crusade" with fourteen ministers accompanying migrant workers in the fields of West Texas.[20] To counteract their efforts, Lucey sent maps of the locations of migrant workers to priests and Catholic Action workers "so that spiritual services may be given to them and they may be kept from Protestant proselytizers." He also began programs to teach seminarians to speak Spanish and imported some Mexican priests to help minister to this growing and underserved population. He brought priests and lay workers from the Southwest together with their counterparts from the North (the first such meeting was held in April 1956 in Grand Rapids, Michigan) to discuss their common problems in ministering to migrant workers. Archbishop Lucey managed to get the Labor Department to assign a person to contact the Growers' Associations and individual farmers to allow the priests to provide religious services for the workers. This action led to a national bishops' committee for migrant workers.

In their efforts to maintain the loyalty of migrant workers the Bishops' Committee for the Spanish-Speaking prepared a kit to be distributed to the workers that included a picture of Our Lady of Guadalupe for the front door of migrants' quarters carrying the inscription (in Spanish): "This is a Catholic home and Protestant propaganda will not be admitted." Obviously the church knew that Catholics were converting to Protestant denominations in significant numbers. The Protestants, while perhaps not passing out propaganda signs for the doors of their converts, were rewarding the most promising among them with scholarships, with a view toward training them to be ministers among their own people or in other Latin American countries in the future.

The bishops recognized as early as the 1950s that the clergy could not minister adequately to this burgeoning population. The final line of the 1958 annual report of the Bishops Committee for the Spanish-Speaking simply read: "Unless we get the laity into this program, the situation is hopeless."[21] But recruiting dedicated Catholics to this apostolate that had "no particular glamour" was an uphill battle. Aside from guarding their continued loyalty to Catholicism, the church attempted to bring economic justice to the migrant workers, often against the powerful growers who exploited them as cheap labor and sometimes defying the government that perceived them as encroachers.

Some courageous visionaries did join the effort. Cesar Chavez, the great Mexican social activist, attracted a great deal of attention to the migrant population not only in California but all over the country. A committee of American bishops mediated the dispute between growers and workers in 1970.[22] Some conservative voices objected to the bishops' efforts saying that they were favoring unionism. One such publication, Twin Circle, editorialized that "large numbers of Catholics have already been alienated from the Church, and thousands of non-Catholics have been embittered by the arbitrary, high-handed action of the bishops' committee."[23] People like Cardinal Roger Mahoney of Los Angeles (as a priest and as Auxiliary Bishop of Fresno) ministered to and brokered talks between the grape growers and the migrant workers that resulted in more equitable wages and contracts for the workers. The migrants' plight received national publicity and became a cause for many social justice-minded Americans. In Chicago the bishops created a National Office for Catholic Migrants in 1960.[24]

By that time there were Spanish-speaking apostolates in fifty-seven archdioceses and dioceses. The Cursillo movement, a Latin-culture oriented retreat program, offered a Catholic spiritual experience to which the Hispanic community could relate. The bishops mixed the quest for political and economic independence with proselytization stating that: "The [Mexican] is

Advocate for farmworkers Cesar Chavez finds Catholic support during a march in Waterbury, Connecticut, July 1974. AP/WIDE WORLD PHOTOS

determined to get organized and he is marching to freedom and justice under the banner of Our Lady of Guadalupe with Catholic priests at his side . . . the Bishops have seen to it that religion was taught to all the people regardless of the fact that some were unlettered and tragically poor. That policy is paying off among the Spanish speaking."[25] Not shying away from the civic implications of their efforts, the bishops urged priests to help the Hispanic population register to vote. "Priests assigned to the Spanish-Speaking apostolate must not imagine that everything political is alien to their vocation. There is a distinction, for example, between encouraging voter registration and engaging in party politics."[26]

The 1950s and '60s brought Cuban refugees to the United States, literally by the boatload, with thousands arriving monthly at the height of the exodus from Cuba. Miami served as the port of entry, and for tens of thousands of Cuban refugees, the final destination. Others found resettlement assistance from Catholic Relief Services. Many of these immigrants were well educated, successful, and anxious to keep their language and culture.

An economic division marked the Spanish-speaking immigrants—some acquiring education, status, and professions, others in the labor class struggling to make ends meet.

Puerto Ricans gravitated north to New York City. By 1964 there were an estimated ten million Spanish-speaking residents in America (one-fifth of all Catholics in the country) coming from various Latin cultures.[27] One of the difficulties in reaching the widespread Hispanic population in America rested with the liturgy—conducted in Latin before Vatican II and in English after. The bishops recognized the need to develop a ritual in Spanish that would be understood and to which the community could readily relate. Latin American bishops already had one which the Americans adapted for their use.

Today the Hispanic Catholic population continues to grow although there is still significant movement to Evangelical churches. The church persists in attempting to address the needs of the Spanish-speaking communities, but with only moderate success. When one pastor realized that the Spanish-speaking Catholics in Miami were reluctant to attend the main church, he set up several store-front churches as missions. These attracted large numbers perhaps because the community was more comfortable with what Evangelical Christians had popularized.

Black Catholic Experience

While the church attempted to nurture its ties with the Hispanic population, the church and society continued to struggle with their relationship to the black community. As African Americans moved north in greater numbers to the burgeoning cities during the twentieth century, they often encountered prejudice, bigotry, and hatred from the pastor to the people in the pews. For example, at Holy Angels Parish in Chicago the pastor routinely requested his few African-American parishioners to sit in six back pews on the right side "and let the white people who built this church sit in the center."[28] As late as the early 1950s, at Holy Name Church in Kansas City, a sign in front urged blacks to attend mass at a neighboring church—until Rev. William R. Barron, O.P., tore down the sign and invited *all* to participate in services.

At issue were a number of closely held traditions and dispositions. Neighborhoods of ethnic clans populated northern cities. Polish immigrants lived in "the Polish neighborhood" and worshiped at the Polish parish where the services were conducted in Latin (as they were in all Catholic churches), but the sermons were delivered in Polish and the parish conducted business in Polish. The same held true for the Germans, Italians, French, and so on. The Irish stood out as the exception that became the norm. Their parishes constituted the territorial parishes, that is, those designated for anyone who lived within certain parish boundaries established by the diocese. Sermons and business were in English, though often English with an Irish brogue, since many of the clergy claimed Irish immigrant ancestry or came directly from Ireland, which had an abundance of priests, many of whom expressed a willingness to go to America. African Americans, who migrated north looking for work in the factories and industries that required skilled and unskilled labor, found themselves outsiders and unwelcome. Many parishioners feared that an encroaching black population would change the character of their neighborhoods and, as many argued, lower the value of their homes. Many white Catholics rationalized that segregation of races was natural and people wanted only to associate with their own race. The Catholic community ignored morality and enforced the segregation laws.

In this situation the Vatican led the way morally while many American Catholics perpetuated the sin of racism. On a number of occasions, the pope or Vatican officials expressed concern for the African-American community. After terrifying race riots in Chicago in 1919, the Vatican condemned the violence and urged bishops to address the issues of the black community. At that time only 2 percent of African Americans were Catholic. The Vatican's admonitions meant one thing; life in the neighborhoods and parishes meant another. Some sectors of the Catholic hierarchy acted responsibly, but others ignored Vatican warnings. Cardinal Spellman opened all Catholic schools in his New York archdiocese to qualified African-American students in 1939, and the Jesuits began admitting black seminarians in 1945, as did St. Louis University. Others, however, including bishops and pastors, ignored Rome's urgings.

Not until 1958 did the American bishops produce a document dealing directly with the problem of racism. "Discrimination and the Christian Conscience" denounced segregation, but many liberals in the church thought the church spoke too late. Further, it did not stem the tide of racism in the country or among Catholics. To accomplish that would take marches and civil disobedience, not pronouncements. It would take the 1960s and figures such as Martin Luther King Jr. to energize churches to fight racism and alter the moral disposition of the United States.

In the 1960s, Americans confronted racism directly—sometimes violently, often nonviolently. John McGreevy describes the era poignantly.

In short, "race" helped mark the cultural changes sweeping through American Catholicism and American society. Between 1964 and 1967, two distinctly Catholic visions of church, community, and authority clashed in the streets, parishes, and Catholic schools of northern cities. Catholic liberals questioned traditional parochial structures while becoming active participants in local civil rights coalitions. Their activism illuminated not only the enduring strength of Catholic racism but the distance now separating various parts of the Catholic community.[29]

Neighborhoods changed. African Americans moved into the cities in increasing numbers, and whites fled to the rapidly growing suburbs.[30] The term "inner-city" became part of the American vocabulary. In popular consciousness it signified poor, minority, few opportunities, run-down, and dangerous. For the African-American population it signified all of these too; but it also meant home, their neighborhood. It meant families, churches, stores, schools and playgrounds.

The population shift had a severe impact on city parishes, most of which had been built during the heyday of immigrant Catholicism. Large complexes often with a convent, school, rectory and church occupied an entire city block or more proclaiming a significant presence in the neighborhood. In the forties and fifties, real estate advertisements mentioned in what parish a house was located. The reputation and stability of the parish became a selling point. The residents themselves described where they lived by parish name and not street name or neighborhood. In many cases the population of sections of the city was overwhelmingly Catholic, so that Jews and Protestants found themselves outsiders in their own neighborhoods. Gradually, African Americans moved in replacing the Polish, Irish, and Italian Americans; the vast majority of them were not Catholic.

The implications for the parish were enormous. The decline in parish income marked the most obvious consequence, but perhaps not the most important. It began a radical social change. For decades Catholics had the run of the neighborhoods. Feast days were celebrated publicly with streets blocked off to accommodate long processions of priests, religious, and parishioners.[31] May processions, filled with hundreds of girls in white dresses and boys in school uniforms, were annual events that bestowed an identity on the neighborhood. For Corpus Christi processions (parades through the streets on the feast of the Body and Blood of Christ celebrated in the spring), police and fire departments cooperated in cordoning off sections of the neighborhood and in setting up temporary wooden structures to serve as altars. Parishioners scrubbed porches, steps, curbs, and streets in preparation for the Benediction Service which would take place. Flowers, ribbons, banners festooned the area, and people talked about the event all summer.

These celebrations made up a part of the rhythm of the neighborhood. The parish school was *the* school. Sports teams, socials, dances, novenas, funerals, missions, weddings, lent, and advent set the calendar and created a place in which people found a common identity. People walked to church. Children walked to the parish school, came home for lunch, went to mass as a group on First Fridays, wore uniforms as had their brothers and sisters before them in the school. There was continuity and cohesion.

There was also xenophobia. Catholics were told from the pulpit and in the classroom that they must not enter a Protestant church or a Jewish synagogue. "Mixed marriages" (between a Catholic and a non-Catholic) were discouraged, though not forbidden in canon law. Catholics who did choose to marry Protestants were not permitted to be married in the sanctuary of the church. They were relegated to the rectory in a quiet and brief ceremony or were allowed to have a ceremony outside of the altar rail in the church. Those who wished to marry non-Christians had an even more difficult task. Children born of a Protestant and a Catholic parent were said to be "the product" of a mixed marriage. In any case, the church ensured that the children would be brought up Catholic by requiring the non-Catholic party to sign a document promising such.[32] In many neighborhoods the words "Catholic ghetto" were not a misnomer.

The style of worship in both mainline Protestantism and Roman Catholicism appears stilted to the eyes and ears of many African Americans. Protestantism denied them saints and sacred objects, and Catholicism offered little leeway in its liturgy for African expression via dance, song, or participation. Black Catholic theologian Diana Hayes notes that contemporary black Catholics "see a structure which has tolerated their presence but not encouraged it. They see a structure which has required that they give up much of what was naturally and validly theirs in order to become a part of a sterile, oppressive system in which many have never felt fully at home."[33] Baptists and Methodists have been the most successful Christian churches to recruit African Americans.[34] Reflecting on the church's failure to reach the majority of the African-American community, especially youth, Edward Braxton, auxiliary bishop of St. Louis, wrote: "Young Black people who are attracted to religious faith, especially men who have been in prison, may be more likely to be drawn to some form of Islam, including Louis Farrakhan's

Nation of Islam, than to the Roman Catholic Church."[35] In one instance that drew national publicity, an African-American priest, Reverend George Stallings of the archdiocese of Washington, D.C., severed his affiliation with Rome to form an independent Catholic church. Stallings denounced the Roman Catholic Church as racist and founded the Imani Temple. Shortly after his split with Rome and the archdiocese, a renegade bishop who had been censured by Rome ordained him a bishop.

Today only about 5 percent of American blacks are Catholic, and they comprise less than 3 percent of the church. There are fewer than 400 African-American priests in America, only a handful of whom are bishops or auxiliary bishops. Father George Clements, who is pastor of a now very different Holy Angels Parish in Chicago, founded the Black Catholic Clergy Caucus to offer a forum for black priests and bishops to discuss the particular problems and opportunities facing the black Catholic community. In a 1975 speech in Minneapolis reflecting on the coming American Bicentennial, Brother Joseph M. Davis, at the time the Director of the National Office for Black Catholics, said:

> [F]rom the beginning of the Catholic Church in America until the present day, Black Catholics have always felt as though they were marginal members of the Church, the step-children so to speak, the objects of the Church's missionary work, its outlet for charity.
>
> Because this may sound like a harsh indictment, we could miss altogether, the truly tragic element that it contains, namely that for these two centuries, despite what they have regarded as less than adequate, human or just treatment within the Church itself, Black Catholics have held their faith in the Church, and continued to push for full inclusion, believing that the Church must one day respond. The presence of black people in the American Catholic Church is nothing less than a living witness of faith, a continual call to justice within the Church.[36]

Father Rudi Cleare of the diocese of Orlando, Florida, worked among the Haitian immigrants as the director of the Office for Black and Haitian Community Ministries.[37] Eighty-five percent of the Haitian immigrants into Florida claim Roman Catholicism as their religion though some among them practice various forms of Voodoo along with their Catholic rites. The Evangelical churches have been successful converting Haitians, partly by allowing untrained Haitian laymen to open churches. The Catholic Church provided social services to the Haitian community that facilitated their integration into American society. Some simply took advantage of the social services the church offered without any reciprocal loyalty to the church; others are eternally grateful to the church for the opportunities it afforded them.

Racism remains a problem to this day. Racist laws were ended but that has not eliminated racism in America or in some churches. As recently as 1997, the Louisiana bishops felt compelled yet again to dispel racist notions in their statement, "Racism's Assumption: That Some Are Superior."[38]

The National Black Catholic Congress, begun originally in 1890 but inactive for most of the century, resumed meeting in 1987 and now convenes in different cities every five years (the most recent meeting convened in Baltimore in 1997). In the summer of 1997, cardinals (including Francis Arinze, a native of Nigeria who heads a Vatican Office), bishops, priests, and laity participated in the dedication of Our Mother of Africa Chapel within the Basilica of the National Shrine of the Immaculate Conception in Washington, D.C., symbolizing a formal national recognition of black Catholics.

Vatican II Launches a New Era

The most dramatic changes in the church since the Reformation and Counter-Reformation period in the sixteenth century occurred as a result of the Second Vatican Council held from October 11, 1962, to December 8, 1965. The Council was called unexpectedly. After the death of Pius XII in 1958, the cardinals met in conclave in the Sistine Chapel in Rome to elect a new pope as has been the custom for centuries. The election is secret, but the process involves balloting by all of the assembled cardinals. Apparently, the cardinals could not agree on one of the front runners, so they elected an elderly cardinal whom they expected to be a short-term caretaker pope until the next conclave. They chose Angelo Roncalli, then Cardinal Archbishop of Venice, Italy. When a cardinal is elected pope he chooses a new name by which he will be called. Cardinal Roncalli chose John XXIII, following a conciliarist pope who had the name John before him. When elected pope he was just shy of his 77th birthday. As expected, his pontificate was short; he died in June 1963. However, he was not the "caretaker" many had envisioned. Instead, he was a man of extraordinary vision. To almost everyone's surprise, shortly after assuming the papacy he announced the Council. Unlike many previous councils of the church that configured creeds and

Dedication ceremony of the Mother of Africa Chapel at the National Shrine in
Washington, D.C., 1997.
COURTESY OF THE NATIONAL BASILICA SHRINE OF THE IMMACULATE CONCEPTION, WASHINGTON, D.C.

dogmas, this was to be a pastoral council dealing with a wide range of concerns that are most easily characterized under the rubric of "the church and
the world."

The changes initiated by this Council continue today to shape the church
universal and in America. A shift from classical culture to modernity
occurred accompanied by a greater appreciation for the immanence of God
instead of the transcendence that pre-Vatican II theology emphasized.

After Vatican II, nuns adopted modified habits; in some religious congregations the women opted for contemporary clothes. Priests marched in
civil rights protests, sometimes against the advice or will of their bishops.
Sermons became "dialogue homilies"; and guitars competed with or
replaced organs in many churches. The social revolution of the 1960s rocked
American society and pitted young people against their parents and other
authorities—from the police, to the president, to the pope. City neighborhoods, so long the preserve of white Catholic immigrants from Europe,
were integrated, usually after much resistance, by increasingly mobile
African Americans. Priests and sisters left the active ministry in large numbers, sometimes accompanied by extensive publicity. Theologians objected

openly to Vatican pronouncements on issues such as artificial birth control and sexual ethics. Many who remained in active ministry did so with the expectation of greater change still, such as the abolition of mandatory celibacy.

Pope John XXIII emphasized that the Council was to be an *aggiornamento*—an opening of the windows to let a fresh breeze blow the cobwebs out of the church's many nooks and crannies. The church has not been the same since. The pre-Vatican II church and the post-Vatican II church may be viewed like cousins, having some family traits in common but being clearly different. While a minority of American Catholics preferred no council at all, the vast majority agree that it breathed new life into the church and opened new possibilities for the way in which the church related to and ministered in the contemporary world. What conservatives and liberals disagree about is the *interpretation* given to Vatican II by post-Vatican II prelates, priests, and people.

The Council drew over twenty-six hundred bishops and over four hundred expert advisers. It was also attended by observers from various Christian churches, including Protestant, Anglican, and Orthodox. Consistent with the church of the time and with a history of patriarchy, there were no women participants at the Council, although twenty-two women were invited as auditors.[39] It was truly a world council, representing a church that was no longer dominated exclusively by Europeans. In keeping with long-standing tradition the official business of the Council was conducted in Latin. The participants of the Council produced sixteen decrees dealing with issues from the self-definition of the church to the church's relation to the state. The Council meetings drew worldwide attention, and media coverage was extensive, including daily press reports. This alone brought the church and the world into contact in an unprecedented way. No doubt due in part to the press coverage, among Catholics worldwide there was an excitement and expectation unparalleled in the church's history. Between the four formal sessions of the Council, bishops returned to their respective countries and dioceses with firsthand news of developments.

The Council introduced new ways to think about the church, or more accurately, retrieved an understanding that had been buried under centuries of cultural and ecclesial accretion. Since the sixteenth century the church had defined itself as a "perfect society," a definition given by St. Robert Bellarmine. The Dogmatic Constitution of the Church (*Lumen Gentium*) stressed that the church is a pilgrim people, not an unchanging institution. By virtue of baptism, every Christian is called upon to minister in the name

Bishops from all over the world gathered with the pope in Rome for the Second Vatican Council, 1962–1965. CATHOLIC NEWS SERVICE

of Christ. This empowered the laity and began, if not the erosion of clericalism (which still exists and has enjoyed a renaissance among some within the recent generation of clergy in the American church), at least the introduction of the notion of the laity as partners in ministry with the clergy. Political scientist and editor of *America* Thomas Reese described this sea-change in the church. "Vatican II caused a revolution in church thinking and practice from the papacy to the local parish. The Council touched almost every aspect of church life from liturgy to political action, from seminary education to catechetics."[40]

Mary Jo Weaver and Scott Appleby have carefully chronicled reactions to this Council in their works *Being Right: Conservative Catholics in America* and *What's Left: Liberal Catholics in America*.[41] Despite the many changes that the Council set in motion, the conservatives do not dispute the legitimacy of the Council, but they do think that the documents of the Council were misinterpreted by ill-advised bishops, permissive clergy, and power-hungry lay people. The liberals, on the other hand, do not think that the reforms initiated by Vatican II have gone far enough, and press for more license and perhaps even a Vatican III. A third group, many of whom are described by Michael Cuneo in *The Smoke of Satan*, rejected the Council outright as the work of the devil and hearken to recreate an ecclesial world untouched by the Council's reforms. While it may still be too early to evaluate the legacy of Vatican II, no one disputes that it was an event in church history of monumental importance for twentieth-century Catholicism.

The document that most immediately affected Catholics was the first one approved by the Council in December 1963, the Constitution on the Sacred Liturgy (*Sacrosanctum concilium*). This decree permitted the celebration of the mass in the vernacular language. Prior to Vatican II, mass was celebrated in Latin, the universal (but dead) language of the church. With the exception of the readings and the sermon, the entire mass was in Latin, including the hymns. The liturgical use of this ancient language, increasingly unknown even to educated persons,[42] contributed to a sense of mystery and allowed those from any country to follow the mass in any part of the world, since the rite and language were uniform. It separated Catholics from Protestants and united immigrant Catholics in America with a common language of worship. However, it also served to distance Catholics from "celebrating" the Eucharist and often reduced them to passive spectators of a mysterious ritual conducted by equally distant priests who were the "celebrants." Altar boys memorized (and usually mumbled) Latin responses to set prayers during the mass, sharing the ritual in a more intimate way than the congregation who were further separated by having altar boys act as official respondents. Women were twice distanced because, in accord with canon law, girls were not permitted to be altar servers. The sanctuary was divided from the nave of the church by an altar rail separating the congregation from the activities at the altar. Laypeople followed the mass using missals that included the Latin on one page and its translation on the opposite page. Catholic publishers of missals benefited greatly from this liturgical style, but it tended to reinforce the notion of the Eucharist as a form of private devotion rather than the common prayer and celebration of the entire people of God, the church. One did not participate in or celebrate the Eucharist, one "heard" the mass. At communion the people knelt at the altar rail to receive the host on their tongues.

Accompanying the transition to the vernacular was a dizzying flurry of liturgical changes that altered significantly the face of Catholicism. Prior to Vatican II, the main altar in churches faced the front wall of the church in the sanctuary. Priests "said mass" facing the altar with their backs to the congregation. They followed complex rubrics that included bowing and genuflecting at different times during the mass. The laity either sat or knelt for most of the mass. At special "high" masses, or for funerals, the main celebrant was accompanied by other priests acting the roles of deacon and subdeacon. After Vatican II altars were turned around (or new ones were installed in front of the existing altars) so that the priest faced the people. Liturgical colors were adjusted, as for example, in the case of funerals, for which the priest now wore white (as a sign of the hope of the resurrection of the dead) instead of black vestments. Latin hymns were translated into English, traditionally Protestant hymns were adopted, and a whole new cottage industry grew up around the creation of liturgical music, much of it accompanied by the guitar rather than the traditional church instrument, the organ, some of it inspiring and some unfortunately lacking aesthetic merit.

Shortly after Vatican II, Catholics who had been required to fast from solid food from midnight the night before receiving communion were required to fast only three hours; eventually that was further reduced to one hour. Many Catholics today do not observe this rule, if indeed they are even aware of such a regulation. Pre-Vatican II Catholics received the host directly on their tongues distributed only by priests. Today they receive the Eucharist (often in the form of ordinary bread instead of the thin wafer) in the palms of their hands from priests and laity who distribute it. They also drink from the cup of consecrated wine. Many pre-Vatican II Catholics would privately and silently recite the rosary during the mass. Today the laity sing, respond to communal prayers offered during the liturgy, greet one another with a handshake of peace, read the scriptures, lead the congregational singing, offer prayers for the needs of the church and world, and stand for much of the celebration.

While Vatican II did not completely alleviate Catholic xenophobia, it did go a long way to open Catholics to other Christians and people of other major religions. The Decree on Ecumenism (*Decretum De Oecumenismo*) reminded Catholics that they are not the only Christians in the world and encouraged them to engage in dialogue and activity that unites Christians. In the past, a person baptized in another Christian church who wished to convert to Catholicism would be baptized again in the Catholic Church. Today, the church recognizes the universal character of the sacrament of baptism and requires those already baptized who wish to join the church, only to make a profession of faith. In the pre-Vatican church, Catholics were admonished from the pulpit not to enter Protestant churches and were not permitted to participate in Protestant worship ceremonies, including weddings and funerals. Today Catholics readily attend and participate in such ceremonies.

During the course of the Council sessions, American bishops were accompanied by private advisers and *periti* (experts) who were usually theologians since most of the bishops, whose time was often occupied with administration, were not professional theologians. One of these *periti* was John Courtney Murray, a Jesuit priest and theologian who taught at Woodstock Seminary in Maryland. Murray possessed a gifted mind and had risen to prominence among theologians for his seminal work on religious freedom.[43] Murray, fascinated by the American experiment in democracy, had written extensively about the church-state relationship, arguing that Catholic teaching and the state's protection of religious freedom were not in conflict. His work was viewed with suspicion by the Vatican, and in 1954 Rome prevailed upon his superiors to silence him and prevent him from writing on issues pertaining to religious freedom. Other theologians had experienced a similar fate from Rome in the 1950s. The French theologians Yves Congar and Henri de Lubac had been silenced by Rome for espousing then controversial views on the nature of the church and the nature of grace. The German Karl Rahner, the most influential theologian of Vatican II and arguably the most influential Catholic theologian of the twentieth century, was also censored by the Vatican in the 1950s for his attempt to reconcile Christian faith with contemporary thought. Murray was exonerated when

Churches added new altars in front of the old ones after Vatican II dictated liturgical changes. UNDA

Cardinal Francis Spellman of New York invited him to act as a *peritus* for the third and fourth sessions of the Council. Murray brought a particular American point of view to the Council deliberations;

> [F]or the Christian society, the freedom of the Church to practice in accord with its beliefs and to join in the shaping of society is the fundamental concern; legal establishment is only one among many means of achieving it. In the case of the United States and in most other modern republics, it would be an inappropriate means. Murray stated repeatedly that the American situation is not that of the Continent.[44]

Finally, fifty years after Leo XIII had condemned Americanism, the American church had an articulate defender of the American situation. Murray was the most influential voice in crafting the Declaration on Religious Freedom proclaimed by the Council. That document recognized the separation of church and state. Another Vatican II document, *Gaudium et*

Spes (Pastoral Constitution on the Church in the World Today) underscored the principles of separation of church and state:

> The role and competence of the Church being what it is, she must in no way be confused with the political community, nor be bound to any political system. . . . In their proper spheres, the political community and the Church are mutually independent and self-governing. . . .The Church does not lodge her hope in privileges conferred by civil authority. Indeed, she stands ready to renounce the exercise of certain legitimately acquired rights if it becomes clear that their use raises doubt about the insincerity of her witness or that new conditions of life demand some other arrangement.[45]

So the document established the church's relationship to governments following the successful model of the United States. This represented one result of the Council. Many other initiatives faced criticism or enthusiasm depending upon what constituency one consulted. The years directly following the Council proved to be some of the most tumultuous in church history and certainly among the most influential in American church history. The church continues to digest and implement the directives of the Second Vatican Council as theologians, pastors, bishops, and laity discern and debate the shape of the church to come.

CHAPTER FOUR

The Post-Vatican II Church in America

Many American Catholics were optimistic at the close of Vatican II. They thought that the rapid pace of change would continue unabated. Others were leery of the changes and longed for the stable church of the 1950s. Tensions between these two groups intensified, and a tug-of-war for control of the church ensued. The American theologian Avery Dulles commented:

> Vatican II has become, for many Catholics, a center of controversy. Some voices from the extreme right and the extreme left frankly reject the council. Reactionaries of the traditionalist variety censure it for having yielded to Protestant and modernist tendencies. Radicals of the far left, conversely, complain that the council, while making some progress, failed to do away with the church's absolutistic claims and its antiquated class structures. The vast majority of Catholics, expressing satisfaction with the results of the council, are still divided because they interpret it in contrary ways.[1]

This struggle was played out in Rome among high-ranking Vatican prelates and in America in pews, convents, chancery offices, and living rooms. Pope Paul VI, the successor to Pope John XXIII, presided over the final session of Vatican II. He also oversaw the implementation of the council decrees.

The years immediately following the Second Vatican Council were tumultuous. The Council instigated a flood of change. Since no one, including the pope, quite knew how to implement all of the initiatives of the

Council, a period of experimentation swept through the church. Catholic University of America theologian Joseph Komonchak claims: "A great deal of what happened was officially authorized. . . . From a theological and canonical perspective, none of these changes was revolutionary, but many of them had more dramatic psychological and sociological consequences than the word *reform* suggests."[2]

An Example of Reform: Vowed Religious Life

An example of this change occurred within the communities of nuns. The renewal of religious life, changes in the lifestyle, ministry, and regulations governing nuns, began in the 1950s under the direction of Pope Pius XII, who issued two major documents *Sponsa Christi* (Concerning the Canonical Status of Nuns of Strict Contemplative Life) 1950 and *Sacra Virginitas* (On Holy Virginity) 1954 on the subject. The Second Vatican Council took up the issue in a document approved on October 28, 1965, the "Decree on the Appropriate Renewal of Religious Life" (*Perfectae Caritatis*). This document encouraged "adaptation to the changed conditions of our times" but also asked religious orders to look to their founders for inspiration as well as scripture and the church's tradition. Since the Council of Trent, the church viewed religious life as a higher calling or a higher state than married life. This document omitted such language, recognizing the members of religious orders as a distinctive part of the church community, but not superior to the laity in the church. American theologian Sandra Schneiders noted, "Whether the Council fathers intended it or not, the decree signaled the beginning of a vast rethinking of the theology of religious life."[3]

This meant that religious orders embarked on new ministries, many moving away from traditional roles in primary and secondary Catholic education to take up social ministries in which the quest for peace and justice took priority. Religious orders reconfigured their constitutions and changed their lifestyles. Habits that had come markedly to distinguish nuns from lay people, and one order from another, were modified or discarded in favor of contemporary clothes. Rigid adherence to regulations ceded to personal responsibility and freedom. Convents with large numbers of sisters living together gave way to smaller communities in houses or apartments. Instead of being appointed by major superiors to minister in certain areas of need, sisters were told to seek their own ministries, to interview for jobs and negotiate salaries for them.

Americans discovered a new spirit of social activism in the 1960s in which sisters, brothers, and priests participated. They opened soup kitchens, moved into inner-city housing projects, and lobbied local, state, and federal government agencies on behalf of the poor and disadvantaged in society. The idealism of Vatican II, coupled with the heightened consciousness of social issues, provided opportune conditions for new ministries to take root. Many sisters and clerics were excited and eager to move in new directions. Some sisters, however, were paralyzed with fear at the prospect of showing their hair, covered so long under the voluminous robes of the founders. And the thought of going "outside" to buy clothes intimidated them. These women had not been responsible for spending a dollar for many years. Now they were given "allowances" and told to "budget."

For a while after the Council, the Vatican continued to encourage and support change. However, this rapid change took its toll on the religious. Between 1958 and 1962 approximately 23,302 women entered American orders; between 1976 and 1980 approximately 2,767 women entered.[4] In addition, thousands of women have left religious life since the close of Vatican II. In 1965 there were 179,954 nuns in America; by 1997 that number had decreased to 86,355. The vast majority of those who left were younger members, leaving an aging population of sisters in which today the median age is 70. This has obvious implications for the future of many orders that are strained financially, have an increasing number of members who require nursing home care, and have little new blood available to sustain the orders' commitments to ongoing ministries.

Dismayed by the sometimes unbridled experimentation that the Council unleashed, the Vatican began to exert its influence to stem the tide. From 1969 until 1983 it issued a number of documents designed to return discipline and obedience, culminating with a section on religious life in the 1983 Code of Canon Law that reiterated that the orders are under the direction of Rome. These laws pertained to "canonical orders," that is, those under the direct authority of Rome. Noncanonical communities of women who make private vows also exist, and are attractive to those women who, for reasons of autonomy and feminist consciousness, do not want to be subject to exclusive male control. A palpable tension existed between renewal and obedience. In *The Frontiers of Catholicism*, political scientist Gene Burns asked: "[H]ow could modernizing reforms and decentralization take place when there were to be no specific reductions of Rome's authority?"[5]

In 1974 women who were disenchanted with the rapid pace of change and the momentum that it created formed the Institute for Religious Life[6] to provide traditionally minded nuns with an alternative to the Leadership Council for Women Religious that represented the majority of religious orders and was in favor of significant reform of religious life.

The decline in the numbers of nuns as well as their lack of financial planning left many orders financially bankrupt. The *Wall Street Journal* reported in May 1986 that nuns in some cases were facing desperate financial circumstances that forced some to go on welfare. Others clipped coupons, took minimum wage jobs, or continued working beyond the normal retirement age. Citing a 1981 bishops' survey, the paper reported that more than a thousand nuns (out of a population of about 115,000) were on public assistance. Many religious orders did not have retirement plans because they were paid so little and did not participate in Social Security. This factor, coupled with a large population of aging sisters and only a few young ones to make up the income difference, led to an estimated $2 billion shortfall. Exemplifying further the harsh nature of their fiscal hardships, one order needed the assistance of a bishops' emergency fund to pay its funeral director for the numerous funerals of their aging community. Many orders began selling off their assets (convents, mother houses, schools) in order to pay outstanding debts or to attempt to accumulate capital for retirement.

In her book, *Sisters in Arms: Catholic Nuns Through Two Millennia,* Jo Ann McNamara predicts an imminent end of the sisterhood: "In the last decade of the twentieth century, with the median age of sisters now set at seventy and rising and no new generation of recruits in sight, the death of the feminine apostolate, at least in the United States and Europe, seems to be inevitable."[7] Her prediction may a bit hyperbolic, but there is little doubt that the size and influence of the sisterhood will be considerably reduced in the twenty-first century.

Rome's attempt to control women religious ran into public opposition in an unpredictable manner. In 1979, on Pope John Paul II's first visit to the United States, the president of the Leadership Conference of Women Religious, Mary Theresa Kane of the Sisters of Mercy of the Union, addressed the pope with the following challenge:

> As I share this privileged moment with you, Your Holiness, I urge you to be mindful of the intense suffering and pain which is part of the life of many women in the United States. I call upon you to listen with compassion and to hear the call of women who comprise half of humankind. As women, we have heard the powerful messages of our church addressing the dignity and reverence for all persons. As women, we have pondered these words. Our contemplation leads us to state that

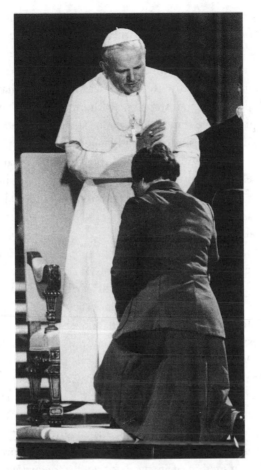

Sister Theresa Kane is blessed by the pope after she challenged him to include women "in all ministries of our church."
CATHOLIC NEWS SERVICE

the church in its struggle to be faithful to its call for reverence and dignity for all persons must respond by providing the possibility of women as persons being included in all ministries of our church. I urge, you, Your Holiness, to be open to and respond to the voices coming from the women of this country who are desirous of serving in and through the church as fully participating members.[8]

Sister Theresa Kane's polite but firm address to the pope proved to be the most public of a number of confrontations between church authority and nuns. In Michigan, Sister Agnes Mansour, a member of the Sisters of

Mercy and the former president of Mercy College in Detroit, was confirmed as the director of the Michigan Department of Social Services in 1983. Archbishop Edmund Szoka opposed her appointment because the department she headed was responsible for Medicaid payments for abortion and because the Vatican's Congregation for Religious was on record that sisters should not accept such political appointments.[9] Although Sister Mansour personally opposed the pro-choice stance, on balance she considered her position an influential one in which she could advance the ethical positions of the church. However, the Vatican assigned then New York auxiliary Bishop Bevilacqua to deliver an ultimatum to her to resign from her government position or from her religious order. Pressured into a decision, Sister Mansour requested a leave of absence from her religious order and eventually ended her formal affiliation.

During a papal visit to San Francisco in 1987, Donna Hanson, the bishop's secretary for social services in Spokane, Washington, told John Paul II: "When I come to my church I cannot discard my cultural experiences. Though I know my church is not a democracy ruled by popular vote, I expect to be treated as a mature, educated, and responsible adult."[10]

Sister Theresa Kane addressed an audience of about six hundred nuns at the Leadership Conference of Women Religious meeting in Philadelphia on August 24, 1980, when she said: "The Roman Catholic Church, as an institution, must recognize and acknowledge the serious social injustices by which its very system is imposed upon women of the Roman Catholic Church. The Church, in its documents, affirms the dignity, reverence and equality of all persons. Until the institutional Catholic Church undertakes a serious, critical examination of its mode of acting toward women, it cannot, it will not, give witness to justice in the world."[11] Perhaps anticipating Sister Kane's tone, Cardinal John Krol of Philadelphia, speaking before her in his welcoming remarks to the conference, asked the sisters "to strive to preserve the unity of the Church by avoiding alienation and divisiveness."[12]

After Vatican II the church began training men for service as permanent deacons.[13] The diaconate is a presbyteral order which the church confers on candidates for the priesthood as the penultimate step to ordination and on men who are to serve in this capacity permanently. Deacons played a role of service in the early church. At that time gender was not a consideration, as the New Testament attests that women functioned as deaconesses in the early church. However, the role disappeared sometime after the tenth century.[14] The post-Vatican II restoration of the diaconate included only males, with some three hundred ordained by 1972. These were designated "permanent" deacons since diaconate for them did not serve as a transitional step to priesthood. The majority of those ordained were married men who would serve in a variety of pastoral ministries on a volunteer part-time basis. Among the tasks they perform are preparing couples for marriage and witnessing marriages, preaching, baptizing, outreach ministry to the poor, and comforting the sick.

In the 1970s a movement began among nuns and other laywomen to restore the diaconate for women. While it is not priesthood, organizers felt that it is an order of ministry that would bring greater respect and responsibility to women. Some obviously believed that it might serve as an entrée to priesthood. There was, after all, historical precedent: women had functioned as deacons in the church in the past. Twelve members of the National Leadership Board of the Sister Formation Conference urged the following at their October 25, 1974, meeting: "1) the prompt restoration of the Diaconate for Women in the Roman Catholic Church, 2) The Ordination of Women to the Priestly Ministry in the Roman Catholic Church, 3) the inclusion of more Women in all decision and policy-making bodies in the Church."[15]

One of the moving forces behind this initiative was Mary B. Lynch, a social worker, feminist, and lay Catholic advocate for women's ordination. She circulated a newsletter, *The Journey*, among nuns and other laywomen who were interested in becoming deacons, and enrolled for courses at the seminary in preparation for ordination about which she was (as it turned out falsely) optimistic when she wrote in 1974: "There is factual data to justify a restoration of the diaconate for women. The Bishops know these facts. As to readiness, we have strong convictions that the Spirit will inspire them to action."[16]

In support of this effort and in an attempt to get the bishops to put this issue on their agenda for a synod meeting in Rome in the fall of 1974, the Sisters of Mercy, meeting for their ninth General Chapter in Bethesda, Maryland, in June, 1974, proposed the restoration of the diaconate for women, supporting their proposal in part with the following:

> When the expanse of the Church's mission is examined, is it feasible to limit the official, public ministry to the male sex alone when fifty-one percent of the persons being ministered to are of the female sex? When all other institutions—family, business, professional, educational—are beginning to recognize the need for complementarity of both sexes in efficiently and effectively fulfilling needs and functions and relating to

persons, can the Church afford to overlook the contributions of the complementarity of the male and female ministries?[17]

This lobbying and advocacy has continued for twenty-five years, but— as we approach the millennium—not much has changed for women in the church.

Bishops

If the period following Vatican II was frustrating for nuns, confusing for the laity, and challenging for priests, it was stressful for the bishops too, as acknowledged by Edward P. Echlin, S.J., of John Carroll University in a speech delivered at a conference in Michigan in December 1971:

> Episcopal isolation is usually defined as an unawareness of the distress and needs of God's people. But there is something more. There is also the distress of the bishops. Recent years have seen the affliction of our leaders. Bishops have been accused and harried not only for their apparently culpable failures but simply for sharing in the same human condition as the people from whom they come. In our agony of reform and renewal we have searched desperately for the scapegoat and found him behind the mitre. In the fastest changing epoch in human history, where generations pass in a decade, no man, including the Catholic bishop, has many answers. No matter how visible their failures or manifest their finitude, bishops too are our brothers.[18]

Archbishop Rembert Weakland of Milwaukee confirmed this assessment saying that "[N]o one seems to worry about who ministers to the bishops."[19] In recent years some bishops have established support groups. Sometimes traveling hundreds of miles, they meet together in an atmosphere of trust and affirmation to share the burdens of their ministries and lives with fellow bishops who understand the pressures they face daily and the expectations of their varied constituencies. These meetings are not designed to conduct business but to rejuvenate their spirits so that they may function sensitively, humanely, and effectively in ministry.

The selection process for bishops involves a lengthy questionnaire sent to numerous evaluators ranging from priests to parishioners. The assessment of candidates covers the following areas: 1) personal characteristics; 2) human qualities; 3) human, Christian, and priestly formation; 4) behavior; 5) cultural preparation; 6) orthodoxy; 7) discipline; 8) pastoral fitness and experience; 9) leadership; 10) administration; 11) public esteem; and 12) suitability. Only those who demonstrate their loyalty to church teachings and policies pass these scrutinies. Some critics of the process fear that it undervalues creativity and vision—qualities that could lead to differences with established policy. Priests who are appointed auxiliary bishops and who fail to follow strict compliance with policies or who publicly question some church positions usually do not advance to become ordinaries of a diocese.

Auxiliary Bishop Thomas Gumbleton, of the archdiocese of Detroit, who is outspoken particularly on issues of peace and justice, within and outside of the church, appears to be one such bishop. Ordained as an auxiliary bishop in 1968, he remains in that position today. Normally, an auxiliary bishop advances to become ordinary of a diocese, unless health or lack of administrative ability prevent him from assuming more responsibility. In the case of Gumbleton, and a handful of other auxiliaries, their liberal views inhibit advancement in the hierarchical order.

While it is true that the office of bishop brings with it public recognition, authority, and a certain amount of power, concurrently those who are appointed to this office have extensive pastoral and administrative responsibilities; and are accountable to Rome, their priests and people. They are subject to significant scrutiny. Some exercise their authority pastorally in such a way that they invite cooperation and receive support. Others rely upon their office so that they separate themselves from those whom they are called to serve and attempt to please Rome exclusively. Bishop Matthew Clark of Rochester, New York, described well the accountability of the office.

[A] bishop must provide for good order while still respecting the freedom and supporting the growth of . . . individual members. As a true servant he stands in the midst of a community to give his very self as a symbol of its unity and a guarantee of its peace. He preaches and celebrates the Mysteries as friend among friends. He proclaims the vision of the whole, not only as the lonely prophet but as one who clothes with words what he sees and hears in the hopes and dreams of the people he serves. When disputes arise, he attempts to help each side to

understand the other's perspective. In serving the gospel while serving
the gospel people, the bishop may have to set limits, call questions, ask
people to respect necessary boundaries. He does so conscious of the
medieval Church axiom: "in necessary things, agreement; in disputed
things, freedom; in all things, charity."[20]

The position of the bishop, then, is a delicate balance of commitments—
to the Vatican, to the American church, to the diocese, but above all, to the
gospel. As Thomas Reese describes them in his book *Archbishop*, most bishops are workaholics whose roles include manager, pastor, judge, spiritual
leader, teacher, and public relations agent, to name a few.[21] One of their
gravest, and sometimes most trying, responsibilities is to lead and govern
the clergy for whom they are responsible. One bishop quipped that there are
only two certainties for those who oversee priests: "You never get a bad
meal and you never hear the truth." At no time in American church history
has the life of bishops been free of tensions, but post-Vatican II bishops
encounter numerous challenges that test even the best-equipped leaders.
These responsibilities are coupled with high expectations for leadership,
pastoral sensitivity, business acumen, and spiritual depth. It is true that they
have plenty of help in discharging their responsibilities and affirmation from
a wide range of constituents from fellow bishops to priests and laity, yet
they also bear a great deal of responsibility.

American Catholics Protest

The Second Vatican Council ended at a critical time in American history.
The 1960s were like no other decade. America was being dragged deeper
and deeper into the conflict in Southeast Asia. Many Americans disagreed
with government policy on Vietnam. Student protests paralyzed colleges
and universities from coast to coast. Catholics, who as an immigrant community had been so anxious to demonstrate their loyalty to America, now
demonstrated in equal numbers with others against U.S. government policy.
Some of the most prominent leaders of the antiwar movement were
Catholic priests and sisters such as Elizabeth McAlister, a member of the
Religious of the Sacred Heart of Mary, and Daniel and Philip Berrigan,
Jesuit and Josephite priests respectively.[22] In the early stages of these
protests, the American bishops were reluctant to side against the govern-
ment though they interfered little with the protesters. By 1968 antiwar sen-

Roman Catholicism relies on bishops to provide leadership and to administer the church.
AP PHOTO/RICK BOWMER

Father Daniel Berrigan and Martin Sheen are
arrested for protesting U.S. "Star Wars"
research.

timent was widespread, and the bishops finally spoke out. They issued a
Pastoral Letter endorsing selective conscientious objection. While most who
were drafted dutifully went to Vietnam, some Catholic students were being
counseled by priests and nuns to object to the war on moral grounds. Some
received conscientious objector status from the Draft Board; others fled to
Canada or other countries.

Much of the enthusiasm generated by Vatican II was tempered in 1968
when Pope Paul VI ignored the advice of a commission he had established
to study the moral implications of birth control, and on July 29, published
the encyclical *Humanae Vitae* (Of Human Life), reiterating the church's
prohibition of any form of artificial contraception for Catholics. This struck
a sensitive chord in Catholic couples' lives. While the church continued to
permit—even encourage—natural family planning, the use of artificial
means to prohibit conception, including the now widely available birth control pill, was deemed sinful. As the encyclical put it: "[E]ach and every marriage act must remain open to the transmission of life." GRAPH 4.1 NEAR
HERE

Historically, many papal encyclicals are little known or noticed by
Catholics. This one created a firestorm. The American reaction was swift

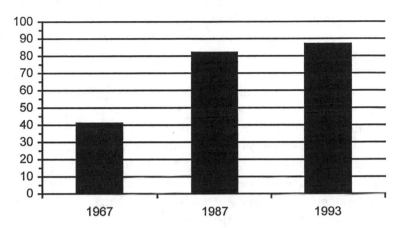

Percent of Catholics Who Approve of Birth Control

and firm. The protest began with theologians who were incredulous that the pope had ignored the advice of his own commission, which would have permitted the practice of birth control. They sensed immediately that this encyclical would cause significant qualms of conscience for American Catholics, who would be forced to choose between their church and their conscience. The emotional and financial expense of having large families was more than many could bear. They were not denying the value of human life, but they were reluctant to bring children into the world for whom they could not adequately provide and care.[23]

A cadre of these theologians were in Washington, D.C., the location of the Catholic University of America. The dissenters were led by Father Charles Curran, a moral theologian on the faculty of Catholic University, who, with the cooperation of ten other theologians, wrote a statement on July 29, 1969, disagreeing with the pope's position and reasoning. Over six hundred other priests and scholars signed the statement which said in part: "Spouses may responsibly decide according to their consciences that artificial contraception in some circumstances is permissible and indeed necessary to preserve and foster the values and sacredness of marriage."[24] Twenty-one dissenting theologians were members of the faculty of Catholic University. They were joined by dozens of priests from the archdiocese of Washington. The dissenters even called a press conference to register their protest. This set the stage for a public confrontation with church authorities.

Patrick O'Boyle, the cardinal archbishop of Washington, wasted no time in responding to the dissent. He demanded that the priests of his archdiocese who were involved recant or face punitive measures. As chancellor of Catholic University, O'Boyle also called the professors of the university to account, initially giving them a matter of days to retract their statement, then setting a deadline of October 1.

The immediate issue was *Humanae Vitae*, but the larger issue was the question of dissent from within the ranks of the church. The American bishops reacted as a body to the dissenting theologians by issuing a pastoral letter, "Human Life in Our Day" which dealt with the reaction to *Humanae Vitae* and established guidelines for dissent. The document said: "The expression of theological dissent from the magisterium is in order only if the reasons are serious and well-founded, if the manner of dissent does not question or impugn the teaching authority of the church, and is such as not to give scandal." For the theologians involved, it was also a matter of academic freedom. The church in the United States had run Catholic universities since the founding of Georgetown in 1789. But the relationship between the church's authority and the independence required to preserve academic freedom had not been tested to the degree that this case required. Theologians want to distinguish between respect for the institutional church's position and submission to it.

Charles Curran became a lightning rod for academic freedom— applauded by many within academic circles for his courage, disliked by others for his confrontation with church authority. The Vatican compiled an extensive file on Curran, examining his writings to determine whether they were in compliance with orthodoxy. Most of the controversy revolved around his positions on sexual ethics. In 1979 the Vatican notified Curran that he was under investigation. This kind of investigation usually had been reserved for European theologians. Earlier in the 1970s, the Vatican had investigated the Belgian-born theologian Edward Schillebeeckx, who taught at Nijmegen in Holland, and the Swiss-born theologian Hans Küng, who taught at Tübingen University in Germany. Curran, however, had attracted the attention of the Vatican as early as 1966. The office investigating Curran was directed by the German Cardinal Joseph Ratzinger, himself a distinguished theologian. Even after much correspondence and a face-to-face meeting between Curran and Ratzinger, nothing was resolved definitively. The Vatican sent its final disposition to Cardinal James Hickey, the successor to O'Boyle as archbishop of Washington and chancellor of Catholic

University. On August 19, 1986, Cardinal Hickey and Father William Byron, the Jesuit president of Catholic University, announced that the church was rescinding Curran's canonical mission, that is, his approval to teach theology in a pontifical faculty, which status Catholic University's theology department had. Then Curran held his own news conference claiming: "I'm from the United States, and there has been friction between the Vatican and the church in the U.S." When asked if he was targeted as an American, he responded "I think so very much," implying that Rome was unhappy with dissenters in the United States and Curran became a convenient scapegoat.[25]

Curran insisted that he was dissenting to the noninfallible teachings of the church, and that it was his right to do so. In January 1987 Cardinal Hickey suspended Curran from his teaching responsibilities. Citing his tenured position as grounds for continued employment, Curran filed a civil law suit in February 1987. After a long trial, in a thirty-six page decision the judge ruled in favor of Catholic University on February 28, 1989. Curran left Catholic University to pursue a number of visiting professorships while considering his academic future. In 1989 he was offered a chair at Auburn University but, for reasons that may or may not have been related to Curran's ecclesiastical censure, the university president rescinded the offer. Curran finally decided to accept a tenured professorship at Southern Methodist University.

The Curran case underscored numerous issues in the American church. While the separation of church and state was the *modus operandi* in the United States, there remained a thorny question about the relationship of the American academy, with its principles of academic freedom and the guarantees of tenure, to the church in church-related institutions of higher education. Increasingly, leading theologians were faculty members of universities rather than seminaries. This meant, in theory at least, that they enjoyed the protection that tenure is meant to provide. However, it was unclear whether academic freedom permitted theologians at church-affiliated universities publicly to dissent from official church teachings, even if those teachings were not infallibly proclaimed but were part of what is known as the ordinary magisterium of the church, such as papal encyclicals.

The Curran case was additionally complicated by the fact that the faculty of theology at the Catholic University of America held pontifical status; that is, they taught in the name of the church and granted degrees that were approved by the church. While there are many Catholic colleges and universities in the United States, only a handful have the prerogative to grant

Controversial moral theologian Father Charles Curran holds a news conference
to protest the church's treatment of academic and clerical critics.
CATHOLIC NEWS SERVICE

pontifical degrees. The chancellor of Catholic University, Cardinal Hickey,
upheld the Vatican's interests.

Those in the academy asked the question: Should a bishop be allowed to
judge the professional competency of a university professor? Would this not
be better left to peers in other institutions of higher education? Further, does
not tenure protect one from retribution if he or she criticizes ecclesial positions? Is it the duty of theologians in church-related institutions to defend
the public teachings of the church at all costs? This issue would surface again
in the 1990s when the church issued an Apostolic Constitution on Catholic
Universities titled "Ex Corde Ecclesiae" (From the Heart of the Church).

The Bishops Challenge American Society

In the 1980s the American bishops addressed a number of sensitive public policy issues. In doing so, they appealed to both the ecclesial community and the civil community, using arguments constructed from the scriptures and from natural law. By grounding their documents in the Bible, they appealed to revelation that underpins all Christian theology. By employing a natural law argument they were being consistent with Catholic theology that has relied on natural law reasoning since at least the time of Thomas Aquinas. Using natural law, they attempted to influence public opinion and government policy by explicitly using a philosophical argument that did not require that the public (and public officials) share the faith disposition of the bishops. The Pastoral Letters ("The Challenge of Peace," 1983, and "Economic Justice for All," 1986) that resulted were not only bold in content, but also the product of an extraordinarily consultative process, something new for the American bishops and for American Catholics. These pastorals addressed all Americans, not simply Catholics. As Theodore Hesburgh, a prominent educator and former president of the University of Notre Dame, remarked: "The bishops do not cease to be citizens by becoming bishops."[26] They have a responsibility to raise moral issues in the public forum.

The impetus for the pastorals came from Vatican II and particularly from the *Pastoral Constitution on the Church in the Modern World* which encouraged the bishops to read the "signs of the times" and to respond to them in ways consistent with the gospel. In the area of war and peace, the bishops' reading of the times indicated the need for a quest for peace, emphasized the unique destructive powers of nuclear weapons, and underlined the need to curb the escalating arms race. The peace pastoral attempted to analyze the moral issues involved in nuclear warfare and to suggest ways to peace. The church has traditionally defended a just war theory which allows for warfare under certain conditions. Nuclear war, the pastoral argued, no longer fit under this rubric since nuclear weaponry cannot compare with conventional weapons. Nuclear weapons are capable of destroying entire countries in a matter of minutes, and they readily violate all principles of proportionality. It is virtually impossible to contain their destructive effect to exclusively military targets. Thus "a limited nuclear war" seems an oxymoron. War, in any form, is no longer morally viable in the modern world, according to the bishops. Citing one of Pope John Paul II's homilies, the document asserts:

Today, the scale and the horror of modern warfare—whether nuclear or not—makes it totally unacceptable as a means of settling differences between nations. War should belong to the tragic past, to history; it should find no place on humanity's agenda for the future.[27]

To some lay people this sounded like a utopian dream. To others it was the only stance possible in an unstable world in which the weaker nations were likely to suffer at the hands of the powerful. The document was careful to distinguish those who are Christian (and Catholic) from those who "do not share the same vision of faith" although the document is ultimately intended for everyone regardless of religious commitment. For Catholics, it is an internal authoritative voice; for other Christians, it is a plea for peace based on Christian scripture; for non-Christian America, it is an appeal to rationality and sanity in a time when all sense of reason could evaporate in the heat of nuclear conflict.

The committee charged with writing the draft of "The Challenge of Peace" included five bishops headed by Cardinal Joseph Bernardin of Chicago. One of the committee members, Cardinal O'Connor, had held the rank of admiral in the Navy and had served as the bishop for U.S. armed forces. Previous to this document, most church statements were the exclusive product of bishops and perhaps theologians. The committee overseeing this pastoral invited comment from a wide range of constituents who reacted to the drafts, including scientists, government officials, the military, politicians, and ordinary Catholics and non-Catholics. The discussions were open and frank. People within and without the church debated the content. Such collaboration was unprecedented. The entire process took thirty months and required the scrutiny of hundreds of potential amendments. When the final draft, titled "The Challenge of Peace: God's Promise and Our Response," was put before the assembled bishops on May 3, 1983, in Chicago, the document passed, 238 to 9.

The road to passage was not always a smooth one, however. Some Catholics who were more hawkish disagreed vehemently with the document's position that first strike nuclear war cannot be justified under any conditions. In general, conservatives inside and outside the church disagreed with the bishops. For example, William F. Buckley Jr. decried the pastoral's message, fearing, in part, that it meant abandoning the fight against communism.[28] Those with a more liberal bent agreed with the document, and those within the church were heartened by the support for the document in circles outside the church. Both sides were surprised and encouraged by the consultative process by which the document was conceived.

Despite the widespread consultation in the creation of the pastoral, and the accompanying publicity it received, many Catholics either ignored it or were unwilling to invest themselves in a quest for peace partly because in the 1980s, as American church historian David O'Brien pointed out: "Episcopal and papal authority is weaker, the church has become more voluntary, and few Catholics are familiar with church teaching on social justice and world peace, even fewer with the natural-law tradition on which so many of these teachings are based."[29]

The second major pastoral letter by the American bishops in the 1980s, under the leadership of Archbishop Rembert Weakland of Milwaukee, dealt with the moral questions underlying the American economy. This was an area which appeared to some as beyond not only the competency but the authority of the bishops. After all, bishops are meant to be shepherds and administrators, not economists. The *Los Angeles Times* reported "that the letter will make the anti-nuclear statement seem like a 'Sunday-school picnic' by comparison."[30] But the bishops thought that it was time to address economic structures that favor the wealthy, spend more on weapons than welfare, foster a permanent underclass, and distribute economic advantage unevenly. The pastoral "calls for the establishment of a floor of material well-being on which all can stand" and "calls into question extreme inequalities of income and consumption when so many lack basic necessities."

The pastoral, "Economic Justice for All: Catholic Social Teachings and the U.S. Economy," dealt with a wide range of economic issues, principal among them being employment, poverty, food and agriculture, and the U.S. role in a global economy.[31] The pastoral was published at a time of high unemployment and its accompanying hardships. The bishops argued that individuals have a right to work, and that every effort should be made to provide jobs in both government and the private sector. While the pastoral acknowledges that some of the reasons for unemployment, such as population growth and women increasingly entering the workforce, are beyond the control of the government or private industry, it is critical of policies such as overseas manufacturing because of lower labor costs, increased defense spending on high-tech weaponry, and lack of job training programs for the unskilled or under-skilled worker. The bishops deplored the fact that one in seven Americans lives below the poverty line in one of the wealthiest countries on earth. This is particularly reprehensible since many of these are children. They also called for an overhaul of the welfare system, not to diminish the assistance given, but to improve it. Theologically, the pastoral favored a preferential option for the poor, a tenet that is biblically grounded, found in Vatican II documents, and stressed in many contemporary liberation theologies.

As adventurous as this pastoral was to address American society on such issues, it reflected the thinking of the universal church as articulated as recently as 1981 by Pope John Paul II in his encyclical *Laborem Exercens* (On Human Work), in which the pope defended work for every individual as a God-given right, along with the right of workers to form legitimate unions. The pope said: "[U]nemployment, which in all cases is an evil, when it reaches a certain level, can become a real social disaster." Previously, Pope Leo XIII defended workers in his 1891 encyclical *Rerum Novarum* (On the Rights and Duties of Capital and Labor) and Pope Pius XI confirmed this in his depression-era 1931 Encyclical *Quadragesimo Anno* (Commemorating the Fortieth Anniversary of Leo XIII's *Rerum Novarum*) claiming that "the opportunity to work be provided for those who are willing and able to work." Pope John XXIII, in his 1963 encyclical *Pacem in Terris* (Peace on Earth), stated "[I]t is clear that human beings have the natural right to free initiative in the economic field and the right to work"; and Pope Paul VI also urged a new economic order in his 1967 encyclical *Populorum Progressio* (Development of Peoples). In addition to these encyclicals, the Vatican II document *Gaudium et Spes* (The Church in the Modern World) stated that "It is the duty of society . . . to help its citizens find opportunities for adequate employment." For decades the church had decried the effects of increasing industrialization. "Economic Justice for All" addresses the problems associated with the deindustrialization of America as America farms out manufacturing to the Pacific rim and the third world, and becomes a service economy.

So the American bishops built on an established tradition. They spoke on similar topics in the past (on unemployment in 1930, on the social order in 1940, and the economy as recently as 1970). However, this was the first time that the bishops, as a body, addressed American society as a whole on this topic and received a spirited public reaction. This prophetic action (in the sense of biblical prophets who brought God's message to the attention of a sometimes reluctant people) reflected the fact that American Catholics and their episcopal leaders no longer thought it incumbent on them to support American public policy at all costs. The Catholic community in America was no longer an exclusively immigrant one seeking confirmation of its patriotism. It had toed the mark long enough to gain respectability and had risen above suspicion that it was beholden to a foreign power in Rome. These pastorals symbolically represent an American Catholic community come of age.

The pastoral on the economy was directed at the American people, Catholic and non-Catholic alike. But it addressed issues of economic justice that affect people all over the world. The economy must serve all of the people, including the poor. The objectives are noble as noted in the pastoral: "[S]ociety has a moral obligation to take the necessary steps to ensure that no one among us is hungry, homeless, unemployed, or otherwise denied what is necessary to live with dignity." Some critics of the economic pastoral challenged the church to live by its own words. Joseph A. Pichler, President and Chief Operating Officer of Dillon Companies, Inc. wrote the following:

> The Church must witness its commitment to self-determination and voluntarism through its own actions as employer, educator, and minister. Church-related institutions must be a sign to all of managerial behavior that respects the dignity of work and of workers. This entails multiple obligations to: avoid all forms of discrimination based upon race, sex, and other arbitrary dimensions; provide employees with full information regarding their performance and status; recognize the right to collective bargaining; limit restraint placed upon employees to those which are necessary for the effective performance of duties; hear and accommodate the personal needs of employees insofar as they are consistent with the task at hand; and avoid actions that would foreclose the freedom of others to seek self-improvement.[32]

Economists took exception not to the objectives of the pastoral but to the methods it proposed to achieve those objectives. Some argued that the bishops were naive or misdirected in their proposals to achieve admirable objectives. For example, the Nobel Prize-winning economist Milton Friedman argued that the means proposed in the pastoral would result in effects diametrically opposed to those the bishops desired.[33] Adhering to the tenets of the pastoral would create more unemployment and weaken the economy. The bishops wanted to invest the government with greater authority over economic matters; Friedman saw little hope that the government could correct what it was largely responsible for creating. He wanted to empower the free market private sector, not the government. Another economist, Walter

Block, senior economist at the Fraser Institute and director of its Centre for the Study of Economics and Religion, was troubled by the bishops' "lack of comprehension of the free marketplace."[34] Carl Christ, an economist at Johns Hopkins University, commented: "Admirable though the aims of the pastoral letter are, they are sometimes [perhaps deliberately] stated in imprecise terms and hence give little quantitative guidance."[35] Clearly, some among the professional ranks of economists thought that the bishops ventured beyond their area of expertise in writing such a document.

And it may have been true that the bishops were beyond their competency as far as economic theory was concerned, but they had not exceeded their moral authority. The gospel is clear in its call for justice and its mandate to care for the poor. In lobbying the American people in such a direct and public manner, the bishops were fulfilling their role as prophetic voices. The details of the letter may be subject to legitimate debate and criticism, but the rationale for such a document is unquestionable in Catholic theology.

Troubles for the Church

At the same time that the church was making its presence felt in the arena of public policy, it was attracting unwanted attention because of the private behavior of some of its clergy. In the 1980s and '90s, a significant number of cases of sexual misconduct involving priests were uncovered. No one knows for certain how long such behavior had been occurring, although it certainly preceded the 1980s. All of the reasons why it came to light during this period may never be known, but some are apparent. From Vatican II on, among Catholics, the pre-Vatican II reverence toward priests had been slowly eroding. The general cultural shift among Americans who became increasingly suspicious of authority in all forms no doubt was a contributing factor. Legal concerns played a role as well. Liability changed from a climate in which people thought it dangerous to disclose knowledge of such matters to one in which it was dangerous not to disclose what one knew. Also after Vatican II priests stepped down from the pedestals where generations of reverential awe had placed them. Interacting differently with the community, priests and sisters revealed themselves as human and vulnerable—and, yes, sinful—to those to whom they ministered. Some laity and clergy, however, deplored the newly introduced informality and pined for earlier customs that distanced clergy from the laity whom they served.

Many clergy and sisters wanted to identify with their people. Some laity found this a refreshing change. Others wanted their clergy and religious to preserve all the external signs of respect the Catholic community had come to expect. In any case, the personal power of the priesthood had not disappeared. And in the privacy of rectories, vacation venues and parishioners' homes, some priests were taking advantage of that authority to seduce children into sexual liaisons. When confronted with such cases, church authorities at first denied such things occurred. In a number of dioceses in which the bishop was informed that a priest had a sexual attraction to children and perhaps had been caught in some compromising situation, the priest was reassigned to another parish where the problem was likely to, and in many cases did, repeat itself. Some priests were quietly sent away for therapy only to return to ministries in which they again had contact with children.

However, many of the victims of this abuse were now adults and, as painful as it was, they no longer maintained their silence. They went to therapists, lawyers, district attorneys, and newspapers.[36] The negative publicity was devastating to the image of the church, and the lawsuits were financially debilitating. Settling out of court, which the church generally preferred to avoid further public embarrassment, cost millions of dollars. Some dioceses teetered on the edge of insolvency. The luster of the priesthood was deeply tarnished by these cases. Although they represented a small fraction of the clergy, the fact that priests were involved shocked and disappointed many Catholics and non-Catholics alike. The fact that the church had denied or mishandled numerous cases early on infuriated many. Lingering questions among the laity about trustworthiness, sexual dysfunction, and institutional accountability are part of the legacy of these unfortunate incidents.

In one notable case, in July 1997 a jury awarded eleven plaintiffs $118 million in a judgment against the diocese of Dallas for its complicity in the illicit sex life of one of its priests, who had had sexual relations with a series of altar boys over a period of years. The diocese defrocked Father Ralph Kos in 1992, too late for these victims. Bishop Charles Grahmann, who had assumed responsibility for the diocese only in 1990, apologized to the victims at a liturgy after the court judgment. This unprecedented gesture made national headlines and was the lead story of one of network television's evening news programs, but the damage had been done: to the victims (one of whom committed suicide in 1992 before the crime was made public) and their families, to the priest, the diocese, and the reputation of the clergy.

Usually these cases are settled by the church out of court before trial in order to spare the victims and the church the pain of public scrutiny. In this case, the amount requested was so large that the church had no choice but to go to trial—a trial that lasted eleven weeks and dominated the headlines of the *Dallas Daily News*. The victims' attorneys argued successfully that the church had ignored signs and warnings (some from other priests) that Father Kos was troubled and a danger to young boys. In July 1998, the diocese and its insurers reached a settlement sum of $35 million. To cover the settlement the diocese sold property and took out loans. The damage to the church in such cases goes far beyond the financial consequences. Catholics' relationship to the church is built on trust and faith. Disclosure of clerical abuse undermines that relationship and sows the seeds of mistrust and doubt.

Bishops, with the help of lawyers, have addressed these abuses more openly in recent years, and many seminaries require psychological screening of their candidates; but the damage has been done and further revelations only confirm that the church often has not effectively managed the serious illnesses of its own priests.

Women in the Church

No issue is more painful in the post-Vatican II American church than its relationship to women. At one point the American bishops attempted to address directly the issue of the role of women in the church. The National Conference of Catholic Bishops formed a committee to investigate the feasibility of writing a pastoral letter on women, much like the ones they had issued on nuclear war and the economy. As indicated, those pastorals ignited extensive and often passionate debate among Catholics and many other circles in American society, including government and the secular press. While many inside and outside the church disagreed with one or the other or both pastorals, few thought they were not worthwhile. The proposed pastoral on women was a different story, however. The six bishops on the committee, which was headed by Bishop Joseph Imesch of Joliet, Illinois, consulted with a number of well-respected women in the American church.[37] The document went through four public drafts over a period of nine years, the final draft of which was rejected by the bishops at their annual meeting in November 1992. At the recommendation of Cardinal Bernardin the rejected draft was released as a committee report so that people would have access to it.

The women's response was: if the church cannot promise women equality, it is best to say nothing at all. Two groups of women, the conservative Women for Faith and Family, mostly laywomen, and the women religious group "Consortium Perfectae Caritatis," in a joint letter to the bishops, warned that if the pastoral were published it would be divisive since it conceded that sexism is a sin but did not confront the sins of feminism. They lamented that the bishops' listening sessions catered to dissident voices. Liberal Catholic feminist groups, including Catholics for a Free Choice and the Women's Ordination Conference, however, urged the bishops to hold new hearings that might spare the church public embarrassment if the document were to be published as it stood in the third draft since it did not admit that the church continues to be guilty of sexism.[38] Even one of their own, Bishop Raymond Lucker of New Ulm, Minnesota, publicly advised the committee to table the pastoral, stating: "We should drop the pastoral, but continue the dialogue. The bishops of the United States should simply make a two- or three-page statement expressing thanks to the countless numbers of people who have participated in the consultations."[39]

A pastoral letter from the American bishops, no matter how well intended, could not resolve the issue of equality when Rome stood firm in its resolve to deny women ordination. Many argued that instead of soothing the wounds that women felt, the timing of such a letter was imprudent and would only stir up further resentment. If the bishops had nothing new to say to women, better to say nothing, they advised. The bishops, many of whom were sympathetic with American women's concerns, listened. They abandoned the effort to produce such a letter. It was a Pyrrhic victory for women.

Rome had particular concerns about this document, and those responsible for writing it were called to Rome in May 1991 to clarify several specific concerns.[40] Pope John Paul II has repeatedly articulated the church's position denying ordination to women. His official statement on the matter was signed on May 22, 1994, the feast of Pentecost, and published on May 30 in the form of an apostolic letter titled *Ordinatio Sacerdotalis* (Priestly Ordination). The letter, which is addressed to bishops, leaves no room for ambiguity about the pope's position concerning the ordination of women. In it he states: "I declare that the church has no authority whatsoever to confer priestly ordination on women and that this judgment is to be definitively held by all the church's faithful." The letter echoes the position taken in an earlier Vatican pronouncement, *Inter Insigniores* (On Women and The Priesthood), issued by the Congregation for the Doctrine of Faith on October 15, 1976, under the direction of Pope Paul VI. The principal arguments for maintaining an all-male clergy are the fact that Jesus chose only men as his apostles, and the consistent practice and teaching of the church.

It was no accident that John Paul II's letter was released shortly after the Anglican church's decision to ordain women. The pope clearly wanted to separate the Roman church from the Anglican church on this issue despite good relations between the churches. Both churches adhere to the same creeds—the main difference being that Anglicans do not recognize the pope as supreme head of the church. Some ecumenists had hoped for a formal union of the two churches, but this apostolic letter made clear a difference on the administration of the sacrament of holy orders that would continue to keep them separate.

Reaction to the pope's letter was swift and extensive. Feminist theologians and many women's groups were quick to condemn it; male theologians (many of whom were in sympathy with women) analyzed and criticized it openly; even American bishops raised questions publicly including a response by Michael Kenny, bishop of the diocese of Juneau, Alaska, who wrote in *America*:

> If, in fact, women can never be ordained and the subject itself is no longer open to review, should the church continue limiting all final and ultimate authority to the ordained and therefore to males only? How can the church present itself to the world as the most just of all societies when its major decisions will continue to rest with men alone? Decisions about married life, social justice, religious life . . . and, yes, ordination?[41]

Other bishops were more cautious in their responses, often emphasizing that the letter affirms the equality of men and women. For example, Archbishop William Keeler of Baltimore said:

> The Catholic Church affirms the fundamental equality of women and men, who are both created in the image of God. The diversity of roles emphasizes the equal dignity of both women and men, who each bring to the glory of creation special gifts, including that of leadership. For example, Catholic women have for generations in our country exercised roles of leadership in hospitals, schools and religious communities, touching the lives of many.[42]

Some bishops pledged their obedience to the pope but expressed discomfort with the letter. For example, Archbishop Rembert Weakland of Milwaukee:

> I certainly will be obedient to this command.
>
> Yet in a spirit of filial loyalty, I must also express my own inner turmoil at this decision. . . . Yet, as a bishop I would not be loyal to the Holy Father if I did not again point out the pastoral problems I now will face in my archdiocese. These have to be the object of my concern because many will be confused and troubled, discouraged and disillusioned.
>
> For example, what effect will this declaration have on so many women and men, especially younger women and vowed religious, who still see this question as one of justice and equality . . . How . . . am I to deal with the anger and disillusionment which will inevitably result? What can I do to instill hope in so many women who are now living on the margins of the church?[43]

But it is not bishops' reactions concerning this issue that are most important. What matters more is the question of how American Catholic women view their relationship to the church. And for many women the relationship is not a healthy one. They feel like second-class citizens in their own church. While the church has seven sacraments, six are for women. Ordination is reserved for men only. The social revolution for women's rights, begun over a century ago with figures such as Sojourner Truth and Elizabeth Cady Stanton, began to exert strong pressure on the church in the 1960s. Radical feminist Mary Daly's observation about the church in her book *The Church and the Second Sex* echoes the belief of many Catholic women today. She wrote in 1968: "There will be no genuine equality of men and women in the church as long as qualified persons are excluded from any ministry by reason of their sex alone."[44]

Criticizing Christian churches, feminist theologian Rosemary Radford Ruether calls for the creation of communities of faith that will parallel those of the church, and give priority to women's concerns because institutional churches

> have become all too often occasions of sin rather than redemption, places where we leave angry and frustrated rather than enlightened and

healed. We do not form new communities lightly, but only because the crisis has grown so acute and the efforts to effect change so unpromising that we often cannot even continue to communicate within these traditional church institutions unless we have an alternative community of reference that nurtures and supports our being.[45]

Many women are frustrated; they have not been given the right to be ordained in post-Vatican II Catholicism, while many of their counterparts in Protestant communions are being ordained (among them Lutheran, Methodist, Presbyterian, and Episcopalian). However, some Catholic women view ordination, for men or women, as continuing an oppressive hierarchical structure that should be dismantled. While the exclusion from ordination has been a painful one for many, Catholic women have been making significant contributions to the church in nonordained ministries. Women have assumed positions of responsibility that were either completely closed to them before Vatican II or previously unimagined. For example, Sister Cecelia Louise Moore, an experienced administrator and trusted leader, was named chancellor of the archdiocese of Los Angeles in May 1997. And Racine Dominican Sister Lisa Lucht is chancellor of the diocese of Green Bay, Wisconsin.

Perhaps the most direct contribution women have made is as full-fledged members of parish staffs. Women have become staff members in parishes in capacities previously reserved exclusively for priests. For example, Nancy Freitas is the director of liturgy in Saint Rose of Lima Parish in Gaithersburg, Maryland, whose Easter Vigil was described in the opening chapter. She is responsible for coordinating, organizing, and preparing the liturgy with input on all matters from the homily to the music. Sue Clark is a pastoral associate in the same parish, overseeing programs, guiding the spiritual lives of parish members, participating in parish planning, and leading other lay people to take responsibility for the parish. She enters the lives of individuals and families as intimately as any priest and uses her rich gifts to serve them in ways well beyond the ordinary. Women, lay and under vows, also serve in diocesan positions as chancellors, members of the tribunal, staff members for bishops, religious education directors, Catholic schools superintendents, and vocation directors. Sharon Kugler, a Catholic laywoman, is the campus chaplain at the Johns Hopkins University in Baltimore serving on the university president's cabinet and leading an interfaith community that includes Evangelicals, Protestants, Catholics, Jews, Muslims, Hindus, and Buddhists. These are a few of the many responsible positions now occupied by Catholic women, suggesting that one need not be ordained to be effective in ministry. By virtue of their baptism Catholics believe all are called to serve and thereby have a vocation to work within the church.

A Watchful Eye

The church, particularly through the United States Catholic Conference Committee on Doctrine continues to keep a close eye on American theologians. One of the most prominent, Richard McBrien, a professor at the University of Notre Dame, whom Tim Unsworth in his work *The Last Priests in America*[46] describes as "the epitome of the American theologian at work—unvarnished, unfiltered, unafraid," is the author of a widely used two-volume work titled *Catholicism*.[47] The book is a thorough compendium of contemporary Catholic theology, covering historical issues, dogmas, sacraments, and practices. Its title and broad scope lead people to think that it is an authoritative work that describes and interprets church teachings in an official manner. It is, however, McBrien himself admits, the work of a single theologian attempting to articulate what contemporary Catholic theology teaches about the church.

The success of the book and its use for catechetical purposes in many churches caused some concern among the American bishops because the book includes what the bishops consider speculative theology. After the first edition of the work in 1980, and a study edition a year later, the United States Catholic Conference Committee on Doctrine initiated a dialogue with McBrien about the content of the book. McBrien was fully cooperative with the committee and willingly made changes to the study edition. Nevertheless, the bishops' committee took it upon itself to make a public clarification of certain elements of the book "in which the presentation is not supportive of the church's authoritative teaching."[48] Theologians dissenting from church teachings are not new, but McBrien's book is a special case since it is not intended exclusively for the scholarly community; it has enjoyed widespread popularity, and some Catholics mistake it for official teaching.[49] His 1994 revised edition of the book also required negotiations with bishops' representatives.

The church maintains a vigilant stance toward theologians. John Courtney Murray and Richard McBrien are two theologians who represent the tensions that can arise between those who construct theologies from within the church and those responsible for governing the church. This tension can be a creative one, encouraging the institutional church to consider new evidence and arguments that will help to shape its theology. On the one hand, the institutional guardians are vigilant to protect the church from faulty theological constructions. On the other hand, the church needs scholars who formulate its teachings with attention to current intellectual developments and in language that conveys its meaning clearly in the contemporary world.

Bishops also come under scrutiny by the Vatican. In 1985, after an investigation of the pastoral practices of Archbishop Raymond Hunthausen of Seattle, the Vatican intervened in the governance of his archdiocese transferring five areas of authority from Hunthausen to Rome-appointed Auxiliary Bishop Donald Wuerl. Rome claimed that Archbishop Hunthausen lacked "the firmness necessary to govern the archdiocese" and failed to uphold orthodoxy in five areas: liturgy, marriage annulments, priestly formation, ministry to homosexuals, and practices at Catholic hospitals. Hunthausen objected to the investigative process that led to his being disciplined and to the power-sharing arrangement established by the Vatican, but for a while the arrangement stood.[50] The Vatican appointed Cardinals Bernardin and O'Connor and Archbishop Quinn to assess the situation. Accepting their conclusion that the governance solution proved unworkable, Rome appointed Auxiliary Bishop Wuerl elsewhere, restored power to Archbishop Hunthausen, and appointed Bishop Thomas Murphy as coadjutor bishop who eventually succeeded Hunthausen as archbishop.

Noninstitutional Developments

Significant Catholic activity at present and in the past forty years occurs outside of the parameters of the institutional setting. Institutional Catholicism, described in some detail in this book, is not the exclusive expression of the faith. Many groups, who for one reason or another find themselves alienated from the institution, continue to work on the edges of Catholicism to bring about change, to offer alternative communities, to provide support to Catholics who find little or no support in institutional expressions of the faith. Some of these groups are identified in this work, others are not. Among these parallel communities are Catholic lesbian and homosexual persons who feel unwanted or otherwise excluded, groups of women who are deeply dedicated to the gospel of Jesus Christ and the Catholic tradition but cannot condone the church's intransigence on certain issues that affect women, Catholics who long for a more democratic church in which their voices will not only be heard but will count when it comes to developing policies and practices, those who refuse to cooperate with what they consider to be a sometimes immoral institution but who also refuse to call themselves anything but Catholic.

Some of this parallel church activity is gender based, as in the case of women who celebrate the Eucharist without a priest. Women-Church Convergence, a coalition of Catholic-rooted organizations acts as a clearing house for feminist concerns which it represents to the institutional church. Even those at one time most directly identified with the church, former priests, continue an affiliation with one another, if not with the institution in a group using the acronym CORPUS (Corps of Reserve Priests United for Service).

Facing the Twenty-First Century

The church embraces the new millennium as a people and an institution shaped by Vatican II and its aftermath. But that formation is as yet incomplete and the church continues to interpret, implement, and aspire to fulfill the vision of the Council documents. Doing so faithfully and effectively, without dividing the church, has posed a challenge since the close of the Council in 1965. Thus far, the church in the United States, as well as worldwide, has managed the transition required by this landmark Council that urged the church to modernize. However, it has not done so without internal disagreements or dueling ideologies.

Perhaps the church would have modernized even if Pope John XXIII did not convene the Council, forced to do so by the inertia of contemporary culture in which it is enmeshed. In the United States, the social upheaval of the 1960s may have spilled over into the church whether or not there was a historic council in Rome. Maybe the post-Vatican II generation's attitude toward the church is affected more by the general decline in trust of institutions after the Vietnam War, Watergate, the civil rights struggle, increased divorce, corporate downsizing, the Clinton impeachment, and feminism's fight against patriarchy among other social movements, than it is by church actions and policies. The institutional church has contributed to its own marginalization in the lives of some American Catholics by refusing to deal openly and directly with myriad problems and issues ranging from sexual abuse by clergy to women's call for equality.

Whether the Council accidentally coincided with this social transformation or was an integral part of it, cannot be definitively known. In the year 2000, the Roman Catholic Church in America faces a host of challenges and opportunities. How it responds to them will affect its future, but it will not make or break this enduring institution, which has survived many trying times in its history.

CHAPTER FIVE

Teachings and Beliefs: Part I

What is it that American Catholics believe? This question is quite different from the question: What is it that the church teaches? The latter question can be answered more easily and definitively. The answer to the former question, no doubt, would differ depending upon whom one asked. This chapter explores some of the foundational beliefs of Catholics and the grounds for those beliefs. The following chapter examines the sacramental character of Catholicism as well as some of its moral teachings and its relationship to other churches and religions. To those outside of Catholicism, the beliefs of Catholics may appear to be uniform and universally held. But to those who profess the faith, it is well known that Catholics differ widely in their beliefs and religious practices. As an example of difference in belief, some Catholics hold that abortion is morally wrong in all circumstances; others believe that there are some circumstances (for example, incest and rape) in which abortion is morally permissible.

Another example of difference in practice: not all persons who identify themselves as Catholic go to church regularly. Catholic teachings range from claims of dogma that are taught officially and definitively (for example, Mary was conceived without sin) and doctrine derived from the regular and consistent teachings of the church and also taught officially but not necessarily infallibly (for example, purgatory); to moral claims (for example, sex outside of marriage is sinful). On the one hand, some Catholics do not know the dogmas and doctrines, although they have been articulated by church councils and taught regularly to the laity. Conversely, some Catholics know well the moral dictates of the church but disagree with them and choose not to follow them in their everyday lives.

Catholics themselves are divided as to how they think about this situation. There are those who hold that the teachings of the church are clear and are to be followed by those who wish to call themselves Catholic. There are also those who hold that some teachings of the church, particularly but not exclusively in the area of sexual morality, even if clear, are neither realistic nor theologically sound. As John Deedy, journalist and former managing editor of the Catholic magazine *Commonweal*, points out, the contemporary American church community is a combination of orthodox and heterodox believers.[1]

Despite these divisions, there are teachings, practices, and beliefs that are generally recognized as Catholic. In order to discuss these, it is important to distinguish theology from spirituality and religious practice. Theology deals with the formation and expression of Catholic beliefs. Spirituality concerns the interior life of the believer. Religious practice is the public expression of one's religious convictions. Each of these is an important component of religion, and each dimension influences the others in a person's religious life. Official theology is formulated by the pope and bishops with the help of theologians. However, sometimes quite independent from the hierarchy, theologians regularly introduce new ideas and theories into the theological landscape. And even apart from bishops and theologians, the laity in many cases constructs its own theology which may or may not coincide with or confirm the official variety.

Using a combination of personal beliefs and experience as norms, laity sometimes justify practices, moral positions, and theological interpretations that are at odds with papal teachings but seem perfectly reasonable to the individuals who hold them. For instance, the church forbids sex outside of marriage, but a significant number of American Catholics do not consider premarital sex between mature adults sinful. In fact, some view it as beneficial since the couple explores an important dimension of their relationship that will help shape their life together in the sacrament of marriage. Or, since a number of anthropologists and psychologists theorize that a certain percentage of the population is innately homosexual, some Catholics condone homosexual relationships on the basis of the church's natural law teaching. If God created some persons as homosexuals, then they should be able to express their God-given sexual nature.

Personal and corporate spirituality are informed by, but different from, theology. The spirituality of the laity involves the Eucharist and other sacraments, Marian devotions, the intercession of saints, personal prayer, retreats of various types, and sometimes spiritual direction by a competent spiritual adviser, among other expressions. The practice of one's religious beliefs includes not only these spiritual exercises but also public acts, such as participation in rituals and in works of charity related to one's beliefs. In some instances a conflict arises between what the church teaches (official theology), what one appropriates internally (spirituality), and what one does (practice). One may, for instance, go to church and pray regularly but act unethically in business or personal affairs, or one may be involved in works of charity but lack a prayer or sacramental life.

Fundamental Catholic theological beliefs are articulated in the Nicene Creed, the original formulation of which dates back to the Council of Nicea in 325 A.D. and which was modified slightly by the Council of Constantinople in 381 A.D. Catholics continue to recite this creed today in the Eucharistic liturgy as the church has done since the eleventh century.

The Nicene Creed
We believe in one God,
the Father, the Almighty.
maker of heaven and earth,
of all that is seen and unseen.
We believe in one Lord, Jesus Christ,
the only Son of God,
eternally begotten of the Father,
God from God, Light from Light,
true God from true God,
begotten, not made, one in Being with the Father,
Through him all things were made,
For us men and for our salvation
he came down from heaven:
by the power of the Holy Spirit
he was born of the virgin Mary, and became man.
For our sake he was crucified under Pontius Pilate,
he suffered, died, and was buried.
On the third day he rose again
in fulfillment of the Scriptures;
he ascended into heaven
and is seated at the right hand of the Father.
He will come again in glory to judge the living and the dead,
and his kingdom will have no end.

We believe in the Holy Spirit, the Lord, the giver of life,
who proceeds from the Father and the Son.
With the Father and the Son he is worshiped and glorified.
He has spoken through the prophets.
We believe in one, holy, catholic, and apostolic Church.
We acknowledge one baptism for the forgiveness of sins.
We look for the resurrection of the dead,
and the life of the world to come. Amen.

The Trinitarian formula, Father, Son, and Holy Spirit, affirms the church's belief in one God who is three persons. Each of these persons of the Trinity is equally God. Further, it affirms belief in the church and the origin and destiny of humanity. This creed sums up the central beliefs of Christians. The Catholic Church has many additional teachings that bind its adherents, but those articulated in the creed are the fundamental teachings.

Similar in content to the Nicene Creed is the Apostles' Creed, which was used at baptism in the early church. It includes most of the claims of the Nicene version with a few additions (such as "he descended into hell," indicating that Jesus's liberation from death applies also to those faithful to God who came before him).

The Soul

Some of the roots of the church's teaching originate in Judaism, Christiani-ty's predecessor and, some say, parent religion. The early Jewish biblical texts are not dualistic, separating body and soul. Around the time of Jesus, some Jewish groups had taken over the notion of a soul and related it to the possibility of personal resurrection and continued life of the individual. Christianity's idea of the soul, its identity and durability, was deeply influenced by the Hellenization of Christianity and the thought patterns of Greek philosophy. In his work *Phaedo*, Plato argued for a dualism of body and soul and contended that the soul constituted the identity of the person. Catholicism today maintains a distinction between body and soul but holds for a unity of body and soul in the sense that the person is an embodied spirit.

While it is true that Christians believe that they will be raised in a resurrection from the dead, made possible by Jesus's resurrection, the belief in resurrection was present among the first-century A.D. Pharisees, a Jewish sect at the time of Jesus. However, this belief was not universal, for it was rejected by the Sadducees, a Jewish religo-political party from the last two centuries B.C. and the first century A.D. The New Testament writer Paul was a Pharisee before his conversion to Christianity. The expectation of the earliest, post-resurrection Christians was that Jesus would return in glory soon, certainly during their lifetime. As the Christian community grew and time passed, the hope for an imminent return of Jesus faded. With the delay of the second coming more evident, and more widely accepted among Christians, the idea of a universal judgment on the last day began to fade. Instead of expecting an immediate return of the Messiah, or having the dead await a final day of judgment for all, the idea that each person was judged immediately after death became increasingly accepted. The thought that the soul was held in some state of abeyance began with the Jewish belief in Sheol, the netherworld, the shadowy realm of the dead, and carried over into early Christianity (influenced by the Greeks). The idea of the immortal soul awaiting the definitive judgment of the Last Day was officially abandoned when the church claimed that the dead are judged immediately after death.[2]

Whether the judgment of the dead is immediate or delayed, and whether or not individual theologians hold for an inseparable unity of body and soul or for body and soul dualism, Christianity maintains that the soul has a beginning when God creates it, but no end.

The Church Magisterium

Who in the church has the right to teach authoritatively on issues regarding faith and morals? The answer to this question is the magisterium. The Catholic moral theologian, William E. May, succinctly defines this authority as "the authority, given by God, to teach in the name of Christ the truths of Christian faith and life and of all that is necessary or useful for the proclamation of these truths."[3] It is the bishops, in union with the pope, who exercise this authority. The bishops have the authority to teach what Catholics are to believe and how they are to live morally.

From the very beginning of the formation of the church, there has been a need for some one or some body to speak authoritatively in its name. The nascent church of the first century came into existence in the midst of a host of religions and cults from which it had to distinguish its beliefs and practices. As the church took shape, it faced the problem of defining itself in relation to internal challenges as well. The four gospels now found in the Bible were not the only ones written. Other so-called Gnostic texts, such as The Gospel of Thomas and the Gospel of Mary, which had somewhat different (although not always radically so) accounts of Jesus, vied for recognition among the growing Christian community. There needed to be an authoritative voice within the Christian community to clarify these matters, to fight heresy, and to preserve that which was developing into orthodoxy. Theologian Francis Sullivan notes: "When conflicts arise . . . those with pastoral responsibility [i.e., the bishops] must have the authority to judge which of the conflicting opinions is in accord with the faith of the Church."[4] This teaching authority is called the magisterium (Latin magister means "teacher").

The magisterium of the church exercises its authority in a number of different ways, but the two principal manners in which this authority is exercised are called ordinary and extraordinary. The ordinary magisterium of the church is the regular and consistent teaching of the pope and bishops via encyclicals and pastoral letters. Such teachings are considered authoritative and true, but they are subject to reform. The extraordinary teachings of the church are solemnly declared by the pope *ex cathedra* (from the chair [of Peter]) and are not subject to reform. The document *Lumen Gentium* (Dogmatic Constitution on the Church) from Vatican II makes it clear that the bishops speak with authority: "This sacred Synod teaches that by divine institution bishops have succeeded to the place of the apostles as shepherds of the Church, and that he who hears them, hears Christ, while he who rejects them, rejects Christ and Him who sent Christ."[5]

Revelation

While the magisterium serves as the teaching authority of the church, the source of the teaching comes from revelation. Revelation is the formal term given to God's message to humankind, God's disclosure to humankind of who God is, how God interacts with humanity, and what God expects of people. The most commonly recognized element of this revelation is the Bible. Catholics believe that the authors of the biblical texts were inspired by God to communicate, in their own words, God's message. Catholics also believe that the church has been endowed by the Holy Spirit with the capacity to discern further the revelation of God's message and will. So while formal revelation closed with the completion of the Bible, revelation continues through the inspiration and guidance of the Holy Spirit within the church.

Most, but not all, of the teachings of the church have their roots in scripture. God's message may come through prophets, saints, and popes, but it is found chiefly in the Bible. The Bible is humanity's record of God's promises, commands, and interaction with human history. According to Catholic theology, the Bible is not considered to have been written or even dictated by God (as, for example, the Qur'an was to Muhammad). Rather, God inspired the writers of the Bible to record God's message. Thus the message is God's, but the writing is humanity's. This understanding of scripture separates Catholics from fundamentalist Christians, who adhere to a literal reading of the Bible, while mainline Protestants share the idea that scripture requires careful methods of interpretation.

Catholics generally believe that the Bible requires interpretation in order to be understood properly. Beginning in the nineteenth century, especially in Germany, Protestants led the way in critical biblical scholarship that employed historical-critical methods of evaluation and interpretation. Although such study was considered radical and was not readily accepted by the Christian community at that time, since then critical exegesis of the scriptures has been widely accepted among mainline Protestant churches and by Catholics. In general, Catholic biblical scholarship lagged behind that of Protestant scholars until Pope Pius XII's 1943 encyclical *Divino Afflante Spiritu* (Inspired by the Holy Spirit) encouraged Catholic biblical scholars to use the available critical tools, in particular the historical-critical methods that had long been used by Protestant scholars.

In 1937 biblical scholars from the United States and Canada formed the Catholic Biblical Association of America and founded the journal *Catholic Biblical Quarterly*. Pius XII's actions allowed Catholic biblical scholarship to come of age. The encyclical helped to erase the shadow of Modernism that hung over Catholic scholars and legitimized what was already happening in scholarly circles. "The Church could not . . . forever deny the critical scientific spirit everywhere characteristic of the age."[6] Since the issuing of this encyclical, Catholics have taken their place among the most respected biblical scholars in the world, including such notables as Raymond Brown, Joseph Fitzmyer, and Roland Murphy. Today John Meier, Elisabeth Schüssler Fiorenza, John Donahue, and Raymond Collins, among others, carry on this scholarly tradition.

Pre-Vatican II Catholics were discouraged from reading the Bible for private inspiration or devotion. Since the church is the official interpreter of revelation, it did not foster Bible study or private interpretation for fear that some would be led in directions different from the way the church interpreted the scriptures. This was a major factor separating Catholics from Protestants, most denominations of which fostered Bible reading for inspiration. Today Catholics are encouraged to read the scriptures, to join Bible study groups, and to use the Bible for personal prayer.

However, Catholic teaching stresses that the Bible is a complex set of books, the content of which is God's message, but the form of which was created by biblical writers who were influenced by their culture, historical period, and personal predilections. Catholics are not literalists reading the scriptures. Catholics believe that the Bible is the word of God but that word needs to be interpreted for our times. This belief distinguishes Catholics from Evangelical Christians who hold to the "literal" meaning of the Bible. Like Catholics, mainline Protestants interpret the Bible; but unlike Catholics, they do so as individuals and do not rely upon the church either to offer a privileged interpretation of the Bible or to act as an intermediary in their relationship with God.

While most Catholics are unacquainted with the sophisticated interpretation process used by scripture scholars, those who preach and teach generally know the theories of interpretation of critical biblical scholarship. Those methods include: 1) *Literary Criticism*, which examines how the literary structure of the biblical text shapes its meaning. The words, images, characters, and expressions help to form and convey the content of the Bible. For example, to understand the story of the good Samaritan from Luke's gospel (10:30–35), it is important to know who Samaritans were at the time of Jesus. 2) *Textual Criticism*, which examines the various surviving ancient manuscripts for variations in the transmission of biblical texts and assesses whether these variations were accidental (scribal error) or intentional (a change for theological reasons, for example). 3) *Source Criticism*, which attempts to determine if a text was derived from a previous source (such as a New Testament saying paraphrasing an Old Testament expression). 4) *Form Criticism*, which attempts to identify the mode of communication that the text uses; for example, a letter, a poem, a speech, a story, or a saying, to name a few possibilities. Determining the form can help in the interpretation of the text. Just as one would read a personal letter differently from a newspaper article, or a poem differently from a legal code, so the biblical texts must be interpreted according to their varying forms. 5) *Historical Criticism*, which attempts to determine the historical accuracy of biblical accounts of events. For example, was it likely that the Romans crucified public criminals in the way that Jesus is said to have been killed? 6) *Redaction Criticism*, which studies the potential changes to source material made by those responsible for compiling and writing the texts. For example, in the gospels they wrote, the evangelists Matthew, Mark, Luke, and John reshaped their material to reflect their own theological understanding. Thus, each of these gospels tells the story of Jesus, using different styles, patterns, and choice of materials.[7]

Within the last decade many biblical scholars have employed an interdisciplinary approach to the study of scripture, using the disciplines of history, anthropology, and archeology combined with social science methods to evaluate and interpret the Bible. In particular, a controversial group called "the Jesus Seminar" has received much attention from scholars and the popular press. The group employs interdisciplinary methods to compare canonical New Testament texts to other noncanonical gospels recorded in the early centuries of Christianity in order to distinguish between what they consider to be authentic sayings of Jesus from additions to Jesus's words by biblical authors. Part of their work attempts to investigate the social setting in which Jesus proclaimed his message, asserting that the context in which he preached can help to interpret properly the message. The best-known Catholic among this interfaith group is John Dominic Crossan, the author of numerous works investigating first-century Christianity.[8]

In recent decades, feminist theologians investigated the male influence on the recording of revelation. While God is neither male nor female, the biblical writers were predominately male. They presented an androcentric (male-centered) story of God's interaction with humanity, a reflection of the patriarchal culture in which the Bible took shape. Feminist theologians argue that the androcentric form is a historical accident and does not constitute the meaning of the texts although the history of effects of androcentrism has colored the interpretation given to scripture, which has been both written and interpreted from a male point of view. Women's biblical scholarship in the past thirty years or so changed the way in which men and women read and interpret scripture. Among other changes, the role of women in the New Testament as witnesses to the resurrection and Jesus's own treatment of women as recorded in the gospels indicates that women, whom Jesus treated as equals to men, were important figures in the life and ministry of Jesus and essential members of the early Christian community after Jesus's resurrection.

Put simply, there is no uninterpreted revelation. The Bible, church teachings, councils, apparitions, or mystical experiences all require some form of interpretation in order to derive meaning. Moses on Mount Sinai had to interpret that the sound he heard was a voice and further determine that the voice was God's. The disciples needed to interpret Jesus's words and actions to understand his message and his person (and at times they misinterpreted and misunderstood). The church via its councils and pronouncements interprets the meaning of revelation and theologians interpret the meaning of the councils. The parish priest interprets the scriptures for the local community of believers. Individual Catholics hear what the church teaches, interpret it, and attempt to apply it in their own lives.

Hearing, appropriating, understanding, and applying constitute a complex process that is not always a conscious one. There can, however, be accurate and inaccurate interpretations; and it is the responsibility of the church through its theologians, bishops, pastors, and teachers to guide the process of interpretation. There also can be disagreements about interpretations. As many American Catholics become more attuned to the process by which the church makes its interpretations, they assume a more critical posture. This critical distance moves some (on certain issues a majority) to arrive at interpretations and conclusions that are at odds with the official ones they read in documents or hear from the pulpit. On the one hand, American Catholics are assuming greater responsibility for their Catholicism; on the other hand, they are shaping their own brands of Catholicism.

This phenomenon goes to the heart of the question of authority. On a numbers of issues, papal pronouncements, preaching, and prayerful supplication do not persuade, convince, or convert American Catholics to the hierarchical church's way of thinking. Many of the people in the pews have thought through and interpreted the issues differently, basing their discernment on personal experience. Reflection leads them to conclude that some of the church's teachings are inconsistent with, or contradictory to, experience in their everyday lives and the moral interpretation they give to that experience. The official teachings seem out of touch and therefore irrelevant. This reaction reflects the crisis of credibility that the hierarchical church faces. Many American Catholics view the hierarchy, and in particular the Vatican, as out of touch with ordinary believers' lives, experiences, and interpretations. This disposition flies in the face of church law since canon law dictates that "The Christian faithful, conscious of their own responsibility, are bound by Christian obedience to follow what the sacred pastors, as representatives of Christ, declare as teachers of the faith or determine as leaders of the Church."[9]

Genuine authority is the ability to call forth a specific response from someone. The response the "Roman" church receives from Americans (among others) is often contrary to the desired one. The response to a number of policies and issues is one of resistance. American Catholics will not stop practicing birth control, will not be silent about women's ordination, will not tolerate an authoritarian approach from Rome, will not listen to bishops who are ideologues, will not turn a blind eye to priests' sexual preference or activity, will not adopt a 1950s "Father knows best" mentality, will not contribute to pay settlements for clerical crime that was condoned by benign neglect or mismanagement on the part of bishops, will not be treated as the "shepherd's flock," that is, as a passive herd. Rome attempts to forbid discussion of certain issues on which the pope has taken positions, but the conversation continues in spite of such caveats. Some bishops, acknowledging this, have asked the Vatican:

> Why then do we still act in ways that leave so many of our people feeling that we treat them like children? Why in their eyes do we seem afraid to consult them on matters of faith and pastoral practice? Why can we not trust that the Holy Spirit will bring about a "consensus ecclesiae?" Why can we not openly dialogue about the ministry of women, the meaning of sexuality and the condition of homosexuality, the situation of the divorced and remarried? Why are bishops, who are called vicars of Christ and servants of local churches, so often excluded from processes which lead to pastoral strategies which will deeply affect their own communities?[10]

Few Catholics dispute that the church has the right to exercise authority. They take issue with how that authority is exercised. American Catholics want to participate in the dialogue on the meaning of revelation for contemporary believers. God's revelation is not static, but a living reality that requires interpretations taking into account contemporary methods of scholarship as well as the experience of those who receive this revelation.

Doctrines, Dogmas, Encyclicals, and Councils

While individual Catholics often believe different things or are unaware of what the church teaches in a specific area, the church's official teachings are carefully laid out in various pronouncements. A doctrine is an official teaching of the church. Doctrines are promulgated by various forms of church authority such as the pope, a synod of bishops, or an ecumenical council, to name a few. The New Testament is the original source for many church teachings. The twenty-seven books of the New Testament tell the story of Jesus's life and death, their meaning for his followers, and the foundation of the continuing community that is the church. Doctrines articulate the explicit and implicit teachings of the New Testament in language of the period in which they are formulated. Over time therefore doctrines are subject to development as insights accumulate and language changes, and so doctrines can be reformulated.

Dogmas are doctrines that are promulgated by the pope, usually in conjunction with an ecumenical council. The teachings of the creed (for example, the Trinity) are dogmas. All are considered definitive teaching by the church. It is a heresy to deny church dogmas; historically, however, theologians have questioned their origin, formulation, and implementation without incurring condemnation.

Encyclicals are formal pastoral letters from the pope addressed to the universal church and, since Pope John XXIII, to all persons of good will.[11] The subject matter of these letters varies widely, from social justice to the church's relation with other religions to pastoral practices. Intended to guide and instruct, these are not infallible although their teachings are supposed to be followed by the faithful. Most Catholics are aware that there are such pronouncements, but they would be hard pressed to name any (including recent ones) and even less likely to be intimately acquainted with their content. Diocesan newspapers cover these letters, but often the text is too long to print in their limited space. *Origins* prints them, but it has fewer subscribers and readers than diocesan papers do. The nations' larger newspapers like the *New York Times* and the *Washington Post* usually cover the release of encyclicals, and occasionally the television media devote a story to an encyclical that strikes them as controversial or particularly timely.

Most of the fundamental doctrines that the church articulates come from councils, which are gatherings of church leaders. The most important of these are ecumenical councils in which the pope convenes the bishops of the church to discuss and proclaim church teaching. The Second Vatican Council (1962–65) was the last such gathering. National councils of bishops are also convened, such as the councils of Baltimore in the last century.

The Infallibility of the Pope

One of the most misunderstood doctrines of the church—by Catholics and non-Catholics alike—is the doctrine of infallibility. Infallibility pertains to

particular statements concerning faith and morals. It is a charism of the
Holy Spirit that is given to the church and exercised through the bishops
and pope. The councils of the church have the authority to teach infallibly.
This is called the extraordinary teaching authority of the church and is exercised to ensure that the revelation given to the church is preserved and
taught properly. For example, the teaching contained in the Apostles' Creed
is an infallible one guaranteed by the presence of the Holy Spirit within the
church. The extraordinary teaching authority of the church is exercised on
occasion to clarify, define, and preserve a central truth of the faith, often
given particular expression to counter heretical ideas. This teaching authority is exercised by the church in the form of a general council, which is representative of the entire church in union with the pope. Papal pronouncements are intended to be taken very seriously by the Catholic community
but they are not, as a matter of course, to be considered infallible. Infallible
teachings must be stated explicitly to be so, as indicated in canon law which
holds: "Nothing is to be understood as dogmatically declared or defined
unless this is clearly manifested."[12]

Infallibility, which was not a formal doctrine until the First Vatican
Council in 1869–70, means that certain statements of the church pronounced
by the pope are immune from error. The document *Pastor Aeternus* (Dogmatic Constitution on the Church), proclaimed at Vatican I, explains:

> When the Roman Pontiff speaks *ex cathedra*, that is, when . . . as pastor
> and teacher of all Christians in virtue of his highest apostolic authority
> he defines a doctrine of faith and morals that must be held by the Uni-
> versal Church, he is empowered, through divine assistance promised
> him in blessed Peter, with that infallibility with which the Divine
> Redeemer willed to endow his Church.

This authority is given first and foremost to the church and is exercised
by the pope.[13] Thus, the pope himself is not *per se* infallible. However, when
he exercises his authority as pope in matters of faith and morals, he may
speak infallibly for the church. Once he does exercise this authority the
church at large does not have the authority to supersede the pope's pronouncement. Speaking to this point, the Fathers of the First Vatican Council wrote that infallible "definitions of the Roman Pontiff are irreformable
of themselves and not from the consent of the Church." In the document
Lumen Gentium (Dogmatic Constitution on the Church), the Second Vatican Council reaffirmed the infallibility of the pope and extended the notion

of the exercise of infallibility to include the bishops who, as a body (not individual bishops) and in communion with the pope, may teach infallibly as well. Vatican II also reminded Catholics that they should obey the pope's teachings even when he does not speak *ex cathedra*. This means obedience to the official pronouncements of the church regarding matters of faith and morals, if they are taught explicitly or implicitly as ones to be held definitively. In any case, the church's authority to teach is to be respected and an appropriate response should greet particular teachings, proportionate to the centrality of the teaching and the degree of authority with which it is taught.

The doctrine of papal infallibility has raised questions inside and outside of the church. At Vatican I, when the doctrine first was proclaimed officially, many bishops opposed it and some left the Roman church over this issue to found the Old Catholic Church, a group from German-speaking countries that continued to practice Catholicism independent of Rome. The church historian and theologian Johann J. I. von Döllinger was excommunicated because he rejected the doctrine of papal infallibility. In recent times, the Swiss theologian Hans Küng has questioned the doctrine in his book *Infallibility?*.[14] Most Protestant theologians continue to view it as a barrier to unity of the Christian churches, and ordinary people of all religious persuasions, including Catholics and those of no religious affiliation, often do not understand it or find it difficult (if not impossible) to accept.

Saints

Saints are ubiquitous in Catholicism and have a very important role in the spirituality of Catholics. Traditionally, Catholics are named after a saint at their baptism, though this practice is not strictly adhered to today since the revision of canon law in 1983 permits non-saints' names provided they are not "foreign to a Christian mentality."[15] Individual parish churches are named for them; each country has a patron saint; the church celebrates their feast days, commemorating their lives in the liturgical calendar; Catholics pray to them to intercede with God on their behalf; miracles are attributed to their intercession and required by the church during the canonization process; the stories of saints' lives are known to many Catholics; statues and paintings of them abound in churches, schools, convents, and rectories. They serve as models and inspirations for millions of American Catholics. A handful of saints were North Americans and thus have attained special prominence for U.S. Catholics. One of these was Elizabeth Ann Seton (nee

Bayley), who was born in New York in 1774; married, widowed in 1803, raised five children, converted to Catholicism at age 29, and four years later founded a religious community and opened a school for poor children near Emmitsburg, Maryland. The Sisters of Charity, which she and some companions founded, became the first indigenous religious society in America. She died in 1821 and was canonized by Pope Paul VI in 1975, becoming the first canonized saint born in the United States.

Another was John Neumann. Although born (1811) abroad in Prachatiz, Bohemia, he migrated to the United States where he worked as a priest and served as the fourth bishop of Philadelphia. He advocated Catholic education and wrote two catechisms that were widely used in his time. Pope Paul VI canonized him in 1977.

A third was Mother Frances Cabrini, the patron saint of immigrants. Born in Italy in 1850, she founded the Institute of the Missionary Sisters of the Sacred Heart and came to the United States in 1889, became a citizen and, with her order, established schools, hospitals, and orphanages. She was canonized in 1946 by Pope Pius XII. More recently, in 1997, the American bishops unanimously supported the cause for sainthood of Mother Mary Henriette Delille, the founder of the Sisters of the Holy Family for black women in New Orleans.

The veneration of the saints, along with the special reverence given to Mary, is another feature that separates Catholics from some Protestant denominations. Certain Protestant denominations, such as Lutherans, name churches after the apostles but do not pay similar homage to anyone who came after the apostles. Other denominations, for instance Baptists and Presbyterians, do not have churches honoring eponymous saints. So the cult of the saints is a uniquely Catholic manifestation of piety. The veneration of specific saints is tied to national and ethnic roots. Even today third- and fourth-generation American Catholics identify with saints who represent their ethnic heritage; Saint Patrick for the Irish, Saint Anthony for the Italians, Saint Casimir for the Poles, to name a few.

Catholics often pray to specific saints for favors, such as Saint Joseph to sell a house, Saint Anthony to help find lost objects, Saint Blaise to prevent ailments of the throat, and, when all else fails, Saint Jude as the patron of lost causes or desperate situations. Statues, medals, and paintings of saints remain common though they are not nearly as widespread as in the pre-Vatican II era.

Not all of the those revered by the faithful were historical figures, however. The existence of some is dubious. Christopher, known as the patron

Italian immigrant Mother Cabrini was the first U.S. citizen to be canonized a saint. AP/WIDE WORLD

saint of travelers, is one; Philomena is another. Roman martyrology notes a
man who carried travelers across a river and one time carried a child who
was Christ in disguise. When historical investigations could not confirm his
existence, the church removed his feast day from the liturgical calendar
although many Catholics and other Christians continue to name children
Christopher (the name comes from the Greek meaning "Christ bearer").
The reverence for Philomena was based on a discovery as recent as the early
nineteenth century when a vial seemingly containing blood was discovered
in a catacomb. The Latin inscription was incorrectly translated Philomena;
a biography was contrived, and a following quickly developed to support
the claim to holiness of the woman buried there. Later more careful investi-

gation proved the translation wrong and the story unreliable, so the church (to its credit) removed her from the list of saints.

Upon her death in September 1997, Catholics all over the world petitioned the Vatican to immediately name Mother Teresa of Calcutta a saint. In the eyes, minds and hearts of millions of people, Catholic and not, she represented exceptional holiness. *Newsweek* devoted its September 22, 1997, cover to the story, outlining the lengthy process for sainthood but intimating that the process might be accelerated in her case.[16] The Vatican politely declined to move so quickly (even though the pope himself was a great admirer of Mother Teresa), electing instead to follow its established regulations for investigating the cause of sainthood. Those regulations require a minimum five-year waiting period before anyone's candidacy can be formally proposed. This is done so that the popularity of a contemporary figure does not sweep the candidate to sainthood without due investigation and enduring influence.

For people considered of heroic virtue to become recognized saints their lives are subjected to careful scrutiny by the church.[17] The Vatican oversees the investigation of their conduct of life, justification for their reputation for holiness, and their activities and writings (if any), and ascertains that validated miracles occurred directly as a result of their intercession. The 1983 Code of Canon Law streamlined the canonization process by combining the cause for Beatification (a step on the way to canonization) and Canonization, and by empowering the local diocese to conduct initial investigations. However, the authority to canonize still rests solely in the hands of the pope.

A person's canonization is a public testimony that this person reached a level of sanctity that assures him or her of heaven and constitutes a model for other Christians. Technically all those in heaven are saints, but it is the public declaration that the church makes of some that indicates with certainty that they have achieved this status. But there are many other factors in this long and thorough process by which one is named a saint. To order the process the Vatican maintains an office called the Congregation for the Causes of Saints, which coordinates the investigation of up to two thousand causes at any given time. It follows the procedures established in the Apostolic Constitution *Divinus Perfectionis Magister* (Divine Teacher and Model of Perfection), which took effect on January 25, 1983, and Canon 1403 of the Code of Canon Law.

The process involves two stages, beatification and canonization, and begins with the local diocesan bishop of the place where the potential candidate died. The bishop informs the pope and submits the cause of the person proposed for sainthood. The cause usually is brought to the bishop's attention by a petitioner, who first proposes the candidate to him. The preliminary phase is a diocesan inquiry that includes consultation with regional bishops, the Holy See, the faithful, and expert testimony. The petitioner selects a "postulator" approved by the bishop, who with the help of an aide (vice-postulator) investigates the person's life and writings (if any). They pay particular attention to the person's reputation for sanctity by investigating whether the person is considered an intercessor by the faithful or a following has arisen around the person. The bishop (or his delegate) then examines the evidence, questions witnesses, and presents what is called the "Acts of the Cause" to the Roman Congregation. During the process the bishop makes the petition public so that the local people may speak for or against the cause. Two consultors appointed by the bishop scrutinize the writings of the proposed candidate to ensure their orthodoxy.

All of the documents from the inquiry are notarized, and copies are sent to the congregation in Rome. Rome appoints a "relator" who oversees the writing of a biography. A group of theologians and a promoter of the faith adjudicate the cause and, if it is approved, pass it on to the prelates. After study, the bishops and cardinals of the Congregation for the Causes of Saints submit their evaluation to the pope who decides whether or not to beatify the candidate. This is a good example of the cooperation necessary between the local diocese and Rome for the church to function efficiently. Before the legal and structural reforms of 1983, the entire process was conducted by Rome. The reforms illustrate not only bureaucratic advances but the Vatican's greater trust in the responsibility of the local church.

Preceding the beatification of a candidate for sainthood is a lesser step in which the pope proclaims the person "venerable" because of a proven life of heroic virtue. The final step from beatified to saint requires proof of one more miracle attributed to the intercession of the person. What qualifies as a miracle is a result that science and medicine cannot achieve on their own; for example, someone who is medically judged to be terminally ill fully recovers after praying to a particular saint for his or her intercession.

There is little qualitative difference between the criteria for beatification and canonization, but saints are recognized with their own feast day in the church calendar, churches are named after them, liturgical prayers are addressed to them, and public recognition is given by the faithful. The entire process is usually a long (often decades) and expensive one. The length of the process serves one function effectively: it helps to determine if a person has a lasting effect on the Catholic community. If the person's reputation for holiness remains strong and vivid at the end of the process this is another testimony to his or her worthiness. This lengthy, costly, detailed process of establishing sainthood is important to Catholics because they believe that the saints intercede for them with God, and are role models for Christian life. To imitate the saints is to live a life of total devotion to God and adherence to the gospel.

Mary

If there is one figure besides the pope that separates Protestant Christians from Catholic Christians, it is the greatest saint, Mary, the mother of Jesus. Both Christian communities acknowledge Mary's role in scripture, but Catholics have a special devotion to Mary. For many Catholics, Marian piety is as important as their sacramental life. Many Catholics pray to her that she might intercede with her son Jesus on their behalf. The church holds Mary in high esteem and has bestowed on her more titles than on Jesus. She is the Patroness of the Americas, commemorated on December 8, the feast of the Immaculate Conception (the belief that Mary was from her conception without stain of original sin), the only human besides Jesus to be so conceived. Protestants are often puzzled by Catholics' fascination with Mary. Some object that Catholics have raised Mary to divine status, making her the fourth person of the Trinity. Theologically, Mary is not divine, but human like all other humans. However, since earliest times the church has taught that Mary was a perpetual virgin. In 1854 Pope Pius IX declared the dogma of the Immaculate Conception and in 1951 Pope Pius XII solemnly declared her Assumption (that Mary was assumed bodily into heaven at her death), fostering the notion that she is greater than human or at least, a specially favored one.

In 1997, an international movement among laity and clergy petitioned Pope John Paul II to declare Mary the co-redeemer with Christ. On August 25, 1997, *Newsweek* ran a cover story titled "The Meaning of Mary"[18] that tells how the pope received petitions with 4,340,429 signatures from 157 countries imploring him to proclaim a new infallible dogma that Mary is the "Co-Redemptrix." A number of influential church figures' signatures were among those collected, including Mother Teresa's, and those of almost 500 bishops and 42 cardinals. Even the rumor that the pope might proclaim such a dogma wreaked havoc with Protestant and other Christian churches, including the Greek Orthodox archdiocese of America. Anglican theologian R. William Franklin said that such a dogma "would be a further nail in

Many Catholics have a deep devotion to the Blessed Virgin Mary, depicted here in sculpture. ARCHIVE PHOTOS/IMAPRESS

the coffin of ecumenism."[19] John Paul II, known to be deeply devoted to the Mother of God, did not act on the petition and responded through Cardinal Ratzinger that such a declaration was not theologically appropriate. Mary had a special role as the mother of Jesus, but such a doctrine might misunderstand her to be an equal to Jesus. Jesus is the savior, not Mary.

One of the fascinations of Catholics all over the world is with apparitions of Mary. Historically, some of the most famous among these are Guadalupe in Mexico, Fatima in Portugal, and Lourdes in France. Many of the faithful believe that Mary appeared to children in all of these places, offering them messages of hope. These have become well-known pilgrimage sites. Millions of American Catholics have journeyed to these places in search of Mary's intercession. In recent years, devout American Catholics have traveled to Medjugorje in Bosnia-Herzegovina, where they report that the sun dances in the sky, the metal links of ordinary rosary beads are turned to gold, and Mary mysteriously shows up in photos of a wall where she is said to have appeared to local peasant children beginning on June 25, 1981.

A Bosnian bishops' commission determined that there was nothing supernatural occurring. This finding was initially overruled by the Vatican, which established its own commission to study the situation and eventually reached the same conclusion. However official denials have not discouraged many pilgrims from continuing to visit the site.

These apparitions are not confined to foreign soil, however. There are numerous locations in the United States where people have claimed to see a vision of the Blessed Virgin Mary; among these are Conyers, Georgia; Bayside, New York; and Leesburg, Virginia. *U.S. News & World Report* covered the events at Conyers in an article titled, "Mary Comes to Georgia."[20] The article states that church authorities have not validated the alleged apparitions to Nancy Fowler on her farm; nevertheless those who visit "stuff bills into collection boxes . . .fill[ed] plastic bottles with 'holy water' from a well," pray and hope to see Mary themselves. They come by the thousands and so strong is their belief, they will not be dissuaded by cautions from church officials. While not denying that Marian apparitions occur, church officials are usually hesitant to confirm them. When they are said to occur, generally by the person or persons to whom Mary appears, the location and the persons involved achieve overnight celebrity. The church is extremely cautious and will not endorse such claims without thorough investigation and evidence. These "apparition-seekers" are an embarrassment to many Catholics, whose faith is based on something stronger than a "face" on the lawn, door, floor, cloud, curtain, or wall.

There is an ancient theological maxim that connects prayer and belief— *lex orandi, lex credendi* (roughly meaning, the content of prayer is the content of belief). Catholics have prayed to Mary since the early centuries of the church. That prayer reveals and has helped to shape what Catholics believe. One of the most popular and enduring prayers recited by Catholics is the rosary, sometimes called "Our Lady's Prayer." The rosary has fifty-five beads connected in a circle with five additional beads leading from the circle to a crucifix. Catholics touch each bead as they pray the "decades" (ten beads). The main prayer recited, the "Hail Mary," is a tribute and petition to Mary:

Hail Mary, full of grace,
The Lord is with thee,
Blessed art thou among women
and blessed is the fruit of thy womb, Jesus.
Holy Mary, Mother of God,

Pray for us sinners now,
and at the hour of our death. Amen.

Every Catholic recognizes this prayer and most have it committed to
memory. It was a mainstay of the pre-Vatican II church. Even though
rosaries continue to sell well in religious goods stores, today many younger
Catholics do not own rosary beads, could not name the various mysteries
which accompany the rosary,[21] and may only encounter this prayer at the
wake of a deceased Catholic, when the priest, deacon, or perhaps a layperson leads the mourners in this prayer. Even on these occasions, however,
today it is likely that the prayer leader will conduct a brief prayer service
using scripture as a base rather than recite the rosary.

Another Marian prayer that pre-Vatican II and Vatican II Catholics grew
up with is the Angelus. Church bells tolled three times a day (morning,
noon, and evening) to remind Catholics to recite the Angelus. This prayer
was recited regularly by Catholic schoolchildren at noon.

PRAYER: The angel of the Lord declared unto Mary.

RESPONSE: And she conceived by the Holy Ghost.
Hail Mary . . .

PRAYER: Behold the handmaid of the Lord.

RESPONSE: Be it done to me according to thy word.
Hail Mary . . .

PRAYER: And the Word was made flesh.

RESPONSE: And dwelt among us.
Hail Mary . . .

PRAYER: Pray for us, O Holy Mother of God.

RESPONSE: That we may be made worthy of the promises of christ.
Let us pray.
Pour forth, we beseech thee, O Lord, Thy grace into our hearts,
that we to whom the Incarnation of Christ, Thy Son, was made
known by the message of an angel, may by His passion and cross be
brought to the glory of his resurrection, through the same Christ
Our Lord. Amen.

The days of church bells tolling as a call to prayer are over, and even
Catholic schoolchildren are no longer familiar with the Angelus. The wor-

ship of the pre-Vatican II church encouraged a passive presence at mass. The Eucharistic liturgy did not involve the laity. Marian devotions, however, invited the laity to participate and sometimes to lead (as in the recitation of the rosary). Private devotion to Mary grew. Novenas (devotional prayers recited over a nine-day period) devoted exclusively to Mary developed. These could be conducted by a group or prayed privately by an individual. Novenas of nine first Fridays of the month observed in a row were very popular in the pre-Vatican II church and continue to be a prayer form today for some Catholics. Many Catholic homes and most Catholic schoolrooms boasted a "May altar" honoring Mary during her month.

Vatican II's emphasis on the Eucharist as the central prayer of the church and the active participation by the laity in that celebration decreased the popularity of Marian devotions. In the 1950s every parish held a May procession that included prayers, hymns, and the crowning of a statue of Mary by a school child, who felt privileged to be chosen for the honor to crown Mary. May is known to Catholics as "the month of Mary." Catholic elementary schools and many parishes continue this tradition, but there are equally as many parishes that have discontinued or reduced the emphasis on this particular devotion. In an era when Christ was seen largely, if not exclusively, in terms of his divinity rather than his humanity, Mary offered Catholics a human side.

The documents of Vatican II include references to Mary, but there is no separate document devoted to her, and the Council refrained from adding new titles to Mary.[22] The Council focused on Mary as she is portrayed in the New Testament, more as a woman of faith than as the mother of God (a phrase which is not used in the New Testament but was used in the church from about the fourth century). According to the Council, she is a model disciple of Jesus and one whose faith Catholics should emulate. One post-Vatican II theological emphasis promoted an appreciation for the humanity of Jesus, especially since a tradition of highlighting his divinity, sometimes at the expense of his humanity, had been in place from the time of the Council of Trent in the sixteenth century. Post-Vatican II theology places Mary in relationship to Christ. While she played a key role in salvation history by being the mother of the savior, she should not be treated as an end in herself. Her importance is in relation to Jesus, who saved her as well as others.

Contemporary theological investigation focuses on the faith and strength of Mary's role as testified to in the New Testament.[23] Feminist theologians object to traditional portrayals of Mary as meek and mild, a docile and dependent woman. They protest that the common Catholic characterization of Mary as "virgin and mother" presents an impossible ideal for women who cannot be both. Elizabeth Johnson, a prominent Catholic theologian, wrote: "The simplest feminist analysis makes clear that in the case of actual women in all historical concreteness, the categories of virgin and mother come nowhere near summing up the totality of what is possible for women's self-realization."[24]

Womanist theologians (black Christian women) object to the artistic depictions of Mary as a fifteenth-century European, since she was in fact a first-century Jew. The fact that Mary was young, poor, and uneducated is usually not highlighted by some of the saccharine presentations history has subjected her to, but black theologians like Delores Williams find an identification with her poverty important: "[t]he Christian Womanist theologian can refocus the salvation story so that it emphasizes the beginning of revelation with the spirit mounting Mary, a woman of the poor."[25]

Some interpreted the Council documents as a signal to limit expressions of Marian devotion. Concerned that Marian piety might suffer a serious decline, Pope Paul VI issued *Marialis Cultus* (Devotion to Mary) in 1974 as an attempt to renew devotion to the mother of Jesus. To further encourage a continued esteem for Mary among Catholics, Pope John Paul II issued *Redemptoris Mater* (Mother of the Redeemer) in 1987, in which he declared 1988 a Marian Year. This year of remembrance of Mary was not designed to undermine the Council's guidance in understanding Mary but was

> meant to promote a new and more careful reading of what the Council said about the Blessed Virgin Mary, Mother of God, in the mystery of Christ and of the Church . . . Here we speak not only of the doctrine of faith but also of the life of faith, and thus of authentic "Marian spirituality," seen in the light of Tradition, and especially the spirituality to which the Council exhorts us.[26]

Mary continues to play a significant role in Catholic piety, as testified to by the millions who practice personal devotion to her. The church dedicates several feast days in the liturgical calendar to Mary, the two most prominent of which are August 15, the feast of the Assumption, commemorating Mary being taken up to heaven body and soul; and December 8, the Immaculate Conception and the patronal feast day of American Catholics. That devotion even carries over into the public world of the internet. The website Catholic Online[27] carries a dedication to Our Lady of Guadalupe and there are numerous other websites dedicated to those who are devoted to Mary. Catholics

Grotto of Our Lady on the campus of the University of
Notre Dame is popular with students and visitors.
UNDA

still gravitate to the grotto of Our Lady at the University of Notre Dame (a
replica of Lourdes), visit Medjugorje hoping to see an apparition of her, travel to Lourdes to dip in the healing waters, and keep rosary beads in the dress-
er drawer. Mary remains a key figure in Catholic art, theology, devotion, and
piety. Interpretations of her today are not as uniform as they were in the
1950s, but her importance to Catholic culture cannot be underestimated.

Symbols

"American Christians . . .want to see, hear, and touch God," Colleen
McDannell observed in her book *Material Christianity*.[28] Catholics have been
fond of putting images of God on their bedroom dressers, on their front
lawns, in their churches. The Puritans who founded New England wanted
to purify Christianity of its Roman excesses. Perhaps no single image of

Children investigate stained glass windows that help to create a sacred space within Catholic churches. AP PHOTO/JACKSON *CITIZEN PATRIOT*, CORY MORSE

those "excesses" is more compelling than the imagery with which Catholicism is replete. Roman Catholicism is a visual and tactile religion. It is filled with statues, paintings, crucifixes, and stained glass windows. Or at least it was. Many contemporary Catholic church buildings in America, with their whitewashed walls, clear windows, unadorned wooden altar and lectern, ape the clean-line aesthetics of Protestantism. Only the sign in front of the church alerts visitors that this is a Catholic church.

Nevertheless, the vast majority of Catholic churches in America are more traditional, reflecting Gothic or Baroque influences, filled with prominent symbols that inform the visitor that this is holy and Catholic ground. Every Catholic church, even the most contemporary, displays the Stations of the Cross, a series of biblical and extrabiblical scenes from Christ's life, depicting in particular the story of the passion and death of Jesus. These stations, which number 14, are usually located on the perimeter walls of the church and may be done in bas-relief, wood, plaster, marble, or another suitable material. Pre-Vatican II and Vatican II Catholics grew up reciting the prayers associated with the stations on the Fridays of Lent and in a special ceremony on Good Friday afternoon. At other times, one could see faithful persons privately "making the Stations of the Cross" in the quiet recesses of the church on any given day of the week. Some of the stations depict scenes recorded in the Bible, such as the women who kept watch at the cross during Jesus's crucifixion. Others, such as the one depicting Veronica wiping the face of Jesus as he carried the cross (the cloth with which she wipes his face has the imprint of Jesus' face on it) have no biblical basis and were created in the tradition by the fervor of piety (in Latin, Ver-iconica means "true image"). Today many churches are locked during the weekdays except for daily mass, preventing the faithful from private prayer in the church, a consequence of the increased crime rate combined with the loss of respect for the sacred space of churches.

Many Roman Catholic churches feature painstakingly executed stained glass windows depicting biblical stories or characters, scenes from the life of Christ, sacraments, the evangelists, saints, and Catholic symbols for the Trinity or the Holy Spirit, among others. These are often quite beautiful, creating an aura of sacred space within the confines of the church. One knows immediately upon entering that this is no ordinary meeting place.

Statues of saints are yet another prominent feature of Roman Catholic churches, although the reforms initiated by Vatican II inspired some purists to put the saints in storage. However, many churches have either maintained or resurrected some statuary; some of it is decent art considering the plaster medium; some of it is kitsch of the worst kind. Statues of Christ abound representing, for instance, the good shepherd, the crucified one, the Sacred Heart of Jesus (a statue associated with a certain piety that has enjoyed widespread recognition), and the final judge. Undoubtedly the two most widely depicted saints are Mary and Joseph. Mary, the mother of Jesus, is often depicted with a light complexion and light hair, clothed in a light blue mantle. The idea apparently is to convey a delicate holiness born of an ethereal quality, since Mary represents many things to Catholics including obedience, purity, motherhood, sanctity, and strength.

Some statues of Joseph portray him as an older man with a white flowing beard, though from biblical accounts it is likely that he was a contemporary of Mary. Others depict a younger Joseph, the patron of workers, holding carpentry tools from his trade. Others have him holding the child Jesus or a bouquet of lilies. Catholics consider him the "foster" father of Jesus since Jesus was not conceived from Joseph but is God's son. Curiously, Joseph appears only in the so-called infancy narratives of the gospels of

Matthew and Luke, playing a particularly prominent role in Matthew's rendition of the birth of Jesus. He does not appear in the Gospels of Mark or John. His place in the history of Catholic piety, however, is second only to Mary's.

There are many other popular saints according to the original ethnic make-up of a parish when the church was constructed and decorated. St. Anthony is a favorite of the Italian-American community, St. Patrick with Irish Americans and St. Stanislaus with Polish Americans. Many churches maintain a long-standing tradition of placing rows of small votive candles in front of statues so that the faithful may light a candle and say a prayer asking for favors through the intercession of the saint.

Paintings, either of saints or religious scenes, are also integral to the decor of many Catholic churches. The art was more than decorative, it was instructive. The ancient and medieval churches had frescoes and paintings on the walls both for decoration and to instruct visually a community many of whose members were not literate. Stained glass windows or paintings depicting the seven sacraments, for example, informed and instructed the people about the sacramental nature of Catholicism. Some contemporary churches have returned to this motif, using abstract art to depict Catholic beliefs.

There are also numerous shrines, sacred places of pilgrimage, throughout the United States.[29] These are not places where miracles or apparitions of Mary have occurred, but they are special because they promote particular devotion to Christ or one of the saints. Canon Law defines a shrine as "a Church or other sacred place to which the faithful make pilgrimages for a particular pious reason, with the approval of the local ordinary" (Canon 1230). The best known of these is the Basilica of the National Shrine of the Immaculate Conception in Washington, D.C., which attracts over one million visitors annually. Shrines are not parishes, so they do not offer all of the services available in a parish. However, usually an order of priests, nuns, or brothers in charge of a shrine cares for the various spiritual needs of visitors.

Among the world's major religious traditions, Hinduism rivals (and probably exceeds) Catholicism in its use of symbols to depict the sacred. The gods are formed in clay images by the hundreds of thousands. Shiva is often represented in temples by dozens of lingams and Hindus adorn their homes with personal shrines to gods and gurus where they perform daily worship rites called *puja*. Islam disdains any physical representation of God. The subtle decorations of the mosque comprise only geometrical patterns that can be extended into eternity indicating the eternal nature of God, and

The Basilica of the National Shrine of the Immaculate Conception in Washington, D.C., is a national symbol of the Catholic presence in America. CATHOLIC NEWS SERVICE

quotations from the Qur'an reminding Muslims of God's revelation. Buddhists revere statues of the Buddha and build stupas to hold sacred objects. Jewish artists and scribes painstakingly transcribe and decorate Torah that are kept in the temple or synagogue.

The theoretical division between the sacred and the profane, so carefully articulated by social scientists like Emile Durkheim and historians of religion like Mircea Eliade,[30] is sometimes in evidence in Catholicism (as for example, in the reservation of the Eucharist) and sometimes absent (as for example, the demystification of the priest as a sacred person after recent revelations about the sexual behavior of some clergy). Although abuses are evident in the history of Catholicism, in general Catholics do not fear the sin of idolatry the way that some other religions or Christian denominations do.

While Protestants elevate the word over the sacrament, Catholics interpret the world in terms of a sacramental encounter with God. One expression of this is the use of "sacramentals" in Catholic practice. Holy water, ashes, crucifixes, blessings, palms, medals, and candles are all used as sacramentals dedicated to reminding the faithful of God's presence in the world. They are not nearly as important or necessary as the Eucharist or the Bible, but they serve as material signs of a spiritual God who cannot be contained, touched or limited by the material world. For some American Catholics, certain of these sacramentals represent their closest ties to the church. They do not participate in Sunday mass weekly, but they would not miss going to church on Ash Wednesday or Palm Sunday when two of these well-known sacramentals are distributed. There is a danger that these sacramentals may be seen as having magic power to remove sins, to convey grace, or to ensure salvation. In order to dispel the notion that these signs are magic, one priest, Father Thomas Shea of the diocese of Providence, Rhode Island, now deceased, described the water used in the Holy Water font as ordinary water "like the kind you find in a river, a lake, your kitchen faucet, or your bathroom toilet." The images may have removed some of the mystery, but he went on to make the point that the water in the font reminds us of our baptismal commitment which begins the process of continual conversion to a Christian life; it is not magic, and it is not effective without human cooperation with God's grace.

The importance of sacramentals, and the use of religious symbols in general, has declined in the post-Vatican II era. This development is not exclusively a result of Vatican II theology, although this no doubt is a contributing factor. It is also a consequence of contemporary American popular culture, which has desacralized almost all dimensions of society. As one frustrated reader of a local newspaper exclaimed after reading about the desecration of graves in a local cemetery, "Is nothing sacred any more?" It may be that sacrality has been removed from the traditionally religious realm and transferred to the secular. For example, the Vietnam Memorial in Washington, D.C., for many is a "sacred" space where people remember relatives and friends who gave their lives for their country. Now instant "shrines" appear at the sight of a tragedy such as a car accident, a shooting, or a murder. Friends and strangers leave flowers, notes, teddy bears, and other objects along the roadside where a tragedy occurred. Some leave identifiably religious symbols such as a cross, but many of these contemporary "sacramentals" are not the symbols of the Catholic tradition. Churches, in the past constructed to inspire awe, now resemble auditoriums. Malls, monuments, and museums are the new forms of "awesome" architecture. For many young persons, professional athletes have replaced priests as the holy untouchables of our culture. The church often fares poorly in the competition for their attention. MTV, sports, and entertainment opportunities capture their allegiance more readily than repetitive liturgies and (in their minds) uninspiring homilies.

CHAPTER SIX

Teachings and Beliefs: Part II

Sacraments

Besides being a visual religion, Roman Catholicism is sacramental; it celebrates God's presence in the world in concrete manifestations such as saints and symbols; the seven sacraments bring this notion to life in the lives of believers. The old *Baltimore Catechism*, the question-and-answer religious education text popular before Vatican II, defined a sacrament as "an outward sign instituted by Christ to bring grace." The three described briefly in the account of the Easter Vigil in chapter 1, Baptism, Eucharist, and Confirmation, are called sacraments of initiation because these are the gateway to the Catholic-Christian community. In the ancient church they were conferred at the same time, as they still are today for adults at the Easter Vigil. But in the ordinary course of events, they are conferred at various chronological intervals of a Catholic's life, as are the remaining sacraments of Reconciliation, Matrimony, Healing of the Sick, and for those men who pursue it, Holy Orders.

Initiation: Baptism, Eucharist, Confirmation

BAPTISM Baptism is the first of the three sacraments of initiation. A Muslim becomes a Muslim by reciting sincerely the creed "There is no God but God, and Muhammad is his messenger." Catholics, like other Christians, become Christian by being baptized in water and the Spirit. The church traces this rite back to New Testament times as witnessed by John the Bap-

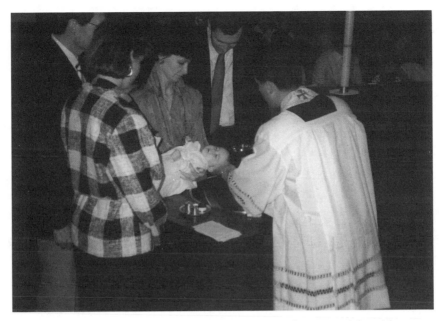

Parents and godparents gather around the font as the priest baptizes an infant girl.

tist's baptism of repentance (Mark 1:4; Luke 3:3; Matt 3:11). John himself acknowledged that his baptism would be surpassed by a baptism with the Holy Spirit.

Infant baptism is the norm in Catholicism. In pre-Vatican II Catholicism there was a fear that a baby who died before being baptized would not go to heaven but to limbo. Thus, parents routinely presented their child for baptism within the first few weeks of life. Limbo was a place neither of permanent punishment like hell, nor of temporary hardship like purgatory, but a place in between purgatory and heaven in which unbaptized babies would neither suffer punishment nor enjoy eternal bliss, but their souls would simply exist in a neutral territory for eternity. There is no scriptural basis for limbo. It was the invention of medieval theologians who were trying to balance the necessity for baptism for salvation (to eliminate the effects of original sin) and the innocence of newborns. Though not officially abrogated, the notion of limbo has all but disappeared in contemporary Catholicism.

Today parents wait several months, sometimes as long as a year, before bringing their child for baptism. Pre-Vatican II baptisms took place in a separate ceremony on Sunday afternoons in the church. While this practice continues, many parishes schedule baptisms during one of the Sunday masses so that the community can participate in this sacrament. Baptism is the

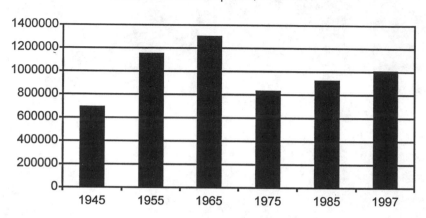

Number of Infant Baptisms, 1945–1997

initiation into the Catholic community, and most parents have their children baptized even if they do not practice their religion with any regularity. For nonpracticing Catholics it is a social and cultural event as much as (or more than) it is a religious commitment. Family history and cultural patterns make it an important symbol, even if for some, a theologically ambiguous one.

Baptism entails rights and responsibilities on the part of those baptized and permits them to share in the ministry of Jesus Christ. It is foundational for all further activity in the church and marks Catholics as followers of Jesus holding them accountable for life in accord with the Good News he preached.

EUCHARIST While baptism initiates one into the church, it is the Eucharist that sustains the church community on a regular basis. The Second Vatican Council confirmed this when it said that the Eucharist "is the fount and apex of the whole Christian life."[1] Those unfamiliar with Christianity are often puzzled by the Eucharist; non-Catholic Christians have their own form of Eucharist but are troubled by Catholic claims that the bread and wine actually become the body and blood of Christ and are no longer bread and wine. The Catholic doctrine, called "transubstantiation," using philosophical language that can be traced back to Aristotle and that was refined by St. Thomas Aquinas in the thirteenth century, holds that at the Eucharist the "substance" of the bread and wine is transformed into the body and blood of Christ while the "accidents" (appearances) remain the same. The Catholic Church teaches that this transformation occurs when the priest who presides at the Eucharist says the words: "This is my body" and "This is my blood" over the bread and wine. The community who then receives the bread and wine is receiving the body and blood of Christ. Catholic theology then also refers to the community of believers as the Body of Christ. How the bread and wine becomes the body and blood of Christ cannot be explained scientifically and is regarded as one of the central mysteries of the faith, along with the Trinity. The biblical evidence for this mystery is the record of Jesus's celebration of Passover with his apostles on the night before he died at which he passed the cup and bread and instructed his followers "take and eat, this is my body given up for you."

The Eucharistic liturgy, which is celebrated daily by the church and attended by active Catholics in large numbers on Saturday evening and Sunday, is divided into two parts—the liturgy of the Word and the liturgy of the Eucharist. The liturgy of the Word, as the term suggests, focuses on the biblical message with readings from both the Old and New Testament. It also includes a call to prayer, a penitential rite asking God to forgive the sins of the community, and a homily delivered by the priest or deacon that reflects on the meaning of the biblical readings for the contemporary Catholic community. While the homily is an integral element of the liturgy, it is not the focal point as it is in Protestant communities that do not share the Lord's Supper at every Sunday service and may do so only monthly or quarterly.

According to the sociologist and priest Andrew Greeley, Catholics have long complained about the quality of preaching in the Catholic church.[2] Unquestionably there are brilliant homilists among the American Catholic clergy, but there is also a great deal of mediocre preaching as well. Some priests work diligently on their homilies; others rely on homily services to provide the material they use in the pulpit on Sunday. Protestant churches signal the importance of preaching in their theology, worship, and nomenclature. Catholics do not point to their parish priest and exclaim: "There is the preacher." However, many Protestant congregations refer to their minister explicitly as "preacher," underscoring the importance of this role for their clergy. The central element of Protestant worship is proclamation and preaching.

The focal point of the liturgy for Catholics is the celebration of the Eucharist. At each mass, Christ is made present in a special way. The liturgy of the Eucharist begins with an offertory during which the gifts of bread and wine, which will later be offered to the community as the body and blood of Christ, are offered to God. A financial offering is also collected from the congregation at this time in order to sustain the needs of the church. In recent years, some parishes have also taken to tithing 10 percent of the offertory income for the poor and needy of the local community, regardless of the religious identity of those who benefit from this gift. The community prays and sings together, greets one another with a sign of peace (usually a kiss or handshake), and receives the Eucharist in holy communion in the form of bread and wine. This celebration binds the community to Christ and one another.

The essentials of the mass just described are in each celebration of the Eucharist, but there are variables that make each celebration different. The composition of the congregation, the liturgical style of the principal celebrant, the quality and form of the music, the level of participation by the people, all make for potentially different Eucharistic experiences. For example, St. Augustine's church in Washington, D.C., is a predominately African-American congregation. The call-and-response style of preaching, the singing of African-American spirituals, and the length of the service (one and a half hours) each reflect the style of black worship.[3]

A mass celebrated at the end of a *cursillo* (Spanish term for short course, as in an introduction to Christ and Christianity) retreat may include personal testimonies of faith, emotional outpourings, spirited singing coupled with affectionate embraces and could last two hours or more. The *cursillo* movement began in Spain in the 1940s and when it spread to the United States in the early 1960s the original retreats were conducted in Spanish. Since then the movement's retreats are conducted in English as well. The teams conducting the retreats are mostly lay people and focus, in part, on self-knowledge, prayer, and evangelization. People who have experienced the retreat, called "Cursillistas," pray and offer sacrifices for those on the retreat and often come to the closing mass for new retreatants, making it a joyous welcoming for those just completing the experience and a reunion for veterans of the experience.

A mass for children receiving their first communion will be directed to the emotional and intellectual capacities of second graders. The homily will be simple, the songs appropriate to the occasion, and the church filled with proud parents, grandparents, siblings, family, and friends. A mass conducted on a youth retreat may include a dramatic presentation of the gospel narrative by teenagers, contemporary secular music with a message mixed with liturgical songs, testimonies of faith and a demonstrative exchange of peace. Mass celebrated in a nursing home has a different ambiance from one celebrated in the chapel of a Catholic high school. All of these celebrations bring Catholics into contact with God and each other, but each has its own character and style.

CONFIRMATION The sacrament of Confirmation does what its name implies—it confirms the person's choice of and commitment to be Catholic. It completes the sacraments of initiation. In the ancient church this sacrament was conferred at the time of baptism (as it remains the custom in Eastern-rite churches today and at the Easter Vigil in the Latin rite for those children and adults who are being received into the church). Normally, however, the church confers this sacrament on young adults from the ages of about thirteen to seventeen. The Jewish faith has a comparable ceremony of bar mitzvah (for boys) and bat mitzvah (for girls). Some flexibility is exercised in different dioceses and parishes as to the age at which Confirmation is conferred. The reception of this sacrament is usually preceded by an intense period of preparation for one to two years. This commonly includes education in the Catholic tradition, a theological understanding of the commitment, a community service project, a retreat, and a discernment of whether or not one wishes publicly and sacramentally to confirm one's commitment to Catholic Christianity. In the past it was an expectation and obligation. Today, many religious educators and pastoral staffs view it as a choice—not their choice, or the parents' choice, but the candidate's choice. Freely making such a commitment requires a certain degree of maturity. At baptism a child's parents speak for him or her making an initial commitment to Christianity. At the time of Confirmation, the young person elects to continue that commitment in the Catholic tradition.

The sacrament commemorates the Pentecost event in the New Testament marked as the birth of the church when the Holy Spirit descended upon the disciples. The church calls that same Holy Spirit to fill the hearts and souls of those being confirmed that they might enter adulthood with a readiness and willingness to live as Christ's disciples in the world.

Sacraments of Vocation: Marriage and Holy Orders

MARRIAGE The sacrament of Marriage is one that Catholic couples look forward to with great hope and anticipation. Marriage is also a time when they want all of the pageantry and ceremony that a sacramental celebration affords. Curiously, even those who have not been to church for years come to reserve the church for their wedding. This may simply be attributable to aesthetics—the church setting is more solemn and magisterial than the court chambers of the judge. Or it may have more to do with the wishes of the parents than those of the couple. To keep the peace or please parents and relatives, they come before the altar rather than the judge's bench. Or it may be something deeper, something sacred, something holy that inspires them to seek the sacrament of Matrimony. They want their vows to one another to be sacred, to be blessed by God, to be witnessed publicly by the Christian community.

As with the other sacraments, the parish is the connection with the larger church. And it is in and through the parish that couples are prepared for the sacrament of Marriage. Marriage is the only sacrament that is not conferred by a priest or deacon; a priest or deacon witnesses the marriage but the bride and groom actually complete the sacrament together. Many contemporary Catholic couples are more influenced by American culture than church doctrine when it comes time for marriage. The age of first marriages had been steadily rising in the 1990s. Young people are not likely to make a commitment to marriage until they have finished their education and settled into a career pattern. In many areas of the country the high cost of housing has forced college graduates to return to their parents' homes after college in order to save money. Rather than each renting an apartment, many young couples move in together for companionship and to save money. The social stigma of living together without the benefit of marriage, so acute in the 1950s, has eased considerably in America. The increasing anonymity, mobility, and transience of the cities and the suburbs means that in many neighborhoods people do not know who lives next door or down the block. What is more, they do not care and would not interfere.

Officially the church disapproves of such practices and considers those in such arrangements guilty of the sin of fornication. In practice, however, many priests do not inquire or wish to know. When these couples approach the door of the rectory to make an appointment to prepare for the sacrament of Marriage they are welcomed. The couple may not be coming to church or living in a wholesome union in the eyes of the church, but turning them away from the altar at the time of marriage may alienate them for the rest of their married lives, and many priests are reluctant to risk permanent dissociation. Some priests, having judged that this has already occurred, do end up turning away the couple.

The sad underside of marriage is divorce. Catholics divorce at the same rate as other Americans. However, the church does not recognize divorce. Referring to the marriage bond, Jesus said: "what God has joined together let no one separate" (Matt 19:6 and Mark 10:9). For Catholics, marriage is not only a contract, it is a sacrament. And sacraments cannot be canceled.

Marriages, however, can be annulled by the church. An annulment signifies that a sacrament was never conferred. The civil dimension of marriage can be nullified by a civil divorce decree issued in the courts. The civil status of the marriage is not affected by the annulment process, and the children from an annulled marriage are legitimate. There are myriad grounds for the church to grant an annulment, from failure to consummate the marriage to the immaturity of one or both of the parties at the time of marriage. The most common reason that the church annuls marriages is psychological incapacity. This is not related to age but the maturity, understanding, and ability of a party to enter into a permanent bond. If at the time of marriage a person was not mature enough to understand and accept the sacramental bond of marriage, after proper investigation and procedures that marriage can be annulled by the church. Thousands of marriages are annulled each year in church tribunals.

Many Catholics and non-Catholics either do not understand or do not accept this legal procedure by the church. Some refer to annulments, as "divorce—Catholic style" or "divorce lite." The situation is further complicated for Catholics who are originally validly married in the Catholic Church but divorced and remarried civilly and who wish to receive the sacraments. If the person has not received an annulment in the church courts, he or she is not permitted to receive the sacraments, since the church considers the second marriage invalid. Some divorced Catholics continue to receive the sacraments even without a formal annulment. Pastoral practice permits an "internal forum" solution as an exception if an annulment is not possible. Relying on conscience and God's forgiveness, a pastoral adviser (usually a priest) reconciles a couple to the church and sacraments, but this practice is frowned upon in hierarchial circles.

Annulments are the source of much pain and some controversy in the contemporary church. In a highly publicized case, when Joseph Kennedy, the son of Robert Kennedy and a congressman from Massachusetts, sought an annulment of his marriage to Sheila Rauch Kennedy, she refused to cooperate with the church or accept the annulment of her marriage. When she did not receive satisfaction from the church she published a book titled *Shattered Faith*[4] criticizing the church's procedures and insisting that her marriage was a valid sacrament freely entered into by mature and knowledgeable adults for which the church had no grounds for annulment.

Lay people encounter canon law most often in marriage cases, in which a person is seeking to marry someone who is not Catholic or not Christian, or is seeking to annul a marriage. Both of these involve matters promulgated in canon law. While the first may be taken care of with the appropriate permissions and documents, annulments often require written and oral testimony to a marriage tribunal within a diocese. The tribunal is composed of judges who are qualified by their formal study of canon law. The tribunal members may be religious women or other lay persons, though the overwhelming majority are priests. Pontifical Catholic universities (those sanctioned by the Vatican to grant degrees) in various parts of the world offer degrees in canon law. The Catholic University of America in Washington, D. C., is the principal institution granting these degrees in America. However, many priests are trained in canon law at European universities such the Gregorian University in Rome and the Catholic University of Louvain in Belgium.

Each diocese has a tribunal or church court. While these tribunals are designed to handle all internal legal matters, the bulk of their work is marriage cases. Unlike civil law, canon law does not recognize divorce. This is because marriage is not a contract, but a sacrament; and if a sacrament is validly entered into, it is permanent. The annulment process, often a mystery even to Catholics, is the church's method for investigating whether or not a sacrament was validly entered into by a couple intending marriage. Since Vatican II, the American church has granted more annulments than any national church.[5] All types of misconceptions surround the annulment process from the idea that only rich or famous people obtain them to the perception that the church is getting rich in the annulment "business." The fact is that anyone who was married in the church may apply for an annulment and the vast majority of annulments are granted to ordinary Catholics who pay a nominal fee to defray some of the costs to process an annulment.

The annulment process is a serious and complex one. Some dioceses have active and efficient tribunals that deal with hundreds of marriage cases annually. How difficult (or in some cases how painful) the process is depends in large part on the personnel on the tribunal and the disposition of the local bishop toward the annulment procedure. As with parish experiences, where you live and who is in charge makes a difference. For some Catholics being granted an annulment gives them a new lease on life (or at least on their institutional religious life); for others it smothers any spark of loyalty, leaving people bitter and disenfranchised.

HOLY ORDERS The one sacrament that is not widely received by Catholics is Holy Orders. In fact, only a small number of American Catholics have even been present for the ordination of a priest. In one sense, this is unfortunate, for this ceremony is rich with word and symbolism that moves the heart and captures the imagination. In another sense, the ceremony symbolizes much that contemporary Catholics, in particular but not exclusively women, object to about the church's structure. Since only males can be ordained, it symbolizes patriarchy; since the ordained men assume roles that tend to elevate them above the laity, it symbolizes hierarchy. Yet priests are taught to approach their position in the church as one of service to the community, not power over it. And there are countless priests in America who live out their daily ministry in just such a fashion. They take seriously the gospel mandate to be a servant to the people of God. They do this at great personal sacrifice and without complaint. Their service is a joy, and they do not count the cost. In return they receive the cooperation, respect, and admiration of the Catholic community whom they serve.

Priests are called to be many things to many people. They baptize the newborn, bury the dead, counsel the confused, comfort the sick, guide the spiritual lives of numerous Catholics, preach the Word, serve as advocates for the voiceless, instruct the ignorant and the well-informed; they live alongside their parishioners, sharing their successes, failures, and struggles. It is a demanding vocation, to say the least. The vast majority of priests in America live their vocation admirably. They are happy with their work, fulfilled emotionally and professionally. At the same time, studies show that they are increasingly overworked, sometimes underappreciated, and subject to the same self-doubts that are manifest in marriages and in other career paths.

Ordination to the priesthood is not the only form of the sacrament. Deacons also are ordained. Some, as transitional, take this step on their way to the priesthood; others—permanent deacons—dedicate themselves to a specific life-long ministry in the church. A number of factors distinguish these two groupings. Transitional deacons who are in training for the priesthood function as deacons for one or two years immediately prior to being ordained priests. Their deaconal ministry may be served partially in the seminary while they are finishing their academic and ministerial training, and partially in a parish setting where they experience the daily routine and challenges of pastoral life. Permanent deacons, married and single men (even though historically there were women deacons in the church, that practice ceased in the early church and has not been revived) prepare within diocesan training programs part-time for a number of years, after which they are ordained by the bishop and assigned work either in

Candidates lie prostrate as part of the ordination to priesthood ceremony.

parishes or in special apostolates. The success of this program may result in the church having more deacons than priests in the future. While theirs is a valuable ministry, it is not a solution to the priest shortage, however, because deacons' responsibilities are limited. They may not preside at Eucharist or hear confessions, although they may baptize, witness marriages, and preach.

Sacraments of Healing: Reconciliation and Anointing of the Sick

RECONCILIATION The sacrament of Reconciliation (formerly Penance), commonly called Confession, is one of the distinctive features of Catholic Christianity. Protestant Christianity's skepticism about clerical elitism and emphasis on the individual's relationship with God, generally safeguard against the ordained minister injecting his or her power into the individual Christian's relationship with God. In Catholicism, the priest acts as an intermediary between God and the community of believers. Catholic theology holds that priests, by virtue of their reception of the sacrament of Holy Orders, are set apart (not above) for sacred duties. One of those duties is to forgive sins. The authority to do so stems from the New Testament command issued by Jesus to his apostles: "Those whose sins you shall forgive, they are forgiven. Those whose sins you shall retain, they are retained" (John 20:23).

The intention of this sacrament is to forgive sins and to reconcile the sinner with God and the church community. Priests are instructed to act in an understanding and pastoral manner to reconcile the sinner. Penitents (those confessing their sins) are required to be contrite for their sins and to resolve, with the help of God's grace, to try not to sin again. Inevitably, the penitent will sin again, but God's mercy is everlasting and there is no limit to the number of times one may be forgiven in the sacrament of reconciliation.

The ritual and the frequency of this sacrament have changed depending upon the historical period. In the ancient church, penance, like baptism, was received only once. There were sometimes harsh penalties associated with it as well. For these reasons most people delayed receiving it until they were dying. In the recent past, before Vatican II, many Catholics would go to confession weekly, usually on Saturday afternoons in a dimly lighted church. Penitents would wait, kneeling in pews alongside a confessional box where a priest would sit for hours hearing confessions, forgiving sins, and meting out penances usually requiring the penitent to say a certain number of Hail Marys and Our Fathers. There would be several confessionals in the church, each with a name over the door identifying the priest inside the confessional. Upon entering the box, the penitent would begin by saying: "Bless me Father, for I have sinned. It has been one week or one month (or whatever length of time) since my last confession. These are my sins." After listening to the penitent's recital, the priest would briefly counsel the penitent to avoid such sins in the future and ask that the penitent recite the Act of Contrition. It is a prayer that every pre-Vatican II Catholic knows by heart:

> O my God, I am heartily sorry for having offended Thee, and I detest all my sins, because I dread the loss of heaven and the pains of hell, but most of all because they offend Thee, my God, who art all good and deserving of all my love. I firmly resolve, with the help of Thy grace, to confess my sins, to do penance, and to amend my life. Amen.

Since the close of Vatican II the manner of celebrating the Sacrament of Reconciliation has changed considerably, and the number of confessions has declined dramatically. In the 1950s and '60s, in any given parish three or four priests would hear confessions for several hours on Saturday afternoon

---

and evening. Today, most parishes do not have the luxury of multiple priests and the small segment of the Catholic population (20 percent according to recent data)[6] who go to confession regularly has eliminated the need for the parish priest to spend long hours in the confessional. In a previous era confessions would be heard every Saturday from perhaps 2 to 4 and 7 to 9 P.M. Today parishes may regularly schedule the sacrament from 4:15 to 4:45 before the Saturday evening mass, and one priest can easily accommodate the small number of penitents, although Catholics are invited to contact a priest at other times if they wish to confess their sins and receive absolution. The post-Vatican II church introduced Penance Services to which the entire parish is invited and during which private confession is celebrated in the context of a celebration including scripture readings, songs, and prayers. The best attended of these communal services are celebrated during the seasons of Advent before Christmas and Lent before Easter. The way in which Catholics go to confession has also changed. Penance "rooms" have been constructed in many parish churches, giving people the option to go to confession in the traditional anonymous fashion or while sitting face-to-face with the priest-confessor. In the face-to-face option, the penitent and priest discuss the quest for the spiritual life and the inevitable failures and successes that accompany such a quest. It is an occasion for nurturing, forgiving, and challenging the repentant Catholic to continue to strive to live the gospel in season and out of season. These "confessions" are less structured and often more encouraging for persons who are willing to discuss their spiritual life openly.

The age of initial participation in the sacrament has varied somewhat, depending upon the rules of the local diocese and the religious education program of the parish. The bishops established national guidelines that children should receive the Sacrament of Reconciliation prior to receiving First Communion. The general guideline is that children must have attained the age of reason (usually around seven years old) so that they can distinguish, in moral categories, the difference between right and wrong and assume conscious personal responsibility for moral acts. Catholics are expected to receive the sacrament at least once a year if they have committed a mortal sin (of such a serious nature that it completely ruptures one's relationship with God).

The decline in the number and frequency of Catholics receiving the Sacrament of Reconciliation is of concern to the church. Have Catholics lost their sense of sin or have they been liberated from an unhealthy guilt that burdened pre-Vatican II Catholics? One priest quipped: "What is the gift that keeps on giving? Guilt. Make a person feel guilty when he's young and he will feel guilty for the rest of his life." Perhaps the noted psychiatrist Karl Menninger was on to something when he titled one of his books, *Whatever Became of Guilt?*[7] However, memories of pre-Vatican II confession conjure up images of sweaty palms and stomach cramps for many Catholics who waited with trepidation in the confessional line. For some, an insensitive confessor made it worse by asking embarrassing questions (often about sexual thoughts or actions), speaking in a stern voice, and reminding the penitent how disappointed God was. One could hardly categorize it as a "celebration" of God's healing forgiveness. It was more a sign of the church's tight grip on the intimate lives of Catholics and of the fear that characterized many people's notion of God.

In the pre-Vatican II era the sacraments of Eucharist and Penance shared a closer interdependent relationship than they do today. Catholics were scrupulous about receiving absolution for their sins before approaching the communion rail, so weekly confession was not uncommon. Today the theological understanding of sin is less juridical, so that the faithful focus upon their fundamental life's direction toward God rather than evaluating every act independently, which often resulted in a "laundry list" of sins. Contemporary churchgoers also receive communion much more frequently than in the pre-Vatican II era. At that time many refrained from receiving communion either because they had broken the prescribed fast (originally from midnight, later three hours—or even one hour—before the reception of Communion) or because they felt guilty of minor unconfessed sins. Of course, all knew that serious (mortal) sin absolutely precluded the reception of the Eucharist. Today the person who remains in the pew during communion is the exception.

ANOINTING OF THE SICK Even at the turn of the twenty-first century, so long after the reforms of Vatican II, some Catholics continue to refer to the sacrament of the sick by its old Latin name, "Extreme Unction," or as the "Last Rites," neither of which term conveys the essence of the sacrament. "I'll (or Let's) call the priest" sounded an ominous death-knell, bringing terror to all hearts. However, the Anointing of the Sick is a sacrament intended to bring spiritual comfort to the sick, not an early death notice. The roots for this sacrament go back to the New Testament Book of James (5:14–15), which reads: "Is there anyone sick among you? He should ask for the presbyters of the church. They in turn are to pray over him, anointing him with oil in the name of the Lord, and the prayer of faith will save the sick person, and the Lord will raise him up. If he has committed any sins, he will be forgiven." During different times in the church's history (including the first half of the twentieth century), the sacrament was administered only when death was imminent. Although it continues to be administered to the dying, sometimes accompanied by the final reception of Holy Communion called Viaticum (meaning "food for the journey"), it is intended not only for those who are mortally ill, but also for all who are sick and who may need an additional sign and source of God's grace to cope with their illness, to be healed, to endure the suffering associated with illness.

The Sacrament of the Sick may be administered to a chronically ill patient, a person about to undergo a serious operation, or someone who is suffering emotionally or mentally. While still administered most regularly in hospitals, parishes conduct liturgical services during which the sick and infirm are anointed in the presence of healthy parishioners. Priests also administer this sacrament in private homes, for those who are unable to attend a communal service; and in nursing homes, either in the context of a service or privately in patients' rooms. If possible, family members are invited to participate in the sacramental ritual, offering prayers and comforting the sick person with their supporting presence.

The sacrament is a sign of God's grace and healing power, but it is not magic or medicine. The oil used in the anointing reminds the recipient of his or her baptism as the priest recites the prayer: "Through this holy anointing, may the Lord in his love and mercy help you with the grace of the Holy Spirit. May the Lord who frees you from sin, save you and raise you up." The church's prayer is for strength, whether to endure an illness, or in severe cases to accept death gracefully. It also reminds the sick person that he or she does not endure these trials alone but is accompanied by the church who prays with and stands by those who are weakened by illness and cannot participate fully in the life of the community.

Prayer and Spirituality

Historically members of the church have separated the spirituality of those in vowed or ordained life from the spirituality of the laity, elevating the former over the latter as testified to in the 1950s by Cardinal Cushing of Boston who wrote: "Religious life has always been regarded as higher in itself than the lay life, and rightly so. . . . The Laity are called to perfection, too, but they are necessarily busy about temporal affairs and subject to numerous distractions."[8] Pre-Vatican II Catholics will recognize the spirituality of a previous era in the following quotation from Monsignor John Boland of Buffalo. Msgr. Boland, a well-known labor activist, served in several civic positions including chair of the Labor Relations Board of New York. His suggested addendum to air raid instructions during World War II betray a mechanistic approach to prayer that borders on ascribing magical powers to it. But his spirituality reflects the common experience of prayer in the early part of this century.[9] In an editorial piece he offered his recommendations for additional spiritual protection in the event of an air raid.

Air raid instructions have been given wide distribution, orally and in print. Everything needful to keep us alive to future danger has been done, everything except in matters that concern our souls and God. To that extent the job is incomplete.

Here are some additional instructions, which you may memorize or clip. (1) Remember during air raids, that the privilege of praying is yours. Aids to prayer should be within easy reach or view, a crucifix, the image of the Sacred Heart, your rosary or rosary ring, spiritual books and leaflets. Holy water which is blessed solely to invoke God's protection against dangers to soul and body, should be available. The thought of God commissioning His angels to watch over you, should give you calm courage. (2) Go to confession often, aware of the fact that when the enemy is overhead, it may be too late. Remain in God's grace by keeping free from mortal sin. The bombs that land will not pass you by just because you are not prepared to meet your maker. If you cannot go to confession, say an act of contrition, for instance, "O my God, I am sorry for my sins because they offend Thee again." (3) Hear Mass on weekdays, too, and receive Holy Communion. (4) Bear in mind your Christian duties toward your neighbors, especially when they have been stricken in body or property. Be models of fearlessness and helpfulness. Your non-Catholic brethren will expect it. (5) Obey the authorities without question, condemning, as they must, violations of the regulations and dim-out deviltry. Your air warden speaks in their name.[10]

This historical example may appear perfectly sensible to some, while others will regard it as a relic that illuminates our understanding of the past, but has little power to inspire. Whatever the reaction, it highlights Catholic attention to the biblical dictum "pray always." Prayer is central to the Christian life, and Catholics pray in a variety of ways.

The form and style of Catholic prayer reflects the diversity of the community. Monks gather at various times to recite the Divine Office. This is the official daily prayer of the church. It is structured to flow throughout the day and into the night. For example, at the Abbey of Genesee in upstate New York, a group of Cistercians of the Strict Observance, commonly known as Trappist monks, follow a full schedule of the liturgical prayer of the church. There are specified prayers, called (from the Latin) Lauds (at daybreak), Terce (mid-morning), Sext (midday), None (mid-afternoon), Vespers (evening), Compline (night), Vigils (middle of the night). Lay people may participate in this series of prayers either as individuals or more likely in small groups; priests pledge to pray parts of this series at certain times during the day; many monasteries structure their days and nights around this universal prayer of the church. This prayer helps to remind the one who prays of God's constant presence. It sets a rhythm to the day, even while the religious person may be engaged in a variety of tasks that seem far from spiritual.

Monks devote their entire lives to the pursuit of holiness through prayer and work. Frank Bianco, a journalist, offers an inside view of Trappist monastic life in his book *Voices of Silence*.[11] The Trappists operate twelve monasteries in the United States, with each monastery home to a small community of monks who intersperse daily work on a farm, a printing press, or a workshop with times of solitude, prayer, and community living. Other monks live similar lives except that they usually staff a school.

The central unifying prayer of the church is the Eucharist. Celebrations of the mass range from the solemnity of the pope gathered with the bishops in St. Peter's in Rome to the informal setting of a group gathered around a coffee table in a living room. This reenactment of the Last Supper is both a prayer and a gift—in which participants pray to God and receive God's gift of his only Son in the form of bread and wine.

The church reserves special spaces dedicated to the pursuit of prayer.[12] As much as prayer requires withdrawing from the world in order to commune with God, it also connects one to the world, as Henri Nouwen, a Dutch priest and spiritual writer who spent much of his adult life in North America until his death in 1997, noted in his book *Gracias!*: "True prayer always includes becoming poor. . . .To lift up your hands to the Lord and show him the hungry children who play on the dusty streets, the tired women who carry their babies on their backs to the marketplace, the men who try to forget their misery by drinking too much on the weekends, the jobless teenagers and the homeless squatters, together with their laughter, friendly gestures, and gentle words—wouldn't that be true service?"[13]

Catholic laity remain connected to the church because it offers opportunities for spiritual growth. In addition to the celebration of the sacraments that are the most common ways in which people participate in the spiritual life of the church, numerous other forms of prayer and spiritual exercises promote spiritual growth. Devotional prayers and services, like the recitation of the rosary and community gatherings with prayers, songs and silence during Advent and Lent, help to build the community and connect people with God. Many parishes have small faith communities that number a dozen or so people who meet regularly to read and reflect on scripture, pray in formal and informal formats, discuss the intersection of their spiritual and secular lives, support one another in the quest for holiness, and share the depth of life together. This form of spiritual community works well to connect people in meaningful ways apart form the usual Sunday worship. These small communities then enrich the larger body of the parish. Retreats continue as a source of spiritual nourishment for millions of American Catholics. The structure of these gatherings varies from completely silent encounters with God for a period of five or seven days, interrupted only by daily meetings with a spiritual director, to youth retreats that include community-building exercises, self exploration, and sharing of one's spiritual and personal life.

One example of Catholic spirituality is the National Marriage Encounter. Marriage Encounter, an organization founded in Spain in 1953 by Father Gabriel Calvo, devised a weekend experience for married couples. The movement spread to the United States via the Christian Family Movement. Today there are two separate divisions: National Marriage Encounter (with ties to the original Spanish movement) and Worldwide Marriage Encounter (an independent American group). The encounter weekend brings couples into dialogue with one another in the presence of God on various aspects of their lives and marriage. Conveners stress that the weekend is intended to strengthen and spiritually enrich a stable marriage, and not offer therapy for a troubled one. The encounter is directed by a team of couples and a priest. The movement has a logo with two wedding rings intertwined with the Greek letters *Chi-Rho* (abbreviation of the name Christ) that couples sometimes attach in sticker form to the rear window of their car as a sign to those who know it that they have experienced the week-end, and as an invitation for others to inquire about it. The movement has been expanded and imitated to include Engaged Encounter (for couples planning to be married), and Beginning Encounter (for those recently divorced or widowed).

Service-oriented efforts represent another form of spirituality. Parishioners or diocesan agencies establish and staff soup kitchens or shelters for the homeless. These endeavors, while they may not appear to be "spiritual" in some people's minds, fulfill the commission that Jesus issued in his Sermon on the Mount in the Gospel of Matthew (chapters 5–7), to seek justice and show mercy. Spirituality encompasses more than one's personal relationship with God; it requires Catholics, indeed all Christians, to care for one another and to form a community of belief and action.

Moral Teachings

The church often assumes the role of moral guardian in American society. Making rules and pronouncements designed to bind Catholics, the church also attempts to influence the larger culture by providing moral norms and guidelines. In practice, Catholics ignore some of the norms the church proposes, and others resent the church for "meddling" in political policy and personal life by attempting to set the moral compass for American society. But moral concerns represent a central element of the church's mission and teaching. Expecting the church to remain silent on ethics is like asking Congress to stop issuing laws. Neither the church nor the government can afford to stand on the sidelines.

Of the many moral matters that could possibly be addressed in this book, a few are presented here. These important ethical issues on which the church holds positions represent some of the teachings of the church regarding moral behavior but clearly not the whole range, which would require a separate volume to cover fully.

Homosexuality

The church holds that sexual intercourse is permissible only within the context of marriage between a man and a woman. It views genital sexual activity between homosexuals or lesbians as sinful. However, in recent years the church has distinguished between homosexual orientation and homosexual activity. In this matter it follows Luther's directive "to condemn the sin but love the sinner." In 1976, the American bishops published "To Live in Christ Jesus" that acknowledged that homosexual orientation is not voluntary. Following a natural law theology, the Congregation for the Doctrine of Faith document *Persona humana* continues to hold that "homosexual acts are intrinsically disordered."[14] The *Catechism of the Catholic Church* confirmed this and stated: "Under no circumstances can they be approved."[15] It calls for homosexuals to live a life of chastity. Yet the Catechism, like the USCC's 1990 document "Human Sexuality," acknowledges that homosexual orientation is not chosen and counsels that homosexuals be treated with respect and compassion and not be discriminated against.

On September 30, 1997, the U.S. bishops released a pastoral letter, the work of the USCC's committee on marriage and family, titled "Always Our Children: A Pastoral Message to Parents of Homosexual Children and Suggestions for Pastoral Ministers." Echoing the *Catechism of the Catholic Church*, it recognizes that the orientation toward homosexuality is "deepseated" in some men and women. The letter does not take up explicitly the anthropological "nurture-nature" debate as to whether homosexual orientation is a part of a person's make-up from birth or if it is a chosen or socially induced orientation. In any case, the letter says that homosexuality is not *experienced* as freely chosen, and it encourages parents to accept their children as homosexual, seemingly conceding that homosexuality is a natural orientation for some. Despite this acknowledgment, however, the document does not endorse a homosexual lifestyle which would include sexual activity.[16] James T. McHugh, Bishop of Camden, New Jersey, writing in the *Philadelphia Inquirer*, made it clear that with the publication of this pastoral letter, the church is not condoning homosexual activity:

> It is important to remember that the role of the church is not simply to put a stamp of approval on whatever someone is doing in order to make that person feel better. The role of the church is to speak the truth in love. At times, this can be difficult to hear and accept. The truth sometimes is. Yet, for anyone, especially the church, to avoid speaking the truth under a veneer of charity is not charitable, but wrong, particularly when certain behaviors are destructive to the physical, emotional and spiritual well-being of a person.[17]

Official documents, as evident so many times in this book, tell only part of the story. Many homosexual persons feel caught between their commitment to their faith and their lifestyle. They do not accept the church's remedy of chastity and as a result find themselves alienated from the community to which they have deep spiritual attachment. Some bishops are sympathetic and encourage ministries to the homosexual community.

Dignity is the name of an organization that serves the needs of the Catholic homosexual and lesbian community. As in the Boston archdiocese, cited in this book, many bishops forbid Dignity access to church property. This distancing from Dignity is the result of a Vatican document issued October 30, 1986, "A Letter to the Bishops of the Catholic Church on Pastoral Care of Homosexual Persons," which referred to homosexual orientation as "an objective disorder" and instructed bishops to withdraw support from any group that condones homosexual acts. Despite these caveats, Dignity headquartered in Washington, D.C., New Ways Ministry headquartered in Maryland, and the Conference for Catholic Lesbians in New York, continue to minister to the Catholic homosexual community, their families, and friends. But these groups do not always receive a warm welcome from the hierarchy. In an editorial in the diocesan newspaper, Cardinal Hickey warned Georgetown University officials not to permit a debate on Catholic teaching on homosexuality on campus since in his view "[New Ways Ministry] is a locally based advocacy group that is distinctly and deliberately ambiguous with regard to the Church's teaching on the wrongness of homosexual activity. . . . the approach of New Ways Ministry is spiritually and pastorally harmful."[18] Despite the warning, the debate took place on campus as scheduled.

Suicide

Those who grew up in the pre-Vatican II church may remember the church's treatment of victims of suicide and their families. Dorothea Varley recalls the funeral of a high school girl who committed suicide when she lived in the Brighton section of Boston in the 1940s. Even though the girl attended a Catholic girls' high school, the priest would neither allow her coffin into the church nor bury her in the consecrated ground of the diocesan Catholic cemetery because the church considered her final act as a mortal sin. Such treatment created outcasts and brought undue shame. At the time, the church considered suicide a willful act of murder. Today, the church understands and accepts that suicide victims are not morally responsible for their acts because of the troubled state of mind that accompanies such a desperate act. Full funeral rites are provided, and the families are treated with the sympathy and compassion they deserve and need at such a difficult time.

Abortion

No moral issue has divided the American Catholic church as much as the controversy about abortion. Even characterizing it as a moral issue is a signal that it should be considered an ethical-moral-religious concern rather than a "social" or "personal" issue, as many political analysts describe it. The debate is long-standing, the bedfellows sometimes strange, and the issue nowhere near resolved despite court rulings and church condemnations. As noted in chapter 1, statistically American Catholics do not differ very much from other Americans in their disposition toward abortion. However, abortion is a lightning rod for discord among Catholics and between the church and society.

The conflict concerning abortion is not so much about the procedure (as it might be with the morality of organ transplants or cloning, for example), although this too can itself be in question, as in the case of what abortion opponents call "partial birth abortions." More often, it is about on whom (or what) the procedure is being performed. Is this a human being, a child? Is it a fetus which may be considered to have a status other than a person? Is a fetus a child? Is a fetus that has reached the developmental stage where it (he/she) is normally viable outside the womb of a different moral and legal status from a fetus that is not viable outside the womb? Who has the right (does anyone?) to decide to terminate a pregnancy: a mother, a couple, a doctor? Is termination a euphemism for murder? These are some of the highly charged questions that surround abortion.

There is passion on both sides. In this case, however, current church teaching is unequivocal: abortion is mortally sinful.[19] On this issue the bishops line up staunchly behind the Vatican. Most priests and sisters support the teaching with little public dissension. Many of the laity, however, do not agree with the teaching and some do not observe it despite the severity of the consequences as stated in Canon 1398 of the Code of Canon Law: "A person who procures a successful abortion incurs an automatic excommunication." The *Catechism of the Catholic Church* notes that the Church is not trying to restrict mercy but to make clear the gravity of the sin.[20]

Abortion is at the same time an intensely private matter and a widely debated public issue. Over this ethical conundrum, private and public morality collide in a battle that has divided the nation as well as affected the church. Individual Catholics dispute with each other, the institutional church via the hierarchy and the offices of the United States Catholic Conference attempts to influence public policy; the church joins its protest with the protests of evangelical Christians in an alliance that some call unholy, and individual bishops and priests have made it the focal point of their ministry. The stances on abortion are as divisive as they are decisive. In a number of highly publicized cases the church has refused the sacraments to Catholics who participate in the rendering of abortion services or who publicly support abortion legislation.[21]

The best-known controversy involved then-Governor Mario Cuomo of New York, a Catholic, who privately opposes abortion but supported public funding of abortions. After being publicly challenged in 1984 by New York's Cardinal O'Connor, who questioned whether or not Catholics should vote for someone (even a fellow Catholic) who did not oppose abortion, Governor Cuomo delivered a speech, "Religious Belief and Public Morality: A Catholic Governor's Perspective,"[22] on September 13, 1984, at the University of Notre Dame, in which he defended his position. He argued that the neutrality on religious questions required by the Constitution in effect protects Catholics' rights to practice Catholicism (including the rejection of abortion) in the same way that it permits other believers to practice their religions. However, "the values derived from religious belief will not—and should not—be accepted as part of the public morality unless they are shared by the pluralistic community at large, by consensus."[23]

It is all too clear to politicians and church officials that the American people do not share one view on the issue of abortion as they do not on a number of moral issues ranging from capital punishment to race relations. Without that mandate Cuomo was reluctant to impose either a denominational or Christian ethic on a religiously diverse nation of believers and nonbelievers, all of whom claimed American citizenship but only a percentage of whom claimed Catholicism. To his mind, abortion, a procedure which as a Catholic he personally opposes, cannot be restricted by the government, which has no right to impose the religious values of a particular denomination or religion on its citizenry. To make his point he cited several Christian and Jewish bodies that support legal abortion. Such public policy does not prohibit the church from instructing its own members about the sinfulness of abortion or attempting to convince the larger body of American citizens that abortion is gravely immoral and should be legally prohibit-

Abortion has divided the country as well as American Catholics.
AP PHOTO/JOE MARQUETTE

ed—which the church does through its preaching, pronouncements and promotion of specific public policies.

In the case of Lucy Killea, a Democrat from San Diego, who ran for office in a heavily Republican district and won, the public opposition to her candidacy by the local bishop may have helped boost voter turnout in her favor. Americans do not take kindly to perceived church interference in the political process.

The challenge to the church's position on abortion has also come from inside the ranks of active Catholics, including some clergy and religious. Father Robert Drinan, S.J., who is personally opposed to abortion, was a five-term representative to Congress from Massachusetts' Fourth Congressional District. However, he supported public funding for abortions for the poor. In 1980, citing canon 285:3 of the 1917 *Code of Canon Law*, which prohibits clerics from holding elected public office, Pope John Paul II ordered Robert Drinan not to seek a sixth term.[24] Drinan acknowledged his priestly vow of obedience and left Congress to take a position at Georgetown University Law Center.

In 1984, a group of 97 Catholics, including 4 male religious and 22 female religious, signed an advertisement titled "Catholic Statement on Pluralism and Abortion" published on October 7 in the *New York Times* that said Catholics held a "diversity of opinions" on abortion and asked for open discussion of the issue.[25] The statement, written by Daniel Maguire, Marjorie Maguire, and Frances Kissling, was circulated among a number of groups including the members of the Catholic Theological Society of America and the College Theology Society. The "Catholic Committee on Pluralism and Abortion" that emerged decided to publish the statement in the heat of the 1984 presidential election because some bishops, namely Cardinals Bernard Law of Boston and John O'Connor of New York, were publicly questioning the abortion position of Geraldine Ferraro, a Catholic and a candidate for the vice-presidency. Like New York Governor Mario Cuomo and Massachusetts Senator Edward Kennedy, she was personally opposed to abortion but would not impose her moral stance on the nation. Unlike Drinan, she had no vow of obedience to the pope, but was committed to follow the law of the land as interpreted by the Supreme Court.

The American bishops formally responded to the statement on November 14 with a letter issued by Archbishop John Quinn of behalf of the National Conference of Catholic Bishops condemning the statement. The church specifically targeted the religious and clergy who signed the document, making it an issue of obedience as well as denial of a church position. The four male signers who were priests or brothers retracted. After protracted negotiations between Rome's Cardinal Jerome Hamer of the Congregation for Religious and Secular Institutes and the religious superiors of the signers, all but two retracted. Barbara Ferraro and Patricia Hussey of the Sisters of Notre Dame de Namur continued to proclaim their pro-choice stance and were dismissed from the order.

In its condemnation of abortion, the church follows a natural law moral reasoning which argues that the natural order is established by God the creator and should be followed as God's mandate. The argument follows that the natural course is birth, and abortion constitutes an unnatural act. By this reasoning, the church attempts to influence public policy on the grounds that its antiabortion stance is in line with principles of moral reasoning based on natural law that have guided Western cultures since the first century. For Catholics, the church has the right to appeal to internal warrants such as revelation, the consistent teaching of the church, and papal pronouncements to guide their moral decision making. In the public realm, however, these touchstones do not apply; and the church relies on philosophical argument that requires neither faith nor membership to make its case. In 1984, Bishop James W. Malone, then president of the NCCB, stated the bishops' position on the church's public appeal clearly:

> In the public arena of a pluralistic democracy, religious leaders face the same tests of rational argument as any other individuals or institutions. Our impact on the public will be directly proportionate to the persuasiveness of our positions. We seek no special status and we should not be accorded one.[26]

The bishops maintain a standing committee on pro-life affairs into which they have poured millions of dollars in their fight to overturn *Roe vs. Wade*. Dioceses and parishes also have pro-life groups that are able to marshal significant political pressure on Congress, the president, and state legislatures. While their attempts to overturn the Supreme Court ruling have been unsuccessful, they have made inroads in other ways, particularly in limiting public funding for abortions. In 1976 Congress passed the Hyde Amendment (sponsored by Representative Henry Hyde of Illinois, a Catholic and a staunch abortion foe) which eliminated the use of federal Medicaid money for abortions.

Since abortion rights or restrictions rest largely with the Supreme Court, in congressional appointment hearings candidates for the court have been painstakingly scrutinized concerning their views on abortion, and only those survived who in a sophisticated (some might say "equivocating") and oblique manner succeeded in masking their views on the issue. Some zealots would make abortion the litmus test (on one side or the other) for sitting on the bench.

Reacting to the 1973 Supreme Court ruling in *Roe vs. Wade* that legalized abortion, the American bishops issued a *Pastoral Plan for Pro-Life Activities* in 1975 in order to coordinate Catholic efforts to counter the court decision. The bishops would fight this ruling nationally through the NCCB, in the states by the dioceses, and locally through the parishes.

In 1989 the bishops reaffirmed their opposition to abortion in a "Resolution on Abortion" that praised the Supreme Court decision *Webster vs. Reproductive Health Services* that permitted the states greater liberty to place restrictions on abortions. The document equates the nomenclature "pro-choice" with "pro-abortion" and states: "No Catholic can responsibly take a 'pro-choice' stand when the 'choice' in question involves the taking of an innocent human life."[27] It further reiterates the bishops' intention to overturn current public policy and law permitting abortions.

In 1995 Pope John Paul II stated that the church's teaching on abortion "is unchanged and unchangeable . . . This doctrine is based upon the natural law and upon the written word of God, is transmitted by the Church's Tradition and taught by the ordinary and universal Magisterium. No circumstance, no purpose, no law whatsoever can ever make licit an act which is intrinsically illicit, since it is contrary to the law of God which is written in every human heart, knowable by reason itself, and proclaimed by the Church."[28]

Upon approval by all the American bishops at a meeting in June 1995, the bishops' Pro-Life Activities Committee issued a document, *Faithful for Life*, linking abortion and euthanasia and condemning both equally forcefully and echoing Pope John Paul II's concerns in his May 19, 1991, document, "On Combating Abortion and Euthanasia." *Faithful for Life* states in part:

> Since the legal floodgates were opened in 1973 by the U.S. Supreme Court's decision in "Roe vs. Wade," an abortion mentality has swept across our land and throughout our culture. The language and the mind-set of abortion—presented in terms of unlimited choice, privacy and autonomy—pervade our entertainment, our news, our public policies and even our private lives. Wrapped so appealingly in the language of self-determination, cloaked so powerfully in the mantle of federal authority, is it any wonder that the logic of Roe has been extended to apply beyond the unborn? Is it any wonder that it appears so explicitly in our public and private conversations about euthanasia? . . . Here we reflect upon these issues in the context of the alarming trend to advance abortion and euthanasia in the name of freedom. But it is a freedom gone wrong.[29]

Parish churches fight the abortion battle from the pulpit via preaching and at the doors of the church (via bulletin inserts) and in the parking lot (via handouts and flyers). However, while many priests regularly preach against abortion, others mention it rarely and do not stress the church's teaching because the people have heard it, and the priests do not want the church to be perceived as a one-issue institution, particularly an issue with which many Catholics disagree. More active pro-life priests find this disposition among their clerical brothers puzzling if not contradictory.

The church's hope to ban abortion was bolstered by the court judgment *Webster vs. Reproductive Health Services* in 1989, which permitted abortion restrictions by the states, such as restricting funding for abortion counseling, prohibiting the use of public funds and personnel for abortions, and permitting viability testing of a fetus at twenty weeks. After this limited victory, the American bishops engaged in a multiyear, multimillion dollar public relations campaign funded by the Knights of Columbus in an attempt to influence voters and public policy. Of this effort, political scientist Timothy Byrnes wrote: "I am not aware of a single politician who has changed his or her position on abortion because of pressure applied by a Catholic bishop. In fact, any politician who did so would surely face a barrage of criticism for 'taking orders' from an ecclesiastical authority."[30]

The Environment

The church's concern for the environment, not always evident in the past, remains tied to its theology of creation, which calls for human stewardship of the earth and its resources. In his 1990 New Year's Day message to the world, Pope John Paul II identified the environment as of chief moral importance and in his World Day of Peace Message, *The Ecological Crisis: A Common Responsibility*, he articulated the church's concern for the natural world.[31] The U.S. bishops' 1991 pastoral *Renewing the Earth: An Invitation to Reflection and Action on the Environment in Light of Catholic Social Teaching* modestly proposed reflections that remained open to correction and invited dialogue between the church and the scientific community to address the problems that beset the environment globally and in America. Calling for more than study, the bishops launched an "Environmental Justice Program" that attempted to address the effects of environmental degradation, particularly among the poor.[32]

Catholic theology regards the natural world as sacramental since nature reveals its creator, God. The church, like government, industry, and individuals, has not always respected the sacramental character of the environment. Pope John Paul II grounds his analysis of the environment in biblical revelation, in particular the first book of the Bible, Genesis, which describes God's act of creation of the earth and humankind's relation to it. He ties environmental destruction in good measure to consumerism that has allowed the profit motive to outweigh ethical considerations. Citing St.

Francis of Assisi as an example, he encourages people everywhere to value and preserve the gift from God that nature represents. The pope suggests that countries should agree to make a safe environment a basic human right. We must assume responsibility for the care of the planet. The pope states: "[T]here is an order in the universe which must be respected, and . . . the human person, endowed with the capability of choosing freely, has a grave responsibility to preserve this order for the well-being of future genera- tions."[33]

In recent years increased sensitivity and efforts coordinated with other Christian communities and with Jews have begun to reverse the trend of religions ignoring environmental concerns. The church engaged in a multi- dimensional effort targeting parishes, seminaries, clergy, public policy mak- ers, and scholars urging them to view the issues as religious as well as civil concerns. The bishops link efforts to preserve the environment to achieving an economy that is both sustainable and just while recognizing that contem- porary economies are necessarily global. They preach an ethic that respects human life from the unborn to the dying and, by extension, pertains to all creation. In practical terms, what impact did the Third World production of basketball shoes or cross-trainers that every American youngster owns have on the environment and workforce of the newly created industrial economies of developing nations? Are Americans, not exclusively, but extensively, because of our heavy dependence on the world's natural resources, responsible for the pollution of rivers, the destruction of rain forests, and the creation of a permanent under-class around the globe? These questions constitute keen challenges to all Americans and should impinge on the consciences of Catholics and non-Catholics alike. The church seeks to be an ethical voice in an expanding and essential conversa- tion about the future of the planet.

Catholics respond to the church's teachings in this area in ways similar to their response on other moral questions. What distinguishes their response to the church's teachings and initiatives on the environment from other ethical concerns like sexuality or reproduction, is the level of agree- ment in principle. Few would disagree that the environment constitutes an important moral dimension but equally few demonstrate awareness, knowl- edge, or willingness to act in an unselfish manner. So in this domain the church teaches but Catholics often fail to abide by that teaching. The ethics of solidarity and the option for the poor that the Church invites Catholics to practice, remain ideals.

However, some strategies proposed by the bishops clash with many

Americans', Catholic and non-Catholic, assessment of social patterns and problems. For instance, the U.S. bishops contend that consumption bears the responsibility for scarcer resources, not population growth. Consistent with their pro-life stance, they oppose population control and instead encourage reduced consumption by first-world inhabitants so that a more equitable distribution of resources may be possible. Many demographers, anthropologists, sociologists, and other observers of human behavior contend that without direct population control, the world will be rendered incapable of supporting the human race and the tide of a rising population must be curtailed by human intervention, and soon. Like its previous pastoral letters on nuclear war and the economy, the church sometimes speaks in a countercultural voice that exhibits an internal coherence but meets opposition from people with different experiences and worldviews, among Catholic citizens as well as other Americans. To some, such a strategy makes the church look naive and renders it irrelevant. To others, it represents the consistency within the church's teachings, be they popular or unpopular with Catholics and other groups in the United States.

"The Seamless Garment"

The church attempts to defend human life against all forces that would diminish or terminate it—nuclear war, capital punishment, abortion, euthanasia, and the like. Cardinal Bernardin termed this approach the "seamless garment" that represents the church's unified defense of life. All over the world the Catholic Church has been a leader in the pro-life movement. The moral teachings of the church classify abortion as one of the most grievous sins. The church insists that it has consistently taught that abortion is morally wrong in all circumstances. The November 18, 1974, "Declaration on Procured Abortion," issued by the Sacred Congregation for the Doctrine of the Faith and ratified by Pope Paul VI, makes this clear saying: "The tradition of the Church has always held that human life must be protected and favored from the beginning," calling its condemnation of abortion "a constant teaching of the supreme Magisterium." In a letter to the bishops of the world, Pope John Paul II directly addressed the political situation under which many Catholics live wherein states have permissive laws with regard to abortion.

> When legislative bodies enact laws that authorize putting innocent people to death and states allow their resources and structures to be used

for these crimes, individual consciences, often poorly formed, are all the more easily led into error. In order to break this vicious circle, it seems more urgent than ever that we should forcefully reaffirm our common teaching, based on sacred Scripture and tradition, with regard to the inviolability of innocent human life.[34]

In a "Pastoral Message On Abortion" issued in Washington, D.C., by the administrative committee of the National Conference of Catholic Bishops on February 13, 1973, the American bishops opposed a Supreme Court decision striking down laws in Texas and Georgia that attempted to curtail abortion, saying: "The Court has apparently failed to understand the scientific evidence clearly showing that the fetus is an individual human being whose prenatal development is but the first phase of the long and continuous process of human development that begins at conception and terminates at death." Further, they praised the Right to Life movement and advised Catholics to be proactive on this issue:

We praise the efforts of pro-life groups and many other concerned Americans and encourage them to:

(a) Offer positive alternatives to abortion for distressed pregnant women;

(b) Pursue protection for institutions and individuals to refuse on the basis of conscience to engage in abortion procedure;

(c) Combat the general permissiveness legislation can engender;

(d) Assure the most restrictive interpretation of the Court's opinion at the state legislative level;

(e) Set in motion the machinery needed to assure legal and constitutional conformity to the basic truth that the unborn child is a "person" in every sense of the term from the time of conception.

And in June 1995, the Pro-life Activities Committee of the American bishops issued yet another statement titled "Faithful for Life." Reflecting on the increasing acceptance of abortion and euthanasia in American society they stated:

Abortion, and now euthanasia, have become socially accepted acts because many have been persuaded that people unfairly lose their freedom when others make claims on them that pose burdens and obligations. . . . It is cruelly ironic that the thought of eliminating one's child or one's parent could be considered an acceptable, even altruistic, action.[35]

The bishops went on in this letter to claim that their intention was both to inform the consciences of Catholics on these grave matters, which is their obligation as teachers of the faith, and to influence public policy, which is their right as citizens of the United States. In addition to issuing official statements, the bishops pursued an aggressive media campaign. In the early 1990s they hired a well-known public relations firm to manage their pro-life campaign, a strategy that resulted in severe criticism from some segments of the Catholic population as well as from non-Catholics. Which strategy to pursue became an issue among the bishops themselves. Cardinal Bernardin, the chairperson of the NCCB's Right to Life Committee, developed a holistic approach to life issues which he termed "the seamless garment" approach, tying abortion, euthanasia, capital punishment, war and society's treatment of the poor into a unified agenda for life. Some among the hierarchy, in particular Cardinal John O'Connor, thought that the combination of issues diluted the anti-abortion focus and detracted from the bishops' goal of reversing the *Roe vs. Wade* Supreme Court decision.

As the Catholic pro-life movement in America gained momentum, it attracted unlikely allies—the Christian right and, specifically, the Christian Coalition. Roman Catholics and the followers of Jerry Falwell had little in common to this point. Catholics viewed Falwell and his followers as fundamentalists, and Falwell's Christian right distanced themselves from Catholics, whom they saw as papal loyalists, social liberals, and theologically misguided.

The pro-life stance by the church extends beyond the womb. American bishops have consistently denounced the death penalty as immoral. Increasingly in the last twenty years, individual states are resuming capital punishment as a sign of their intolerance of violent crime. The move toward tougher laws and the execution of criminals convicted of certain crimes like the murder of a police officer finds widespread support in American society. But not all citizens back this form of punishment and the Catholic Church considers itself a leading opponent of the death penalty, this despite the fact that many individual Catholics favor capital punishment.

Traditionally, the state justifies capital punishment by claiming that it constitutes the best way to preserve good order and promote justice. Many citizens believe this. However, others argue that capital punishment is neither deterrent nor just. The church stands with these critics of capital pun-

ishment although the *Catechism of the Catholic Church* states: "[T]he traditional teaching of the church has acknowledged as well-founded the right
and duty of legitimate public authority to punish malefactors by means of
penalties commensurate with the gravity of the crime, not excluding, in
cases of extreme gravity, the death penalty."[36] In his encyclical, *Evangelium
Vitae* (The Gospel of Life) John Paul II wrote that cases in which the death
penalty should be permitted "are rare if not practically nonexistent." In
1974 the U.S. bishops declared their opposition to capital punishment and in
a 1980 statement they acknowledged both the Catholic tradition permitting
capital punishment and the popular sentiment to continue the practice. In
part the document said: "We recognize that many citizens may believe that
capital punishment should be maintained as an integral part of society's
response to the evils of crime, nor is this position incompatible with Catholic
tradition. We acknowledge the depth and the sincerity of their concern."
The document went on to urge them to change their minds and resist the
use of the death penalty in the United States.

Even in the case of Timothy McVeigh, the convicted terrorist whose
April 1995 bombing of the federal building in Oklahoma City killed 181
people and injured scores more, the U.S. bishops' Domestic Policy Committee chairman Bishop William Skylstad of Spokane said that "to execute
Mr. McVeigh would tragically perpetuate a terrible cycle of violence and
further diminish respect for life." And in the case of an African American
convicted of killing a Baltimore police officer, Baltimore Cardinal William
Keeler, Delaware Bishop Michael Saltarelli, and Washington, D.C., Cardinal James Hickey sent a letter on June 6, 1997, to the Maryland Court of
Appeals asking the court to examine and correct "the racial disparity in the
imposition of the death penalty in Maryland."

For the same reasons, the church also opposes all efforts to legalize
assisted suicide. When Oregon voters chose twice (Oregon Death with Dignity Act, 1994 and 1997) to permit doctors to prescribe lethal dosages of
medication to patients who request it, are diagnosed to have less than six
months to live, and who observe a fifteen-day waiting period before receiving the drugs, the church protested and spent almost $4 million to oppose
the legislative initiative. These examples of the church's protection of life
reflect Cardinal Bernardin's notion of a "seamless garment," that is, the
church's pro-life position extends chronologically, from before birth to
death, and to all members of society, from the unborn to the convicted mur-
derer. While the pro-life movement conveys in most people's minds an
antiabortion stance, for the church it is broader than this.

The Catholic Church and Other Christian Churches

The Reformation in the sixteenth century divided the Christian church in the West into Protestants and Catholics. Henry VIII further divided Catholics into Anglican and Roman. These divisions have been further compounded through the centuries, so that today multiple Christian churches fill the religious landscape in America. A brief excursion through almost any city or town reveals the variety: the First Presbyterian, Friends Meeting House, African Methodist Episcopal, Church of Jesus Christ of Latter-day Saints, St. Mark's Episcopal, Trinity Lutheran, Southern Baptist, American Baptist, United Church of Christ, Unitarian and others.

While Catholics and Protestants today stand closer to each other in belief and practice than they were a generation ago, differences continue between them. It is important to note that Protestant churches differ significantly with each other and generalizations do not apply to all non-Roman Catholic Christian churches but, given this caveat, some general comparisons are possible. In most mainline Protestant churches clergy are male and female. Roman Catholicism ordains only men. Protestants do not recognize the pope's ecclesial authority. Their churches tend to be less hierarchical than Catholic ones. Protestant churches usually celebrate fewer sacraments than the seven that the Catholic Church recognizes. Catholics celebrate the Eucharist at daily mass and every Sunday; Protestants generally celebrate it less frequently, quarterly in some churches, more or less frequently in others. The order of worship in Protestant churches can vary from week to week while the Catholic celebration of the Eucharist regularly follows the same patterns. The scripture readings at mass are determined by the church and used universally. Protestant ministers often exercise the right to choose the biblical texts for their services. Protestant churches emphasize preaching and commonly have sermons that are at least twenty minutes long. Homilies at Catholic mass are briefer, usually between ten and twenty minutes long. Protestants do not view their clergy as intermediaries with God as Catholics often hold the priest to be, but prefer a personal and direct relationship with God without going through the church or pastor as an intermediary. Catholics call their priest "Father," Protestants prefer the term "Pastor." Catholics are required by the church to attend church on Sundays. Protestants are encouraged but not required to do so. These constitute some of the differences between Protestants and Catholics.

Sixty percent of the world's Christians are Catholics. The Second Vatican Council addressed the relationship of the Roman Catholic Church with other Christians in the Decree on Ecumenism (*Unitatis redintegratio*). The decree acknowledged that the Christian church is not coterminous with the Roman Catholic Church, but that other baptized persons are also members of the Christian community and the reign of God that Jesus proclaimed is what the church itself is striving to achieve.[37] Since that time the Roman church has engaged in dialogue about unity with the separated Christian churches of the East and West. Pope Paul VI met with the Eastern Orthodox patriarch, the archbishop of Canterbury (representing Anglicanism), the leaders of the Oriental Orthodox Churches, each time signing declarations committing their respective communities to strive for full communion. Pope John Paul II, who holds Christian unity as a high priority, met with other spiritual leaders in Assisi in 1986, to dialogue and pray for world peace, and he preached at an ecumenical prayer service in Columbia, South Carolina, during his visit to the United States in 1987. The progress is significant between some churches. For example, Catholics and Lutherans agreed on a theology of justification, a theological mark of division between the two communities since the Reformation.

Local churches engage in such pursuits as well, exchanging pulpits occasionally, dialoguing, and cooperating in joint social action ventures. Nevertheless, ecumenism moves slowly, encountering theological and practical roadblocks. The admission of women to ordination in many Protestant churches and the Episcopal church while Rome stands firm against the possibility; the aggressive proselytizing methods of some evangelicals; and the primacy of the pope, are but a few. Some think that religious ecumenism is passé, arguing that the endeavor to underscore the unity of humankind takes priority to the task of bringing unity to the church, resulting in a so-called secular ecumenism. In the past ten years or so, enthusiasm for the ecumenical movement, no longer a novelty, has waned as people see few visible signs that the variety of Christian churches is diminishing. Reunifications and mergers within denominations changed the face of the Lutheran and Presbyterian communions in recent years, but unity between Roman Catholics and other Christian communities remains only a theoretical possibility.

Catholic theologians conduct their research in a truly ecumenical spirit, drawing upon the insights, arguments, and conclusions of Protestant scholars with regularity, especially in biblical studies, history, liturgical studies, and philosophical theology. The church holds a "Week of Prayer for Christian Unity" annually and some local congregations establish "covenant relationships" that result in mutual cooperation. Priests in all areas of the country regularly participate in ministerial associations that include members from a variety of denominations. Non-Roman Catholics with a particular expertise in areas as diverse as social service and sick-care, often serve in positions in Catholic parishes or institutions.

The U.S. bishops maintain a Secretariat for Ecumenical and Interreligious Affairs that oversees ecumenical dialogue with Episcopalians, Lutherans, Baptists and the Orthodox among others, and also fosters contact with Jews, Muslims, Hindus, Buddhists, and other religions.

The Catholic Church and Non-Christian Religions

One hundred years ago in America a plethora of churches offered a Christian smorgasbord. In most cities and in many towns synagogues and temples added diversity to the largely Christian landscape. Today a drive down New Hampshire Avenue in Silver Spring, Maryland, discloses a landscape that testifies to the religious pluralism in America. In a short stretch one encounters seemingly other worlds: a Gujarati Hindu temple, a Cambodian Buddhist temple, a Korean Christian church, a Vietnamese Catholic church, a Hispanic Pentecostal church, a Ukrainian Orthodox church, and an Islamic mosque. And these are not far from a Jain temple, a synagogue, and various mainline Protestant churches.

This is no longer Robert Handy's Christian America.[38] Not only has the Catholic ghetto vanished, the demise of Christian hegemony is quickly following. As Diana Eck and the Harvard Pluralism Project have demonstrated on their compact disk, *On Common Ground*, the religious landscape in the United States is rapidly being transformed with ancient world religions previously not in widespread evidence, taking their place alongside Judaism and Christianity. Today the mosque is erected in the shadow of the Catholic church, the synagogue is adjacent to the Hindu temple, and the Pentecostal church borders the Buddhist shrine. This is more than a visual panoply; it constitutes a theological challenge to a tradition that historically has considered itself the sole vehicle to salvation.

Roman Catholicism for much of its history claimed that membership in the church (via baptism) was necessary for the possibility of salvation. Because the world has shrunk to the proportions of a global village, the church after the Second Vatican Council was challenged to construct a new ecclesiology and soteriology (understanding of salvation). It had to consider itself not only in relation to the modern world, as Vatican II stressed, but also in relationship to the major world religions. This new ecclesiology is not to be a mere accounting of differences, or further assessment of what characterizes the church as unique or superior. Rather, it is a genuine attempt to understand itself and its role as one among several significant religious traditions. This new vision of ecclesiology draws from the rich tradition of Catholic theology and reinterprets some of that tradition.

The well-known but often misinterpreted phrase of Cyprian (c. 206–258) *extra ecclesiam nulla salus* [outside the church no salvation] had largely shaped the form of the Catholic response to other religions until the twentieth century. In its history the Catholic Church has witnessed periods of both tolerance and intolerance in its understanding of non-Catholics and non-Christians. Cyprian's phrase, strictly interpreted, meant that only those who were members of the visible church enjoyed the possibility of salvation. Thus, from the early centuries, there was a Catholic provincialism regarding the doctrine of salvation.

While a tradition of exclusivity of salvation took shape, it was sometimes softened by more conciliatory stances. For example, the Second General Council of Nicea, in 787, held the tolerant position that Jews who did not wish to convert to Christianity should be allowed to live openly as Jews. Again in 1076, Pope Gregory VII wrote to the Muslim king of Mauretania that Muslims and Christians worship the same God in different ways. However, this tradition of relative tolerance was countered by a number of rigidly intolerant claims. For example, in 1302, Pope Boniface VIII wrote: "We are required by faith to believe and hold that there is one holy, Catholic and apostolic Church; we firmly believe it and unreservedly profess it; outside it there is neither salvation nor remission of sins."[39] He further demanded that all people must submit to the Roman pontiff to be saved. The Council of Florence in 1442 continued this intolerant approach, claiming that those who were not living within the Catholic Church would be condemned to hell unless they converted before their death. The Council of Trent (1545–63) dealt with the issue by speaking about a "baptism of desire" for those who, through no fault of their own, were deprived of the formal sacrament of baptism, but who still may be saved. A mediating tone echoing Trent was struck further in the nineteenth and twentieth centuries. It excused those who were ignorant of the truth from culpability. Pope Pius IX (1846–78) again reiterated that invincible ignorance was cause for exoneration.[40] Pope Pius XII, in the encyclical *Mystici Corporis*, wrote that non-Christians could be saved if they were bonded to the church "by some unconscious yearning or desire."[41]

Although the document "Declaration on the Relationship of the Church to Non-Christian Religions" (*Nostra Aetate*) is the shortest produced by the participants of the Second Vatican Council, it deals with a question most pressing for the church in the next century: What is the relationship between the Catholic Church and the major world religions? The document itself does not treat explicitly the intricacies and delicacies of the theological ramifications of an interreligious dialogue. In a commentary published shortly after the time of the Council, theologian and general editor of a four-volume commentary on Vatican II John Oesterreicher correctly observed: "In it [*Nostra Aetate*], a Council for the first time in history acknowledges the search for the absolute by other men and by whole races and peoples, and honours the truth and holiness in other religions as the work of one living God."[42]

This disposition was first articulated in Vatican II, during which the church declared that: "The Catholic Church rejects nothing which is true and holy in these religions. She looks with sincere respect upon those ways of conduct and of life, those rules and teachings which, though differing in many particulars from what she holds and sets forth, nevertheless often reflect a ray of Truth which enlightens all men."[43] Pope John Paul II reaffirmed this positive assessment describing other religions as "so many reflections of the one truth," and seeing the spirit of God in non-Christians.[44] This recognition of the positive elements in the world religions connoted a new era in ecumenism. It signaled an openness to dialogue, beyond the world of separated Christian churches, with those who do not recognize Jesus Christ as "the way, the truth, and the life" (Jn 14:6) in any exclusive manner.

The document, *Nostra Aetate*, carefully and gently encouraged Catholics to "prudently and lovingly, through dialogue and collaboration with followers of other religions, and in witness of Christian faith and life, acknowledge, preserve, and promote the spiritual and moral goods found among these men, as well as values in their society and culture." This attitude is reflected in other documents of the Council as well,[45] indicating the seriousness of the participants' attempts to promote respect for dialogue with the other major religions of the world.

It is unlikely that, at the time of the document's promulgation (October 28, 1965), those who voted in favor of it, brief as it was, recognized fully the implications or complexities of what they were promoting, namely, interreligious dialogue on a world scale. Certainly they were well aware of the major shift in the Roman Catholic Church's position from mere tolerance of other religions to positive recognition. Prior to the Council the church held

that only those who were baptized (or who desire baptism, or were not ignorant of Jesus Christ) could be saved. A new theology developed with the
Council that espoused the view that even those who are not Christians enjoy
the possibility of salvation because Jesus died and rose for all. So a non-
Christian who worships God and lives a moral life may also be saved.

Centered Pluralism

The church continues to issue documents, to teach, to preach, and to offer a
set of beliefs. American Catholics, however, believe and practice them
imperfectly. The vast majority of Catholics hold to the central theological
teachings about the Trinity, the divinity of Jesus, grace, the reality of sin,
the need for salvation, the sacraments as points of contact with God, and
the validity of the Gospel message. In fact, they recognize that these are an
essential part of what makes them Catholic. But some (on some issues, the
majority) think that the church lacks insight in its interpretation and implementation of Jesus's message. They consistently ignore some teachings
because they find them irrelevant, out of date, intrusive (in the case of birth
control), or against their sense of Jesus's example. It is by no means a
homogenous community when it comes to beliefs and practices. Nevertheless, Catholics look to the church as a spiritual guide, a place where God's
presence is felt, touched, communicated, a community that believes together, even if some (or many) differ with some official teachings.

Christ remains at the center of their beliefs and practices. It is Jesus's
example, his teachings, his actions that they try to emulate. They want to be
like him, to act like him, to surrender to God's will as he did. But individuals fall short and need forgiveness. So does the church as a whole. American
Catholics, not unlike their contemporary Catholic counterparts elsewhere,
can be said to manifest a "centered pluralism." They hold God, Jesus, the
Holy Spirit at the center of their spiritual lives. They publicly identify with
the church as Catholics. But a theological pluralism marks their belief and a
pragmatic pluralism their practices.

CHAPTER SEVEN

Institutions, Roles, and Organizations

Those outside of it know, and Catholics know from experience, that the church is not a democracy. It is, in fact, one of the most hierarchical organizations in the world. While people join, and worship in, the local church, concurrently they become members of a world church. Every Roman Catholic community in America exists in relation to all other Catholic churches, and all are under the leadership of the Vatican in Rome. The pope is the head of the church. Although the official doctrine of papal infallibility was not promulgated until the First Vatican Council in 1871, historically the pope has been the first among equals. In other words, the primacy of the pope is separate from and prior to his infallibility. The church traces this authority to the scriptures which, Catholics believe, record that Peter was appointed the leader of the Apostles.

Papal authority has been exercised in different ways by different popes, and it has been challenged by internal forces as well as by princes, kings, and warlords. At times the pope was a prisoner in his own castle and at other times a ruler with considerable land. The modern Vatican City-State is a shrunken version of the papal states that once included parts of what are today Italy and France. The current Vatican City-State is an enclave of about 100 acres in Rome established as an independent political entity in an agreement with Italy in 1929. If the pope no longer controls significant territory, he remains the head of the Roman Catholic Church, an empire judged less by its land holdings than by its hold over the reins of orthodoxy in the church.

The democratic principle of one person, one vote, does not pertain with-

in the church. However, the pope is himself elected by his peers, the College of Cardinals. This body is made up of priests who have been elevated
to the level of cardinal, the highest rank below the pope within the church.[1]
In recent times the College of Cardinals has had a membership of about
one hundred twenty, with all regions of the globe represented. Next in rank
are archbishops, who oversee a large diocese (called an archdiocese) and
technically, several bishops (the next rank) in surrounding dioceses. In practice, they rarely interfere with the internal matters of a suffragan bishop
(one under their authority). In archdioceses and large dioceses, bishops have
auxiliary bishops to assist them. In the diocesan structure, bishops oversee
the work of priests, deacons, religious sisters, brothers, and laity.

Religious orders of men and women have their own internal structures
of authority, traditionally with a father or sister general, provincials and
superiors, and in more recent nomenclature with presidents and vice-presi-
dents. In this hierarchical order, the laity are below all of these.

But this hierarchical structure is only one conception of church, or
ecclesiology. The Vatican II document "The Church in the Modern World"
used the term "People of God" to describe the church, ushering in an ecclesiology of egalitarianism and empowerment to the laity. Since that time the
two ecclesiologies have collided with each other regularly. The Council
called upon all Catholics to take seriously their baptismal vows and therefore take greater responsibility for their faith life and the life of the church.
Such an ecclesiology softens the distinction between hierarchy and laity
although it does not eliminate it.

Regardless of which ecclesiology one adopts, the influence of the church
reaches into every dimension of a Catholic's religious life, from baptism to
burial. Dioceses oversee organizations and budgets for everything from
seminaries to cemeteries. There are particular rules for clerics and for the
laity, and regulations that pertain to both. The presence of structures, regulations, and directives implies neither knowledge nor compliance, but indicates the wide-ranging organizational structure of the church.

The Church as Educator

Catholic schools have helped to shape the lives of millions of Catholics
and, more recently, many non-Catholics who attend them. Since Vatican II,
however, enrollment in Catholic elementary and secondary schools has been
cut in half (despite small annual increases in the last six years). Catholic

Number of Catholic Elementary Schools, 1945–1997.

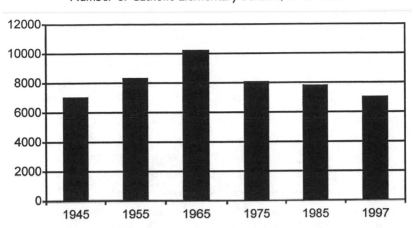

education peaked at a population of 5.5 million nationwide in the mid 1960s. At its peak in 1965, the Catholic system accounted for 12 percent of all American elementary and secondary students.[2] Between 1965 and 1989, the overall number of students attending elementary and secondary schools declined. Then, that trend reversed: between 1990 and 1995, the number of students increased by 79,000. In 1996 the census was down almost half to 2.6 million from its peak of 5.5 million.[3] There seem to be many explanatory factors, including demographics, economics, personnel changes, and a paucity of resources.[4] The population shift from cities to suburbs has deeply affected Catholic schools, many of which were built in the heyday of "brick and mortar" bishops who oversaw the construction of thousands of schools in the nineteenth and early twentieth centuries to accommodate the burgeoning immigrant Catholic population. Schools are increasingly expensive to operate and in some cases it is difficult to pass the costs along to students' families. The great majority of school personnel are lay persons who are paid larger salaries than the nuns received when they constituted the administration and faculties of Catholic schools. The human and financial resources of parishes require reallocation to cover burgeoning needs, and schools are often no longer accorded the priority they received from a previous generation.

Even though it was over sixty years ago, Thom Davis of Montgomery Village, Maryland, says his Catholic school days remain fresh in his mind.[5] The Immaculate Heart of Mary nuns at St. Joan of Arc Parish School in Philadelphia were tough, but fair. The tougher they were, he recalls, the more he learned. For example, one nun started all of the students off with 100 points, which everyone loved. Then she would randomly call on students during the term and each time a student answered wrong, she deducted five points. After three-quarters of the class failed, no one thought too highly of her system.

Thom recalls discipline and religion as high priorities in the school. Each week after school the children would line up under Sister's careful eye for confession. The nuns also proved ready and able with a ruler and their bare hands to enforce discipline. Thom recalls having missed a morning of school to visit the dentist, the pain from which was exacerbated by a slap to the face by a Sister who was unaware of his dentist visit and disapproved of his tardiness. That incident required a visit to the nuns by his mother to assure them that she would discipline Thom when necessary. Despite the disciplinary measures, Thom developed friendships with some of the Sisters and he and his friends visited a few of them after the nuns were transferred to another school.

The Oblates of Saint Francis De Sales priests and brothers at Northeast Catholic High School commanded respect also, except for a couple who the boys quickly realized had a drinking problem. Thom, a talented athlete, knew that academics were the school priorities, and he excelled in both.

Alex Chacón attended Santa Teresita Elementary school from fourth to eight grade in the late 1980s and Bishop Mora Salesian High School in the early 1990s, both in East Los Angeles. His parents sent him to Catholic elementary school because the public school system was, as he describes it, "a disaster."

> One day I got beat up by the local gang who were recruiting at the public elementary school. When I declined their invitation to join, they responded violently. Fortunately, all this happened within the eyesight of my mother who was waiting for me at the corner after school. After that incident she decided to put me in Catholic school—a tough decision because my parents are not wealthy but they figured the I'd be safe and learn more in Catholic school. When I got there it was culture shock—uniforms every day, nuns and Catholic laity teaching classes, prayer before every class, and mass once a month at the church next door to the school. But I found that my new classmates were there largely for the same reasons I was. Their parents, like mine, also took an interest in their welfare and education, something that was less com-

mon in the public school. I learned discipline and the importance of service to others, a value that the school stressed.

After elementary school, they sent me to the nearby all-boys Bishop Mora Salesian High School. There were only two Salesians on the staff, one a priest who taught religion and the other a Brother who worked there since the school opened in 1956 and who, now retired from teaching and coaching, served as a maintenance person at the school. We all took religion seriously. I learned to love education and developed an ambition to go to college, which was something my parents never expected. Most kids in the inner city where I come from ended their academic career after high school, if not before, either to go to work or to become involved in illegal activities. The school supported me and gave me (as well as almost the entire student body) financial aid—as a result the school regularly operates on the edge of bankruptcy. The vice-principal, a non-Hispanic in a school that was 99 percent Hispanic, who became like a second father to me, was a Georgetown grad who recognized my abilities and encouraged me to apply to his alma mater. In imitation of him, after graduation from Georgetown in the spring of 1998, I have a contract to teach at my high school to help others fulfill their dreams as I have done. It may not pay like Wall Street, but the satisfaction exceeds the compensation.[6]

Christine Hawes, a sixth-grader at Stone Ridge School of the Sacred Heart in Bethesda, Maryland, says she enjoys Catholic school because the class size is small and the teachers are always available to help. Even though the school is not located in her neighborhood, she has lots of friends at school because "they don't allow cliques and all the kids are friendly."

"Schoolwork is a little harder and we wear uniforms and the school is more strict but that probably turns out better," she says, reflecting the academic quality of the program and the discipline at the school. "They're pretty serious about religion. We take classes and get grades in it, and we have to go a service once a week and mass once a month at school. We have seven or eight nuns in the school but I only know two of them; the headmistress of the middle school and my religion teacher. We don't have service projects yet, but the high school spends one afternoon a week doing something for the community outside the school." One other factor that she thinks distinguishes her school from the public school is parental involvement. "We have a lot of fund-raisers and activities that parents volunteer to help with. It helps you to get to know all the families."[7]

In the early nineteenth century, there was little distinction between Catholic and public schools—at least in terms of how they were treated by the state. Until 1825 Catholic schools in New York City received public funds, and as late as 1890 Catholic schools received aid for the teaching of nonreligious subjects in Massachusetts, Connecticut, New Jersey, and Wisconsin. Nonetheless, fierce debates about the necessity for Catholic schools took place among the bishops who attended the three plenary councils of Baltimore held in 1852, 1866, and 1884. The councils recommended that schools be established in every parish in a diocese. Many bishops wanted to impose severe penalties, such as removal from their position, for pastors who did not comply. They also wanted to obligate parishioners to support the schools. Others wanted to force Catholics to send their children to these schools by denying the sacraments to parents who failed to enroll their children in the parish school. The public schools represented not only an alternative to Catholic education, but, in the minds of the bishops, a system of Protestant education in which children would read the Protestant version of the Bible, be exposed regularly to Protestant theological ideas, and encounter anti-Catholic sentiment.

Among the chief reasons for the success of Catholic schools was the dedication, hard work, and loyalty of nuns. Lay faculties in Catholic schools are a recent phenomenon. Until the middle of the 1960s, Catholic schools were staffed almost exclusively by nuns or, in the case of boys' schools, by priests and brothers. The majority of women's religious orders in the United States, whether founded here or in Europe, have been engaged in ministries of education. Orders of brothers, such as the Christian Brothers, and priests, such as the Holy Cross Fathers, have also been dedicated to this ministry. While theirs was a labor of love, it was also inexpensive labor. Most nuns lived in convents adjoining the schools they taught in and received little or no salary.[8] Sometimes they had to earn a pittance of a salary twice: once by teaching, and again by selling Christmas cards, candy bars, and magazines, using their students as door-to-door salespersons, or by holding paper drives every few months—all to raise money which the pastor "allowed" them to bank as salary. This made it possible for parishes to have their own schools and to charge modest tuition rates that were affordable for an immigrant population, the majority of whom earned blue-collar wages.

The parish school, while it still exists in many parishes, is in jeopardy. In 1967 there were 94,000 religious in the schools: by 1994 there were fewer

Number of Catholic Schoolteachers, 1945–1997

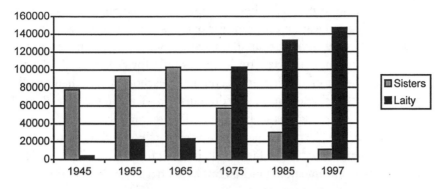

than 20,000. In 1994 sisters made up only 12 percent of school staff. Most Catholic schoolteachers and principals are lay people. These personnel require larger salaries, which in turn translates into either higher tuition charges or larger subsidies from the parish or diocese. While they have not committed their lives under vows as religious sisters do, these lay faculty make sacrifices to teach in Catholic schools since they are paid considerably less than their public school counterparts.[9] Bishop Kenneth Untener admits: "[W]e also did not pay religious women, especially when they taught in schools, as professionals, so we now have trouble with teacher salaries."[10] Many teachers choose to work in Catholic schools, however, because conditions are often much better than in public schools. Discipline is easier to maintain, parents are interested and involved, the children are more easily motivated, and religiously based values are held in common.

On average, it cost $184,372 to run a Catholic elementary school in 1980. By 1993 that cost had escalated to $537,838.[11] Part of the increase is due to inflation, but this amounts to only about one-third of the total. The other two-thirds are expenses related to redesigning the curriculum, and increased operating expenses from higher insurance premiums to more adequate benefit packages. The introduction of high technology to the classroom has also increased the budget for Catholic schools as it has for all schools. Fundraisers have been a way of life in Catholic schools for a long time, but it is difficult to expect students (and their parents) to raise sufficient additional funds to make up the shortfall by candy sales, hot cross buns, and auctions. Most parish budgets are stretched thin already, so that parish administrators are hard pressed to increase significantly their subsidies to the schools. The same is true for dioceses. The issue of fairness also must be considered.

With parish schools serving an average of 280 children, is it just to spend a larger portion of the parish budget annually in the service of so few? The decision to do so or not is further complicated by the need to subsidize a quality religious education program for public schoolchildren, who constitute a majority of their age group in the parish. Some parishes have adopted a cost-based tuition which sets tuition rates on a formula that divides the cost by the number of children in a school. The school would then be self-supporting with a single tuition schedule instead of a complex set of rates that have different categories such as Catholic and non-Catholic or in-parish and out-of-parish. The parish may offer a scholarship fund for poorer families but this amount would be far less than previous subsidies. The difficulties with this arrangement, as pointed out by Father Peter Daly in the weekly paper of the Washington, D.C. archdiocese, the *Catholic Standard*,[12] is that tuition may rise dramatically, permitting Catholic education only for the economically elite.

Exacerbating the troubles of Catholic schools is the fact that when overall financial contributions by Catholics began to decline in the mid-1960s, parishes reduced school subsidies in order to balance their budgets.[13] Inner-city schools are particularly burdensome financially, though the service they provide to the local communities is immeasurable. In some situations they are the first to be closed since they are often underenrolled and underfunded. In 1988 the archdiocese of Detroit closed 31 parishes, some with schools. In 1990 the archdiocese of Chicago closed 28 churches and 18 schools, including the largest high school seminary in the country; but in 1997 Cardinal Hickey of the archdiocese of Washington, D.C., announced a project called "Faith in the City" to infuse inner-city schools with $1 million that would allow the diocese to link schools in a consortium, raise enrollment and, it was hoped, save them. The effort centralized management and altered the curriculum. Part of the effort included a media campaign to raise awareness and recruit donors to support the effort. In February 1997 the Archdiocesan Catholic Schools Office ran the following radio spot:

> ED MCGEHRIN: Invest in quality, get consistent performance and predictable results.
> VOICE OVER: It's a strategy Edward McGehrin, member of the Stockbrokers' hall of fame, follows with his investments, including the education of his seven children.
> ED: Catholic schools work! That's why I sent my own kids there and why I help fund scholarships for other kids too.

VOICE OVER: Catholic school students excel in math, reading, and science, finish school, and go on to college. They come from diverse social, religious, and ethnic backgrounds, and learn not only academics, but faith and values that guide them long after they've left the classroom.

ED: For a person in business, helping Catholic schools is more than a good idea. It's a good investment.

VOICE OVER: Counsel a student on career opportunities, sponsor a computer program, provide a scholarship for a youngster in need. There are many ways you can help. To learn more, call the Archdiocese of Washington at 1–800–469-EXCEL. That's 1–800–469-E-X-C-E-L. Catholic Schools—the *Good News* in Education.[14]

This radio advertisement is as interesting for what it does not stress as it is for what it does. It is not directed toward recruiting potential students. Clearly it is aimed at those who can make a significant financial contribution to the cause of Catholic schools or can offer their business expertise to students. The ad underlines the potential tangible (and largely secular) results one can expect from Catholic education: "consistent performance," "predictable results," education as an "investment" like a stock or commodity; excellence in math, reading, and science; completing school, going on to college. It describes the student body as being "from diverse social, religious, and ethnic backgrounds" and the curriculum as one that teaches "faith and values" along with traditional academic disciplines. The phone number is 1–800-EXCEL, *not* 1–800-FAITH.

This advertisement appeals to those who can make a difference through their contribution of time, expertise, and financial resources—and this is all to the good. On the other hand, it gives the impression that Catholic schools are a way to get ahead in a competitive world more than being avenues to carry on the tradition of Catholic faith—and this makes them sound like any other private school in a setting where the public schools have failed.

The moneys collected from the archdiocese's fundraising efforts will go to support Catholic schools that most need it, namely schools located in Washington, D.C.'s poorer neighborhoods where children would not have such an opportunity to excel except for the continued presence of Catholic education. Even though the majority of the students in these schools are not likely to be Catholics, the church is carrying out a fundamental part of its gospel mission to care for those who are poor and underprivileged.

The rationale for this ministry goes back to Jesus himself and has been

Catholic schools advertise their secular as well as religious benefits.
COURTESY ARCHDIOCESE OF MILWAUKEE

taught consistently by the church in its history, and particularly in the social encyclicals of the twentieth century. It is a story repeated in many cities in America. In *Catholic Schools and the Common Good*, the authors trace the evolution of a Catholic high school in California that "functioned as a some- what elite finishing school" for white upper-middle-class girls in the 1950s, to one that educates young black inner-city women, almost half of whom are not Catholic. While the researchers laud Catholic high schools for con- tributing to the common good, just as the advertisement for Catholic schools in Washington stresses the competitive edge these schools afford their stu- dents, the researchers concede: "Many of the girls look upon [the Catholic high school] as a ticket to a prestigious college and a high-paying career, a vision shaped by parental hopes and media images."[15]

In 1994 a superintendent of Catholic schools in Orlando, Florida, sent a survey to a representative group of parents inquiring, among other things, why they sent their children to Catholic schools. The top three responses were 1) college preparation; 2) safety; 3) discipline. Neither faith formation nor development of character (a separate category from discipline) was in the top ten responses, illustrating that many families view Catholic schools as alternatives to public ones for reasons unrelated to religion.

Standing by its commitment to Catholic schools in the cities, the church is following the lead of the Second Vatican Council's "Declaration on Christian Education" that supported Catholic schooling. On the national level the American bishops developed their commitment to a social justice focus in the schools in the 1972 document "To Teach as Jesus Did." The 1979 document from the bishops "Brothers and Sisters to Us," urged "the continuation and expansion of Catholic schools in the inner city and other disadvantaged areas." Nonetheless, it is a struggle to keep schools open in these neighborhoods. With some frustration, the Florida bishops noted the problem stating: "As the costs and regulatory burdens have increased, the availability of a Catholic school education for low-income and socially disadvantaged families of all races has diminished."[16]

In one recent ten-year period (1983–93), 823 Catholic elementary schools closed.[17] Not all of these were inner-city schools. During this period over 500 rural parish schools closed. These closings seem an irony in the light of the American bishops' commitment to Catholic education expressed in their November 1990 pastoral letter "In Support of Catholic and Elementary Schools." In that letter they promised to provide Catholic education for those families who wanted it, stabilize the financing of these operations, and pay just salaries to those who staff them, all by 1997. While they have not achieved all of these desired goals, Catholic schools are not about to disappear.

Eighty-six percent of Catholic schools continue to be parish-sponsored. One way that parishes have attempted to address challenges is for a number of parishes in an area to cosponsor a regional Catholic school. This structure reduces the number of facilities, distributes the financial burden, and provides a wider recruiting base from which the school can draw its students. For example, in the Detroit suburb of Plymouth-Canton, the archdiocese and four parishes collaborated to construct a new $7.22 million school that opened in the fall of 1997. Another potential solution is for the state to issue tuition vouchers to families who choose to send their children to private schools, including religious schools. However, this option continues to meet with constitutional challenges concerning the separation of

Number of Catholic Elementary Students, 1945–1997

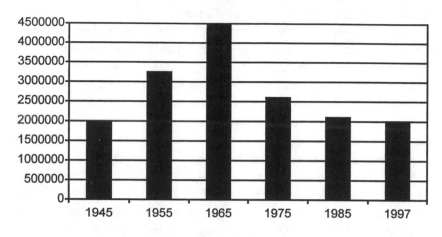

church and state, and for the time being cannot be counted on as a viable option to resolve the financial dilemma Catholic schools face.

For all of the fiscal headaches they create, schools do present a valuable opportunity to a parish. Primarily they provide daily contact with children and families. A parish is meant to be a community, and this is one important way to build one. Usually at least some of the teachers in the school will be parishioners who contribute to the community-building mission of the parish. The pastor and assistant pastor (if a parish is fortunate enough to have one) and the parish staff can have regular contact with the children, and through them with their families. Involvement is the key to a vibrant parish, and enrollment in the school represents a commitment on the part of families who send children to their parochial school.

One fact of Catholic education that has not gone unnoticed in the public sector is that Catholic schools do more with less. In a speech on August 14, 1995, New York Mayor Rudolph Giuliani, a graduate of Catholic schools, suggested that public schools emulate the parochial system. The statistics support his idea: the archdiocese of New York and the Brooklyn diocese educate a combined 151,000 students at a cost of about $3,000 per student, compared to more than one million public school students whose costs are $8,000 per student; the drop-out rate for the parochial schools is 0.1 percent, compared to 18 percent for public school students; and Catholic school pupils pass the Regents' Competency Tests at a much higher rate than public school students do. Similarly, in 1997 the superintendent of the Chicago public schools began studying Catholic schools in the archdiocese of Chicago, try-

Uniforms and single-sex education are two characteristics that distinguish many Catholic school students. AP PHOTO/MARK LENNIHAM

ing to learn the secret of their success. Spending far less per student than the public schools, Catholic schools achieved better results when measured by standards such as attendance, reading level, and standardized test scores. In controversial books by Andrew Greeley and James Coleman,[18] the researchers interpreted data to conclude that economically disadvantaged Catholic school students do better than similar students in public schools.

Catholic schools may produce better academic results than public schools, particularly city schools, but in the end this is not their raison d'être. They were created to educate young Catholics in the faith and to pass the tradition on to the next generation. The responsibility for this crucial mission, once the exclusive preserve of sisters, has now generally been entrusted to the hands of lay people.

Catholic Health Care

Even a cursory reading of the Gospels informs the reader that an essential part of Jesus's ministry involved curing the sick. Jesus's cures were occasional and often involved the restoration of the soul as much as the body.

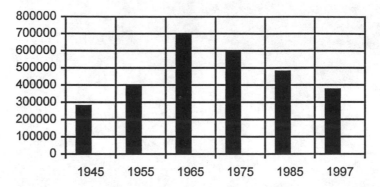

Number of High School Students: Diocesan and Parish, 1945–1997

Following in his footsteps but not emulating his itinerant ways, the church has developed an elaborate system of hospitals, nursing homes, hospices, and other health care facilities. If its only concern were the body, its task would be easier. The church's belief that each person has a God-given soul created at the time of conception, and the costs and complexity of contemporary medicine, have made its attempt to deliver state-of-the-art quality health care immensely complicated. Catholic hospitals, medical schools, and health care facilities operate under internal ethical constraints. Every living person, from the moment of conception until natural death, is a child of God whose life must be respected in all stages. In practice this means no abortions, no fetal-tissue research, and no assisted suicides. The church's prohibition of artificial birth control means no pills, condoms, or diaphragms. The church is certainly within its rights to prohibit such procedures and to refrain from distributing certain drugs or appliances. However, the health care system in America, from medical schools to outpatient clinics, relies on government funds to accomplish its mission. Government regulation accompanies government assistance.

In his study of Catholic health care, historian Christopher Kauffman makes a distinction between caring and curing, but suggests that each has a role in the tradition of Catholic health care.[19] In the nineteenth century, religious sisters offered a high degree of personal care for patients in hospitals even though many of the infirm had chronic incurable diseases or died in the hospital. The story is told of a visitor to a leper hospital who saw a Sister changing the putrid bandages of a patient. "I wouldn't do that for a million dollars!" he said in disgust. "Sir," answered the Sister, "neither would I." Today, with technology dominating health care and the quest more exclusively directed toward a cure, nuns highlight the spiritual dimension, an aspect of healing easily eschewed in an industry increasingly driven by machines and economic considerations. In addition to these differences, Kauffman noted the decline in the explicit religious character in contemporary Catholic hospitals. "The Catholic subculture, with its ethnic and devotional foundations so dominant in the pre-Vatican II world, is barely visible in the contemporary hospital."[20]

As early as 1727, sisters came to America to minister to the sick when twelve French Ursulines arrived in New Orleans. By 1820, sisters outnumbered priests. "What this means, really, is that for nearly all of the nation's history, women have comprised the majority of those serving in professional Catholic ministry here."[21] The Catholic Health Association (CHA), the political and structural entity representing Catholic health care, was established (then as the Catholic Hospital Association) in 1915. The CHA began an affiliation with St. Louis University in the 1940s. Sisters comprised the majority membership although priests headed the organization until a change in the bylaws in 1965 permitted nuns to be president. By that time there were about 860 Catholic hospitals in the United States and 71 percent of the population held private hospital insurance. Medicare and Medicaid came into existence at this time. The income derived from the combination of private insurance and federal dollars kept hospitals in the black and permitted them to care for indigent patients. Thus "there were hundreds of Catholic hospitals located in small towns and in heavily Catholic urban areas where physicians, priests, school sisters, and laity could confidently refer uninsured patients and friends."[22]

By 1975 the number of Catholic hospitals declined to 671 and the number of nuns working in them went from 13,618 to 8,980, due in part to the general decline in numbers among sisters and also due to choices some made to provide health care in other settings or to pursue other forms of ministry. In 1997, of 586 Catholic hospitals (about 10 percent of nonfederal hospitals in the United States), 542 were affiliated with CHA, and all Catholic health care facilities combined employed almost 700,000 Americans.

Within Catholic hospitals the spiritual care previously provided exclusively by priests and nuns evolved into pastoral care provided by teams of priests, nuns, lay people, and representatives of other Christian denominations who received formal Clinical Pastoral Education preparing them for this specific ministry. At the same time the composition of hospital professional and support staff and patients was changing, with an increasingly non-Catholic presence among both. Catholic hospitals reflected the religious pluralism of America, particularly in large cities and in places where the Catholic hospital was the sole health care facility. These facilities, like all hospitals, relied heavily on government programs for payment, further complicating if not, in the eyes of some, compromising their Catholic identity and mission. Catholic health care systems developed from the rapid changes and economic pressures encountered by Catholic health care facilities in the 1970s and '80s.

The very place where CHA found its home, St. Louis University, faced the consequences of declining revenues and increased expenses that confronted all hospitals. In 1997 the Jesuit university decided to sell its hospital to Tenet Healthcare Corp, a for-profit corporation.[23] The decision to sell, made by the president and board of directors of the university, met with strong resistance when Justin Rigali, archbishop of St. Louis, joined by Cardinals Hickey, Law, and O'Connor, argued that the university was not free to sell off its hospital since it was an intrinsic part of the Catholic church in St. Louis. Rigali contended that if sold, it would no longer be a Catholic hospital. Different interpretations of arcane points in Canon Law regarding the "alienation of property" (Canon 1257) clashed with one another.[24]

This case brought to the public's, and in particular to the Catholic community's, attention the question of ownership and episcopal governance of church-affiliated institutions. These institutions, as well as other Catholic organizations like colleges and universities, usually are incorporated under civil law, which allows them to function as independent entities. The Catholic religious orders who founded them relinquished ownership to independent boards during the 1960s and '70s. St. Louis University president, Father Lawrence Biondi, a Jesuit, assured the university's board of directors that the agreement with Tenet ensured that the hospital would continue to function as a Catholic facility. Tenet bought the hospital when it bid $100 million more than a competitive bid from two Catholic health care systems that combined in an effort to buy the facility.

The question of Catholic identity is an increasingly complex one as various institutional forces give their own definition to "Catholic" and may require adherence to specific rules, the display of particular symbols, a certain moral or religious practice, or explicitly Catholic personnel. Sometimes conflicts arise over the issue of Catholic identity. This concern is not a new one. Dorothy Day experienced pressure from church officials to drop the title "Catholic" from the Catholic Worker movement and newspaper because of her left-leaning political views that some thought bordered on communism. She responded: "If you feed the poor, they call you a saint. If you ask why they are poor, they call you a communist."[25] It all depends on who interprets the titles. Narrow juridical interpretations limit the scope of what may be called Catholic. Broader or more porous definitions risk sacrificing the specificity of the designation.

The Church's Legal Code: Canon Law

Most Catholics are vaguely aware that the church is internally governed by its own legal code called the Code of Canon Law. Those who have sought an annulment after divorce encounter the legal process of the church. The church's clerical ranks from priests to the pope are keenly aware of it at all times. It is a universal code governing the Latin or Western church (not the Eastern or Oriental churches in union with Rome) that provides for uniform procedures within a church that claims nearly 900 million members worldwide.

Although it has been a part of the church since the Middle Ages, the code that governed the church until its revision in 1983 dated from 1917. By the time of the Second Vatican Council, Pope John XXIII decided that it was outdated and needed to be modernized. In 1963, shortly before his death, he appointed a commission to revise canon law. He thought that it should reflect the spirit of the conciliar reforms, so the work of the council needed to be completed before canon law could be reformed. Thus, the commission's work was deferred until 1967. Initially the pope thought that the revision of the code would not take long. In November 1965 Pope Paul VI established a commission to revamp the code in the light of Vatican II's contributions. The revisions took years because its process was lengthy and tedious, involving extensive consultation with bishops' conferences and canon lawyers from around the world. An indicator of the importance of canon law to the church is that the final revision was done by Pope John Paul II himself in consultation with a few handpicked canon lawyers. The revised code was promulgated on January 25, 1983, and took effect on November 27, 1983. It was innovative and traditional at the same time—preserving some laws verbatim, modifying others, and incorporating conciliar reforms in others.[26]

While it is a code of law, it is also intended to be a pastoral guide to Catholic belief and practice. One of America's foremost canon lawyers, Ladislas Örsy, reminds Catholics that: "The *Code*, in spite of its title, is more than a book of legal rights and duties. . . . To interpret any given rule in such a multilayered document requires a sophisticated approach; an unwary reader may easily attach a sanction to an exhortation or miss the seriousness of a legal obligation."[27]

The internal mechanisms of the Catholic Church are no less complex than those of government or international business. Although not normally visible to the ordinary lay person, canon law plays a significant role in church matters behind the scenes. Canon law governs workings of the church and applies equally to the church in the Americas as it does to the church in Europe, Africa, or Asia. While there are accommodations for national practices, such as the abolition of certain holy days of obligation or transferring their observance to the nearest Sunday,[28] it is a universal code. As with many universal norms, there is a benefit and a liability. On the positive side, the church operates consistently throughout the world. On the negative side, all parts of the world are not alike. Canon lawyers are keenly aware of this conundrum and understand that "[T]he idealist view has been held that the norms of canon law are immutable. But in reality the opposite seems to be the case. Both in the past and today, canon law has been influenced by the different cultures in which Christians have lived."[29]

The 1983 Code consists of 1,752 canons (laws), compared with 2,414 canons in its predecessor, and is divided into seven books.[30] These books can be categorized under the rubric of governing, teaching, and sanctifying. They guide all aspects of church life, protecting the rights of individuals and specifying obligations. While canon law is not technically theology, a theology is implicit and the code of 1983 endeavored to imbue legal prescriptions with an appropriate theological character that reflected the pronouncements of the Second Vatican Council. The difference between theology and canon law is that "Theology emerges from the consciousness of the whole Church as fruit of faith seeking understanding. Canon Law emerges from the consciousness of legitimate authority as the fruit of faith seeking decisions and actions."[31]

In general, the revised code incorporates an ecclesiology that sees the church as the people of God, specifying that the laity may work in the apostolate of the church. However, it continues certain restrictions. For example, Canon 1024 limits ordination to males. The code covers multiple concerns from the proper husbanding of church resources, to the proper rubrics for the celebration of sacraments, to the governance of schools.

Many of these laws pertain exclusively to bishops in their role as leaders and administrators. One of the first obligations of a new bishop is an oath professing his faith and loyalty. Canon 380 prescribes: "After he has been promoted but before he takes canonical possession of his office, he must make a profession of faith and take an oath of fidelity to the Apostolic See according to the formula approved by the same Apostolic See."[32] Thus, bishops are bound to Rome first and foremost. Though their episcopal authority as successors to the apostles derives from God, the judicial exercise of it depends on Rome and they act as liaisons between the Vatican and the American Catholics whom they serve. Bishops face difficult dilemmas when these two constituencies collide. They are bound by canon law but their pastoral sensitivity sometimes conflicts with legal proscriptions leaving them in the middle between enforcing the law and making exceptions for good pastoral reasons. The same is true for priests, some of whom ignore the letter of the law in favor of the spirit.

Catholic Charities

The gospel mandates to feed the poor and to care for the orphan constitute ministries to which the church devotes considerable resources and energy.[33] Historian of American Christianity, Elizabeth McKeown, sees charity as the key component of the church's social mission.

> Although the Catholic Church adjusted its social programs in response to national and international developments, it insisted on the importance of the ancient ideal of charity. Personal service and almsgiving continued to hold a central place in Catholic teaching and practice, even as the Church championed a modern program of social justice aimed at removing the root causes of human need.[34]

In its history, the church established a welfare system that cared for its own and reached out to non-Catholics in a network run by clergy, religious women, and laity. The organization founded in 1910, the National Conference of Catholic Charities (NCCC), had a large contingent of mostly volunteer lay women in its ranks before World War I. The 1920s and the New Deal in the 1930s witnessed the professionalization of Catholic social workers. After World War II the church's advocacy for the poor and its work for justice became as important as its direct services. Since the 1960s, the church increasingly serves non-Catholics through its many charities. In 1994 Catholic Charities U.S.A. succeeded the NCCC, engaging 200,000 volunteers in its mission to improve the lot of the poor as the largest private system in the nation.[35]

Another aspect of the church's mission to the needy is its international arm, Catholic Relief Services (CRS). Founded in 1943, CRS, with its world headquarters located in Baltimore, is the U.S. Bishops' development and relief agency to assist the poor outside of the United States. Many Catholic schoolchildren become acquainted with CRS through its Operation Rice Bowl, a program of fasting, prayer, education, and almsgiving conducted during the holy season of lent. A readily identifiable component of that program is the distribution of small cardboard boxes varying called "mite boxes" or "rice bowls," in which children collect money to give to the needy through CRS's collection efforts at schools and churches.

With the money it collects through this and other direct fundraising efforts, CRS supports ongoing relief projects in over 80 countries in Africa, Asia, Europe, and Latin America as well as providing emergency aid at times of natural and human-generated disasters. The work that CRS does complements efforts by the United Nations and the International Monetary Fund to provide a reasonable standard of living to the world's developing peoples. Domestically, the church has an annual appeal called the Campaign for Human Development which, since its founding in 1970, has raised over $250 million and funded thousands of self-help projects. The motivation for this form of charity, besides human compassion, is the conviction that all people everywhere are children of God and thus deserve to be treated as such. The organization of CRS involves some priests, brothers, and sisters, but comprises mostly lay people who share the church's desire to fulfill the gospel mandate to feed the hungry, give drink to the thirsty, welcome the stranger, and clothe the naked (Matthew 25:31–46).

Mission or Maintenance?

The church struggles to maintain a delicate balance between mission and maintenance. The mission of the church to proclaim the gospel in season and out requires forgiving, healing, challenging, supporting, nurturing, informing, and forming. The maintenance of the church demands organization, structures, laws, budgets, personnel boards, fiscal responsibility, and hierarchy, all of which should be devoted to making the mission possible and successful. As with any institution, the necessity for maintenance can easily obscure or overcome the more foundational goals of the mission so that the church expends its energy and the talent of its members on the preservation of institutional identity, character, and longevity. The perennial temptation seducing the church remains the regularity with which the gospel vision is interrupted or displaced by quotidian concerns that often

assume an unmerited significance—a leaky roof requires fixing, a personnel decision leads to consultations, a church or a diocese needs a budget, a
bishop cannot work without a staff. Structures are necessary but they have
the potential, even the tendency if left unchecked, to become ends instead of
means. They also furnish a defensible distraction from the mission of
preaching the gospel.

Mother Teresa ran the Missionary Sisters of Charity without a computer or even a typewriter. While it is unrealistic for the church to follow such
a practice, it is equally unrealistic for it to operate in the same way as a for-
profit corporation. The real danger exists that the church will spend the
bulk of its energy and efforts preserving its power, its structure, its institutional presence. Inordinate attention to rules and regulations may stifle creativity and undermine the belief that the Holy Spirit permeates the church,
giving it a prophetic charism. Jesus's parables consistently surprise the hear-
er because the unexpected emerges. A church that prefers maintenance to
mission will not provide the unexpected prophetic voice that society needs
to hear. It will be too busy with its own self-preservation.

The prophetic role of the church demands that it distance itself from
society; its institutional role requires it to be an integral part of society. The
church's primary concern cannot be itself, yet it risks deterioration if it fails
to attend to internal necessities. Structure insures continuity but impedes
creativity. The institutional church should not seek to control its members,
but it risks a desultory path if it neglects to hold them accountable to some
degree. Without denying that the people of God are the church, an institutional expression of this reality is necessary. The church only represents the
reign of God to the world; it is not identical to it. It must humbly admit
when it is wrong, forcefully pursue God's justice in the land, and promote
an open dialogue among its own and with the world at large. Its pronouncements must be relevant without sacrificing principle. It must hear
the world and be heard, comfort and challenge, stand firm yet be open to
change.

Filled with paradoxes in its history, the church is the home of monks
and contemplatives; denouncer of heretics and proclaimer of saints; the
people of God and a hierarchy of bishops; sometimes a home for the poor
and sometimes a tax deduction for the wealthy; nurturer of Augustine,
Aquinas, Teresa of Avila, and Dorothy Day; Daniel Berrigan, Andrew
Greeley, and Antonin Scalia; bastion of male leadership under the patronage of Mary; a pilgrim people and the most enduring institution in human
history; led by the Spirit, governed by canon law; called to holiness, filled

with sinners; comforter of the sick, challenger of the healthy; a sacrament of salvation and a social construction of reality.

The church is in many ways a complex set of paradoxes. Different Catholics have different experiences and expectations of the church. Following the insights of the American theologian Avery Dulles in his now classic work *Models of the Church*,[36] it is possible to examine the church from multiple perspectives. Some would say that the church is above all a community, adopting Vatican II language of the people of God which displaced earlier descriptions like "a perfect society." The church as community vision values the growth of the individual as part of a larger body that is united as much by relationships among members as by their corporate relationship to Christ. The development of community is as important as the message and mission; in many ways community building is the mission.

Some view the church as other-directed, that is as servant to the world. It is a minority in service to the majority, a light to lighten the world. The church is an agent of social change upholding a gospel of action as well as proclamation. For these, the church should not be busy so much with teaching catechism or organizing pot-luck suppers as with trying to change the social structures that permit racial injustice, government bureaucracy that hurts the poor, or war. In this view, priests and laity should spend less time in worship and ritual and more time in soup kitchens. For the church to be a sign of the kingdom of God, it must be about the task of transforming society.

For others, however, the church is primarily neither community nor servant, it is institution. The church is the pope and the bishops, the priests, sisters, and brothers, the schools and the parishes. In order to function effectively, the church needs an identifiable structure. The church with its authority, magisterium, and organization is *the* church. They argue that no ideal or vision can perdure without a structure to carry it forward to the next generation.

Still others identify the church as herald of the Good News of Jesus Christ. Its duty is to proclaim and save. They say that the world is sorely in need of hearing the gospel, the Good News of the death and resurrection of Jesus, and if we do not announce it, who will? Others may form community, or serve the poor, as well as or better than Catholics do. The church is here first and foremost to proclaim Jesus as Lord.

A final group view the church as sacrament. In Edward Schillebeeckx's terms, it is the "sacrament of encounter with God."[37] The charisma of the church is to be holy and facilitate communion with Christ through worship and sacraments. The church is holy and a place to put one in touch with the sacred. It is the place where sacraments are dispensed to the faithful. Therefore it should be about the cultivation of piety and the sanctification of its members. It is not organizational or communal primarily; it is religious.

To those who see in the church different possibilities, the words of the New Testament writer Paul, in his first letter to the Corinthians, help to explain why the church has so many dimensions. "There are different gifts but the same spirit; there are different ministries but the same Lord; there are different works but the same God who accomplishes all of them in every one of us" (1 Cor. 12:4–7).

CHAPTER EIGHT

Catholic Popular Culture

Catholicism represents not only a "culture within a culture," but it also interacts with and influences American culture as a whole. There is a symbiotic relationship in which Catholics are assimilated into American culture, and American culture assimilates a Catholic presence. For instance, the majority of Catholic school-age children attend public schools and are influenced by the larger culture represented by public schools. Yet a sizable number of non-Catholic children attend Catholic schools and are exposed to and influenced by Catholic culture. While the line between the common culture and Catholic culture is much finer in the second half of the twentieth century than it was in the first half, it still exists. In some areas (schools, newspapers, and hospitals, for example), the church continues operations that parallel those of the common culture. In other domains (politics, economics, and morality, for example), the church seeks to influence decision making, policies, and structures. There exists, then, both a Catholic culture and Catholic culture's influence beyond the Catholic community.

The number of instances of this relation between the two cultures is too numerous to describe or investigate. This chapter explores a few of the ways in which Catholicism manifests a separate cultural entity and some of the ways in which it influences popular American culture.

The Church and the Media

Print

Since the advent of the printing press and the publication of the first Gutenberg Bibles, the church has had an interest in putting its message in print.

The oldest Catholic newspaper in this country, *Le Propagateur Catholique*, was published in New Orleans in 1810. The pioneer Catholic newspaper in English, *United States Catholic Miscellany*, appeared in Charleston, South Carolina, in 1822. Today in America there is a vast publishing industry connected to Catholicism; some of it educates, some analyzes, some proselytizes, and some criticizes.

At the local level, every diocese in America has its own newspaper. These papers usually are weeklies designed to keep the local Catholic population informed. They regularly cover news from the Vatican, publish official church statements from Rome, communicate statements and developments originating from the National Conference of Catholic Bishops, cover national news that relates to Catholics or issues of concern to Catholics, and perhaps most important, act as a voice for the local bishop and diocese. These papers generally avoid controversial reporting and print only those stories that are consistent with church policy. Some of these diocesan papers carry syndicated columns written by theologians, clergy, religious, or lay persons. The subject matter of these articles is, therefore, not under the control of the local editor, and occasionally controversial subjects are covered in these articles. Sometimes these papers are quite provincial in their coverage with headlines such as "Six People Die in Crash, Two Catholic." This biased provincialism has its counterpart in the secular press when a story with an international scope identifies only the Americans involved.

If editors deem the subject matter or analysis to be inappropriate they can omit the column from their paper. Controversial priest-sociologist and novelist Andrew Greeley experienced such a boycott of his column by a number of Catholic newspapers. The editor of a diocesan newspaper may be a member of the diocesan clergy, a sister or a lay person, but the publisher is the diocese or bishop. The objective is to have a copy of this paper in each Catholic home in the diocese each week. Funding such an ambition is a different story, however. Reliance upon individual subscriptions leaves it to the choice (and the budget) of individual churchgoers or families. To subvene this, some dioceses circulate their papers through the parishes, either by distributing them after masses in the foyer of the church or having them sent directly to registered parishioners and billing the parish for the cost. Advertising covers some of the cost of publishing a diocesan paper, but with the increasing costs of printing, it is often not enough to cover expenses, and many papers require a subsidy from the diocese.[1]

In addition to local newspapers, there are a few national Catholic newspapers. These tend to fall along ideological lines. Two of the most well known are the *Wanderer*, favored by conservatives, and the *National Catholic Reporter*, which takes a liberal position on most issues. These weeklies are run as mail-order operations. *NCR* began in October 1964 in response to the Second Vatican Council. It is an independent paper, edited and published in Kansas City, Missouri, by lay people. The paper also maintains a website (NCR Online). Circulation is approximately 50,000. The same organization publishes Sheed and Ward books, Credence Cassettes, the liturgical magazine *Celebration*, and the magazine *Praying*. The *Wanderer*, begun in 1867, has a current circulation of approximately 37,000.

In addition to newspapers and books, Catholic weekly magazines reach a number of readers, Catholic and non-Catholic alike. *Commonweal* and *America* tend toward the liberal side and *Crisis* and *Our Sunday Visitor* toward the conservative. *Commonweal* is edited by Catholic lay people, and *America* is a Jesuit publication. *Origins*, a publication of the bishops, is a weekly resource useful in obtaining official information and views of the bishops. It publishes papal documents and often provides insightful commentaries by theologians and bishops.

The Catholic Press Association in the United States was founded in the nineteenth century "for the purpose of stationing agents at important news centres who should telegraph truthful, full and early intelligence of events interesting to the faithful."[2] The association continues its original mission to report news interesting to Catholics and affecting the church. The Catholic Book Publishers Association publishes a Catholic Bestsellers list under the categories Hardcover, Paperback, and Children and Young People.

The Catholic book industry is extensive and diverse, ranging from Bibles to textbooks. A large commercial interest in religious education is served by publishers such as Sadlier and Silver Burdett. Prayer books, hymnals, sacramentaries, lectionaries, and ritual books abound for liturgical use. Although contemporary Catholic theologians are not constrained to publish their work with Catholic presses, and many prominent theologians use secular or traditionally Protestant publishing houses, a number of Catholic presses are dedicated to theology and spirituality, some prominent ones being Paulist Press, Orbis, and Sheed and Ward. These are complemented by university presses such as those of the Catholic University of America and Loyola University of Chicago, which publish works primarily for scholars.

The church exerts some control over the content of Catholic books by granting its imprimatur to those books that it approves, meaning that they contain nothing contrary to faith and morals and are unlikely to spiritually or theologically misinform, and thus harm, readers.[3] In addition, the church indicates that a book is free from doctrinal error by giving it a *nihil obstat*, though this does not constitute an endorsement of the book. The imprimatur is granted by a bishop and the *nihil obstat* is given by a theologian who is charged by the bishop with this responsibility. While this system remains in place, the 1983 revised code of canon law significantly narrowed the scope of the imprimatur to works that enjoy the privilege of a semi-official capacity, meaning biblical and liturgical texts, prayerbooks, catechisms, textbooks for religious education, and books displayed or sold in churches. In order to receive an imprimatur, the work must agree with the teaching of the Church on faith and morals as proposed by the magisterium. The church's enforcement of this regulation caused a stir in a few instances, the most noteworthy when it withdrew the imprimatur in 1984 from a popular catechetical work by Anthony Wilhelm, *Christ Among Us*.[4] Canon lawyer James Coriden wrote: "This revised standard means that the imprimatur now comes closer to the status of a seal of approval from writings which are not at all at variance with official teachings."[5]

In practice many theologians do not seek the imprimatur or *nihil obstat*, and the majority of Catholic laity in America either do not know about the system or do not particularly care if a book has these ecclesiastical approvals or not. In the case of a Catholic publisher for religious education texts, however, lack of these approvals can be the death knell for a religious education textbook since these are not speculative theology but are specifically intended to offer the official teachings of the church.

Much of the material published in national and local Catholic newspapers originates from the Catholic News Service (CNS), the oldest and largest news wire service. Both print and broadcast media (including Vatican Radio) rely on CNS for stories about Catholicism and reports on issues relating to Catholics. CNS was created by the U.S. bishops in 1920 and operates under the jurisdiction of the United States Catholic Conference but maintains editorial and financial independence. In addition to its own cadre of reporters, CNS maintains professional ties with other U.S. and international news organizations in order to cover the world as accurately and fully as possible.

Film

The movie-going habits of Catholics who grew up before and during Vatican II were influenced by the National Legion of Decency, an office funded by the American bishops to monitor and assess the moral content of movies. Indeed, as James Skinner, a Canadian professor of film and history attests in his book *The Cross and the Cinema*, "More than any other expressive art form or popular entertainment, the motion picture has had to bear the continuous scrutiny of moral watchdogs."[6]

Shortly after the beginning of widespread distribution of "talkies" in the late 1920s, the church began to advocate publicly for censorship of films. Influential American bishops such as John Cantwell of Los Angeles (the home of the burgeoning movie industry), in collusion with the wealthy publisher, Martin Quigley Sr., convinced the newly appointed Apostolic Delegate to the United States, Most Reverend Amleto Giovanni Cicognani, "to indict the motion picture business in his first public utterance at a Catholic Charities convention in New York in October 1933."[7] At the same time, the bishops formed an Episcopal Committee on Motion Pictures that became the predecessor to the Legion of Decency. Many bishops and priests were already unilaterally condemning the movie industry and decrying individual films from their pulpits with significant results, as revenues for these films fell dramatically. To introduce consistency and to shift the onus from the industry to the individual, the bishops' committee formed the Legion of Decency that asked each Catholic to pledge the following oath:

I wish to join the Legion of Decency, which condemns vile and unwholesome motion moving pictures. I unite with all who protest against them as a grave menace to youth, to home life, to country and religion.

I condemn absolutely those salacious motion pictures which, with other degrading agencies, are corrupting public morals and promoting a sex mania in our land.

I shall do all that I can to arouse public opinion against the portrayal of vice as a normal condition of affairs and against depicting criminals of any class as heroes and heroines, presenting their filthy philosophy of life as something acceptable to decent men and women.

I unite with all who condemn the display of suggestive advertisements on billboards, at theater entrances and the favorable notices given to immoral motion pictures.

Considering these evils, I hereby promise to remain away from all motion pictures except those which do not offend decency and Christian morality. I promise further to secure as many members as possible for the Legion of Decency.

I make this protest in a spirit of self-respect, and with the conviction that the American public does not demand filthy pictures, but clean entertainment and educational features.[8]

On every December 8 for years, millions of Catholics took an abridged version of this pledge during the mass honoring Mary's "Immaculate Conception." To assist them in their discrimination when choosing movies, and to rectify the inequities of individual dioceses issuing lists of acceptable and unacceptable films, the Legion of Decency established a rating system to assess films. Located in New York near St. Patrick's Cathedral, the organization was staffed by members of the International Federation of Catholic Alumnae, a group that had been rating movies under two positive categories, suitable for viewing in a church hall or suitable for mature audiences, since 1924. In 1935 they established the following classification system: A-1—Morally Unobjectionable for General Patronage; A-2—Morally Unobjectionable for Adults; B—Morally Objectionable in Part for All; C—Morally Objectionable for All (Condemned). Three years later they added S. C. (Special Category, changed to A-4 in 1963) to cover films used in education, or directed to a specific audience such as doctors, that were explicit but not morally objectionable in content. In 1957 they redefined A-2 to include adolescents and added A-3—Morally Unobjectionable for Adults.

Concurrent with the formation of the Legion of Decency, and in response to the same issue of censorship, the motion picture industry established its own Production Code Administration that served the function of self-regulation. This system had a significant impact on the industry. "Some pictures had been withdrawn and were destined not to see the light of day for a generation; others were aborted in the script-writing stage because of the impossibility of creating a finished product acceptable to the Production Code Administration; still others were scrubbed clean before being allowed to venture into first-run release."[9] For example, scenes of the bedroom, even that of a married couple, always showed twin beds.

While the Legion of Decency's pledge may strike the contemporary Catholic moviegoer as an excessive form of censorship, it does find an echo today in many people's disenchantment with the gratuitous violence that seems ubiquitous in contemporary formulaic films that have requisite car chases, explosions, and excessively armed heroes, although these movies continue to be box office successes. What appears to be less disturbing to the contemporary viewer is the treatment of sexual matters on screen. At the time of the foundation of the Legion of Decency, in the Catholic mind, objectionable subject matter included references to divorce, extra-marital or pre-marital sex, exposure of a woman's legs, and even on-screen kisses lasting longer than a few seconds.

In 1934 Cardinal Dennis Dougherty of Philadelphia took the drastic measure of forbidding Catholics in his archdiocese from going to the movies at all, saying that movie theaters constituted an "occasion of sin."[10] Compliant Catholics obeyed the cardinal's prohibition. Some Protestants joined the protest, causing business to decline 40 percent and forcing some movie theaters to close. Even personal visits from wealthy movie industry mogul Samuel Goldwyn could not persuade Dougherty to lift his prohibition.

The combined Production Code and the Legion of Decency maintained their moral hegemony over the movie industry into the 1950s. After much wrangling, some film makers, such as Howard Hughes (producer of *The Outlaw*, 1946) and studios such as United Artists, ignored the ratings system. European films, in which the standards of morality appeared more lenient, like Fellini's *La Dolce Vita*, were also increasingly making their way into American theaters. Even though intense pressure was exerted on movie theaters not to show such films, profit motives and the preferences of the viewing public often won out. Post-World War II moviegoers wanted more realistic films. As historian Frank Walsh notes "[T]he regulations [Production Code] drafted during the first year of the Great Depression seemed out of date in the postwar era."[11] In 1956, the Production Code was liberalized, and in 1959 the Legion of Decency's pledge was rewritten. In 1965 the Legion changed its name to the more innocuous National Catholic Office for Motion Pictures.[12] By 1970 parishes no longer led parishioners in the pledge. In 1982, B and C ratings were replaced by an O (morally offensive) rating. The Office for Film and Broadcasting of the United States Catholic Conference continues to rate movies today, although most post-Vatican II Catholics are neither cognizant of the church's code nor interested in the church's ratings of the moral content of movies.

In addition to diocesan newspapers, movie reviews are available on the World Wide Web via the internet. It is hardly surprising that a sampling of reviews in March 1997 from the Motion Picture office of the bishops compared with the same films as reviewed in the *Washington Post*[13] reveals that the church continues to maintain a stricter code. For example, the newspaper, under the heading "Okay for 6 and Up," comments the following about the movie *That Darn Cat* (PG): "Teen and her cat solve kidnapping in fairly entertaining remake. Sensitive portrayal of cranky teenhood. Less scary than the 1965 version." Under the heading "Preferably 10 and Up" it describes *Vegas Vacation* thus: "Lamest installment of vacation spoofs, though naive Griswold family still wins a few laughs. Mild comic sexual innuendo; crude language."

The Office of Film and Broadcasting, an arm of the Conference of Catholic Bishops and the United States Catholic Conference that is currently responsible for rating films and television programs, writes this about *That Darn Cat*: "Because of frequent slapstick violence, the U.S. Catholic Conference classification is A-II—adults and adolescents. The Motion Picture Association of America rating is PG—parental guidance suggested. *That Darn Cat* is a shoddy remake of the 1965 Disney comedy in which a teenager is convinced her cat has found a clue to the whereabouts of a kidnap victim, then gets a hapless FBI agent to follow the frisky feline around town. The resulting mayhem and chaos is overdone in a mistaken attempt at humor." Of *Vegas Vacation* it says: "Because of comic sexual innuendo, the allure of gambling and mild profanity, the U. S. Catholic Conference classification is A-III—adults. The Motion Picture Association rating is PG— parental guidance suggested. *Vegas Vacation* is a witless comedy with Chevy Chase and Beverly D'Angelo as the parents of two teenagers on the loose in a Vegas gambling resort. Their misadventures are mostly dull, entirely predictable and woefully unamusing."

As is evident from this sampling of ratings, the church is stricter than both the film industry and the news media when evaluating movies on a moral scale. However, as long as such films continue to fill theaters and the coffers of the film industry, the American public, Catholics included, is not likely to boycott violent movies, and long ago they gave up their inhibitions about sex on the screen.

The movie industry itself, however, introduced a new rating system in 1968, in response to the public's desire to know whether a film contained nudity, inappropriate language, or violence. In 1997, after public pressure and congressional inquiries, the television industry followed suit with a voluntary ratings system for television programs. One of the reasons for the new system was that in the 1990s television shows, particularly those shown after nine at night, had become more, not less, explicit. Warnings euphemistically alert viewers to "adult" language and situations.

The battle for moral control of the big screen continues today, even if the heyday of the church as a voice that receives a wide hearing is over. In February 1992, Cardinal Roger Mahoney, archbishop of Los Angeles, "told the Anti-Pornography Coalition that the motion picture industry was an 'assault against the values held by the vast majority of the people in American society,' "[14] and requested that the Hollywood Production Code be rein-stated. The church continued to be concerned about the influence of films on morality in an era when advocates of censorship were about to attempt unsuccessfully to limit pornography on the internet, a medium without the history and cultural influence of films, but an increasingly influential one. As historian Gregory Black comments in his book, *Hollywood Censored*: "Cardinal Mahoney's plea is for a return to those heady days when prelates and censors, who presumed they spoke for the American people, controlled what people saw and heard at the movies."[15]

Pre-Vatican II and Vatican II Catholics will remember well the influ-ence of the church in the entertainment sphere. Parents regularly consulted the weekly list of film ratings in the diocesan newspaper before they would allow their children to go to the movies. They themselves would not want to be seen coming out of a movie theater that was showing a movie that had been condemned by the Legion of Decency. Well-known films like *The Blue Angel* (1930) with Marlene Dietrich, *Two-Faced Woman* (1941) with Greta Garbo, and *The Pawnbroker* (1965) with Rod Steiger were condemned, or altered before distribution in order to receive a respectable rating. The church had a huge influence over this element of American culture. The Vatican was no less interested in the influence that films were having on Catholics. Pope Pius XII, speaking to the World Congress of the World Union of Catholic Women's Organizations in Rome in 1957, told them to hold fast to the truth that they are in a fundamental relationship to God "when you find yourselves at the mercy of the ebb and flow of ideas which novels, movies, and theater constantly spread among the masses and which impart a thoroughly vitiated concept of womanhood."[16]

Cecil B. DeMille's *The Ten Commandments* is the last movie with a reli-gious theme that some older Catholics have seen or can name. Yet there have been other films of note that have had a Christian theme, if not specif-ically Catholic. In the 1960s, *Godspell* was a successful Broadway play and a movie casting Jesus in the figure of a carefree clown. This was followed on stage and film by the very human characterization of Jesus in *Jesus Christ Superstar* in 1973. These two plays also enjoyed commercially successful soundtracks. Franco Zeffirelli's *Jesus of Nazareth* (1978), filmed in the Holy Land, attempted to be aesthetically sensitive and theologically accurate. The controversial director, Martin Scorsese, adapted the Kazantzakis novel *The Last Temptation of Christ* for the screen in 1988. The film included a contro-versial dream scene in which Jesus marries Mary Magdalene, rallying some Catholics to stage old-fashioned protests outside theater entrances. In 1988, the film *Romero* chronicled the life and death by assassination of the El Salvador bishop and champion of human rights Oscar Romero.[17] The 1989 film *Jesus of Montreal* depicted a contemporary setting for a parallel story to the gospels. The 1995 film *The Priest* engendered the strongest reaction. The movie depicts a pastor who is sleeping with his housekeeper, an alcoholic priest, a young priest who struggles with his homosexuality, and an uncaring bishop—hardly an endearing image of men of the cloth. It is a far cry from the "Catholic" Bing Crosby 1940s films *Going My Way* and *The Bells of St. Mary's*, which depicted priests as moral giants and gentle souls, and won a host of Oscars including best actor (Crosby) and best picture (*Going My Way*). The current generation of film makers no longer maintains the self-imposed strictures that guided studios at least until the 1960s. In that era films were not allowed to ridicule faith, priests, or ministers, and rituals commanded a respectful representation.[18] Today the film and the television industry is less concerned about offending religious sensibilities.

Television

The church has not ignored the opportunity to proselytize presented by the medium of television. Alongside the names Billy Graham, Jim Bakker, and Jimmy Swaggert stand Bishop Fulton J. Sheen and Mother Angelica. In the 1930s, Sheen, a priest from the diocese of Peoria, Illinois, became a weekly guest in the home of millions of Catholics and others on his radio show "The Catholic Hour." From 1951 to 1957 he had a television show called "Life Is Worth Living," and in 1966 another one called "the Bishop Sheen Program" (he was named auxiliary bishop of the archdiocese of New York in 1951 and bishop of Rochester, New York, in 1966). A spellbinding preacher, Sheen brought the message, and was the public face of Catholicism to a generation of Catholics and non-Catholics alike.

On August 15, 1981, Eternal Word Television Network began on cable television. Since its humble beginnings, EWTN evolved into the largest religious cable network, broadcasting to over 55 million homes in 38 countries on 1,500 cable systems. The charismatic figure of the network is Mother Angelica. Her show "Mother Angelica Live" has brought a conservative Catholicism into millions of American homes. In addition, programming includes a teaching series on the Catholic Catechism called "Pillars of Faith," and a teen-young adult segment called "Life on the Rock." The network, and Mother Angelica in particular, has used the medium of cable television effectively. Her conservative views, however, coupled with her occa-

The well-known host of Eternal Word Television Network, Mother Angelica, brings traditional Catholicism into millions of American homes daily. CATHOLIC NEWS SERVICE

sional criticism of the positions of some prelates, has drawn unwanted attention from a few bishops. After she criticized the pastoral letter on Sunday liturgy issued by Cardinal Roger Mahoney of Los Angeles on her program of November 12, 1997, calling upon Catholics in Los Angeles to practice "zero obedience" to the letter, Cardinal Mahoney complained to the Vatican about her. The cardinal wanted her to exhibit more deference to the bishops' teaching authority. In a later show (November 18) she expressed regret for her remarks.[19]

Not all efforts to use the mass media succeed. In 1995, after thirteen years of operation and a $10 million investment, the bishops discontinued their television venture, the Catholic Telecommunications Network of America. In this case there was someone willing to try to fill the void. In

1996 Bishop Charles Grahmann and producer Bobbie Cavnar of Dallas, Texas, launched ICN, the International Catholic Network, with private donations.

Prime time television introduced a new show, *Nothing Sacred*, on ABC in the fall of 1997. The main character, a young priest nicknamed Father Ray (played by Kevin Anderson), struggles with his calling to be a selfless minister to God's people, and with his own doubts about some of the church's teachings, especially those dealing with sexuality. Even before the show aired, the Catholic League criticized the pilot for what it considered a negative portrayal of the priesthood, and after the first episode Cardinal Hickey of Washington in his weekly column described the main character as a "stereotypical, cardboard figure of a priest, a cipher for someone's partially formed idea of what a priest is like."[20] The New York-based Catholic League for Religious and Civil Rights coordinated a petition drive via its website[21] to urge sponsors to cancel their advertisements on the show. Several, including national brands Dupont and Kmart, fearing a customer backlash, pulled their ads from the show. The *Tidings*, the newspaper of the archdiocese of Los Angeles, editorialized against the action of the Catholic League; and Cardinal Roger Mahoney personally greeted Kevin Anderson at a mass in Los Angeles during which he said that he thought the show invites people to discuss the church. Mahoney's archdiocese includes Hollywood, and he is the author of a 1992 pastoral letter titled "Filmmakers, Film Viewers: Their Challenges and Opportunities."[22] The show received poor ratings (whether due to its quality or the effects of the Catholic League-led boycott is unclear), causing ABC to cancel it in March 1998.

Radio

Despite the ubiquitous character of television and the information revolution engendered by the computer, radio remains an important medium of communication for the church. In the heyday of radio the church's best-known voice was that of Father Charles E. Coughlin, a pastor from Royal Oak, Michigan, who attracted an audience of millions with his Sunday radio broadcasts. Coughlin did not shy away from political affairs. Nor was he averse to changing his mind and the minds of his listeners. At the beginning of the Roosevelt years he was an ardent supporter of the New Deal. Over time he retreated from Roosevelt and saw the New Deal as a raw deal for Americans. He became increasingly fearful of communism; his message turned unapologetically anti-Semitic and his politics sympathetic to Hitler.

His inflammatory rhetoric drew so much attention to the church that Cardinal Mundelein of Chicago stepped in to denounce Coughlin's message. Shortly after America's entrance into World War II Coughlin left the air and was no longer a voice to or for Catholics.

Today with high definition television, surround-sound home systems, the VCR, and DVD, radio is no longer the dominant medium that it was in the 1930s. The Catholic presence on radio has not disappeared, however. In March 1996 EWTN began broadcasting in English and Spanish to AM and FM stations around the world via the satellite reach of the established television network. Programming includes a news service that keeps Catholics informed of papal pronouncements and stories of interest to Catholics. An organization called UndaUSA (*unda* is Latin for wave), part of UndaWorld, the International Catholic Association for Radio and Television, began in 1972 in the United States with national offices in Dayton, Ohio. The organization brings together writers, directors, producers, media specialists, and students who want to further the mission of the church through electronic media. The Catholic Broadcasters Association also seeks to bring the gospel to Americans via the air waves.

Catholicism On-Line

In the document *Communio et Progressio* (The Church and Computer Culture), issued in conjunction with World Communications Day on May 27, 1989, Pope John Paul II wrote:

> With the advent of computer telecommunications and what are known as computer participation systems, the Church is offered further means for fulfilling her mission. Methods of facilitating communication and dialogue among her own members can strengthen the bonds of unity between them. Immediate access to information makes it possible for her to deepen her dialogue with the contemporary world. In the new "computer culture" the Church can more readily inform the world of her beliefs and explain the reasons for her stance on any given issue or event.[23]

Like many other institutions, the church took a few years to catch on to the online age of internet connection and websites. Today, however, the universal church, and the American church in particular, is connected to and invested in modern communications technology. A brief glance at the elec-

The cast of the television show *Nothing Sacred* brought a liberal view of contemporary Catholicism to network TV.
PHOTOFEST

tronic sources appendix in this book will demonstrate how committed the church is to getting its message across electronically.

From the Vatican to the National Conference of Catholic Bishops, Catholics now have electronic access to a wealth of information from and about the church. For example, Catholic Online[24] attempts to fulfill the pope's wishes for instant access to information and for loyalty:

> Catholic Online proudly declares our desire always to be distinguished and well-known for a particularly "Catholic" Christian character. We openly proclaim our faithfulness to the Holy Father, Pope John Paul II and his successors, in union with the Catholic Bishops throughout the world. The Catholic laity and clergy who administer and staff Catholic Online are convinced that, in the tradition of the Church's always bold willingness to make use of means of social communication available in every age of her mission of evangelization, the new and challenging medium of the Internet and cyberspace must have a strong, visible and above all faithful Catholic presence embracing both the Eastern and Western Catholic traditions and Churches.

The Vatican Web Page,[25] available in six languages (English, Dutch, French, Spanish, Italian, and Portuguese), posts important papal documents, includes news and an on-line tour of the Vatican Museum. The book *Catholicism on the Web* by the editor of the *National Catholic Reporter*, Thomas Fox, lists over five hundred Catholic websites, and the number is growing daily.[26] The proliferation of Catholic websites has some church officials worried. In February 1997, Cardinal Roger Mahoney of Los Angeles voiced his concern to the Pontifical Council for Social Communications at the Vatican. "There are too many 'Catholic websites and services' that are questionable" he wrote. "The Church needs to take immediate steps to authorize and authenticate electronic services that utilize the name 'Catholic,' while disallowing those that are illegitimate and so informing unsuspecting users."[27]

Those who operate the Catholic Online website are aware of the vagaries of cyberspace and have already anticipated Cardinal Mahoney's warning, adding this caveat:

> [I]t may happen from time to time that Catholic Online might inadvertently provide a link or list a site for some individual or organization which espouses teachings not consistent with its manifestly expressed goals or which conflict with Catholic teachings or the Church's duly appointed pastors in an inappropriate way. In that case, recognizing that at times errors can be made, the staff and administrators of Catholic Online humbly request your cooperation and understanding, and furthermore invite you to inform us without delay of anything unsuitable which may have through oversight been included in our menus and web pages so that they may be opportunely reviewed and reevaluated.

As with virtually all dimensions of American life, computers provide new avenues for information, creativity, conflict, proselytization, and connection for the church. The American bishops, most dioceses, and many parishes already have websites by which they can disseminate information, invite interaction, and extend the church's reach into the home and workplace in new ways. The church's considerable collection of art is accessible via computer, and Rome can communicate its message worldwide without delay and without the pope having to leave the Vatican. Where they do not exist already, in the near future religious education programs will have an on-line component, parish registration will take place on-line, and the minutes of parish committee meetings will be posted on the web as parishes now post copies of their weekly bulletin. While none of this activity is the equivalent of personal contact, and the church is not about to become a virtual community, it does speed communication and provide more ready access to information. Even in the tradition-laden domain of Catholicism, it is a brave new world.

Literature

The literary world in America has always been dominated by writers from a Protestant background. Even as late as the latter part of the nineteenth century, the ghosts of American Puritanism were still being wrestled with in the novels of Nathaniel Hawthorne and the stories of Mary Wilkins Freeman—both descendants of American Puritans. It was not until the twentieth century that Catholic writers really began to lay claim to their own corner of the literary world. From the beginning of the century, as greater numbers of European Catholic immigrants poured into the country, Catholics could boast at least one prominent writer in every literary generation. Though many, like Kate Chopin, F. Scott Fitzgerald, and Jack Kerouac, were more Catholic by birth than practice, others consciously worked at creating a distinctly Catholic identity. Most eminent among these were Flannery O'Connor and Walker Percy (a convert to Catholicism), both Southern and both writing in the middle part of the century. In novels like O'Connor's *The Violent Bear It Away* and Percy's *The Moviegoer*, characters live desperate lives in search of grace and salvation in a world that leans less toward the sacred than the profane. Together, O'Connor and Percy can be credited with inaugurating the modern Catholic literary tradition in America.

Since the 1960s that tradition has come into its own. In recent years, American Catholic writers have been among those receiving the highest literary awards. For example, Pulitzer Prizes for Literature went to John Kennedy Toole in 1981 for *A Confederacy of Dunces*, William Kennedy in 1984 for *Ironweed*, and Oscar Hijuelos in 1990 for *The Mambo Kings Play Songs of Love*. In 1997, the National Book Award for general nonfiction went to James Carroll for *An American Requiem*, and the PEN/Faulkner Award for fiction went to Ron Hansen for *Atticus*. Today among critically acclaimed Catholic writers like Hansen and Carroll, Alice McDermott, and Andre Dubus, there is an effort to create literature that concerns itself with the sacramentality of everyday life. In the pages of their books, readers almost always find themselves on holy ground, even when the stories have to do with the breakup of a marriage or the breakdown of a religious vocation. As writers they are not afraid to voice their doubts, and yet they maintain their belief in a God who loves and forgives and brings meaning to the world. That they are making the right connections is evidenced by their popularity with critics and readers of all faiths.

Two American Catholic writers whose novels fall short of being literary masterpieces but consistently appear on the bestseller lists are Andrew Greeley and Joseph Girzone. Both are Catholic priests (thought Girzone is no longer in active ministry) and both use their novels to teach lessons of faith. The similarities end there, however. Greeley, a respected sociologist, is also a prolific writer of racy mass-market novels. Competing in the same market as Danielle Steel, Greeley offers his readers strong Irish-American (often clerical) heroes, beautiful Irish-American heroines, and enough sex to keep readers interested. By his own admission, Greeley is not trying to write great literature. Instead, he is trying to bring spiritual truths to people who might never consider picking up the Bible or the *Catechism of the Catholic Church*.

This is true also of Girzone. His books, particularly his "Joshua" novels, have become staples in both general and Christian bookstores. The character of Joshua is Christ come back to earth in the person of a simple but wise and miraculous carpenter. The stories tend to be gentle and goodhearted parables that over and over answer the question "What would Jesus do?" They are sometimes critical of the Catholic establishment and are aimed at an ecumenical readership, where they have found a home with many evangelical Christians. Like Greeley, Girzone is mostly concerned with spreading the Gospel message.

A Cultural Force and the Force of Culture

As Catholics assimilate into the larger culture, along with many other groups, distinguishing characteristics fade. Catholics blend in with others. Larger cultural forces influence them as they do all Americans. Their need for a Catholic ghetto now past, many attempt to forget that one ever existed. Assimilation hastens their homogenization. A shrinking minority of Catholic children attend parochial schools. Catholics, outsiders for most of American history, now appear as insiders in so many dimensions that affect the larger American culture. They hold key positions in publishing, the film industry, television, and technology, to name a few of the sectors that significantly influence the larger culture.

The church represents, on the one hand, a cultural force, and on the other, an institution shaped by the force of culture. While the church no longer exhibits the sway on culture that it did in the pre-Vatican II era when it deeply and directly influenced the cultural lives of Catholics and, in an incidental way, many non-Catholics, it still constitutes a presence and influence. As long as networks air programs like "Nothing Sacred," Catholics tune into cable shows featuring Mother Angelica, or the popular British art critic Sister Wendy, studios produce movies like *The Priest* and *Agnes of God*, publishers continue to release novels with Catholic themes like those of Greeley and Carroll, newspapers like the *New York Times* and the *Atlanta Constitution* carry stories about the pope, the bishops, or the laity, the church maintains a place in popular culture. Every time a Catholic signs a petition after mass to stop partial-birth abortion, assisted suicide, or capital punishment, the church seeks to influence culture. But, at the same time, the culture exerts a strong influence on Catholics. MTV, the nightly news, newspapers, books, films, the internet, advertising, and so many other cultural forces shape the way Catholics think and behave, and influence the ways in which Catholicism is viewed by everyone in America.

Catholics still constitute a presence in the larger culture. Bishops publicly defend the sanctity of human life in all its phases. Many Catholics ask to be excused from work on Good Friday afternoon. Catholic newspapers and journals find their way onto coffee tables in many homes. Shreds of palm hang loosely behind crucifixes and holy pictures in bedrooms and kitchens. Children in every state wear uniforms identifying them as members of parochial schools. Catholic culture is not gone, but it may take a sensitive eye to see it in the twenty-first century.

CHAPTER NINE

Challenges

At the turn of the millennium the Roman Catholic Church in America faces the twenty-first century with many strengths, and not a few challenges. Catholics persistently identify with Catholicism, even if one third of them never bother to register in a parish and many disagree with some of the teaching of the church. The situation that the contemporary American church faces looms no larger on today's horizon than did those of previous eras. John Carroll nurtured an infant church amidst a host of troubles from lack of native clergy to the necessity to forge an American identity. The American church at the turn of the nineteenth century struggled with its identity vis-à-vis the Vatican. The social and ecclesial changes of the 1960s found the church struggling to embrace modernity without sacrificing its historical identity. At the end of the twentieth century the church experiences divisions and disagreements among some of its members and with its relationship to Rome. If history is a guide, then the American church will weather the present difficulties. It would be foolish to pretend that the church is without serious problems. It would be naive to hold that these problems are insurmountable.

Secularism has existed from at least the time of the Enlightenment, yet it has captured neither the majority of Americans in general nor American Catholics in particular. American Catholics are comfortable with their allegiance to both the church and the country as they have been throughout their history. They support the church with their energies and funds (though statistics indicate that they contribute less of their income today than in the past).[1] Most continue to find meaning in the liturgy, sacraments, and spiritual guidance offered.

At the same time, however, the church faces significant challenges which, if ignored or left unresolved, could result in deeper divisions, irreconcilable fragmentation, and costly defections. Is the Roman Catholic Church in America ready to embrace the new millennium? The answer is a dialectic yes and no. On the positive side, American Catholicism is deeply rooted in American culture, has a sizable constituency that is growing ever larger, is generally financially sound, and is more diverse than at any time in its history. On the negative side, the church continues to struggle with a number of long-standing intractable problems, and it faces new and sometimes more complicated challenges in the twenty-first century.

Some of the troubling problems are: the continued decline in the number of clergy and religious; the role of women in the church; the ethical and sexual conduct of clergy; the number of inactive Catholics and Catholics who are leaving the Roman Church for other Christian communions or (to a lesser degree) other religions; sexual and reproductive ethics (including but not limited to birth control, premarital sex, abortion, AIDS education, homosexuality); democratization of structures; church-state relations; ecumenical relations; secularism. Some of the challenges looming larger in the twenty-first century are: meeting the needs of the changing ethnic composition of the church (especially the growth in the Hispanic community); the roles and identities of Catholic schools and universities; tensions between the Vatican and America, relations with non-Christian religions, and bioethics.

The Church and Women

As noted in chapter 4, the Catholic Church's relationship to women is a troubled one. There is a long history of patriarchy in the Roman Catholic Church. Of the thirty-two doctors of the church (those who are acknowledged as having made great contributions theologically and spiritually such as Augustine and John Chrysostom), only three are women.[2] The contemporary church needs to listen more carefully to the voices of women—because they deserve to be heard after generations of being shut out and because the church cannot sustain itself without their continued contributions. If women are alienated from institutional identification, both women and the institution will suffer. Many women are not anxious for the demise of the church, but they are increasingly impatient with the Vatican's disposition toward women and the American hierarchy's inability to institute changes. Reflecting the frustration of many American women, one student wrote: "Holy Father, if you wish to save the church, if you truly believe in the full equality of humankind, then the church must change. As long as women continue to be the *subjects* of letters, *issues* and not people, *they* and not we, we will not be content. If the Catholic Church wants to survive, then it had better change quickly to include the lives and experiences of the women who comprise over half its mission."[3]

The church's intransigence on women's position in the institution has cost it the loyalty of many women. Leah Speltz in Wausaw, Wisconsin, converted to Catholicism from the Presbyterian denomination when she married a Catholic. She thought it a good idea to have a unified religious identification. After trying to raise three daughters in the church, Speltz left Catholicism and returned to the Presbyterian church in which women have been ordained since 1956 and where the local congregation was served by a woman pastor. Her daughters were confirmed at First Presbyterian.

Some within the church would dismiss these as "voices from the margin," but that would be an inaccurate assessment and an unwise decision. Women compose a significant proportion of the volunteer workforce of the church. They are also the mothers of seminarians and priests. If they are alienated, it is unlikely that they will encourage or support sons who are considering a vocation to the priesthood. Women are often the first teachers of the faith to their children. If they are alienated so may be the next generation of Catholics.

But these arguments are ancillary to their fundamental concern, which is justice. In a church that preaches justice, that opposes nuclear war, capital punishment, and racism, is it just to preclude women on the basis of gender, not competency, from assuming positions of authority in ordained ministry, they ask? Feminist theologians have informed, and in some cases awakened, the consciousness of Catholic women. What theology has not done, the broader culture has. Women's opportunities in education, the professions, and the personal realm have all expanded dramatically in the past thirty years. In the minds of many women, the church has simply not kept pace, and its arguments from tradition prove unconvincing.

If anything, the church's attempted prohibition of discussion of women's ordination galvanizes opposition, tempting them to withdraw whatever support they may be giving the institution. The Women's Ordination Conference, a Catholic advocacy group, printed and distributed surrogate dollar bills for women to deposit into the collection basket in lieu of their regular contribution. The bogus bills indicate that financial support is being withheld because of the church's unjust treatment of women. And it is not simply women who are concerned. As testified to in journalist and

Altar girls now outnumber boys in many parishes and dioceses.
AP PHOTO/ANDY ROGERS

Catholic parishioner Jim Naughton's book, *Catholics in Crisis*, men are willing to stand firm with them and to sacrifice for justice.[4] Naughton chronicles the story of how one man's protest of the prohibition of women's ordination ignited a firestorm that divided a parish and brought unwelcome
scrutiny from authorities.

One group that is keenly aware of the ambiguity that women feel about
the church is the Catholic Theological Society of America (CTSA) which
issued a statement in June 1997 during its annual meeting. The statement,
after a year of consultations and revisions, passed by a vote of 216 to 22
with 10 abstentions. It was a response to a ruling issued by the Vatican's
Congregation for the Doctrine of the Faith, headed by Cardinal Joseph
Ratzinger, that prohibited further public discussion of the ordination of
women. Peter Steinfels of the *New York Times* reported that "Leaders of the
society went out of their way to couch their arguments in tones respectful
of church doctrine and not set themselves up as . . . 'a counter-magisterial.'
"[5] Nevertheless, the statement claimed that discussion of the issue should
continue and that "legitimate questions" can be raised concerning the Vatican's arguments for excluding women from ordination. Despite the respect-

ful tone, some, including Matthew Lamb of Boston College, strongly disagreed with the statement, labeling it inadequate and misleading because it
borders on advocacy for women's ordination although it neither explicitly
calls for it nor does it explicitly dissent against Vatican teaching. Also criticizing the study, Cardinal Bernard Law of Boston accused the CTSA of
being "an association of advocacy for theological dissent."[6]

In September 1997 the Committee on Doctrine of the NCCB sent a letter to all of the American bishops responding to the document of the CTSA
saying that: "The Church affirms that it is in the divinely instituted, sacramental character of the priesthood that the reason for its reservation to men
is to be found." It reasserted the church's position and argued that the current position has always been the disposition of the church on this matter;
thus it constitutes a teaching of the ordinary magisterium. The result was a
continued stalemate on the issue of women's ordination with some liberal
and moderate theologians claiming that the practice of ordaining only males
could change, and the official position claiming the opposite.

In any event, nothing along these lines will change during the pontificate of John Paul II. While it is unlikely that his successor will be much different from him ideologically, the problems created by the declining number of American clergy will have to be addressed. Although the door to
women priests or noncelibate clergy seems closed tight at present, it is not
locked, and any number of events could reopen a serious investigation of
the merits of these changes.

Sexual and Reproductive Ethics

The church's concern with sexual and reproductive ethics goes back to biblical times. It has never been easy to regulate sexual behavior, but the church
was probably more successful in pre-Vatican II times than it has been since.
Moral issues concerning sexual activity, preference, conception, and procreation have been sharply contested at the end of the twentieth century. The
notion of "free love" in the 1960s in America directly conflicted with church
morality. With more and more young people eschewing marriage at the end
of the century until their middle—or late—twenties or beyond, many couples live together before marrying.

The church continues to oppose sex outside of marriage. Birth control
is opposed by official church pronouncement, even though Catholics practice it as readily as all other Americans. Abortion is considered a mortal sin

by the church, but even on this grave issue Catholics are divided as to whether or not they agree with church teaching and just as many Catholics as non-Catholics have abortions.[7] The church has foresworn its condemnation of homosexuals, but maintains its opposition to homosexual activity.

The Vatican is not unaware of the resistance by contemporary Catholics to its proposed ethical norms. The gap exists not only on issues relating to reproduction and sexuality, but encompasses a deeper fundamental shift in the way that Catholics assess ethical situations. The encyclical issued by John Paul II, *Veritatis Splendor* (The Splendor of Truth) on August 6, 1993, acknowledged the divide between the church's ethical teachings and their acceptance by the faithful.

> [A] new situation has come about "within the Christian community itself," which has experienced the spread of numerous doubts and objections of a human and psychological, social and cultural, religious and even properly theological nature, with regard to the Church's moral teachings. It is no longer a matter of limited and occasional dissent, but of an overall and systematic calling into question of traditional moral doctrine, on the basis of certain anthropological and ethical presuppositions. At the root of these presuppositions is the more or less obvious influence of currents of thought which end by detaching human freedom from its essential and constitutive relationship to truth. Thus the traditional doctrine regarding the natural law, and the universality and the permanent validity of its precepts, is rejected; certain of the Church's moral teachings are found simply unacceptable; and the Magisterium itself is considered capable of intervening in matters of morality only in order to "exhort consciences" and to "propose values," in the light of which each individual will independently make his or her decisions and life choices.[8]

The church has not been able to prevent or curtail much of what it opposes in the arena of sexual activity. While the church has placed a ban on birth control, for example, the ban is heeded by a small minority of American Catholics. Andrew Greeley connects the church's loss of authority directly to its ban on artificial contraception in the 1968 encyclical *Humanae Vitae*. Greeley argues that the church lost its hold on people when it attempted to interject its will on couples in the intimacy of their bedroom in a matter that many saw as purely personal. The decision whether or not to use birth control, of course, does have societal and public consequences;

but couples did not think that these concerns or the commitment of the church, based on the morality of natural law (that all acts of intercourse be open to procreation) outweighed their personal decisions. In the minds of many Catholic couples, the emotional and economic costs of caring for a child into adulthood were weighed against the church's interest in a consistent moral ethic, and in most cases the church lost.

The church permits one form of regulation, the rhythm method, but most couples find this method cumbersome; and some think that, although natural, the monitoring it requires is more mechanical than artificial birth control, so they opt instead for artificial means.

Another ethical issue closely related to birth control, but more controversial, is abortion. The church has been unwavering in its defense of the unborn. Catholics, however, have not responded in lockstep with the Vatican. The bishops have invested themselves, the resources of the church, and the power of their political weight in this issue. Despite the hierarchy's clear and consistent condemnation of abortion, many American Catholics are not in agreement. In fact, American Catholics differ little in their position on abortion from American Protestants. Some inactive Catholics, cited it in Gallup surveys (along with the prohibition on birth control and views on church authority) as one of the reasons for their lack of participation in the church.[9]

The church concerns itself with sexual activity independent of procreation issues. Put simply, sexual acts outside of marriage are sinful. Fornication, adultery, and homosexual sex are judged immoral by the church. Of course, every American knows that the church's teaching does not mean that Catholics do not engage in such sexual activity; it only means that they should not do so. What the common culture increasingly tolerates (if not accepts), the church continues to forbid. There are few American Catholics who do not know someone who is sexually involved with another person outside of marriage, either in a relationship between single heterosexuals or homosexuals, or in an extra-marital relationship. Couples who live together before marriage may encounter disapproval from parents and families on religious grounds, but many are doing it nonetheless. Many homosexuals continue to hide their sexual identity for fear of reprisals, yet some live in openly gay relationships in which they might even adopt a child or, in the case of lesbian relationships, one of the partners bears a child for the couple. With divorce no longer exceptional in America, many divorced persons live with a new partner at least for a period without marrying. Many of these arrangements include "blended" families in which children are brought up seeing their unmarried Mom or Dad living in what seems to them a normal relationship.

The church's stringent ethics regarding sexual behavior are clearly countercultural. But this does not imply that the church should adopt the mores of the common culture. It means that the church faces a more difficult task proclaiming and enforcing its sexual moral code. Many Catholics do not take it seriously; or, if they agree with it, they have developed ways to appease their consciences when they transgress. In the view of some Catholics, the church's position renders it increasingly irrelevant in a world that tolerates all manner of sexual relationships. Yet the church consistently opposes lifestyles for Catholics that undermine the sacramental nature of marriage. Further, the church defends a traditional view of the institution of marriage against either legislation or public policies that would alter the exclusive bond between a man and a woman which marriage recognizes. Bishops Joseph Charon, chair of U.S. bishops' Committee on Marriage and Family, and William Skylstad, chair of the Committee on Domestic Policy, issued a statement opposing same-sex unions on July 24, 1996, that said in part: "[W]e oppose attempts to grant the legal status of marriage to a relationship between persons of the same sex."[10] And Cardinal Anthony Bevilacqua of Philadelphia wrote to the mayor of Philadelphia on June 7, 1996 expressing his strong opposition to extending benefits to city worker's partners in same-sex couple relationships.[11]

The institutional church can continue to make pronouncements that attempt to prevent what it considers immoral sexual activity and reproductive practices. However, it has not changed the minds of the majority of Catholics who ignore the church's teachings in these areas and conduct their sexual and reproductive lives in a way indistinguishable from other Americans. For the church's part, it is caught in a dilemma—either hold the line and risk irrelevance or change and risk being viewed by conservative Catholics as a capitulator to secular mores.

Priests and Nuns: Decline in Numbers and Morale

In America, statistics help to tell the story. At the time of Vatican II there were about 180,000 nuns in America. Today there are fewer than 100,000, a 45 percent loss. In 1966, 35,070 diocesan priests were active; Sociologists Schoennherr and Young[12] predict that by the year 2005 there will be 21,030, a 40 percent loss. Church membership in 1965 was 44,790,000. They predict it will reach 74,109,000 in 2005. The ratio of priests to parishioners in 1975 was 1:1,100; in 1990 it was 1:2,200; by the year 2005 it will be 1:3,100. More than 40 percent of the dioceses in the United States have at least one parish headed by a non-priest, and many dioceses have multiple parishes without clerical leadership.[13]

The church has not been able to reverse the tide despite efforts to encourage vocations. In 1975 the church even changed its counting practice as recorded in the official *National Catholic Directory* to include priests who were working abroad as missionaries among the domestic count. It will take more than adjusting accounting procedures to solve the shortage, however.

A droll, but nevertheless poignant, example of the strain that accompanies the contemporary priesthood for many, is illustrated in the story of one priest who took a respite from the responsibilities and routine only to realize that his situation was symbolic of a entire system under pressure. While on vacation, Father Michael Kirkness of the diocese of Billings, Montana, went to mass one Sunday at the local parish. Now a prison chaplain, at the time he was the only priest serving a parish in rural Montana, and, although the people were wonderful, he was weary from being a "sacramental machine" in the parish church and its three missions that he served. Father Kirkness elected to attend mass instead of presiding because he needed a break, and he did not have the emotional strength to preside and preach. He noticed, a few pews in front of him, a former classmate, who was there with his wife and two children. He had left the priesthood years earlier. Liturgy began a few minutes after the hour, when a retired priest made his way to the altar. The vacationing priest reflected with friends that afternoon: "This is a sign of the future church. In fact, come to think of it, it's already here. I'm afraid it will only get worse before it gets better."

One of the greatest challenges for the church in the twenty-first century is a matter of numbers—a concern that strikes at the heart of the church's sacramental life. Will the church in America have enough religious and clergy to sustain the present level of service to the Catholic community? While women religious are no less dedicated and have an importance often overlooked in favor of the clergy's contribution, it remains true that the church depends in a unique way upon priests for its sacramental life. If the Vatican continues to insist on a celibate clergy and continues to confer the sacrament of ordination only on males, then the statistics indicate a priest-parishioner ratio that puts a greater burden on fewer clergy and may deny a growing proportion of the faithful easy access to the sacraments.

From 1920 to the mid-1960s the number of priests in America grew at a

Number of Sisters, 1945–1997

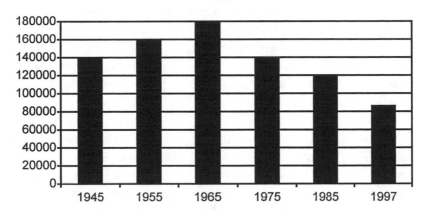

steady rate.[14] From the mid-1960s to the present, the number of clergy has declined (especially in relation to the number of Catholics, which has increased). Two separate but not unrelated factors contribute to this statistic—fewer ordinations and a sizable number of resignations. One of the consequences of this trend is a higher median age among active clergy since younger clergy leave the active ministry in greater proportion to older clergy. For example, while 13,631 men were ordained for the diocesan priesthood between 1966 and 1984, 6,938 men resigned the priesthood in the same nineteen-year period, a gross loss of 19.5 percent. Adding to the difficulties caused by this shrinkage, the vast majority of priests who resigned were under 50 years old, leaving a middle-aged and older clergy to serve a growing number of baby-boomer and younger Catholics. According to sociologists Richard A. Schoennherr and Lawrence A. Young "[B]y the time members of a typical class ordained in the late 1960s or early 1970s reached age 35, 19% would have resigned. By the time the class celebrates its 25th anniversary—when most would have reached age 52—37% would no longer be in the active priesthood."[15] If present trends continue, by the year 2005 "Nearly half of the active priests in the United States will be 55 or older, while just a little over an eighth will be under 35."[16] The statistics from one archdiocese, Philadelphia, from 1965 to 1995 tell the story: the number of priests declined from 1,720 to 1,290; sisters from 6,540 to 4,285; and the Catholic school population from 306,000 to 156,000—while the Catholic population grew from 1,325,000 to 1,439,000.

The condition of most religious order priests is no better, and sometimes worse. For example, in 1992 "54 percent of all women's religious communities, 36 percent of the communities of nonordained men, and 22 percent of clerical men's communities [had] no new members applying at all."[17]

These statistics are not intended to alarm but to inform. Unless the church successfully addresses the problem of the declining number of clergy, severe consequences will ensue. The Catholic community relies on priests to provide most sacraments (deacons can baptize and witness marriages). The sacrament that is central to Catholic faith and spirituality is the Eucharist. This is the sacrament in which the community is meant to come closest to Christ and at the same time proclaims itself in a unique way as the Body of Christ. Daily mass, even though attended by a small percentage of parishioners, is a staple of parish life, and Sunday mass is an obligation. In many parishes daily mass is no longer a given. In many parishes on days when the pastor is away for pastoral reasons—continuing education, retreat, diocesan business, or a much deserved day off—there is no priest to replace him and the community substitutes a Eucharistic service presided over by a religious sister, lay pastoral associate, or active lay person using bread previously consecrated by the priest. More acute is the need within parishes that have no resident priest and who may not have mass every weekend. These parishes are presided over by a nonclerical administrator assigned by the bishop, so that there is pastoral service available. However, sacramental ministry occurs irregularly, depending upon the availability of a priest. In some instances, for example in rural areas, one priest will perform sacramental rites in several parishes on a rotating schedule. What this unsatisfactory arrangement does to the relationship between priest and parishioners one can only guess.

Priestless parishes are by no means the norm in America. However, there are enough of them for the church to provide a rite for worship in parishes where there is no priest. A ritual book aptly titled "Sunday Celebrations in the Absence of a Priest" details what a community can and cannot do in fulfilling its Sunday obligation. One liturgist sent a twelve-page questionnaire to the Catholic bishops in the United States and Canada to ascertain what they have been doing in cases where there is no priest available. In appended comments, one priest responding for his bishop wrote:

> For the past ten years or so, our senate of priests has encouraged the Bishops to prioritize the parishes to see which ones would lose their resident pastor first. This was only done this past year. Up to that time, our Bishop's response was, "Pray for vocations; God will provide." But over the years, churches which had one or even two associates have lost

them. We've gotten some elderly priests to help out. These from religious orders. We have been stretched as far as we can go. Last year one of our priests retired. The pastor of the neighboring parish was named pastor at the parish of the retired priest. So we now have the situation of having one priest as pastor of two parishes and three missions. . . . We only have four seminarians, several of whom are older men. I am not trying to be negative here, but I am trying to be realistic.[18]

Some refuse to admit that there is a serious vocation problem that threatens the American church. For example, Elden Curtiss, archbishop of Omaha, wrote: "I personally think that the vocation 'crisis' in this country is more artificial and contrived than many people realize. . . . It seems to me that the vocation 'crisis' is precipitated and continued by people who want to change the church's agenda, by people who do not support orthodox candidates loyal to the magisterial teaching of the Pope and bishops, and by people who actually discourage viable candidates from seeking priesthood and vowed religious life as the Church defines the ministries."[19] While professor of liturgy Kathleen Hughes predicts that the bishops will not put this on the agenda for discussion by the National Conference of Catholic Bishops until the shortage affects the large dioceses in the East like New York and Washington, its impact is being felt by priests who work in chancery and diocesan offices in those regions. In Providence, Rhode Island, for example, priests whose primary assignment is to work in the diocesan chancery office now hold other part-time assignments in parishes, some even as pastors of smaller parishes. As a consequence they go from their day job in the diocesan office to their night and weekend job in the parish. This not only divides their attention, it exhausts them in the process.

Sometimes even East coast parishes are rendered priestless for periods, as in the instance of St. Joachim Parish on Cape Ann, Massachusetts.[20] The pastor, Father Ronald J. Gariaboldi, broke his leg in an accidental fall in church. Fortunately, Father Gariaboldi's collegial leadership prepared the people to take over the ordinary operations of the parish smoothly in his absence. However, even though this happened during Lent, when more people attend daily mass, the archdiocese of Boston could provide neither a full-time replacement nor a priest to offer daily mass. The Vatican's 1973 "Instruction on Holy Communion and Eucharistic Devotion Outside of Mass" treats lay-led communion services as "exceptions," so the archdiocese supplied a priest for Sunday mass but discontinued daily mass/Eucharistic services while the pastor convalesced.

One way that religious orders attempt to combat the decline in vocations is by advertising regularly for new recruits. ELYSE RIEDER

The rite devised for priestless parishes is not very original or creative. Essentially it follows the rite of the mass, substituting an "Act of Thanksgiving" for the Eucharistic prayer and using previously consecrated bread for communion. These rituals may be presided over by a nun, a brother, or a layperson. Responses from parishioners vary. In an analysis of a Southwestern diocese, one researcher found varying degrees of acceptance of priestless liturgies.[21] In his study, sociologist Cornelius Hughes asked Catholics of the diocese, almost half of whom were Hispanic: "If your parish were unable to provide Mass on a Sunday, which of the following would you most likely do?" Thirty-four percent "would attend a communion service provided in place of the Mass;" 52 percent "would find another Catholic church even though very inconvenient;" 10 percent "would not go to church that Sunday;" and 4 percent "would go to a non-Catholic Sunday service." Since two-thirds chose some option other than attending a priestless service, Hughes concluded that there is significant disappointment with priestless Sundays. But his further research indicated that they are objecting to the fact that the Eucharist is not celebrated, rather than to the fact that a priest is not presiding. When asked about their reaction to who might preside at a Sunday liturgy if there were no priest available, they "would welcome or accept" a religious (79 percent), a deacon (73 percent), or a layperson (63 percent). The issue then is not so much who presides, but what they are presiding over (clearly preferring a Eucharist to a Eucharistic service).

Not all parishes respond to the priestless Sundays so openly. In January 1992, Holy Trinity Church, a small parish (52 families) in Conrath, Wisconsin, was wracked by this dilemma. In an attempt to stop the church from closing their parish due to the lack of priests, at least half of the families came together as Holy Trinity *Episcopal* Church and attempted to buy the church building from the Catholic diocese.[22]

The church's response to the decline in clergy and its incumbent consequences has been constrained in part by the church disciplines required of clergy, in particular, but not exclusively, celibacy. In the pre-Vatican II era vocations to the priesthood were robust. There are several quantifiable reasons for this. Families were larger. It was not unusual for Catholic parents to have five or six children. The numbers also made it easier for parents to encourage one of their sons to become a priest since the family name often would be carried on by another son, who would marry.

The post-Vatican II generation come from smaller families. Today a large family may have three children, with the average being two, and many families having only one child. It seems to constitute more of a sacrifice on the part of parents to give their only son, or in some cases, their only child to the church. It is true that families did this in the past. Many priests today are only sons or only children. However, the allure of the priesthood is not today what it was forty or fifty years ago. Contemporary American society emphasizes "quality of life" when, as Archbishop Francis Stafford aptly described it: " 'Quality of life.' . . too often refers to one's car, one's home, or one's stereo system."[23] This materialism or consumerism, at least has diminished the desire of many young people to pursue a life of obedience, celibacy, and for many priests in religious orders, poverty. (One couple, on the way home from church after a sermon on vocations asked their two boys in the back seat of the car if either of them would like to become a priest. Matt pointed at Chris and Chris at Matt saying simultaneously, "He would.")

But it is not the lack of material comforts that distances many young men from the priesthood. Indeed, many diocesan priests drive expensive cars, live in the largest house in the neighborhood (albeit a rectory), and own expensive stereo systems and other modern household conveniences. It is something deeper. The priesthood is no longer the only road to an education, status, and professional responsibilities as it was for the immigrant peoples of the first half of the twentieth century. Immigrant families were loyal to the church, respected and often admired the clergy, and they were poor. They could not afford to provide higher education for their children. A son who entered the seminary was assured of a high quality education (granted within certain academic parameters) at the expense of the diocese or religious order. Many priests from the pre-Vatican II generation were the first in their family to receive a college education.

Today higher education is readily available and, while increasingly expensive, it is affordable to the majority of Catholics who are third- and fourth-generation Americans. It remains out of reach for many recent immigrants and their children, but these conditions will also change as these immigrants are assimilated into American society and as community colleges increasingly reach out to offer affordable education to this population. So education is no longer the lure for vocations that it once was. Neither is social mobility. For previous generations of Catholics, to become a priest was to advance in a social hierarchy, especially within Catholic circles although the priesthood also enjoyed a prestige (even if a bit mysterious and sometimes misunderstood) outside of the Catholic community. As "a man of the cloth," "Father" was known and respected within his local community. Scott Appleby describes the priest of the 1940s.

> The priest was, in the theological terminology of the day, *alter Christus*. Accordingly, his competence in religious questions went unchallenged by a laity that perceived him as "a man set apart" from the crowd. His parishioners presumed him to be a man of holiness by virtue of his ordination. The church, itself an institution set apart from the sin of the world, guaranteed this. In training the priest for public service, seminaries and clergy conferences held up the image of "the Christian gentleman" as the model of priestly behavior in sanctuary, rectory, and marketplace. Such a man would conduct himself at all times with dignity and reserve, polite to a fault, stern in defense of principle.[24]

Much of the magic of the priesthood has been tarnished by the behavior of priests themselves—behavior that some suspect happened for decades undiscovered or unreported. The disclosure of priests' sex abuse scandals in the 1980s and '90s created "a whole new set of images and new stories," says Father Robert Bullock, a pastor in Sharon, Massachusetts. "This scandal is having a terrible effect on the future of the celibate, male, ordained priesthood."[25] Nationwide there have been over 400 reported cases of sex abuse by priests. Considering that there are 48,000 priests in America, this is not an extraordinary number of cases. However, the priesthood has represented a lifestyle that is meant to be above reproach. These scandals, therefore, make a deep impact on the psyche of the American people.

Priests have long been trusted with the care of the young—spiritually, ethically, and religiously. The breach of that trust will take decades to amend. Jason Berry chronicles cases of abuse in his book *Lead Us Not into Temptation*.[26] Victims established a group with the acronym VOCAL (Victims of Clergy Abuse Link Up) in order to provide support and advice to one another.[27] Legal settlements, in and out of court, have cost the American church tens of millions of dollars and put some dioceses on the edge of bankruptcy. The problem has been compounded by the fact that in some cases bishops knew of priests' offenses and yet continued to assign them to pastoral work.[28] Instead of confronting and correcting the problems, they moved the problem priests to new assignments where they were able to act out their sinful and illegal behavior among unsuspecting faithful.

Among the more noted cases was that of James Porter, a former priest living in Wisconsin, who in 1993 was sentenced to eighteen to twenty years in prison for molesting twenty-eight children while he was a priest in Massachusetts. The victims came forward years after the crime because it took them that long to come to terms with what had happened to them when they were altar boys. This case garnered national attention from the press, but almost every diocese in the country has suffered some embarrassment and legal action because of sex abuse by priests. Not all the accusations proved accurate, however. In perhaps the most watched incident, a former seminarian accused Cardinal Bernardin of sexual abuse in a case brought on by the surfacing of supposedly suppressed memories. The memories proved to be false and the man apologized, but not until the cardinal and Catholics all over America had suffered painfully. The cardinal graciously accepted the apology and forgave the man—a noble example of Christian behavior.

As a result of highly publicized cases, all priests are tarred with the same brush and find themselves trying to avoid suspicion. As Father Virgil Elizondo, a leader in the Catholic Hispanic community, said: "I try to eliminate some of the risk by being more public in my dealings with people." Richard Sipe has done an extensive study of priests' relationship to their vow of celibacy in his book *A Secret World: Sexuality and the Search for Celibacy*.[29] In it, he juxtaposes Hollywood caricatures of priests thus:

> Catholic priests ordained prior to 1960 were generally viewed as public icons of strength, virility, honesty, and dedicated service. To follow that conception from the height of its Hollywood portrayal, during the 1940s especially, into the 1980s is to witness it mutate into precisely its opposite. The priest of today emerges more generally as a weak man of questionable masculinity or outright wimpishness. He is seen as at least less than honest or at worst hypocritical and is surrounded by an aura of monumental irrelevance.[30]

Sipe's description has some truth to it, as all caricatures do. But it is not at all an accurate depiction (nor does he intend it to be) of the many priests who work hard, touch the lives of their parishioners in ways that are effective and at depths where few others touch them, struggle with many of the same questions that other Catholics contend with, and try to live as compassionately and humanly as our culture will permit.

The concern for priests' morale has not escaped the notice of the American bishops. The Committee on Priestly Life of the National Conference of Catholic Bishops issued a document in 1988 that begins on a positive note but quickly admits a problem: "Although there are present today powerful individual examples of priestly ministry shared in creative and energizing ways which continue the ministry and mission of the church, it is also clear to us that there exists today a serious and substantial morale problem among priests in general."

The numerically significant exodus of priests from the active ministry after Vatican II has slowed considerably in the past ten years, but it has nevertheless taken its toll. Many young talented priests left, and their departure left the American church depleted. Those who remained while their friends were leaving felt the loss keenly. Those who have been ordained since have not made up for the loss in terms of numbers or quality. According to many insiders, recently ordained priests tend to be more institutionally oriented and less innovative. This makes for greater stability in the ministry, but some ask at what cost? The same is true for nuns, only the numbers are greater and the impact even more severe, so severe that many orders will not survive, and decades or centuries of service to the American church will come to an end, in the words of the poet T. S. Eliot, "not with a bang but a whimper."

The loneliness that some feel in a life of celibacy is heightened when the community of the priesthood or sisterhood is so diminished by resignations and lack of vocations. Rectories built for four or five priests who might form a small community of support now are home to a single priest, if they have not been turned into parish centers or sold outright. Motherhouses of religious communities of nuns are virtual nursing homes for the aging sisters, or they, too, have been sold to pay the nursing care bills. Now every retirement hurts, not because a priest or sister is not entitled to it, but because those still working will have more to do. In some dioceses and religious orders of nuns and priests, retirement has become a euphemism for death. No matter how old they are, their contribution is needed.

Many hard-working, sincere, and committed priests and nuns continue to serve in active ministry. Many of these are more than happy to share ministerial responsibilities with the laity. They are not threatened by lay involvement or power. In fact, they welcome it. The more the laity assume ownership for their parishes, the stronger the parish. These priests and nuns understand their role increasingly as educators and enablers. Their pastoral plan is to hand over to the laity areas of responsibility such as finances, much of the administrative duties, building maintenance, and other areas that require time-consuming attention but are ancillary to their central ministry to preach the gospel by word and action. They also readily share ministerial duties that directly involve pastoral care. Ultimately they remain responsible for proper oversight of all dimensions of parish life, but they need not micro-manage every aspect of parish life and administration. Practicing such a principle of subsidiarity frees them to concentrate on aspects of ministry that permit them to serve people in a direct and personal manner. It may also free them to read, pray, think, and rest—all critical elements that too often are truncated because there are too many immediate demands on their time.

A notable example of the demands and variety in priestly ministry is Father Michael Nash, a priest of the diocese of Juneau, Alaska.[31] Since his ordination in 1980, Father Nash, one of eleven priests in the diocese of Juneau (an area many times the size of other American dioceses), has served the townspeople of Alaska and the Native American villages, in particular the Tlingit tribe in Hoonah, Angoon, and Klawock; and the Haida tribe in Craig. He shared this remote ministry with Sister Marguerite Gravel, C.S.C., who came to Alaska from Manchester, New Hampshire, to work among the Native peoples. Father Nash, a commercial commuter pilot before he entered the priesthood, flies his own light plane to many of his

Number of Seminarians, 1945–1997

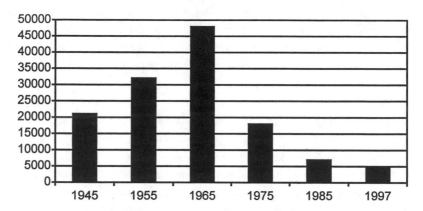

Number of Priests, 1945–1997

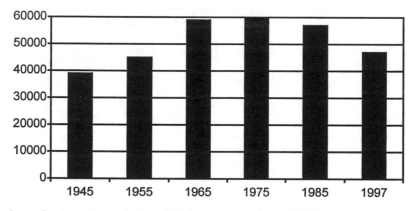

SOURCE: *THE OFFICIAL CATHOLIC DIRECTORY, 1997.* FIGURES ARE AS OF JANUARY 1, 1997

mission sites that include logging camps, fishing villages, fishing lodges, and native villages, often celebrating the Eucharist in private homes or churches rented from Protestant denominations. Where there are no churches, Father Nash carries everything with him, referring to his "church in a box."

Are there sacrifices involved in this rural ministry? Indeed there are, but he is quick to note that they are no greater for him than for the people he serves. His sacrifices differ from those of priests and sisters who serve in other areas of the United States, but everyone who signs on for a life of ministry encounters unexpected sacrifices and reaps unexpected rewards. It is the nature of ministerial life and Father Nash takes it all in stride without hubris or undue humility.

The church addresses the priest shortage in a number of ways, none of which has resolved the shortage crisis. The first thing is to build larger churches, mini-cathedrals in the suburbs. Packing thousands of parishioners into one Sunday liturgy eliminates the need for an extensive mass schedule, a burden that overworked and overextended priests in their fifties and sixties have a difficult time coping with physically and emotionally. Fewer masses with larger congregations eliminate the need for more priests. A second tactic hearkens back to the nineteenth and early twentieth century— to import priests from foreign countries. The Irish seminary All Hallows supplied the American church with a regular complement of priests for decades. While Ireland no longer has a surplus, other countries do. Priests from the Philippines and parts of Africa are appearing at American altars with increasing frequency. One of the four regional seminaries in Nigeria has over 700 seminarians. Although from a different culture and a different expression of the church, many of these are willing to come to America to serve. The problem is that it may take some time before they are acclimated to American culture and the American church. Some dioceses have chosen to redouble their efforts to recruit vocations to the priesthood. A few bishops have assumed responsibility for recruitment, encouraging young men to think about the priesthood and personally following up on potential candidates. The church also admits candidates to the priesthood who would not have been considered forty years ago. These include older men, divorced men, widowers, and Episcopalian priests who embrace Roman Catholicism.

These efforts have not yielded bumper crops. Seminaries built in the heyday of vocations in the 1940s to the early '60s are either underutilized by the small number of seminarians in the 1990s, sold, or converted to other uses such as retreat centers or diocesan office buildings. The average age of seminarians in theologates (graduate schools) in the 1950s and '60s was about twenty-four. Today seminaries are regularly receiving students for whom priesthood is a second vocation or who simply choose to enter the seminary later than previous generations. Numbers are down and age is up.

The American church could do with far fewer seminaries today. However, a certain "territorialism" is rooted in the American church culture. Bishops who have seminaries in their dioceses usually want their own seminarians to attend them for two reasons: it keeps the student census up, and it allows them to carefully monitor their education and suitableness for ministry. Most bishops, however, do not have the luxury (burden?) of a diocesan seminary, so they send their candidates to regional, national, or international seminaries. Some seminaries, for example, Mundelein, the diocesan seminary for the archdiocese of Chicago, act as a diocesan seminary, training priests for the archdiocese of Chicago; a national seminary, training priests for other American dioceses; and an international seminary, taking in candidates from other countries.

Biomedical Issues

One plot of complicated terrain for American Catholicism is the ethical implications of medical and biological advancements. First of all, it requires a high degree of intelligence and education simply to understand the disciplines. Second, the moral implications of contemporary research and practice are enormous. Third, everything changes seemingly at the speed of light with further research, new discoveries, and advanced techniques. As one example, few immigrant Catholics would have thought that at the end of the century, the country, indeed the world, and the church would be faced with the possibility of cloning. This is only one (albeit extraordinary) possibility among a host of complex medical and biological issues with significant ethical implications including, but not limited to, euthanasia, assisted suicide, transplantation, pharmacologically induced changes, sex changes, in vitro fertilization, and cryogenics. Bioethics is a genuinely interdisciplinary field in which a handful of experts are able to speak competently.

The church has a stake in what happens in laboratories, hospitals, clinics, and research facilities since the very character of human life can be changed by what happens in these arenas. The problem for the church is what to say and when to say it in a research environment that sometimes has more scientific capability than moral restraint. A committee of experts convened by President Clinton to investigate the medical and moral effects of cloning concluded that we should not do it with humans because it is unethical. Such constraints on science are few and far between, however, and even the cloning debate did not end, as Dr. Richard Seed demonstrated in late 1997 with his intention to proceed expeditiously with human cloning before legislation rendered the procedure illegal.

The field of bioethics is in many ways still in its infancy, but few would dispute its importance. Philosophers debate the nature of the human person, lawyers scramble to find language to protect individual rights, doctors sincerely want to help their patients, and theologians seek to lead the conversation toward the moral high ground without seeming to inhibit progress. Adding to the complexity from the theological side is the proliferation of various theological methodologies in addition to the traditional natural law approach historically favored by Catholicism. If the church insists too much on promulgating its moral stance, it may sacrifice its credibility as a serious conversation partner with modern science, law, and medicine. If it retreats and allows others to take the lead, it risks reducing its voice to an echo of the tones of larger cultural forces.

On March 25, 1995, Pope John Paul II issued the encyclical *Evangelium Vitae* (The Gospel of Life) that dealt with specific ethical dilemmas. The pope expressed the church's concern that in places all over the globe, societies are more tolerant of practices previously considered immoral, and that in many instances legislative bodies are legalizing such practices in an attempt to curry favor with the electorate. To the pope, all of this constitutes evidence of serious moral decline, as he indicated in the encyclical.

> The fact that legislation in many countries, perhaps even departing from basic principles of their constitutions, has determined not to punish these practices against life, and even to make them altogether legal, is both a disturbing symptom and a significant cause of grave moral decline. Choices once unanimously considered criminal and rejected by the common moral sense are gradually becoming socially acceptable.[32]

On certain issues the position of the church is clear. Abortion, as is evident from previous discussions in this book, is one. Euthanasia is another. Capital punishment is a third. However, in many countries the church's opposition on moral grounds to such practices fails to persuade governments to enact legislation against them. In the United States, abortion is legal, laws prohibiting euthanasia are being challenged or changed in states such as Oregon, and capital punishment is the ultimate penalty in many states. John Paul II described such a climate as a "culture of death." Behind this moral decay, according to the church, lies a desire to accord excessive privilege to individual conscience. As *Veritatis Splendor* described it:

> The individual conscience is accorded the status of a supreme tribunal of moral judgment which hands down categorical and infallible decisions about good and evil. To the affirmation that one has a duty to fol-

low one's conscience is unduly added the affirmation that one's moral judgment is true merely by the fact that it has its origin in the conscience. But in this way the inescapable claims of truth disappear, yielding their place to a criterion of sincerity, authenticity and "being at peace with oneself," so much so that some have come to adopt a radically subjectivistic conception of moral judgment.[33]

The church recognizes the value of individual conscience as a moral guide. However, when individuals rely exclusively on conscience without properly being informed by reference to available authoritative church teachings, the reliability of conscience is severely diminished. As Kevin Wildes, a bioethicist and philosopher, notes, "the arguments in *Evangelium Vitae* cannot be a matter of indifference to Catholics or institutions that identity themselves as Catholic."[34] Catholics are expected to listen to the church's teaching and heed it. In practice, some of the teachings conflict with either the individual's experience or conscience (or both). Then the individual is forced to choose between the church's direction and his or her own moral compass. The pope prefers Catholics to accept the wisdom of the church in moral decision making, but the reality is that personal freedom, cultural and social forces, and often scientific development, all mitigate against such acceptance. To the pope, human dignity requires limitations on personal choices and constraint in medical practices, since we are created beings who owe our existence to God. Catholicism reminds us that we are not, in the end, complete masters of our own destiny. We ought, not thoughtlessly or foolishly, but in a deeply reflective way, to surrender our will to the will of God. After all is said and done, as one wisdom saying of the Ash Wednesday liturgy reminds people as they receive a smudge of ash on the forehead, "Remember, you are dust and to dust you shall return." The problem arises when trying to determine just what constitutes "the will of God" in complicated decisions that require scientific, medical, and moral expertise. The Bible provides negative (Thou shall not kill) and positive (Do onto others as you would have them do unto you) ethical norms that are foundational, but obviously it cannot provide concrete reference to the moral choices faced by contemporary Catholics—the administration of powerful drugs that can relieve pain but have the potential to end life, the preservation of sperm and eggs for future use in vitro fertilization, withholding food or hydration from a terminally ill patient, or genetic manipulation to improve or perfect a baby.

Catholic Identity

The thorny question of Catholic identity arises often in the contemporary church in institutions ranging from colleges and universities to hospitals. What constitutes a "Catholic" institution—history and heritage, simple nomenclature, episcopal approbation, self-designation? These are not trivial questions; and the issue has led to protracted discussions, if not negotiations, in a number of instances. It is one thing for Cardinal Mahoney to warn that websites may not be truly representative of Catholic thought and policy even though they may designate themselves as Catholic. Most people are well aware that postings on the web have no gatekeeper in general and certainly no ecclesial gatekeeper in particular. In such cases "searcher beware" is common knowledge. More complicated, however, are the instances of known Catholic institutions such as universities, hospitals, and social service organizations. What if they are not following to the letter the dictates of the church? What if they think they are, but others (the Vatican, bishops, or a certain segment of the Catholic population) disagree? Who adjudicates which institutions may call themselves Catholic and which may not, keeping in mind that even the Vatican and bishops know that there is room for legitimate differences?

The discussion of Catholic identity occupies any number of American Catholic institutions at present. One example that is illustrative is the case of Catholic colleges and universities. These are complex institutions that serve a number of different purposes in American culture and in the church. First of all, they are institutions of higher learning. Education must be their primary mission. But education is a multidimensional enterprise. It involves teaching and learning; but beyond that generic classification lies a complex web of nuance. Who are authorized to teach, and what are they expected to teach? This may seem a facile question if one thinks of a discipline such as physics, for example. Universities hire scholars who are trained in the field, who can communicate in the classroom, and who can conduct research. Those who fail at either of the latter two criteria usually do not receive tenure.

But what about a biologist who works within or in cooperation with a medical school on a Catholic campus? Should he or she be permitted to teach the biological dimensions of abortion methods or how an abortion can be performed most safely? May this scientist conduct any research that has ties to or implications for abortion? What about the use of fetal tissue for experiments? What if the biologist is not Catholic and not even religious, yet he or she is one of the most highly regarded scholars in the field? Should the university decide at the onset that it will not hire such a person but seek out someone who is Catholic or who at least agrees to work within the ethical confines of Catholic teaching? What if this results in faculties that do not enhance the academic reputation of the university? Should the university sacrifice its academic pursuit of excellence in favor of a Catholic agenda? Will this result in a decline in applications to the institution from highly qualified candidates because potential students rank first-rate academic programs over Catholic values or identity? The dilemma is equally complex in the humanities. Should the philosophy department hire a brilliant atheist? Should government/political science departments hire professors who oppose the church's public policy efforts? Do economics departments in Catholic colleges have room for someone who opposes the bishops' teaching in the pastoral on the economy? Can theologians offer dissenting views about birth control, christology, or papal infallibility in their courses and publications? Are members of the psychology department permitted to challenge the church's position on homosexual behavior?

More complicated still is the question of who determines Catholic identity and who adjudicates whether an institution no longer adequately represents Catholicism. One must bear in mind that the issue of what Catholicism is remains ambiguous to some degree. If being Catholic means strict adherence to the official teachings and pronouncements from Rome and the bishops on all matters, then the majority of American Catholics are not Catholic, since they disagree with a number of teachings and practices.

In August 1990 the Vatican issued a document tilted *Ex corde Ecclesiae* (From the Heart of the Church) on these very matters. The document, which examines the relationship between Catholic universities and the church, appeared after years of dialogue among and between academics and Vatican officials that produced a succession of documents.[35] Catholic colleges and universities multiplied in the nineteenth and twentieth centuries, fueled by religious orders who founded institutions to serve the immigrant Catholic population and to give their religious congregations significant roles in higher education. While some colleges and universities were founded by individual bishops, only the Catholic University of America, established in 1887, originated under the direction of the national body of bishops and Rome. In 1904, the National Catholic Educational Association (NCEA) began with the objective of assisting secondary and higher education to implement their mission to educate Catholics. In 1949, the Vatican recognized the International Federation of Catholic Universities (IFCU)

which, in 1963, became an independent association headed by Theodore
Hesburgh. By the 1960s, numbers in the orders began to decrease; lay faculty often outnumbered order members; and trustee boards, composed
increasingly of laity, exhibited a more distant relationship to the institutional church. Watching this with interest, Roman authorities sought a juridical
connection between Catholic institutions of higher education and bishops.
In 1965, the IFCU proposed a dialogue to produce a statement that would
articulate the distinctive character of a Catholic university and that initiated
an ongoing conversation about Catholic higher education and its relationship to the church. At issue was the role of the university as a mediator
between faith and culture. Alice Gallin of the Association of Catholic Colleges and Universities describes the dilemma: "Some persons, beginning
from the point of view of the church, see the relationship as one of instru-
mentality—the university is the arm of the church and assists it in its task of
preaching the gospel to all nations and cultures; others begin with the broad
understanding of the life and purpose of any university, and then struggle
to express the way in which such a task might have a legitimate connection
with the mission of the church."[36]

In 1967, the IFCU's initiative led to an American response (among oth-
ers worldwide) called the "Land O'Lakes Statement: The Nature of the
Contemporary University." The statement stressed academic freedom and
institutional autonomy while striving to preserve the visible presence of
Catholicism within American Catholic universities. At a 1972 meeting in
Rome, all of the international responses to the question of Catholic identity
in higher education were melded into a single document, "The Catholic
University in the Modern World." The Vatican's Congregation for Catholic
Education requested clarifications on the commitment to Catholicism and
on self-regulation, but the document remained as a guide until 1990 when
Ex corde Ecclesiae appeared.

Father Theodore Hesburgh, then president of the University of Notre
Dame, described the role of Catholic universities in a speech at Seton Hall
University:

Universities today are, through their distinguished faculty, committed
to a wide variety of intellectual attitudes: agnosticism, scientism, rela-
tivism, subjectivism, with all their variations too numerous to mention.
I would submit that I can live with all these commitments, freely chosen
and sincerely embraced, especially since all of these other commitments
are limited to one or another way of knowing, while our commitment
is open to all ways of knowing, science, theology, artistic or poetic intu-

ition, hypothesis, analysis, and synthesis of all kinds, but each with their proper freedom and limitations.[37]

The context for American Catholic universities differs from their European counterparts, which are usually funded by the state and operate under a concordat with Rome for the appointment of theology professors but not others. American universities receive their accreditation from independent agencies that monitor the quality of education according to academic standards that are unrelated to the religious mission of an institution. The benefits from this scrutiny are both tangible and intangible. First, it evaluates Catholic universities by the same standard as other American higher education institutions, public and private; second, it results in recognized accreditation that increases the public value of the degrees granted; third, it allows Catholic universities to compete on a level playing field for grant and scholarship money.

Not unlike European universities, American universities receive government aid, but the diversity of forms for that aid ranges widely from research dollars to federally underwritten student aid. With government assistance comes government regulation and certain legal obligations. American Catholic universities must operate within the rule of law established in the United States. The delicate balance between separation of church and state on the one hand, and local or federal government aid to higher education (including Catholic institutions) on the other hand, means in practice that Catholic colleges and universities sometimes must permit (not condone) the establishment of groups or free speech practices that are in conflict with their professed beliefs. For example, gay rights groups who openly support homosexual lifestyles, and pro-choice groups who support a woman's right to choose abortion, have found a place on some Catholic campuses because college administrations legally must not discriminate against them.

Some fear that Catholic colleges and universities who interpret *Ex corde Ecclesiae* too liberally will soon follow the path that many originally Protestant denominational universities have trod, that is surrendering their religious (for example, Methodist, Presbyterian or Lutheran) character and being identified only historically with these churches. Princeton, Harvard, and Yale all have Protestant roots they long ago abandoned; and Duke and Syracuse exhibit little institutional connection to their Methodist roots, even though all of these institutions maintain divinity schools or religious studies departments.

An important piece of the puzzle when trying to construct a complete picture of Catholic universities and their mission resides in Canon 812 of the Code of Canon Law, which states: "It is necessary that those who teach theological disciplines in any institute of higher studies have a mandate from the competent ecclesiastical authority." While it mandates that Catholic colleges and universities teach theology, *Ex corde Ecclesiae* "Guarantees its [the university's] members academic freedom, so long as the rights of the individual person and of the community are preserved within the confines of the truth and the common good."[38] The delicate balance among ecclesial oversight by bishops, academic freedom, as determined not by church authorities but by national organizations such as the American Association of University Professors and secular regional accreditation boards, and institutional autonomy, requires careful nuance. Undeniably, the church has a vested interest in the teaching, research, deliberations, and conclusions of scholars who work within its institutions of higher learning. Concurrently, the church benefits from the unfettered exploration of ideas and would be imprudent to hamper research that customarily advances knowledge.

It is perhaps an irony that colleges and universities founded to permit Catholics the opportunity to advance intellectually, socially, and economically, no longer are the haven for immigrants that they once were. Recent Hispanic, Asian, African, and other immigrants generally cannot afford the steep tuition charges at private Catholic colleges. The most prestigious among these now reflect market forces and charge about the same as Ivy League schools. The smaller and less competitive ones cannot survive unless their annual tuition approaches at least $10,000.

Rising tuitions also threaten the mission of Catholic colleges to educate and form a diverse group of leaders for the next generation. Despite sincere efforts on the part of institutions and administrators to provide scholarships and financial aid, students from lower and even middle income backgrounds often cannot afford to attend Catholic institutions of higher learning. In many areas of the country, the problem extends to high schools as well. Many Catholic families cannot stretch the budget far enough to afford Catholic secondary education for their children. The church therefore ends up educating the economically elite.

The same concerns surround Catholic hospitals and are particularly sensitive in teaching and research hospitals associated with universities. All health care facilities have been beset with economic difficulties with the rise of managed care. With HMOs determining fee schedules, it is increasingly difficult for hospitals to remain fiscally sound. Catholic hospitals are sometimes at a disadvantage since they do not offer the complete range of services in the Obstetrics and Gynecology departments (for example, they do not offer birth control or abortion services). Health care providers must inform their clients of these restrictions, which may result in a decline in patients for Catholic facilities participating in the HMO. Diminished patient base translates into a decline in revenues that health care facilities can ill afford in a highly competitive environment. While some Catholic patients will choose a Catholic hospital because of its religious identity and ethical values, many prefer the most highly regarded facility medically (regardless of its ethical stance), and will choose it for care unrelated to specific ethical concerns.

While the church needs to function in a complex society, it must also stand for something and therefore sometimes can do neither what is most expedient financially nor take what, at the time, is the popular course. It stands in the difficult position in which it risks irrelevancy to some and lack of conviction to others depending upon its course of action on any number of complex ethical decisions.

Secularization of Rituals

A cultural development over which the church has little control is the secularization of rituals. What this means is that American Catholics, not unlike adherents of other denominations, increasingly are marking milestone events with quasi-liturgical rituals that substitute for church rituals. Two of the most apparent examples are marriage and death. In previous generations Catholic couples (and their families) would consider nothing less than a church wedding. It was the desire of the couple, and the expectation of their guests, that a wedding be celebrated in church, usually with the sacrament witnessed within the context of a mass. Today, it is not uncommon to have a nonreligious or quasi-religious ceremony precede the wedding reception in the same facility. The services offered by the banquet facility include the ceremony, photos, receiving line, band, drinks, and dinner in a convenient "wedding package." Or, the couple will hire a justice of the peace or a minister to conduct the ceremony at a location of their choice outside a church setting. Weddings in the park, on the beach, and in the hotel lobby are attracting Catholics who see no compelling need to be married in the church, yet who may still call themselves "Catholic."

Or, at the end of life, Catholics and their families are electing to hold funeral services in funeral homes, with or without a priest or religious representative present. Funeral directors or family members conduct the "service." Persons involved in the funeral industry are receiving an increasing number of requests for such arrangements, although in some areas of the country more so than in others. Usually the deceased are persons who drifted away from Catholic practice without formally leaving the church or joining another denomination.

Of course, there have always been baptized Catholics who maintained no active affiliation with the church. What is different today is the level of acceptance of these arrangements by relatives and friends who attend such a wedding or a funeral. People are neither surprised nor do they often raise objections when couples marry outside the church or a funeral is conducted exclusively within the funeral home. For some Catholics, church ceremonies are becoming optional.

The Changing Composition of the Church

The face of church in the twenty-first century, not unlike the nineteenth and twentieth centuries, will be ethnically diverse. The rising Hispanic presence constitutes one notable community that will demand increasing attention. In 1991 Andrew Greeley reported that the Hispanic birth rate was 20 per 1,000, whereas the national rate was 15.5 per 1,000.[39] There are over 25 million Americans of Hispanic origin, a figure that may be increased if one included those who are undocumented and therefore difficult to include in any census of the population. Estimates of how much of this community identifies themselves as Catholic range from 60 to 80 percent.[40] Conservative estimates place the Hispanic Catholic population at about 15 million, making them about one-fourth of the U.S. Catholic population. About 60 percent of U.S. Hispanics come from Mexico, 13 percent from Puerto Rico, and 5 percent from Cuba, and 8 percent from other (mostly Latin American) countries.

Latinos clearly differ from one another in background, style, and preferences. The following description by sociologists of religion Wade Clark Roof and Christel Manning illustrates this point.

> The scene is Los Angeles, California, on a Sunday morning, and on first glance it is not all that unusual: a Roman Catholic Church in a Hispanic neighborhood with hundreds in attendance. But on closer look, there are some peculiarities: some people are leaving, others are just arriving. Those leaving are Mexican Americans, those arriving are from Central America—mainly Salvadorans and Nicaraguans. This Sunday they hold

The diversity of Roman Catholicism in America today is illustrated by the Asian-style architecture of the Vietnamese Martyrs Shrine built by the diocese of Orange, California.
COURTESY VIETNAMESE MARTYRS SHRINE

their own services at different hours, each celebrating their own ethnic
and religious traditions. On the first Sunday of the month they gather
for joint Eucharist in which prayers are recited using both traditions.[41]

The Hispanic community differs from the majority of Catholics in a
number of ways. Many who have recently immigrated do not speak English
well and are learning the language and customs of the country. By and large,
Hispanics represent an undereducated population in which less than 10 percent have graduated from college, and high school drop-out rates remain as
high as 40 percent.[42] Their spiritual needs, arising from a faith that revolves
around religious devotion and popular tradition rather than doctrines and
church pronouncements, often go unmet. The priest-theologian Orlando
Espin notes that "popular Catholicism reads the gospel texts quite literally,
enriching its interpretation of them with non-canonical traditions, and especially with commonsensical wisdom."[43] In many ways, their religious habits
hearken back to the Anglo population 1950s Catholicism, favoring religious
medals around their necks, statues in their homes, and family-based prayer.

One result of the church's lack of attention to their spiritual needs is
that between 1980 and 1990 five million Hispanic Catholics left the Catholic
Church. The Reverend Ricardo Chavez, spokesman for the California
Catholic conference, reports that Hispanics leave the church at the rate of
about 100,000 a year.[44] They often move to Evangelical or Pentecostal

churches where they are more likely to find a form of worship and spirituality that suits their penchant for popular religion—a place where the theology is less complex, the ritual more dynamic, and the emotional quotient high. Alan Figueroa Deck views this as a complex phenomenon that eludes naive characterizations.[45]

As the Hispanic community acculturates and increasingly identifies with American habits and ideas, they tend to assimilate a more secular perspective, note sociologists Gerardo Marín and Raymond Gamba.[46] At the same time, however, many wish to maintain their ethnic identity proudly thinking of themselves as Chicanos or Latinos. One survey found no significant differences in religious views between high school seniors of Hispanic and non-Hispanic origin, indicating that second generation Catholics of Spanish origin are rapidly assimilating into the larger culture. For instance, they prefer mass in English and "often do not feel that they fit into their parents' churches, nor do they feel fully accepted in Anglo culture."[47]

Hispanics lack adequate representation in the hierarchical and institutional church, with 21 active bishops, 1,600 priests, and 2,000 nuns in 1997. The church encourages vocations among the Hispanic community but, as in other ethnic groups, the response is inadequate to serve the needs of this diverse and growing community. In places where a large Hispanic population resides, for example California, dioceses require that all priests learn Spanish. In other areas, the community seeks out Spanish-speaking clergy and some dioceses designate particular parishes or centers with bilingual staff to serve them. In *Transforming Parish Ministry*, Jay Dolan notes that often the poor among them settle in cities, although the suburbs are seeing an increased Latino presence.[48] In terms of income and influence they are the underclass of the American church.

But they are also the future, or at least a big part of it. The church must serve them better, recognize them more, encourage them to take part as leaders. The church cannot afford to ignore them, underserve them, or otherwise disregard their concerns. It must attempt to integrate Hispanics while at the same time it must respect their language, cultures, and religious practices. They represent a significant part of the church at present and a growing presence in the future.

Challenged, Not Undone

The fact that the church faces significant challenges on a number of fronts does not mean that it is in danger of dying, collapsing, or disappearing.

Some of the problems that the Roman Catholic Church in America faces can be overcome with greater effort, more sensitivity, and clear vision. Others appear beyond its immediate control. This is due, in part, to its ties to Rome, which prevent it from embarking on national initiatives that conflict with the Vatican's agenda, and in part to American culture which shapes Catholics in the same way that it shapes other citizens. A number of American cultural forces work against the church's agenda, forcing Catholics consciously to resist or oppose elements of culture that society as a whole accepts. Of course, Catholics do not always do so. Like other Americans, religious and nonreligious, they regularly follow cultural patterns. A church embedded in a culture cannot avoid this dialectic.

The church can, however, shape its response to culture, inform and form its constituency, offer alternatives where possible, and provide reasons to resist cultural pressures when necessary. In order to do so effectively, the church must know its members, respect their thinking, listen to their voices, and take them seriously. And in some regards this occurs: Cardinal Bernardin's ongoing Common Ground Project that attempts to bring conservatives and liberals into constructive conversation, for example. In other respects, the hierarchical church conducts itself as if it were the sole adjudicator of what benefits the Catholic community, for example, the continuing ban on birth control. No one can reasonably expect all Catholics to think alike, just as no one can expect all Americans to agree on federal or local public policy initiatives. The church is accustomed to differing views among its membership. On those issues in which some transgress, there is forgiveness. On matters on which they disagree, there remains dissent. In either case, the official church usually approaches change cautiously and effects it slowly.

CHAPTER TEN

The Future

The complex story of American Catholicism is one of allegiance and independence; obedience and autonomy; assimilation and separatism; creating a Catholic subculture and then trying to escape it. It is a story of a community who wants to be loyal to its church and its country. It is cardinals who follow the Vatican's sometimes unpopular directives; bishops who want to identify with their people but at the same time want to be cardinals; priests who minister tirelessly but are feeling increasingly overburdened and underappreciated; and lay people who campaign either for more democratic structures, or more central control, or who ignore the institutional implications of their religion altogether.

In the first half of the nineteenth century, Alexis de Tocqueville wrote in *Democracy In America*: "The [people] of our days are naturally little disposed to believe; but as soon as they have any religion, they immediately find in themselves a latent instinct that urges them unconsciously towards Catholicism. Many of the doctrines and practices of the Roman Catholic Church astonish them, but they feel a secret admiration for its discipline, and its great unity attracts them."[1] Not only has its unity attracted them, it has maintained their interest. American Catholics seem to like the universal character of the church while at the same time objecting to certain practices and beliefs that underlie this unity. Most do not envy their Protestant brothers and sisters and they do not wish to emulate the divisions that Protestant Christianity displays. Besides, declaring independence from Rome would not resolve all of the issues that differentiate American Catholics from each other. There would still be those who favor and those who oppose women priests, noncelibate clergy, local autonomy and universal compliance, more rules and fewer rules.

The combination of Vatican II and the cultural revolution in the 1960s in America left Catholics reeling. Perhaps the American canonist James Provost is correct when he reflected that it will take a long time for the church to absorb Vatican II in its entirety. But his prediction that "[W]e must anticipate a period—perhaps a century or two—of unsettled times"[2] is not very comforting to Americans who are accustomed to change but fear anarchy. Nevertheless, it may take much longer than forty years for the church to implement Vatican II wisely. Or, since the world evolves so quickly, it may require a Vatican Council every fifty years simply for the church to keep up with cultural and social change.

In their 1984 book *How to Save the Catholic Church*, Andrew Greeley and Mary Durkin asked: "By the turn of the millennium, will there be anything left of Catholicism in the United States, except perhaps some ethnic customs, to distinguish it from other Christian Churches. . .?"[3] My answer, as I have tried to make clear in this book, is, "yes." But the Catholicism of the twenty-first century will differ markedly from that of the previous century.

First of all, there will be a new pope. John Paul II is energetic, but he is not well. Unquestionably, he has put his stamp on Catholicism globally—a carefully crafted one created over two decades. The likelihood is that his legacy will loom large over the church as it embraces the twenty-first century. He has meticulously groomed the next generation of episcopal leadership. But while one can confidently predict what the hierarchy of the church will look like in the national and international arena in the near future, the local leadership, particularly at the level of the parish, is changing rapidly. Pastoral ministry no longer equals clerical ministry. The male and female lay professional presence has changed the face of institutional Catholicism. To some degree, lay women replace the sisters who toiled before them in various ministries—sisters whose numbers have shrunk so that even a consolidation of orders (an unlikely event) or a narrower focus of ministry will not result in a presence and influence that even approach that of forty years ago.

Of course, the laity who take up the mantle of professionally caring for the church are themselves of all different stripes—some more doctrinally rigid, some wishing to revive the subculture of a previous era, some maneuvering for the day when they can operate without clerical "interference," some eschewing all politics in the church, all wondering what the future will bring and praying that the Holy Spirit will lead them in the right direction. Increasingly, the laity are taking responsibility within the church. In 1950, 17,000 lay people worked full-time for the church; by 1997 that number grew to 177,000. Lay influence grows daily and it is bound to have a long-term impact.

American Catholics are diverse in their beliefs, practices, levels of affiliation, loyalty, and identification with the church. Journalist Paul Wilkes accurately observed:

> Indeed, there is more room in Catholicism than a person might imagine. From Bible-quoting fundamentalist Catholics to Catholics who have found a spirituality rooted in Buddhist meditation, from Catholics who celebrate the mass in an uproarious charismatic celebration to those who prefer the quiet dignity of a Tridentine Mass, the church is broad enough for all.[4]

In many ways diversity serves the church well. And there is no sign that a homogeneous community is on the horizon. The followers of Jesus in the Roman Catholic Church reflect the ways in which he himself served. The director of a soup kitchen is doing Jesus's work of feeding the hungry. The hospice volunteer or nurse is comforting the dying as Jesus would have them do. The university theologian follows Jesus's example as a teacher. The protester against capital punishment or abortion emulates Jesus's cries against injustice and immorality. The inspiring preacher brings Jesus's parables and narratives to life for a new generation. The religious education teacher suffers the little children to come unto her as Jesus instructed his disciples to allow him to do. The retreat director uncovers a path to God as Jesus did for those willing to listen to him. The liturgical scripture reader proclaims the Word of the Lord. The finance committee chairperson insures that the resources to do Jesus's work are sufficient to the task. The parish social life committee members help to create a community that knows each other by name instead of a group of anonymous churchgoers. The youth minister nurtures tomorrow's leaders with respect for their presence in the church today. The pastor spends himself so that others may know the gospel and encounter the living God. The rich talents of many in this diverse community enable the church to serve a wide variety of needs and will enable it to continue to flourish in the twenty-first century.

A Church with Staying Power

Those who loudly proclaim that Catholicism is drawing its dying breath are most likely not very well acquainted with history. The church has defied prognosticators in the past and will do so in the present. It is neither dying nor in crisis. While it is not without troubles, Roman Catholicism, with its deep roots and staying power, is growing in America. I agree with the contemporary Jesuit theologian Thomas Rausch that "In spite of the divisions in the Catholic community today, the church is still very much alive and healthy."[5] History has witnessed corrupt popes, clergy with concubines, and laity with swords. The American church within recent memory has seen bishops caught in sexually compromising situations, priests arrested and tried for pederasty, entire orders of nuns dying for lack of vocations, and laity divided between conservatives and liberals. All this, and people remain loyal. All this, and baptisms are up. All this, and the Sunday 10 o'clock mass remains crowded. All this, and people still find here something with which to identify, a tradition worth holding on to, a tradition worth investing themselves in.

But the church faces continuing challenges. Ironically, despite the crowded masses at many churches, statistics indicate an overall decline in church attendance to about one-third of the Catholic population. Of the sixty million Catholics in America, one-third do not even bother to register in a parish, one-third do not attend church regularly, and one-third regularly participate.

The church remains important in the lives of Catholics, but it must compete for their attention and allegiance with social, cultural, and economic forces that pull them in different directions. While not a new tension for Catholics in America, the price for disobedience to church practices is lower now than a generation ago. Contemporary Catholics do not fear the institutional church to the degree that previous generations did. Unlike their grandparents who held church rules as mandatory, today's Catholics more readily perceive compliance as voluntary. The days when the church dictates in all facets of a Catholic's life are gone. In the 1950s Catholicism had cultural supports and an institutional regime that cannot be retrieved in the beginning of the twenty-first century (despite the nostalgia and efforts by some to do so). The areas in which the church carries significant authority in a believer's life are fewer than in the past and the authority is of a different type. The educational level of American Catholics today is much higher overall than in the first half of the twentieth century, the economic status greater, and the social stigmas for noncompliance with church dictates have greatly diminished. In other words, if the church wants followers to comply with its teachings, it had better persuade them because it surely will not be able to order them to obey. Threats of eternal damnation fall on deaf ears.

Will American Catholicism follow the way of several Protestant denominations and of Judaism, and divide into different bodies like Missouri Synod Lutheranism and the Lutheran Church in America, or Orthodox, Conservative, and Reform Judaism? It seems unlikely. Somehow, for all their differences among themselves and with Rome, American Catholics cling to their single identity as Catholics, even though that identity implies a pluralism of beliefs and practices. While some Catholics, disenchanted with Vatican oversight, may entertain thoughts of an independent "American Catholic Church," they have not proposed concrete measures that would give birth to such a stepchild of Roman Catholicism. The overwhelming majority of American Catholics are content to be *Roman* Catholics and are not inclined to favor a separate "American Catholic Church."

A Church Moving Toward the Laity

The face of Catholicism will be different in the twenty-first century. One of the major differences is the make-up of local leadership. Increasingly it is a church of the laity. A curious and certainly unintended consequence of the priest shortage, brought on at least in part by the intransigence of the Vatican on women's ordination or a married clergy, is the laity assuming greater responsibility for day-to-day operations and ministry. Tasks previously reserved exclusively to the clergy and nuns, such as pastoral counseling, religious education, youth ministry, sacramental preparation, hospital ministry, pastoral administration, and liturgical planning, now are the domain of lay professionals, volunteers, or a combination of both.

There remain many among the laity who are uncomfortable with the de-clericalizing of the local church leadership. Barbara Mullen of St. Michael's Parish in Wausaw, in the diocese of Lacrosse, Wisconsin, hesitates when confronted with the new situation of parishes staffed mostly by lay people. "If I have a problem, I feel more comfortable approaching a priest than discussing it with a layperson. Increasingly that opportunity is being taken away from me."

What she faces, many others also experience and all American Catholics will soon face. The decline in vocations continues, leaving the church with little choice but to consolidate its personnel and to replace clergy in pastoral positions with laity. Everyone from the bishops to the parishioners needs to adjust to this new situation. In what ways it is for better or worse remains to be seen, but that it will happen is a virtual certainty.

Bishop Joseph A. Galante of Beaumont, Texas, instituted a program called "Liturgy Renew" in his churches for weekend masses in part because he was alarmed when he read a survey that indicated that only one-third of Catholics believe in the real presence of Christ in the Eucharist.[6] This represents one belief among many that is being challenged, disbelieved, or ignored by the faithful in a church grounded in doctrines. In some cases, Post-Vatican II Catholics are not taught the dogmas of the church. In other instances, they find them simply not credible. One religious education teacher devoted an entire class to the explanation of the Eucharist, detailing the philosophical conditions and theological assertions about the real presence of Christ in the Eucharist, including an explanation of transubstantiation to the degree that he understood it and in language that, to the best of his ability, would convey meaning to his eighth grade class. When he finished his presentation, one incredulous student blurted out: "You expect me to believe that!" The teacher's appeal to mystery as a last-ditch effort to salvage the session met equally with disbelief and disinterest from the entire group.

Contemporary Catholics exhibit skepticism over claims that their grandparents willingly embraced. In a world in which scientists are working on cloning, humans can live on space stations for months at a time, and the internet can retrieve information from around the world almost instantaneously, there is very little mystery left in moon light through the window, never mind epiphenomenal theological claims.

The Catholic subculture, that often paralleled the larger American culture and provided opportunity and identity for Catholics, so vibrant and evident in the 1950s, has dramatically declined at the turn of the twentieth century. One remainder is the clerical culture, which itself is divided among priests and bishops who encourage mutual decision making, shared ministry, and empowerment of all; and those whose identity is in their authority by virtue of ordination—an identity ontologically different from, and an authority over, the laity. The clerical culture persists; but the Catholic subculture, such a prominent feature from the immigrants to the third-generation Americans, while still visible to those who seek it, is less evident today. The days of "Father knows best" are pretty much gone. Today, Father does not always know best. He is no better educated than his congregation, and sometimes less so. He may know some theology and canon law, but these are not the determining forces of life in the suburbs. The members of his profession have feet of clay, and those feet have been exposed in a multiplicity of embarrassing situations. Even those above suspicion or reproach have not escaped the loss of stature suffered by the profession. People still love their priests, but they do not defer to them simply because of their clerical status. Catholics disagreed with their pastors in the past, but the high regard for the priesthood and the fear of punishment (from God or the church) tempered their disagreement. Today, respect and fear do not function in the same way. Doctors, lawyers, and TV talk-show hosts have as much or more authority as priests in Catholics' lives. Often the ultimate court of appeal is that of experience, no matter how myopic, unreflective, or particular one's experience may be. Arguments from authority are unconvincing to the majority of contemporary American Catholics.

The vast majority of Catholics are no longer ruled by the church in their personal or public life. They practice birth control at the same rate as other Americans, go to the movies after consulting newspaper and television reviews and hearing of hits by word of mouth (few check the NCCB ratings), go to church less regularly than the previous generation (in this regard they are becoming more like Protestant worshipers), make political choices based on many factors, only some of which have religious implications, and want the best education for their children (be it parochial, public, or private). If they are not convinced of the church's position by virtue of reason and experience, they are unlikely to be convinced by an appeal to tradition or authority. Preserving traditions for the sake of tradition does not make good sense to many of them.

The church is founded on tradition. But that tradition is not Catholic culture; it is the message of Jesus. As long as the church preaches, teaches, and lives that message, it is true to its roots. The rest is mutable. The best teacher of this lesson is church history. The church in its infancy struggled for recognition. In the medieval period, some popes were prisoners and some fathered children. In its heyday the church dominated Western culture. At the end of the twentieth century, its days of cultural hegemony are long gone. In the twenty-first century it will find its place as one cultural force among many—Christendom is ended, but Christianity survives. The church in America served as the cultural focal point for an immigrant community. In an era when most citizens no longer identify themselves as Irish, Polish, Italian, or German but simply as American, their religious identity is subservient to their sense of being autonomous individuals.

The majority of American Catholics are neither radical liberals nor reactionary conservatives. They live their faith somewhere in the middle of these extremes. The extremists, however, garner a great deal of attention, probably more than they deserve. Writing for *Our Sunday Visitor*, David Carlin describes this group well:

> What Catholicism needs is a third way, a *via media* ("middle way") that rejects the unrealistic extremes of progressivism and traditionalism while retaining positive elements of both. . . . It is this *via media*, I suspect, that most churchgoing Catholics are quietly attached to. But they are too quiet. All the noise and the passion are found in the left and right wings, none in the center.[7]

Echoing this idea, Mary Jo Weaver commented jokingly that in addition to *Being Right* and *What's Left*, describing conservative and liberal Catholics respectively, she should write a book about the majority of Catholics and title it *Who Cares?* It may, however, be risky to equate silence with apathy, lack of "noise and passion" with lack of conviction and caring. It is the majority of Catholics who support their parish—sometimes at a great financial burden to themselves; it is the "silent" ones who fill the pews and try to participate in changing liturgies, unfamiliar hymns, occasionally experimental innovations. It is those in the *via media* who volunteer in soup kitchens or in children's instruction classes. It is they who organize the parish bazaar, collect food for Thanksgiving, Christmas, and Easter baskets; set up Christmas "Giving Trees," serve the free Thanksgiving dinner, deliver Christmas gifts to foster homes, nursing homes, and hospitals—while some among the "noisy" ones are complaining and criticizing, or dreaming of a "new" or "different" church.

Assimilated Catholics: Benefits and Dangers

Despite the efforts of conservative Catholics, the Catholic subculture of the pre-Vatican II era is eroding if not disappearing in most places in America. While liberal Catholics do not mourn this loss, there is a price to pay for assimilation. Catholics themselves protested against the Catholic "ghetto" of the 1940s and '50s and longed to be assimilated into the larger American culture. Since the 1960s they have been assimilated—to the point that many are now virtually indistinguishable from others in the society. A simultaneous consequence of this successful assimilation is the loss of group identity, lack of a common vision, detachment from specific marks of identification, and appropriation of practices and values esteemed by the common culture, whether or not they adhere to Catholic principles. In brief, they face the danger of being American, but not Catholic.

It is well known among sociologists of religion, church historians, and Protestant administrators that mainline Protestant churches have been shrinking in membership in the latter half of the twentieth century. A complex of reasons account for the decline including but not limited to decreasing birth rates, changing ethnic composition of society, movement to other Christian churches, and aging of the baby-boomers. Some Protestant churches see alliances as the answer to declining numbers, but thus far this has not produced an upswing in membership. Could the same fate await the Catholic church? Will assimilation result in greater loss? Statistics on church attendance indicate that the church of the twenty-first century will have a smaller core membership that participates regularly while at the same time the number of baptized Catholics grows.

One possible cause of declining numbers and waning influence is the loss of a clear message within Christianity. The mid twentieth-century theologian H. Richard Niebuhr wrote about the ways in which Christ's message conflicts with the habits of culture, suggesting that the church must stand against the world. Perhaps all Christian churches could benefit from such a bold stance in terms of a clear identity that sets them apart from society. An "easy" Christianity—polite, accommodating, nonconfrontational—smoothes the harsh edge that Jesus's message includes. Perhaps Catholics should be different, radically different, in the ways in which they interface with American society. Maybe Catholic Christianity, like all forms of Christianity, has been too accommodating of secular cultural and social developments.

But such a call for difference seems unlikely to occur on a wide scale. Most Catholics like their Christianity to fulfill their spiritual needs but not at a cost of severely disrupting their lifestyle. Willing to sacrifice to a degree for their religious convictions, most Catholics maintain a threshold that keeps them from embracing a radical commitment that would impinge on all areas of their lives. Compartmentalized religion means comfortable religion for the vast majority.

The Many Cultures of American Catholicism

In all likelihood, American Catholics will continue in the twenty-first century to form a community that is bound by a core of central beliefs and

divided by a multiplicity of practices, moral stances, and theological differences with Rome and with each other. One parish that advertises "God's
People in Great Variety" captures the essence of American Catholicism. No
procrustean bed suits them; no single characterization describes them; they
are not circumscribed by any one definition. They boast a rich tradition that
binds them but is continually developing and changing. They identify with
Rome but often think and act as if the American church, or their own parish
for that matter, is the whole of Catholicism. The Catholic subculture so
prominent in the 1950s has evolved into less homogeneous manifestations.
For some it signifies spirituality, for others sacramental life, for others moral
guidelines, and for still others social bonds. For fully one third of American
Catholics, the church holds little attraction or relevance.

There is no single answer to the question "What does it mean to be a
Catholic in America in the twenty-first century?" But that question had no
single answer in any previous century either. The portrait offered in this
book testifies to the variety of expressions that American Catholicism manifests. Only by surveying the different parts can one see the whole.

Select Profiles of American Catholics

Joseph Cardinal Bernardin
Born April 2, 1928; Died November 14, 1996

Among the most influential prelates in the second half of the twentieth century, Cardinal Bernardin was the archbishop of Chicago from 1982 until his death in 1996. Named "Most influential religious leader" in a 1976 poll by *U.S. News and World Report*, Cardinal Bernardin held many important positions during his priestly career, including president of the National Conference of Catholic Bishops and the United States Catholic Conference, a member of several pontifical commissions, and chairperson of the Pro-Life Committee of the NCCB. Architect of the bishops' pastoral letter on nuclear war, he won the Albert Einstein Peace Prize in 1983. He fostered closer relations between Jews and Christians, both in Cincinnati where he was archbishop, in Chicago, and nationally. A capable administrator, he never lost his pastoral connection with the priests and people in his charge and proved to be a master of consensus building. Despite his busy schedule, he used to visit his mother daily in her nursing home.

Shortly before his death, he initiated the Catholic Common Ground Project, a dialogue between conservatives and liberals in the church that continues today. Known as "Joseph, your brother" from the time of his introduction to the Chicago community, his death was mourned by people of all religions in the city who viewed him as a leader, a spiritual model, and a friend.

Corinne Claiborne "Lindy" Boggs
Born March 13, 1916

U.S. Representative to Congress from Louisiana from 1973 to 1991, Corinne Boggs succeeded her husband (Thomas) Hale Boggs Sr. after he was killed in a helicopter accident. Born in Louisiana, she acknowledges the deep influence of the nuns who educated her in her youth in her 1994 autobiography, *Washington Through a Purple Veil*. A defender of civil rights, she found allies in the church to support her social and political activities on behalf of minorities and she spoke in Congress for women's rights as well as attending to the needs of her Louisiana constituents. In 1976 she served as chairperson of the Democratic National Convention, the first woman to do so.

In addition to her public duties, she is the mother of the ABC News commentator Cokie Roberts, Washington lobbyist and lawyer Tommy Boggs, and Barbara Sigmund (d. 1990), who started her own political career working in the Kennedy White House, worked with the Domestic Peace Corps, and ran for political office. Lindy Boggs, a faithful Catholic all of her life, has served her country and the church admirably. In recognition of this, President Clinton appointed her Ambassador to the Vatican in 1997.

Thea Bowman, F.S.P.A.
Born December 29, 1937; Died March 30, 1990

Born in Canton, Mississippi, the granddaughter of a slave and a convert to Catholicism, Thea Bowman joined the Franciscan nuns, earned a doctorate in English Literature from Catholic University of America in 1972, and became a highly respected educator and liturgist. She taught that black spirituality is for all, not just blacks, thus introducing Catholics to the riches of African rituals and African-American folk songs. A gifted singer, she recorded spirituals and performed Gospel music for those unfamiliar with it and those for whom the only religious music was Gospel.

She held a charter membership in the National Black Sisters Conference, helped found Black Catholic Studies at Xavier University in New Orleans, was a moving force behind the Black Catholic Congress, and crisscrossed the country conducting workshops and liturgical celebrations. Six days before her death she was named the recipient of Notre Dame's Laetare Medal, an honor posthumously awarded to her. She was mourned by blacks and whites, bishops, priests, and lay people, the ordinary and the extraordinary, for she touched them all and left a legacy to the American church.

William F. Buckley
Born November 24, 1925

Self-described cradle Catholic and conservative commentator, William Buckley began his publishing career in 1951 with *God and Man at Yale* and in 1997 published *Nearer, My God: An Autobiography of Faith.* As host of the PBS television show "Firing Line" and a widely syndicated columnist, Buckley is one of the best-known conservatives in America.

He founded the *National Review* in 1955. His Catholic faith has been a grounding bedrock throughout his life. A defender of papal authority, Buckley's Catholicism, like his social and political views, is of the conservative variety although he generally supports the reforms instituted by Vatican II. Buckley frequently writes about and discusses theology, often tackling difficult questions such as the problem that evil and suffering pose for believers, the infallibility of the pope, and the meaning of Jesus's crucifixion for the salvation of the world. In this way, he has brought Catholic doctrine to the attention of a wide audience that he commands by virtue of his television appearances, columns, and books.

Mary Ann Glendon
Born October 7, 1938

Harvard Law School Professor Mary Ann Glendon has served on several Vatican committees and, the first woman to head a Vatican delegation, she represented Pope John Paul II at the United Nations Fourth World Conference on Women held in Beijing, China, in September 1995. Born in Dalton, Massachusetts, she grew up there until she went to college at the University of Chicago where she also received her law degree at age 21. She worked in the civil rights movement in Mississippi, married and later divorced an African-American lawyer with whom she had one child, and is currently married to a retired Jewish lawyer and writer. They have two daughters.

A strong supporter of the Vatican's opposition to abortion, at the Beijing conference she represented a position that was unpopular with many attendees but one which the church holds firm. She sees family planning programs, particularly when imposed by developing countries, as methods to alleviate poverty by eliminating poor people. Many observers including Glendon thought that the preceding conference, held in Cairo, was dominated by radical feminist interests and at the Beijing conference they wanted to represent motherhood and family life in a more positive light. She openly opposes the Supreme Court's *Roe vs. Wade* decision and favors economic policies that aid the poor. A prolific writer, among her numerous books is one that expresses her views on the family, *Abortion and Divorce in Western Law*.

Andrew Greeley
Born February 8, 1928

Priest, sociologist, and novelist. Most American Catholics probably know the name of Andrew Greeley, and many have an opinion of his work. A priest of the Archdiocese of Chicago, Greeley is also a widely published sociologist who teaches at the universities of Chicago and Arizona, is a Research Associate at the National Opinion Center at the University of Chicago, a columnist commenting on church issues, and the author of over 30 best-selling novels, most of which have plots and themes that are intertwined with Catholic identity.

He was educated in Chicago Catholic schools, St. Mary of the Lake Seminary, and the University of Chicago. Greeley has been a lightning-rod for Catholics—some saying that he is irreverent and hyper-critical of the institutional church and the hierarchy; others saying that he has only been pointing to conditions, flaws, and misdirection in the church that are apparent to the attentive observer but to which the bishops seem to turn a blind eye.

His website (www.Agreele@aol.com) is no doubt one of the most sophisticated among American clergy.

Theodore M. Hesburgh, C.S.C.
Born May 25, 1917

Theodore Hesburgh, a member of the religious order the Congregation of the Holy Cross, the (15th) president of Notre Dame University from 1952 to 1987, is one of the most influential voices on higher education in America. The *New York Times* said of his 1990 autobiography: "One should have to have been unconscious not to have heard of Father Hesburgh at some time during the last four decades." Born in Syracuse, New York, he was educated at the University of Notre Dame, Gregorian University in Rome, and the Catholic University of America, from which he received his doctorate in theology in 1945. Ordained in Sacred Heart Church on the campus of Notre Dame on June 24, 1943, he began teaching at Notre Dame in 1945.

He has held 14 presidential appointments dealing with civil rights, atomic energy, and third world development. He was appointed a member of the

U.S. Civil Rights Commission in 1957 (from which he was dismissed by President Nixon in 1972 after he complained publicly of lack of progress on civil rights). From 1963 to 1970 he was president of the International Federation of Catholic Universities. He received the Medal of Freedom from President Johnson in 1964. He has been a member of the National Science Board, as well as a member of several papal commissions. He is a director of the Chase Manhattan Bank and a trustee of the Rockefeller Foundation (the first priest to be named to either), and has been the recipient of over one hundred and twenty honorary degrees. His tenure as president of the University of Notre Dame was the longest held by any president of an American institution of higher education.

A skilled fund raiser, he improved the reputation and visibility of Notre Dame nationally and internationally. The main library at Notre Dame was named after him upon his retirement. He has remained active overseeing the creation of an international peace studies center.

The Kennedy Family

Many non-Catholic Americans have become acquainted with Catholicism through the public events marked by religious ceremony within the Kennedy family. The election of John F. Kennedy as president in 1960 initiated a new era for Catholics in public life. His televised funeral mass permitted Americans to see the liturgy of Catholicism with commentators explaining the significance of various parts of the ritual.

The baptisms, weddings, and funerals of other family members, including that of assassinated presidential candidate Robert, further exposed Catholicism to the American public. Even Congressman Joseph Kennedy's divorce brought Catholic practices into the public eye.

Michael Novak
Born September 9, 1933

In the 1960s Michael Novak stood for liberal ideas, championed Vatican II, and was considered by many to signify a new democratic form of Catholicism. Since then, his political and religious views shifted to the right and he has become a "neo-conservative."

The author of dozens of books, Novak is a social critic and philosopher who began his career after studying for the priesthood in Rome and subsequently at Harvard. He has taught at a number of leading American universities, been director of humanities at the Rockefeller Foundation, and a fellow at the American Enterprise Institute for Public Policy Research. His 1983 book, *Confessions of a Catholic*, criticized the post-Vatican II church and its theology. He also published articles and letters critical of the American bishops' pastoral letters on war and the economy. He is a strong supporter of Pope John Paul II's attempts to curb post-Vatican II theological speculation and to direct the church toward more traditional interpretations and practices. In 1998, with his daughter Jana, he cowrote a popular book, *Tell Me Why: A Father Answers His Daughter's Questions About God*.

John Cardinal O'Connor
Born January 15, 1920

The eighth archbishop of New York, Cardinal O'Connor, an influential leader and a powerful voice on issues ranging from the church's pro-life stance to Jewish-Christian relations, has held influential positions both on Vatican commissions and the National Conference of Bishops. A native of Philadelphia, he served from 1952 to 1979 as a chaplain with the United States Navy and Marine Corps, rising to the rank of rear admiral before becoming bishop for the armed forces in 1979. He served briefly as bishop of Scranton before being named archbishop of New York in 1984.

Not shy with the press, Cardinal O'Connor consistently and vigorously defends even unpopular church policies. He has coauthored books with former New York City Mayor Edward Koch and Nobel prizewinner Elie Wiesel. He is a progressive about issues of social justice and a staunch defender of the church's doctrinal positions. On the day that CBS 60 Minutes news program featured Dr. Jack Kevorkian involved in active euthanasia, from the pulpit O'Connor strongly condemned Kevorkian as a proponent of America's "culture of death." In 1997 he received the Fiat Lux Award from Clark University for his contribution to Holocaust education. A tireless worker, the fact that he has remained archbishop of New York beyond the normal retirement age of 75 indicates the confidence that Pope John Paul II has in his leadership.

Helen Prejean, C.S.J.
Born April 21, 1939

Sister Helen Prejean is an internationally known opponent of the death penalty. She published her extraordinary autobiography protesting the death penalty in 1993 in a best-selling book titled *Dead Man Walking*. The book became a successful film by the same name and Susan Sarandon won an Academy Award for her portrayal of Sister Prejean.

A native of Baton Rouge, Sister Perjean has worked in Louisiana all her life joining the Sisters of St. Joseph of Medaille in 1957 when she was 18 years old. Her religious community pledged itself to "stand on the side of the poor." Since 1982, when she began her correspondence with death-row inmate Elmo Patrick Sonnier, she has devoted her ministry to counseling death row inmates and the families of their victims. She accompanied Sonnier to his electrocution. Since that time, she has decried the immorality of capital punishment while concurrently advocating for victims' rights.

She founded "Survive," a victims' advocacy group, served as a board member and chair of the National Coalition to Abolish the Death Penalty, lectured nationwide, received several honorary doctorates, and received the Laetare Medal from the University of Notre Dame in 1996.

Rosemary Radford Ruether
Born November 2, 1936

A theologian and a lay woman, Rosemary Radford Ruether teaches at Garrett-Evangelical Theological Seminary in Evanston, Illinois. Educated at Scripps College and the School of Theology at Claremont, she is internationally recognized as one of the foremost feminist theologians in America. Her works range from a critique of the patriarchal structure of Christianity (*Sexism and God-Talk: Toward a Feminist Theology*), to ecological concerns (*Gaia and God: An Ecofeminist Theology of Earth Healing*), to the practice of ritual (*Women-Church: Theology and Practice of Feminist Liturgical Communities*).

Her theological work is at the forefront of a movement among women to appraise critically the treatment of women in the Christian tradition. This includes deconstructing the androcentric categories which guide Christian theology, criticizing the patriarchal character of revelation and tradition, and giving women a genuine voice in theological conversation. A leading feminist theologian, she has combined concern for the environment with a recognition of women's contributions, experiences, and struggles within Christianity.

Antonin Scalia
Born March 11, 1936

A member of the U.S. Supreme Court since 1986, Antonin Scalia is a devout Catholic who with his wife, Maureen, has nine children, one of whom is a priest in the diocese of Arlington, Virginia. Born in Trenton, N.J., he was educated at Georgetown, Fribourg (Switzerland), and Harvard Law School. He practiced law in a private firm and for the government, and taught at Virginia, Georgetown, Chicago, and Stanford before he was appointed by President Reagan and confirmed by Congress as Associate Justice.

A conservative member of the court, on many occasions in talks outside the court chambers he has spoken in defense of religious beliefs and practices and is unequivocal about his Catholicism. On the court, he has advocated closer ties between the church and state, favoring clergy-led prayer at graduations, public funds for religiously affiliated school programs, and anti-abortion legislation. He was one of four dissenters when the Supreme Court reaffirmed the right to abortion in 1992. He resigned from Georgetown's Board of advisers over differences with the way the university interpreted its Catholic identity and the freedom of expression it permitted students who disagree with Catholic teachings.

Martin Sheen

Born August 3, 1940

Movie actor, father of actors Charlie Sheen, Rene and Emilio Estevez, and dancer Ramon Estevez, Martin Sheen is an active and devout Catholic. He defends the poor, practices civil disobedience based on conscience, and understands Catholicism as a call to justice.

Born in Dayton, Ohio, Sheen (birth name Ramon Estevez) grew up in a pious Roman Catholic family. A self-described liberal Catholic, he is a social activist who has been arrested over 50 times in his fight to gain rights for the poor, stop the nuclear build-up, and protest unjust government policies. His activism has taken him abroad, including a trip in 1997 to Manila in the Philippines to head an international fact-finding mission investigating the plight of the urban poor. In 1988 he fasted with Cesar Chavez to protest the poor working conditions and low wages of migrant farm workers. Along with a group of religious leaders, he was arrested in 1997 supporting strawberry workers in their fight to join the United Farm Workers.

Sheen appeared in several films dealing with Catholic figures and themes including *Fallen Angel: The Dorothy Day Story* (1996, Paulist Films).

In addition to his antinuclear war protest and his efforts to help the working poor, Sheen is a participant in Greenpeace's efforts to preserve the environment. In 1995, he and Greenpeace founder Paul Watson were beaten by seal hunters on the remote Magdelene Islands in the Gulf of St. Lawrence while trying to convince them to refrain from killing seals and selling their pelts. He was arrested while also protesting nuclear testing in Nevada with (now deceased) astronomer Carl Sagen.

David Tracy
Born January 6, 1939

Most Catholics probably do not recognize this name, but among theologians in America and internationally, David Tracy is one of the best known and most influential of the last quarter of the twentieth century. Born in New York, Tracy is a priest from the diocese of Bridgeport, Connecticut, who was educated at the Gregorian University in Rome and holds the Andrew Thomas Greeley and Grace McNichols Greeley chair at the University of Chicago Divinity School, where he has taught since 1969.

A part of Tracy's legacy is the number of the theologians whom he has trained during his career—a generation of American scholars of religion. His early work on the Jesuit philosopher Bernard Lonergan grounded Tracy's epistemology, and his later work on hermeneutics established him as one of the foremost theological thinkers in America. He combines interpretation of classics with sophisticated philosophical analysis of the sources of revelation in Christianity and other religious traditions in a theory of participatory understanding. He seeks to address a variety of audiences in his work, engaging texts, context, and persons in a conversation that is able to disclose meaning. His books *Blessed Rage for Order* and *Analogical Imagination* thoroughly chronicled the development of contemporary theology.

Time Line

1634   The first Roman Catholics arrive in Maryland aboard two ships, the *Ark* and the *Dove*.

1789   Pope Pius VI (1775–1799) ratifies the changes in "Ex hac Apostolicae," making the American Catholic Church a formal ecclesiastical entity with Baltimore as the first diocese.

1789   Georgetown University, America's oldest Catholic university, founded on the banks of the Potomac in Maryland.

1790   John Carroll becomes the first American bishop.

1830   The first wave of Catholic immigrants enters the United States from across Europe.

1882   Knights of Columbus founded by Father Michael McGivney at age 29 to answer a need for Catholic men to have a lodge to call their own.

1887   The Catholic University of America founded in Washington D.C. by the U.S. bishops.

1891   Rosary and Altar Society for women established.

1892   Pope Leo XIII sends an apostolic delegate to the United States for the first time.

1899   Pope Leo XIII, in *Testem Benevolentiae*, encyclical letter to Cardinal Gibbons of Baltimore, cautions American Catholics against any "among you who conceive of and desire a church in America different from that which is in the rest of the world."

1907   Pope Pius X calls modernism "the synthesis of all heresies" in the encyclical *Pascendi Dominici Gregis*.

1908   The American church no longer considered a missionary church by Rome when Pope Pius X signed the apostolic constitution *Sapienti Consilio*.

1909   Holy Name Society established for men for prayer and support of the church.

1910   Pope Pius X requires clerics to take an oath against modernism; not rescinded until 1967.

1911   The American bishops set up their own missionary enterprise, the Maryknoll Catholic Foreign Mission Society of America, Inc.

1919   National Catholic Welfare Council, the official organization of American bishops, established.

1928   Al Smith, a Catholic, encounters anti-Catholic sentiment in his unsuccessful bid for U.S. presidency.

1928   *Opus Dei* founded in Spain.

1931–1942   Father Charles Coughlin discusses Catholic concerns and social issues in radio broadcasts heard by millions of Americans.

1933   Catholic Worker Movement founded by Peter Maurin and Dorothy Day in which Catholics embrace voluntary poverty to fight the involuntary poverty endured by the poor.

1959   Cardinal Angelo Roncalli of Venice, nearly 77 years old, elected Pope John XXIII in 1958.

1960   John F. Kennedy is the first Catholic elected president of the United States.

1961   Congress passes immigration legislation.

1962–1965   The Second Vatican Council takes place in Rome.

1965   Pope Paul VI visits New York to address the United Nations to urge nations to end all war.

1965   The second wave of Catholic immigrants begins coming largely from Latin America and Southeast Asia.

1968   Catholics United for Faith, a lay organization, founded in St. Paul, Minnesota, to oppose dissent and pluralism within the church.

1968   Pope Paul VI issues encyclical "Humanae Vitae," prohibiting Catholics from practicing birth control.

1968   Eighty-seven Catholics, including some prominent (ordained) theologians, dissent from the teaching of "Humanae Vitae" in a statement published in the *New York Times*.

1969   Thomas Merton, monk of Gethsemane Abbey and leading Catholic writer, suffers an accidental death while attending a conference in Thailand.

1973   The U.S. Supreme Court in *Roe vs. Wade* rules that abortion is legal.

1979   Pope John Paul II comes on his first papal visit to the United States, visiting Boston, New York, Philadelphia, Chicago, and Washington.

1983   National Conference of Catholic Bishops issues pastoral, "The Challenge of Peace: God's Promise and Our Response," dealing with nuclear war.

1983   Revised Code of Canon Law, completely updating the 1917 Code, promulgated by the Vatican.

1983   Archbishop Raymond Hunthausen of Seattle under review by Vatican for unorthodox practices leading to shared administrative responsibilities with a Rome-appointed auxiliary.

1984   Official diplomatic relations between the United States and the Vatican are established when President Ronald Reagan and Pope John Paul II agree to have America represented to Rome by an ambassador.

1984   Four male religious and twenty-two female religious sign *New York Times* ad that said Catholics held a "diversity of opinions" on abortion and asked for open discussion of the issue.

1986   National Conference of Catholic Bishops issues pastoral, "Economic Justice, for All: Catholic Social Teaching and the U.S. Economy."

1987   Pope John Paul II returns to the United States visiting Miami, South Carolina, New Orleans, New Mexico, Arizona, Los Angeles, San Antonio, San Francisco, and Detroit.

1992   Approval of the new *Catechism of the Catholic Church*, a compendium of the teachings of the church, the first universal catechism in 400 years.

1993   Pope John Paul II attends 8th World Youth Day held in Denver.

1995   Pope John Paul II comes to the United States, visiting New Jersey, New York, and Baltimore.

1995   Harvard Law Professor Mary Ann Glendon represents the Vatican at international conference on women held in Beijing, China.

1998   Pope John Paul II criticizes the U.S. embargo policy against Cuba during a visit to that country.

NOTES

Introduction

1. Jaroslav Pelikan, *The Riddle of Roman Catholicism: Its History, Its Beliefs, Its Future* (Nashville: Abingdon, 1959), 12.

2. Jay P. Dolan, *The American Catholic Experience: A History from the Colonial Times to the Present*, 2d ed. (Notre Dame, Ind: University of Notre Dame Press, 1992), 453.

3. Eugene Kennedy, *Tomorrow's Catholics Yesterday's Church: The Two Cultures of American Catholicism* (New York: Harper and Row, 1988).

4. Walter J. Burghardt, *Tell the Next Generation: Homilies and Near Homilies* (New York: Paulist, 1980), 74.

1. Who Are American Catholics?

1. Monika K. Hellwig, *Understanding Catholicism* (Mahwah, N.J.: Paulist Press, 1981), 51.

2. Canon law distinguishes between nuns and sisters; nuns are members of religious orders and are cloistered; sisters are members of religious congregations and are involved in active ministries such as teaching and social work. In this work, the terms "religious women," and "nuns" refer to either designation. Although most Catholics consider nuns in a special ecclesial category, they are actually lay persons. In this work they are sometimes distinguished from lay people in order to discuss their contributions and concerns independently from lay persons who do not take vows that bind them to the church in a special way as nuns do.

3. "Mass with a Female Touch," *Chicago Tribune*, February 15, 1998. See also Shelia Durkin Dierks, *WomenEucharist* (Denver: Woven Word, 1997).

4. For a detailed history and description of the parish, see James A. Coriden, *The Parish in Catholic Tradition: History, Theology, and Canon Law* (Mahwah, N.J.: Paulist Press, 1997).

5. Jim Castelli and Joseph Gremillion, *The Emerging Parish: The Notre Dame Study of Catholic Life Since Vatican II* (San Francisco: Harper and Row, 1987), 194–95.

6. James D. Davidson et al., *The Search for Common Ground: What Unites and Divides Catholic Americans* (Huntington, Ind.: Our Sunday Visitor, 1997), 38.

7. The results of an extensive study conducted in the 1990s show that Vatican II and Post-Vatican II Catholics' attitudes toward church teachings and practices are less inclined to agree with the church than are those of pre-Vatican II Catholics. See James D. Davidson et al., *The Search for Common Ground.*

8. James D. Davidson and Andrea Williams, "Generations of Catholics: Results of Focus Groups." Paper presented at the annual meeting of the Association for the Sociology of Religion, Miami, 1993; and, "Catechism Catholics, Council Catholics, and Christian Catholics: A Theory of Catholic Generations." Paper presented at the annual meeting of the Religious Research Association, Albuquerque, 1994. D'Antonio, Davidson, Hoge, and Wallace make use of these theories identified in chapter 4, "Three Generation of Catholics: Pre-Vatican II, Vatican II, and Post-Vatican II," William V. D'Antonio, James D. Davidson, Dean R. Hoge, and Ruth A. Wallace, *Laity American and Catholic: Transforming the Church* (Kansas City: Sheed and Ward, 1996), 65–82. For those unfamiliar with it, Opus Dei is a conservative group sanctioned by the pope that will be discussed later in the book.

9. Robert A. Ludwig, *Reconstructing Catholicism For a New Generation* (New York: Crossroad, 1996), 42.

10. James D. Davidson et al., *The Search for Common Ground,* 24.

11. Cf. Jay P. Dolan, *The American Catholic Experience,* 196.

12. Davidson et al., *The Search for Common Ground,* 45.

13. Ibid., 126.

14. *Marco Island Eagle,* July 24, 1996. The church has permitted cremation since 1963 but never offered explicit guidelines for the final disposition of cremated remains. Lacking these, people created their own personal rites as in the case cited. In 1997 20 percent of all funerals in the United States involved cremation, and the percentage is growing. The Committee on the Liturgy of the National Conference of Catholic Bishops issued a document, "Reflections on the Body, Cremation, and Catholic Funeral Rites" in May 1997 to address just such matters. The document instructs Catholics about the final disposition of the remains and specifically addresses the practice described. "The practice of scattering created remains on the sea, from the air, or on the ground or keeping created remains in the home of a rel-

ative or friend of the deceased are not the reverent disposition that the Church requires." Instead the church requires entombment in a grave, mausoleum, or columbarium.

15. Andrew M. Greeley, "On the Margins of the Church: A Sociological Note," *America*, March 4, 1989, 194.

16. William V. D'Antonio et al., *Laity American and Catholic: Transforming the Church*, 1.

17. James J. Bacik, *Tensions in the Church: Facing the Challenges and Seizing the Opportunities* (Kansas City: Sheed and Ward, 1993), 14.

18. Mary Jo Weaver and R. Scott Appleby, *Being Right: Conservative Catholics in America* (Bloomington, Ind.: Indiana University Press, 1995), 56 (quote from Philip Gleason).

19. "Attendance at Mass Still Declining," *Our Sunday Visitor/Gallup Poll Report*, *Our Sunday Visitor* 27 (January 1985): 5. Social scientists warn that securing an accurate count for churchgoers is a very difficult and complex process. Many would argue that the 44 percent figure is too high and estimate attendance at between 29 and 33 percent. When tallying the numbers one must address questions such as the accuracy of self-reporting, self-definition, and the times of the year that counts are conducted. Barry Kosmin and Seymour Lachman, *One Nation Under God: Religion in Contemporary American Society* (New York: Harmony, 1993) estimate 29 percent attend weekly. A 1991 survey relying on self-reporting indicated that 51 percent of Catholics attend church weekly. However, Mark Chaves and James C. Cavendish concluded that the rate is half that. See "More Evidence on U.S. Catholic Church Attendance," *Journal for the Scientific Study of Religion* 33, no. 4 (1994): 376–81.

20. Peter L. Berger, *A Far Glory: The Quest for Faith in an Age of Credulity* (Garden City, N.Y.: Doubleday, 1992), 44.

21. Michael W. Cuneo, *The Smoke of Satan: Conservative and Traditionalist Dissent in Contemporary American Catholicism* (New York: Oxford University Press, 1997), 26.

22. Bacik, *Tensions in the Church*, 55.

23. Walter M. Abbott, ed., *The Documents of Vatican II* (New York: Herder and Herder, 1966), 60.

24. Oath required of Father Lawrence Madden at his installation as pastor of Holy Trinity Parish, Washington D.C., October 1993. Cited in Jim Naughton, *Catholics in Crisis: An American Parish Fights for its Soul* (Reading, Mass.: Addison-Wesley, 1996), 252. This formulation of the oath, published by the Congregation for the Doctrine of the Faith in the official bulletin of the Holy See, *Acta Apostolicae Sedis*, on January 9, 1989, was designated to be taken by those who function "in the name of the church."

25. Tom Verde, BBC report on "The Latin Mass," August 1997.

26. For a thorough study of the advancement of women in pastoral positions, see Ruth Wallace, *They Call Her Pastor: A New Role for Catholic Women* (Albany: SUNY, 1992).

27. Canon 536 stipulates that if the bishop deems it opportune, parishes are to have councils who may exercise only a consultative vote.

28. Throughout this work the American bishops are often treated as a unified body who think and act alike. It is wise early on to note the caveat of Timothy A. Byrnes, who reminds us that "[We] have a tendency to overstate the cohesiveness of the National Conference of Catholic Bishops. We use the phrase 'the bishops' to describe a large group of men with varied temperaments, varied approaches, and on many questions, varied opinions." "The Politics of Abortion: The Catholic Bishops" in Timothy A. Byrnes and Mary C. Segers, *The Catholic Church and Politics of Abortion: A View from the States* (Boulder: Westview, 1992), 21.

29. Andrew M. Greeley, "Why Do Catholics Stay in the Church?" *New York Times Magazine*, July 10, 1994.

30. Andrew M. Greeley, *The Catholic Myth: The Behaviors and Beliefs of American Catholics* (New York: Scribner's, 1990), 146–47.

31. Mary Jo Anderson, "Trojan Horses: Catholic Dissidents Network" *Crisis* 15, no. 2 (February 1997), 29.

32. Michael Walsh, *Opus Dei: An Investigation into the Secret Society Struggling for Power within the Roman Catholic Church* (San Francisco: Harper, 1989), 176.

33. Bernard Lonergan, "Dimension of Meaning," in Frederick Crowe, ed., *Collection: Papers by Bernard Lonergan* (New York: Herder and Herder, 1967), 266.

34. "Lay People Will Count in the '80s," *Davenport Messenger*, February 21, 1980.

35. According to David C. Leege, about 85 percent of core Catholics (those with definite parish connections) attend the parish within the boundaries of their residences. "The American Catholic Parish" in Francis J. Butler, ed., *American Catholic Identity: Essays in an Age of Change* (Kansas City: Sheed and Ward, 1994), 78.

36. Mary Jo Weaver and R. Scott Appleby, *Being Right*, xi.

37. Monika Hellwig, "American Culture: Reciprocity with Catholic Vision, Values, and Community," in Cassian Yuhaus, ed., *The Catholic Church and American Culture: Reciprocity and Challenge* (Mahwah, N.J.: Paulist Press, 1990), 74.

38. www.truecatholic.org.

39. Quoted in Cuneo, *The Smoke of Satan*, 25.

40. Mary Jo Weaver, "Who Are Conservative Catholics?" in Weaver and Appleby, eds., *Being Right*, 6.

41. One of those who is suspicious of the motives and activities of Opus Dei is Michael Walsh, whose book *Opus Dei* attempts to expose the structure and practices of the organization.

42. www.call-to-action.org.

43. www.dignityusa.org/spp.html.

44. www.sacred-heart.com.

45. *New York Times*, February 28, 1990, B4.

46. Michael Novak, *Confession of a Catholic* (San Francisco: Harper and Row, 1983), 8. Quoted in Weaver and Appleby, *Being Right*, 23.

47. Ibid., ix.

48. Cardinal Joseph Bernardin, "Called to Be Catholic: Church in a Time of Peril," *Origins* 26, no. 11 (August 29, 1996): 169.

49. While most documents in Latin easily yield verbatim translations into English, some do not. Thus, either the literal translation or the common English title is used throughout the book, depending upon the document.

50. Kenneth Untener, bishop of Saginaw, Michigan, wrote an insightful analysis of the debate among cardinals and bishops that ensued after Cardinal Bernardin's and Archbishop Quinn's statements. See "How Bishops Talk," *America* 175, no. 11 (October 19, 1996): 9–15.

51. Bishop James McHugh, "What Is the 'New Situation'?" *Origins* 26, no. 11 (August 29, 1996): 175–76.

52. Mary Jo Anderson, "Shaky Ground" *Crisis* 15, no. 2 (February 1997): 26.

53. Andrew Greeley, "Polarized Catholics? Don't Believe Your Mail!," *America* 176, no. 6 (February 22, 1997): 11–15.

54. Maureen Currey and Flora Van der Zon, letters to the editor, *Detroit News*, October 10, 1995.

55. Paul Wilkes, "The Seven Secrets of Successful Catholics: Pass It On" *U.S. Catholic* 62, no. 9 (September 1997): 8–15. The other six marks of successful Catholics are: 1) members of a faith community; 2) rely on their conscience and good judgment—but never alone; 3) regularly do things that call them out of themselves; 4) live in the moment, recognizing daily opportunities for holiness; 5) always remember that God is merciful and forgiving; 6) believe in prayer and pray regularly.

56. This is particularly true of some radical feminists such as Mary Daly, who argues for a post-Christian understanding of Christianity in the "Feminist Postchristian Introduction" to her second edition of *The Church and the Second Sex* (Boston: Beacon Press, 1985), 15–52 and chronicles her disagreements with the church in her autobiography, *Outercourse: The Be-Da``zling Voyage* (San Francisco: HarperCollins, 1992).

57. This information comes from a personal interview with Judy Scott.

58. Personal interview.

2. A Brief History: Colonial Times to 1900

1. John Deedy, *American Catholicism: And Now Where?* (New York and London: Plenum, 1987), 4.

2. An attempt by President Truman to appoint an ambassador was accompanied by protests and conflict.

3. Cf. James Hennesey, *American Catholics: A History of the Roman Catholic Community in the United States* (New York: Oxford University Press, 1981), 11.

4. Ibid., 14.

5. Ibid., 20.

6. Jay P. Dolan, *The American Catholic Experience: A History from Colonoial Times to the Present* (Notre Dame, Ind.: University of Notre Dame Press, 1992), 56.

7. Ibid., 75.

8. Cf. Stephen J. Vicchio, "The Origins and Development of Anti-Catholicism in America," in Stephen J. Vicchio and Virginia Geiger, eds., *Perspectives on the American Catholic Church, 1789–1989* (Westminster, Md.: Christian Classics, 1989), 84–103.

9. Hennesey, *American Catholics*, 42.

10. Quoted in Cyprian Davis, *The History of Black Catholics in the United States* (New York: Crossroad, 1991), 35.

11. Hennesey, *American Catholics*, 43.

12. Margaret Susan Thompson, "Women and American Catholicism, 1789–1989," in Vicchio and Geiger, eds., *Perspectives on the American Catholic Church 1789–1989*, 126; see note 8.

13. Dolan, *The American Catholic Experience*, 89.

14. Ibid., 97.

15. Patrick W. Carey, *The Roman Catholics* (Westport, Conn.: Greenwood Press, 1993), 21.

16. Dolan, *The American Catholic Experience*, 111.

17. There is a split among historians over the interpretation of Carroll's episcopacy, with James Hennesey exemplifying the "classical" interpretation that Carroll forged a new vision yet led the American church in a direction that was properly attuned to Rome, and a "revisionist" history exemplified by Jay Dolan that claims Carroll missed the opportunity to create a uniquely American church. See George Weigel's analysis of the split, "Telling the American Catholic Story," *First Things* 7 (November 1990): 43–49.

18. Davis, *The History of Black Catholics in the United States*, 39–40.

19. Jo Ann Kay McNamara, *Sisters in Arms: Catholic Nuns Through Two Millennia* (Cambridge: Harvard University Press, 1996), 596.

20. Dolan, *The American Catholic Experience*, 124.

21. Stephen Michael DiGiovanni recounts the story of the struggles of the Italian immigrants in New York at the end of the nineteenth century and their favorable treatment by an Irish-American bishop in *Archbishop Corrigan and the Italian Immigrants* (Huntington, Ind.: Our Sunday Visitor, 1994).

22. Richard M. Linkh, *American Catholicism and European Immigrants (1900–1924)* (New York: Center for Migration Studies, 1975), 35.

23. John Cogley and Rodger Van Allen, *Catholic America: Expanded and Updated* (Kansas City: Sheed and Ward, 1986), 66.

24. Dolan, *The American Catholic Experience*, 167.

25. As cited in Dolan, *The American Catholic Experience*, 180–81.

26. Dolan, *The American Catholic Experience*, 189.

27. Charles Morris chronicles the history and profiles some of the key figures of Irish Catholicism in America in *American Catholic: The Saints and Sinners Who Built America's Most Powerful Church* (New York: Times Books, 1997).

28. See Davis, *The History of Black Catholics in the United States*, 96.

29. John T. McGreevy, *Parish Boundaries: The Catholic Encounter with Race in the Twentieth-Century Urban North* (Chicago: University of Chicago Press, 1996).

30. David O'Brien, *Public Catholicism* (New York: Macmillan, 1989), 9–10.

31. See George Weigel, "Telling the American Catholic Story," *First Things*, no. 7 (November 1990): 43–49.

32. Gerald P. Fogarty, *The Vatican and the American Hierarchy from 1850 to 1965* (Stuttgart: Anton Hiersemann, 1982), 180.

33. David J. O'Brien's biography, *Isaac Hecker: An American Catholic* (Mahwah, N.J.: Paulist Press, 1992), chronicles Hecker's disputes with the Vatican and with some among the American hierarchy.

34. Richard J. Gelm, *Religious Authority: American Catholics Since the Second Vatican Council* (Westport, Conn.: Greenwood Press, 1994), 21.

3. A Brief History of Catholics in America: 1900 to the Second Vatican Council

1. R. Scott Appleby has chronicled the intellectual development and the subsequent ecclesial conflicts of several American priests involved in the modernist movement in *Church and Age Unite!: The Modernist Impulse in American Catholicism* (Notre Dame, Ind.: University of Notre Dame Press, 1992).

2. John Cogley and Rodger Van Allen, *Catholic America: Expanded and Updated* (Kansas City: Sheed and Ward, 1986), 8.

3. Ernest Audran, "A Retrospect on Events that Made Possible the Late Baltimore Convention," unpublished speech, 1889, 2/11 University of Notre Dame Archives (hereafter UNDA), Audran, Ernest CAUD.

4. Cf. Patrick Henry Callaghan Papers, 1/1 UNDA.

5. Cf. Douglas J. Slawson, *The Foundation and First Decade of the National Catholic Welfare Council* (Washington, D.C.: Catholic University of America, 1992), 22–69.

6. Quoted in Thomas J. Shelley, "Gibbons, James, Cardinal (1834–1921)," in Michael Glazier and Monika K. Hellwig, eds., *The Modern Catholic Encyclopedia* (Collegeville, Minn.: Liturgical Press, 1994), 343.

7. Charles R. Morris, *American Catholic: The Saints and Sinners Who Built America's Most Powerful Church* (New York: Times Books, 1997), 135–38.

8. Cogley and Van Allen, *Catholic America*, 78.

9. William D. Miller, *Dorothy Day: A Biography* (San Francisco: Harper and Row, 1982), 252.

10. For an insight into Maurin's philosophy, see James Terence Fisher, *The Catholic Counterculture in America, 1933–1962* (Chapel Hill: University of North Carolina Press, 1989). Maurin, who was twenty years Day's senior, died in 1949. Dorothy Day died in 1980.

11. William D. Miller, "Dorothy Day," in John J. Delaney, ed., *Saints Are Now: Eight Portraits of Modern Sanctity* (Garden City, N.Y.: Doubleday, 1981), 32.

12. Ibid., 37.

13. Dorothy Day, *The Long Loneliness: The Autobiography of Dorothy Day* (New York: Harper, 1952; San Francisco: Harper, 1997).

14. Letter from Merton to Day, December 29, 1965, cited in Monica Furlong, *Merton: A Biography* (San Francisco: Harper and Row, 1980), 293.

15. Ibid., 238.

16. Ibid., 240.

17. Samuel A. Mills "Parochiaid and the Abortion Decisions: Supreme Court Justice William J. Brennan Jr. versus the U.S. Catholic Hierarchy," *Journal of Church and State* 34, no. 4 (1992): 753.

18. Excerpt from the minutes of the 26th annual meeting of the Bishops of the United States, November 15, 1944, Archbishop Robert Emmet Lucey, UNDA, CLUC 12:13/8.

19. Congress ended the practice when it voted to discontinue Public Law 78 (the Bracero Law) as of December 31, 1964.

20. Most Reverend Robert E. Lucey, "Remarks," November 16, 1955, UNDA, CLUC 12:13/8.

21. Minutes of the November 12, 1958, meeting, UNDA, CLUC 12:13/8.

22. The ad hoc committee members were Auxiliary Bishop Joseph Donnelly of Hartford (chair), Archbishop Timothy Manning of Los Angeles, Bishop Hugh Donahue of Fresno, Bishop Walter Curtis of Bridgeport, and Bishop Humberto Medeiros of Brownsville, Texas.

23. Editorial, *Twin Circle*, July 12, 1970. The bishops' committee sharply criticized the paper and the editorial writer, Fr. Daniel Lyons, S.J., for attempting to publicly undermine their efforts.

24. In 1964 this ceased to function and the Chicago office became a branch of the San Antonio office that replaced it as the national headquarters under the continued direction of Archbishop Lucey.

25. "Report of the Bishops' Committee for the Spanish Speaking," July 1966, UNDA CLUC 12:13/8.

26. Archbishop Lucey, "Memorandum," January 15, 1968, UNDA CLUC 12:13/8.

27. The Spanish-speaking population was concentrated in nine states: Arizona, California, Colorado, Florida, Illinois, New Jersey, New Mexico, New York, and Texas.

28. John T. McGreevy, *Parish Boundaries: The Catholic Encounter with Race in Twentieth-Century Urban America* (Chicago: University of Chicago Press, 1996), 57.

29. Ibid., 205.

30. From 1960 to 1970 Chicago's black population increased from 22.9 percent to 32.7 percent; Detroit's from 28.9 to 43.7; Cleveland's from 28.6 to 38.3; Buffalo's from 13.3 to 20.4; Boston's from 9.1 to 16.3; and Milwaukee's from 8.4 to 14.7. McGreevy, *Parish Boundaries*, 180.

31. An excellent study of this phenomenon is Robert A. Orsi's *The Madonna of 115th Street: Faith and Community in Italian Harlem* (New Haven: Yale University Press, 1985).

32. This practice was changed in the revised Code of Common Law in 1983 to require the Catholic party "to do all in his or her power" to share the Catholic faith with the children.

33. Diana Hayes, "Black Catholic Revivalism: The Emergence of a New Form of Worship," *Journal of the Interdenominational Theological Center* 14 (Fall 1986/Spring 1997): 103.

34. See J. Deotis Roberts, "The Status of Black Catholics," *The Journal of Religious Thought* 48, no. 1 (Summer/Fall 1991): 73–78.

35. Edward K. Braxton, "The View From the Barbershop: The Church and African-American Culture," *America* 178, no. 4, February 14, 1998, pp. 18–22.

36. Joseph M. Davis, "Black Catholics in America: A Living Witness of Faith, A Constant Call to Justice in the Church," manuscript, UNDA, CDAV 156 1/12.

37. Personal interview.

38. Statement issued January 16, 1997, *Origins* 26, no. 32, January 30, 1997.

39. For an insightful portrait of the women who were present for the Council, see Carmel McEnroy, *Guests in Their Own House: The Women of Vatican II* (New York: Crossroad, 1996).

40. Thomas J. Reese, *Inside the Vatican: The Politics and Organization of the Catholic Church* (Cambridge: Harvard University Press, 1996), 38.

41. Mary Jo Weaver and R. Scott Appleby, *Being Right: Conservative Catholics in America* (Bloomington: Indiana University Press, 1995). *What's Left* is forthcoming from Indiana University Press.

42. Even Francis Cardinal Spellman of New York had to have someone speak for him in Latin in a public address at Vatican II.

43. William R. Luckey traces Murray's intellectual development in "The Contribution of John Courtney Murray, S.J.: A Catholic Perspective," in Robert R. Hunt and Kenneth L Grasso, eds., *John Courtney Murray and the American Civil Conversation* (Grand Rapids, Mich.: Eerdmans, 1992), 19–43.

44. J. Leon Hooper and Todd David Whitmore, eds., *John Courtney Murray and the Growth of Tradition* (Kansas City: Sheed and Ward, 1996), xii.

45. Walter M. Abbott, ed., *The Documents of Vatican II* (New York: Herder and Herder, 1966), 287–88.

4. The Post-Vatican II Church in America

1. Avery Dulles, *The Reshaping of Catholicism: Current Challenges in the Theology of the Church* (San Francisco: Harper and Row, 1988), 19.

2. Joseph A. Komonchak, "Interpreting the Council: Catholic Attitudes Toward Vatican II," in Mary Jo Weaver and R. Scott Appleby, *Being Right: Conservative Catholics in America* (Bloomington: Indiana University Press, 1995), 18.

3. Sandra M. Schneiders, "Religious Life (Perfectae Caritatis)," in Adrian Hastings, ed., *Modern Catholicism: Vatican II and After* (New York: Oxford University Press, 1991), 159.

4. Cf. Helen Rose Ebaugh, Jon Lorence, and Janet Saltzman Chafetz, "The Growth and Decline of Catholic Nuns Cross-Nationally, 1960–1990: A Case of Secularization as Social Structural Change," *Journal for the Scientific Study of Religion* 35, no. 2 (1996): 171–83.

5. Gene Burns, *The Frontiers of Catholicism: The Politics of Ideology in a Liberal World* (Berkeley: University of California Press, 1992), 137.

6. Now replaced by the Council of Major Superiors of Women, which represents about 6 percent of American sisters.

7. Jo Ann Kay McNamara, *Sisters in Arms: Catholic Nuns Through Two Millennia* (Cambridge: Harvard University Press, 1996), 631.

8. Barbara Ferraro and Patricia Hussey, *No Turning Back: Two Nuns' Battle with the Vatican Over Women's Right to Choose* (New York: Poseidon, 1990), 153.

9. The document "Religious Life and Human Promotion" reads in part: "Religious have shown that they are conscious of the fact that their involvement in human promotion is a service of the Gospel to humanity, not a preferential choice of ideologies or political parties. [I]n any such involvement, they see the risk of loss of the identity proper to religious life and to the church's mission." For a study of this issue see Christine Kurtzke Hughes, "Vanishing Habits: The Roman Catholic Hierarchy and American Women Religious Since Vatican II," M.A. thesis, Georgetown University, 1994.

10. Quoted in Jane Redmont, *Generous Lives: American Catholic Women Today* (New York: William Morrow, 1992), 38.

11. "The Root Evil Must Be Eradicated," *Davenport Messenger*, September 4, 1980, 10.

12. "Avoid Alienation and Divisiveness," ibid.

13. The idea of restoring the permanent diaconate was under consideration even before Vatican II, as indicated by Pope Pius XII in his talk "Guiding Principles of the Lay Apostolate," to the Second World Congress of the Lay Apostolate on October 5, 1957, in which he said: "The duties connected with Minor Orders have long been performed by laymen, and We know that thought is being given at present to the introduction of a diaconate conceived as an ecclesiastical office independent of the priesthood," National Catholic Welfare Conference, 1957, 4.

14. An ordination rite for deaconesses still existed in the tenth century. See J. Massyngberde Ford, "Order for Ordination of a Deaconess," *Review for Religious* 32, no. 2 (1974): 308–14, in which she translates this rite.

15. Press Release, Sister Formation Conference, 1325 Massachusetts Ave., N.W. Washington, D.C. 20005. University of Notre Dame Archives (hereafter UNDA), CMBL 2/03, Mary B. Lynch.

16. Mary B. Lynch, *The Journey*, no. 13 (September 1974), 3, UNDA, CMBL 4/06.

17. "Request for the Restoration of the Diaconate for Women," UNDA, CMBL 2/01, Mary B. Lynch.

18. Edward P. Echlin, "Theological Frontiers of the Deacon's Ministry," Proceedings of the Second National Workshop on Permanent Diaconate Training and Ministry, December 6–8, 1971, Farmington, Mich., UNDA, CMBL 2/32, Mary B. Lynch.

19. Thomas J. Reese, *Archbishop: Inside the Power Structure of the American Catholic Church* (San Francisco: Harper and Row, 1989), 364.

20. Matthew H. Clark, "The Pastoral Exercise of Authority," *New Theology Review* 10, no. 3 (August 1997): 1–17.

21. Reese, *Archbishop*, 78–80.

22. The recent biography, *Disarmed and Dangerous: The Radical Lives and Times of Daniel and Philip Berrigan* by Murray Polner and Jim O'Grady, chronicles their religious and political lives (New York: Basic Books, 1997). Elizabeth McAlister and Philip Berrigan secretly married each other and later left their religious orders.

23. Source of statistics on approval of birth control, William V. D'Antonio et al., *Laity American and Catholic*, see note 8, ch. 1.

24. Quoted in Larry Witham, *Curran Vs. Catholic University: A Study of Authority and Freedom in Conflict* (Riverdale, Md.: Edington-Rand, 1991), 26.

25. Ibid., 42.

26. Philip J. Murnion, ed., *Catholics and Nuclear War: A Commentary on the Challenge of Peace, the U.S. Catholic Bishops' Pastoral Letter on War and Peace* (New York: Crossroad, 1983), vii.

27. *The Challenge of Peace: God's Promise and Our Response* (Washington, D.C.: United States Catholic Conference, 1983), para. 219.

28. William F. Buckley Jr., "Dubois Memorial Lecture," in *Right Reason* (Garden City, N.Y.: Doubleday, 1985), 111–20.

29. David J. O'Brien, "American Catholics and American Society," in Murnion, ed., *Catholics and Nuclear War*, 26; see note 26.

30. Quoted in John W. Houck and Oliver F. Williams, eds., *Catholic Social Teaching and the U.S. Economy: Working Papers for a Bishops' Pastoral* (Washington, D.C.: University Press of America, 1984), 4.

31. See Douglas Rasmussen and James Sterba, *The Catholic Bishops and the Economy: A Debate* (New Brunswick: Transaction Books, 1987); Walter Block, *The U.S. Bishops and Their Critics: An Economic and Ethical Perspective* (Vancouver: Fraser Institute, 1986); John W. Houck and Oliver F. Williams, eds., *Catholic Social Teaching and the U.S. Economy;* see note 30.

32. Joseph A. Pichler, "Capitalism and Employment: A Policy Perspective," in John W. Houck and Oliver F. Williams, eds., *Catholic Social Teaching and the U.S. Economy*, 67; see note30. For a study of the church's relationship to unions within

its own organizations including schools, hospitals, and other church employees, see Patrick J. Sullivan, *U.S. Catholic Institutions and Labor Unions, 1960–1980* (Lanham, Md.: University Press of America, 1985).

33. Milton Friedman, "Good Ends, Bad Means," in Thomas M. Gannon, ed. *The Catholic Challenge to the American Economy* (New York: Macmillan, 1987), 99–106.

34. Walter Block, *The U.S. Bishops and Their Critics*, 11.

35. Carl Christ, "Unemployment and Macroeconomics" in Thomas M. Gannon, ed., *The Catholic Challenge to the American Economy,* 117; see note 33.

36. One group established a website called "Survivors Network of Those Abused by Priests" (SNAP) at www.teleport.com/snapmail/index.html that provides information and support to victims.

37. The bishops on Imesch's committee were: Matthew Clark of Rochester, N.Y.; Thomas Grady of Orlando, Fla.; auxiliary bishops Alfred Hughes of Boston and Amedee Proulx of Portland, Maine; and Archbishop William Leveda of Portland, Ore. Consultants were: Dr. Mary M. Brabeck of Boston College; Sister Sara Butler of the Missionary Sisters of the Most Blessed Trinity; Dr. Ronda Chervin of St. John's Seminary Theologate, Camarillo, Calif.; Dr. Toinette M. Eugene of Colgate Rochester Divinity School, Rochester, N.Y.; and Dr. Pheme Perkins of Boston College. Staff members were Sister Mariella Frye, NCCB consultant, and Dr. Susan A. Muto of Duquesne University. Toinette Eugene eventually resigned from the committee.

38. Cf. *Origins* 22, no. 6 (June 18, 1992): 91.

39. Raymond Lucker, "Drop the Pastoral, But Continue the Dialogue" *Origins* 22, no. 6 (June 18, 1992): 91–92.

40. Cf. Thomas J. Reese, *A Flock of Shepherds: The National Conference of Catholic Bishops* (Kansas City: Sheed and Ward, 1992), 265.

41. Michael H. Kenny, *America* 171, no. 3 (July 30–August 6, 1994): 16.

42. Archbishop William Keeler, *Origins* 24, no. 4 (June 9, 1994): 53.

43. Archbishop Rembert Weakland, *Origins* 24, no. 4 (June 9, 1994): 55.

44. Mary Daly, *The Church and the Second Sex* (Boston: Beacon Press, 1985 ed.), 197.

45. Rosemary Radford Ruether, *Women-Church: Theology and Practice of Feminist Liturgical Communities* (San Francisco: Harper and Row, 1985), 5.

46. Tim Unsworth, *The Last Priests in America: Conversations with Remarkable Men* (New York: Crossroad, 1991), 196.

47. Richard P. McBrien, *Catholicism*, completely revised and updated edition (San Francisco: Harper, 1994).

48. U.S. Bishops' Committee on Doctrine, "Father Richard McBrien's 'Catholicism,' " *Origins* 15, no. 9 (August 1, 1985): 129.

49. Roach A. Kerestzty laments the rise in dissent, from the left and the right, evident in the contemporary American church in "Theological Dissent in the North American Church," *Communio* 2 (1987): 94–114.

50. See "U.S. Bishops Consider Hunthausen Case," *Sojourners* (January 1987): 8–9; and Thomas J. Reese, *Archbishop*, 337–44.

5. Teachings and Beliefs: Part I

1. John Deedy, *American Catholicism: And Now Where?* (New York and London: Plenum, 1987).

2. For further information on this subject, see Karl Rahner, "Hell," *Encyclopedia of Theology* (London: Burnes and Oates, 1975), 602–4.

3. William E. May, "Catholic Moral Teaching and the Limits of Dissent," in William E. May, ed., *Vatican Authority and American Catholic Dissent* (New York: Crossroad, 1987), 88.

4. Francis A. Sullivan, *Magisterium: Teaching Authority in the Catholic Church* (New York: Paulist Press, 1983), 30.

5. *Lumen Gentium*, paragraph 20. In Walter M. Abbott, ed., *The Documents of Vatican II* (New York: Herder and Herder, 1966), 39–40.

6. Robert Bruce Robertson, *Roman Catholic Exegesis Since Divino Afflante Spiritu: Hermeneutical Implications* (Atlanta: Scholars Press, 1988), 18.

7. For a thorough survey of the methods of biblical scholarship, see Raymond E. Brown, *An Introduction to the New Testament* (New York: Doubleday, 1997).

8. Among Crossan's works are *The Historical Jesus: The Life of a Mediterranean Jewish Peasant* (San Francisco: Harper, 1993); *Jesus: A Revolutionary Biography* (San Francisco: Harper, 1995); and *The Birth of Christianity: Discovering What Happened in the Years Immediately After the Execution of Jesus* (San Francisco: Harper, 1996).

9. *Code of Canon Law: Latin-English Edition* (Washington, D.C.: Canon Law Soviety of America, 1983), canon 212.

10. Bishop Matthew H. Clark, "The Pastoral Exercise of Authority," *New Theology Review* 10, no. 3 (August 1997): 10.

11. Another form of papal pronouncement whose nomenclature was used more widely in an earlier era is a "bull" derived from the Latin *bulla* referring to the seal on papal letters. It simply means an official correspondence from the pope.

12. *Code of Canon Law*, canon 1323, para. 3.

13. For a brief history of the development on the doctrine of infallibility, see Richard P. McBrien, *Catholicism* (San Francisco: Harper, 1994) 759–765 and the

entry on "infallibility" by John T. Ford in Richard P. McBrien, ed., *HarperCollins Encyclopedia of Catholicism* (San Francisco: Harper, 1995), 664–65.

14. Hans Küng, *Infallibility?: An Inquiry* (Garden City, N.Y.: Doubleday, 1971).

15. *Code of Canon Law*, canon 855: "Parents, sponsors, and the pastor are to see that a name foreign to a Christian mentality is not given."

16. Kenneth L. Woodward, "Requiem for a Saint," *Newsweek*, September 22, 1997, 22–36.

17. For a thorough study of the canonization process, see Michael Freze, *The Making of Saints* (Hunting, Ind.: Our Sunday Visitor, 1991). Kenneth Woodward has also done a thorough study of the process, titled *Making Saints* (New York: Simon and Schuster, 1991). For a historical appreciation, see Peter Brown's Haskell Lectures at the University of Chicago, *The Cult of the Saints: Its Rise and Function in Latin Christianity* (Chicago: University of Chicago Press, 1981).

18. Kenneth L. Woodward, "Hail, Mary," *Newsweek*, August 25, 1997, 48–56.

19. Ibid., 48.

20. *U.S. News & World Report*, October 27, 1997, 70–76.

21. The fifteen mysteries are: *Glorious* 1) Resurrection; 2) Ascension; 3) Descent of the Holy Spirit; 4) Assumption; 5) Coronation; *Joyful* 1) Annunciation; 2) Visitation; 3) Nativity; 4) Presentation; 5) Finding in the Temple; and *Sorrowful* 1) Agony in the Garden; 2) Scourging; 3) Crowning with Thorns; 4) Carrying of the Cross; 5) Crucifixion.

22. The principal Marian text is chapter 8 of the document *Lumen Gentium* (Light to the People).

23. For a helpful survey of the contemporary direction in Mariology, see Anthony J. Tambasco, *What Are They Saying About Mary?* (New York: Paulist Press, 1984).

24. Elizabeth A. Johnson, *She Who Is: The Mystery of God in Feminist Theological Discourse* (New York: Crossroad, 1992), 52.

25. Delores S. Williams, "Womanist Theology: Black Women's Voices," in Ursula King, ed., *Feminist Theology from the Third World: A Reader* (Maryknoll, N.Y.: Orbis, 1994), 85.

26. *Redemptoris Mater*, para. 48. *Origins* 16, no. 3 (April 9, 1987): 763.

27. Catholic Internet Network, see www.catholic.org.

28. Colleen McDannell, *Material Christianity: Religion and Popular Culture in America* (New Haven: Yale University Press, 1995), 1.

29. See *Catholic Shrines and Places of Pilgrimage in the United States*, prepared by the Office of Pastoral Care of Migrants and Refugees of the United States (Washington, D.C.: United States Catholic Conference, 1994).

30. See Emile Durkheim, *The Elementary Forms of Religious Life*, translated

with and introduction by Karen E. Fields (New York: Free Press, 1995); Mircea Eliade, *The Sacred and the Profane: The Nature of Religion*, translated from the French by Willard R. Trask (New York: Harcourt, Brace, 1959).

6. Teachings and Beliefs: Part II

1. *Lumen Gentium*, ch. 2, para. 11. In Walter M. Abbott, ed., *Documents of Vatican II* (New York: Herder and Herder, 1966), 28.

2. Andrew Greeley, "Priests Should Make Preaching Their Number One Job," *U.S. Catholic* 58, no. 3 (1993): 13–17.

3. See Mary Pope and Richard Collman, "Epiphany at the Mother Church of African-American Roman Catholicism," *Anglican and Episcopal History* 63, no. 4 (December 1994): 535–39.

4. Sheila Rauch Kennedy, *Shattered Faith* (New York: Pantheon, 1997).

5. The increased number of annulments granted in the United States concerned Pope John Paul II, who warned tribunals not to be too lenient. See Michael L Farrell, "Annulments: 15,000% Increase in 15 Years," *National Catholic Reporter* 21 (November 16, 1984): 1, 9.

6. James D. Davidson et al., *The Search for Common Ground: What Unites and Divides Catholic Americans* (Huntington, Ind.: Our Sunday Visitor, 1997), 26.

7. Karl A. Menninger, *Whatever Became of Sin?* (New York: Hawthorne, 1973).

8. Richard Cardinal Cushing, "The Age of Lay Spirituality" (Boston: Daughters of Saint Paul, undated), University of Notre Dame Archives (hereafter UNDA), 8 CMBL Mary B. Lynch, 4/01.

9. For a valuable historical study of devotional practices, see Ann Taves, *The Household of Faith: Roman Catholic Devotions in Mid-Nineteenth-Century America* (Notre Dame, Ind.: University of Notre Dame Press, 1986).

10. John P. Boland, "Add . . . Air Raid Regulations," August 21, 1942, UNDA, Boland, Monsignor John P. 1888–1968, 41 CBOL Box 2. Manuscript of an editorial (apparently) to the *Union and Echo* paper.

11. Frank Bianco, *Voices of Silence: Lives of the Trappists Today* (New York: Paragon, 1991).

12. For an extensive list of places dedicated to such pursuits, see Janet Joy, *A Place Apart: Houses of Prayer and Retreat Centers in America* (Trabuco Canyon, Calif.: Sources, 1995).

13. Henri J. M. Nouwen, *Gracias!: A Latin American Journal* (San Francisco: Harper and Row, 1983), 11.

14. *Persona humana*, Declaration on Certain Questions Concerning Sexual Ethics, December 29, 1975, para. 8.

15. *Catechism of the Catholic Church* (New York: Doubleday, 1995), para. 2357.

16. Some misinterpreted the document as condoning homosexual activity. James T. McHugh, bishop of the diocese of Camden, N.J., responded to one such misreading in a commentary titled "Church Holds Firm on Homosexuality," *Philadelphia Inquirer*, November 1, 1997, A13, in which he explains that the church has always asked parents to love their children but: "This does not mean, however, that the American bishops think parents should accept their children's homosexual behavior."

17. McHugh, "Church holds firm . . . ," ibid.

18. Cardinal James Hickey, "Crucifix Controversy Symbolizes Deeper Debate at Georgetown," *Catholic Standard*, November 13, 1997.

19. A number of voices have argued that historically the church's teaching on abortion has not been consistent and that a certain pluralism of views can be found in the tradition. This argument was most forcefully articulated in a signed full-page viewpoint in the *New York Times*, October 7, 1984, titled "Statement on Pluralism and Abortion." The ad stated that "a diversity of opinions regarding abortion exists among committed Catholics" and called for "a recognition that there is no common and constant teaching on ensoulment in Church doctrine, nor has abortion always been treated as murder in canonical history." Ninety-seven persons signed the document, including twenty-six religious sisters, two male religious, and two priests. The Vatican Congregation for Religious and Secular Institutes, under the direction of Archbishop (later Cardinal) Jerome Hamer, O.P., sought and received retractions from all of the signers except Barbara Ferraro and Patricia Hussey, both Sisters of Notre Dame, who eventually left their religious order rather than retract their statement. For a fuller treatment, see Barbara Ferraro and Patricia Hussey, *No Turning Back: Two Nuns' Battle with the Vatican Over Women's Right to Choose* (New York: Poseidon, 1990) and Frances Kissling; "Special Report II: The Vatican Attack on the Catholic Statement on Pluralism and Abortion, 1984–1986," *Conscience* 7, no. 3 (1986): 9–16.

20. *Catechism of the Catholic Church*, paragraph 2272.

21. Examples of such behavior include Bishop Leo Maher of San Diego, Calif., denying communion to Lucy Killea, a Catholic who ran for State Senate and supported a pro-choice stance; Bishop Rene H. Gracida of Corpus Christi, excommunicating Catholics who served as directors of abortion clinics; and Bishop Louis E. Gelineau of Providence, refusing to confirm the daughter of the director of Planned Parenthood.

22. For a text of the speech, see Patricia Beattie Jung and Thomas A. Shannon, eds., *Abortion & Catholicism: The American Debate* (New York: Crossroad, 1988), 202–16.

23. Ibid., 207.

24. For an American canonical perspective on this prohibition, see James H.

Provost, "Clergy and Religious in Political Office: Comments in the American Context," *The Jurist* 44 (1984): 276–303.

25. See Mary E. Hunt and Frances Kissling, "The New York Times Ad: A Case Study in Religious Feminism," *Journal of Feminist Studies in Religion* 3, no. 1 (1987): 115–27 for more on this statement.

26. *New York Times*, November 13, 1984, A22, as cited in Timothy A. Byrnes and Mary C. Segers, *The Catholic Church and the Politics of Abortion: A View from the States* (Boulder: Westview, 1992), 3.

27. U.S. Bishops, "Resolution on Abortion," *Origins* 18, no. 24 (November 16, 1989): 395–96.

28. *Evangelium Vitae*, 62. *Origins* 24, no. 42 (April 16, 1995): 711.

29. The document can be found in copyrighted electronic form (© Trinity Communications 1995) on the Catholic Resource Network, www.ewtn.com/library/BISHOPS/FAITHFUL.TXT.

30. Timothy A. Byrnes, "The Politics of Abortion: The Catholic Bishops," in Byrnes and Segers, *The Catholic Church and the Politics of Abortion*, 19.

31. Pope John Paul II, *The Ecological Crisis: A Common Responsibility*, December 8, 1989.

32. For a thoughtful theological study of environmental issues, see Drew Christiansen and Walter Grazer, eds., *"And God Saw That It Was Good": Catholic Theology and the Environment* (Washington, D.C.: United States Catholic Conference, 1996).

33. Ibid., paragraph 15.

34. Pope John Paul II, letter to the world's bishops, "On Combating Abortion and Euthanasia," *Origins* 21, no. 8 (May 19, 1991): 36.

35. Untied States Catholic Conference, "Faithful for Life: A Moral Reflection," (Washington, D.C.: 1995), 10.

36. *Catechism of the Catholic Church*, number 2266.

37. For an informative study of ecumenism since Vatican II, see Thaddeus D. Horgan, ed., *Walking Together: Roman Catholics and Ecumenism Twenty-Five Years After Vatican II* (Grand Rapids, Mich.: Eerdmans, 1990).

38. The American religious historian Robert T. Handy's influential book, *A Christian America* (New York: Oxford University Press, 1971), a standard work for scholars of American religion, today needs to be complemented by Harvard University's Pluralism Project, mapping the contemporary religious landscape in America, directed by Diana Eck. This project has produced an excellent resource that captures the contemporary religious face of the United States on the compact disk, *On Common Ground: World Religions in America* (New York: Columbia University Press, 1997).

39. *Denzinger* 1957, nos. 468–69.

40. "It must . . . be held as certain that those who are affected by ignorance of the true religion, if it is invincible ignorance, are not subject to any guilt in this matter before the eyes of the Lord. Now, then, who could presume in himself an ability to set the boundaries of such ignorance, taking into consideration the natural differences of peoples, lands, native talents, and so many other factors?" *Singulari Quadam* 1854. *Denzinger* 1957, nos. 1647–48.

41. For further examples, see Eugene Hillman, *Many Paths: A Catholic Approach to Religious Pluralism* (Maryknoll, N.Y.: Orbis Press, 1989), 30 34.

42. "Declaration on the Relationship of the Church to Non-Christian Religions," "Introduction and Commentary," trans. by Simon and Erika Young and Helda Graef in H. Vorgrimler, ed., *Commentary on the Documents of Vatican II*, vol. 3 (London: Burnes and Oates, 1969), 1.

43. *Nostra Aetate*, paragraph 2. Walter M. Abbott, ed., *Documents of Vatican II*, 662: see note 1.

44. *Redemptor Hominis*, 1979. *Origins* 8, no. 40 (March 22, 1979): 632.

45. See, for example, *Ad Gentes*, paragraphs 11, 12, 16, 34, 41; *Gaudium et Spes*, paragraphs 3, 23, 58, 92; and *Apostolicam Actuositatem*, paragraph 14. In Walter M. Abbott, ed., *Documents of Vatican II;* see note 1.

7. Institutions, Roles, and Organizations

1. Historically not all cardinals were clerics, although according to canon law since 1917 all cardinals must be ordained priests and since 1962 they must also be bishops. In the Middle Ages, during periods of intrigue within the Vatican, some cardinals were not clerics but were named to the college of cardinals by the pope as political favors or for the incumbent pope to curry favor with the cardinals and stack the college in his favor.

2. Anthony S. Bryk, Valerie E. Lee, and Peter B. Holland, *Catholic Schools and the Common Good* (Cambridge: Harvard University Press, 1993), 32.

3. "Diocese to Focus $1 Million on 16 D.C. Schools: Catholic Elementaries Show Enrollment Dip," *Washington Post*, January 30, 1997, 1 and 10. In 1996–97 the total increased by more than ten thousand to 2,645,462 (source, *Catholic Standard* April 10, 1997, 3).

4. Cf. Harold A. Buetow, *The Catholic School: Its Roots, Identity, and Future* (New York: Crossroad, 1988), 310.

5. Personal interview, March 1998.

6. Personal interview, April 1998.

7. Personal interview, April 1998.

8. Nuns were often at the mercy of pastors financially and in other ways. Some

bishops established salary requirements so that nuns would be treated equally although they still received minimal amounts. The following historical example is from Bishop Daniel Francis of the Diocese of Fall River, Mass.: "Parishes employing religious communities of women as teachers in schools of the parish and providing said religious with a suitable convent will, henceforth, out of church funds, pay for each teacher so employed an annual salary of $200 and will, in addition to the lodging provided in the parish convent, supply light, fuel and water for said convent and keep the same in good repair." Letter dated July 23, 1908 from James C. Coyle, 1850–1931, University of Notre Dame Archives (hereafter UNDA), 141 CCOY III-1-b.

9. In 1992, the median salary for a Catholic high school teacher was $24,700, compared to $33,800 for public school teachers. Joseph Claude Harris, *The Cost of Catholic Parishes and Schools* (Kansas City: Sheed and Ward, 1996), 21.

10. Kenneth E. Untener, "Our Sunday Worship Experience: What It Is, What It Could Be," in Francis J. Butler, ed., *American Catholic Identity: Essays in an Age of Change* (Kansas City: Sheed and Ward, 1994), 39.

11. Harris, *The Cost of Catholic Parishes and Schools*, 70.

12. Peter Daly, "Eyeing Cost-Based Tuition for Catholic Schools," *Catholic Standard*, June 19, 1997, 8.

13. Harris, *The Cost of Catholic Parishes and Schools*, 2.

14. From the Catholic Education office of the archdiocese of Washington, D.C.

15. Bryk, Lee, and Holand, *Catholic Schools and the Common Good*, 9.

16. "The Education of Black Youth," Statement of November 1, 1996. *Origins* 26, no. 26 (December 12, 1996): 435–436.

17. Frederick H. Brigham Jr., *United States Catholic Elementary and Secondary Schools, 1993–1994* (Washington, D.C.: National Catholic Educational Association, 1994), 11.

18. Andrew Greeley, *Minority Students in Catholic Schools* (New Brunswick, N.J.: Transaction Books, 1982); and James S. Coleman, Thomas Hoffer, and Sally B. Kilgore, *High School Achievement: Public, Catholic, and Private Schools Compared* (New York: Basic Books, 1982).

19. Christopher J. Kauffman, *Meaning: A Religious History of Catholic Health Care in the United States* (New York: Crossroad, 1995), 2.

20. Ibid., 246.

21. Margaret Susan Thompson, Foreword to Suzy Farren's *A Call to Care: The Women Who Built Catholic Health Care in America* (St. Louis: Catholic Health Care Association of the United States, 1996), iv. In prose and historical photos, the book chronicles the health care contributions of dozens of religious orders and scores of individual sisters.

22. Ibid., 278.

23. Pamela Schaeffer, "Cardinals Claim Rights in Hospital Dispute," *National Catholic Reporter*, October 24, 1997, 3.

24. For an analysis of the nuances, see John J. Danagher, "The New Code and Catholic Health Facilities: Fundamental Obligations of Administrators," *The Jurist* 44 (1984): 143–52.

25. The quotation comes from a film, *Entertaining Angels*, in which Dorothy Day says this to the archbishop.

26. For a fuller analysis of the new code in relation to Vatican II, see James Provost, "Strategizing the Application of Life to Church Order," in James Provost and Knut Walf, *From Life to Law* (Maryknoll, N.Y.: Orbis: 1996), 116–24.

27. Ladislas Örsy, "The Revision of Canon Law," in Adrian Hastings, ed., *Modern Catholicism: Vatican II and Afterward* (New York: Oxford University Press, 1991), 210.

28. *Code of Canon Law: Latin-English Edition* (Washington, D.C.: Canon Law Society of Americs, 1983), canon 1246, para. 2.

29. Provost and Walf, *From Life to Law*, vii.

30. The books are: 1) General Norms; 2) The People of God; 3) The Teaching Office of the Church; 4) The Sanctifying Office of the Church; 5) The Temporal Goods of the Church; 6) Sanctions; 7) Processes.

31. Ladislas Örsy, "Theology and Canon Law: An Inquiry Into Their Relationship," *The Jurist* 50 (1990), 408.

32. The current oath in place since 1989 consists of four paragraphs. The first is the well-known Nicene-Constantinopolitan Creed; paragraphs two, three, and four are as follows:

"With firm faith I believe also all that is contained in the word of God, written or handed down, and is proposed by the church—either through solemn judgment or through the ordinary and universal magisterium—as divinely revealed and to be believed.

"I also firmly embrace and hold all and each that are definitively proposed by the church concerning the doctrine of faith and morals.

"Moreover, I adhere with religious *obsequium* of will and intellect to the doctrines which either the Roman Pontiff or the college of bishops enunciate when they exercise the *magisterium authenticum* even if they intend to proclaim those doctrines by a nondefinitive act."

This is Ladislas Örsy's translation in his book, *The Profession of Faith and the Oath of Fidelity* (Wilmington: Michael Glazier, 1990), in which he analyzes the context and content of the oath. It is the same oath that Father Lawrence Madden (as pastor, not bishop) professed at Holy Trinity Church as cited in chapter 1.

33. For a comprehensive history of domestic and international Catholic missionary work, see Angelyn Dries, *The Missionary Movement in American Catholic History* (Maryknoll, N.Y.: Orbis, 1998).

34. Elizabeth McKeown, "Catholic Charities," in Michael Glazier and Thomas J. Shelley, eds., *The Encyclopedia of American Catholic History* (Collegeville: Minn.: Liturgical Press, 1997), 242.

35. For a thorough study of Catholic charities in the twentieth century see Dorothy M. Brown and Elizabeth McKeown, *The Poor Belong to Us: Catholic Charities and American Welfare* (Cambridge: Harvard University Press, 1997).

36. Avery Dulles, *Models of the Church* (New York: Doubleday, 1974; expanded ed., 1987).

37. Edward Schillebeeckx, *Christ the Sacrament of Encounter with God* (New York: Sheed and Ward, 1963).

8. Catholic Popular Culture

1. For example, *Catholic Northwest Progress*, the newspaper of the archdiocese of Seattle, required a $650,000 subsidy in 1993. Reported in Joseph Claude Harris, *The Cost of Catholic Parishes and Schools* (Kansas City: Sheed and Ward, 1996), 96.

2. *Catholic Mirror*, Baltimore, December 29, 1877.

3. For the details of this position, see James A. Coriden, "The End of the Imprimatur," *The Jurist* 44 (1984), 339–56.

4. Anthony J. Wilhelm, *Christ Among Us: A Modern Presentation of the Catholic Faith* (New York: Paulist Press, 1973, 2d rev. ed., 1975).

5. Coriden, "The End of the Imprimatur," 340.

6. James M. Skinner, *The Cross and the Cinema: The Legion of Decency and the National Catholic Office for Motion Pictures, 1933–1970* (Westport, Conn.: Praeger, 1993), 1.

7. Ibid., 34.

8. Quoted in Skinner, 37.

9. Ibid., 57.

10. Charles Morris, *American Catholic: The Saints and Sinners Who Built America's Most Powerful Church* (New York: Times Books, 1997), 166.

11. Frank Walsh, *Sin and Censorship: The Catholic Church and the Motion Picture Industry* (New Haven: Yale Universitiy Press, 1996), 278.

12. In 1980 this office merged with the National Catholic Office for Radio and Television and later became the Department of Communication of the United States Catholic Conference.

13. "Beyond the Ratings Game," "Weekend," *Washington Post*, March 7, 1997, 33.

14. Gregory D. Black, *Hollywood Censored: Morality Codes, Catholics, and the Movies* (New York: Cambridge University, 1994), 1.

15. Ibid., 2.

16. Pope Pius XII, "The Three Apostolates of Modern Woman," (Washington, D.C.: National Council of Catholic Women, 1957), 3.

17. The fascinating story behind the movie is told by the producer in Ellwood E. Kieser, *Hollywood Priest: A Spiritual Struggle* (New York: Doubleday, 1991).

18. For a rich description of these days, see Les and Barbara Keyser, *Hollywood and the Catholic Church: The Image of Roman Catholicism in American Movies* (Chicago: Loyola University Press, 1984) 93–156.

19. For an account of the behind-the-scenes negotiating in this dispute, see *National Catholic Reporter*, December 5, 1997.

20. Cardinal James Hickey, *Catholic Standard* 47, no. 38 September 18, 1997.

21. www.catholicleague.org.

22. See "Mahoney Welcomes Actor," *National Catholic Reporter* 34, no. 3 (November 7, 1997): 8.

23. Speech available on the World Wide Web at listserv.american.edu/catholic/church/papal/jp.ii/computer-culture.html.

24. www.catholic.org/declares.html.

25. www.vatican.va.

26. Thomas C. Fox, *Catholicism on the Web* (New York: MIS, 1997).

27. Cindy Wooden, Catholic News Service, "Some 'Catholic' Internet Sites Questionable, Says L.A. Cardinal," *Catholic Standard* (March 6, 1997): 4.

9. Challenges

1. In 1960 Catholics contributed 2.2 percent of their income and only 1.1 percent in 1990. See Andrew M. Greeley, *The Catholic Myth: The Behavior and Beliefs of American Catholics* (New York: Scribner's, 1990), 11.

2. St. Teresa of Avila and St. Catherine of Siena, both proclaimed doctors by Pope Paul VI in 1970; and St. Therese of Lisieux proclaimed a doctor by Pope John Paul II in 1997.

3. For further exploration of this point, see Chester Gillis, "Feminist Theology, Roman Catholicism, and Alienation," *Horizons* 20, no. 2 (Fall 1993): 280–300

4. Jim Naughton, *Catholics in Crisis: An American Parish Fights for Its Soul* (New York: Penguin Books, 1997).

5. Peter Steinfels, "Catholic Theologians Urge Discussion on Female Priests," *New York Times*, June 8, 1997, 32.

6. Bernard Law, "The CTSA: A Theological Wasteland," editorial in *The Pilot*, archdiocese of Boston newspaper, June 18, 1997.

7. For a statistical analysis, see Stanley K. Henshaw and Kathryn Kost, "Abortion Patients in 1994–1995: Characteristics and Contraceptive Use," *Family Planning Perspectives* (July/August 1996): 140–58.

8. John Paul II, *Veritatis Splendor*, para. 4. *Origins* 23, no. 18 (October 14, 1993): 297–334.

9. See Richard J. Glem, *Religious Authority: American Catholics Since the Second Vatican Council* (Westport, Conn.: Greenwood Press, 1994), 100.

10. "Bishops' Statement," *Catholic Almanac 1997*, compiled and edited by Felician A. Foy, O.F.M and Rose M. Avato (Huntington, Ind.: Our Sunday Visitor, 1996), 51.

11. "Domestic Partners," *Catholic Almanac 1997*, 51–52.

12. Richard A Schoennherr and Lawrence A. Young, *Full Pews and Empty Altars: Demographics of the Priest Shortage in the United States Catholic Dioceses* (Madison: University of Wisconsin Press, 1993).

13. William V. D'Antonio, James D. Davidson, Deon R. Hoge, and Ruth A. Wallace studied this phenomenon in *Laity American and Catholic: Transforming the Church* (Kansas City: Sheed and Ward, 1996), 122. Their statistics are for 1992 but the situation in most dioceses only worsens each year due to retirements, deaths, and a dearth of ordinations. Priestless parishes are not unique to America. The situation is similar in Europe as testified to by the story of St. Verena's Parish in Volkertshausen in Southwest Germany where Fr. Engelbert Ruf was asked by his bishop to oversee five parishes. As reported in the *National Catholic Reporter*, February 21, 1997.

14. Cf. Richard A. Schoennherr and Lawrence A. Young "Quitting the Clergy: Resignations in the Roman Catholic Priesthood," *Journal for the Scientific Study of Religion* 29, no. 4 (1990): 463–81.

15. Ibid., 473. In 1966, 21 percent of diocesan priests were between the ages of 25 and 34 and 18 percent were between the ages of 55 and 64. By the year 2005, 12 percent will be between 25 and 34 years old, and 28 percent will be between 55 and 64 years old.

16. Schoennherr and Young, *Full Pews and Empty Altars*, 32.

17. Patricia Wittberg, *The Rise and Decline of Catholic Religious Orders: A Social Movement Perspective* (Albany, N.Y.: SUNY, 1994), 1.

18. Kathleen Hughes, *Studia Liturgica* 26 (1996): 114–15.

19. Elden Curtiss, "Crisis in Vocations? What Crisis?" *Our Sunday Visitor* 84, no. 23 (October 8, 1995): 18.

20. John Deedy, "A Taste of Priestlessness," *America* 177, no. 2 (July 19–26, 1997): 4–6.

21. Cornelius G. Hughes, "Views from the Pews: Hispanic and Anglo Catholics in a Changing Church," *Review of Religious Research* 33, no. 4 (1992): 364–75.

22. "Catholic Parish Turns Episcopal," *Christianity Today*, March 9, 1992.

23. J. Francis Stafford, "This Home of Freedom: A Pastoral Letter to the Church of Denver," *This World* 18 (Summer 1987): 89.

24. R. Scott Appleby, "The Era of the Ombudsman, 1930–1954," in *Transforming Parish Ministry: The Changing Roles of Catholic Clergy, Laity, and Women Religious* (New York: Crossroad, 1989), 8.

25. "Catholic Priests Under a Cloud," *Christian Century*, February 17, 1993.

26. Jason Berry, *Lead Us Not Into Temptation: Catholic Priests and the Sexual Abuse of Children* (New York: Doubleday, 1992).

27. The address is P. O. Box 1268, Wheeling, IL 60090.

28. This practice is nothing new. Bishops have been dealing with priests with personal and psychological problems since the beginning of the American church. Many bishops feel that it is one of the most difficult challenges of their position. The problems of deviant sexual practices are different, however, from previous generations. A letter from Bishop Matthew Harkins of Providence, R.I., to Father James Coyle, pastor of St. Joseph's Parish in Newport, R.I., dated May 5, 1900, illustrates the practice.

> *My dear Fr. Coyle,*
>
> *In accordance with our conversation yesterday, [an assistant priest] goes to you today. I have made him aware of the conditions of going to you. a) that he is to abstain entirely from the use of intoxicating liquor; b) that he is to be guided by you even more strictly than an ordinary assistant; c) that he is not to remain with you indefinitely but that he is liable to change at any time; d) that in his conduct while with you will depend his appointment to some position as assistant.*
>
> *I trust that with the help of the Lord your kind interest may be of great service to him.*
>
> *Sincerely yours in Christ,*
> *Matthew Harkins*
> *Bp. of Providence*

As a postscript to another letter to Father Coyle dated April 8, 1904, Bishop Harkins wrote: "Good advice—prudent direction—and fraternal correction are useful for young priests." From Coyle, James 1850–1931 UNDA 141 CCOY III-1-b.

29. A. W. Richard Sipe, *A Secret World: Sexuality and the Search for Celibacy* (New York: Brunner/Mazel, 1990).

30. Ibid., 18.

31. This information comes from a personal interview with Father Nash, November 1997.

32. John Paul II, *Evangelium Vitae*, para. 4.

33. *Veritatis Splendor*, para. 32. *Origins* 20, no. 18 (October 14, 1993): 297–334.

34. Kevin Wildes, "In the Service of Life: *Evangelium Vitae* and Medical Research," in Kevin Wm. Wildes, S.J. and Alan C. Mitchell, *Choosing Life: A Dialogue on Evangelium Vitae* (Washington, D.C.: Georgetown University, 1997).

35. Alice Gallin has collected these in a book, Gallin, ed., *American Catholic Higher Education: Essential Documents, 1967–1990* (Notre Dame, Ind.: University of Notre Dame Press, 1992); and Philip Gleason analyzes them in "The American Background of 'Ex corde Ecclesiae' " in John P. Langan, ed., *Catholic Universities in Church and Society: A Dialogue on Ex Corde Ecclesiae* (Washington, D.C.: Georgetown University Press, 1993), 1–27.

36. Gallin, *American Catholic Higher Education*, 1–2.

37. "The Catholic University Must Be an Oasis," *Davenport Messenger*, April 3, 1980.

38. *Ex Corde Ecclesiae*, n. 12. *Origins* 20, no. 17 (October 4, 1990): 265–276.

39. Andrew M. Greeley, "The Demographics of American Catholics: 1965–1990." In Andrew M. Greeley, *The Sociology of Andrew M. Greeley* (Atlanta: Scholars Press, 1994), 545–64. Original article in *Religion and the Social Order* 2, 37–56.

40. The *Catholic Standard* (October 30, 1997) reported that the percent of Hispanics in the United States who say they are Catholic was 78 percent in 1972–75, 72 percent in 1982–85, and 67 percent in 1990–94.

41. Wade Clark Roof and Christel Manning, "Cultural Conflicts and Identity: Second-Generation Hispanic Catholics in the United States," *Social Compass* 41, no. 1 (1994): 171–84.

42. Statistics from Rosendo Urrabazo, "Pastoral Education of Hispanic Adults," *Missiology: An International Review* 20, no. 2 (April 1992): 255–60.

43. Orlando Espin, "The God of the Vanquished: Foundations for a Latino Spirituality," *Journal of Religious Culture* 27, no. 1 (Winter 1997): 70–83.

44. *San Jose Mercury News*, February 28, 1990, 12A.

45. See Alan Figueroa Deck, "The Challenge of Evangelical/Pentecostal Christianity to Hispanic Catholicism," in Jay P. Dolan and Alan Figueroa Deck, eds, *Hispanic Catholic Culture in the U.S.: Issues and Concerns* (Notre Dame, Ind.: University of Notre Dame Press, 1994): 409–39.

46. Gerardo Marín and Raymond J. Gamba, "The Role and Expectations in Religious Conversions: The Case of Hispanic Catholics," *Review of Religious Research* 34, no. 4 (June 1993): 357–71.

47. Roof and Manning, "Cultural Conflicts and Identity: Second-Generation Hispanic Catholics in the United States," 180.

48. Jay P. Dolan, *Transforming Parish Ministry: The Changing Roles of Catholic Clergy, Laity, and Women Religious* (New York: Crossroad, 1989), 281–320.

10. The Future

1. Alexis de Tocqueville, *Democracy in America*, vol. 2, book 1, chapter 6 (New York: Vintage Books, 1945), 30.

2. James Provost, "The Church in a Post-Council Era of Transition," *Origins* 26, no. 42 (April 10, 1997): 691-695.

3. Andrew Greeley and Mary Greeley Durkin, *How to Save the Catholic Church* (New York: Viking Press, 1984), xv.

4. Paul Wikes, *The Good Enough Catholic: A Guide for the Perplexed* (New York: Ballantine, 1996), xx.

5. Thomas P. Rausch, "Divisions, Dialogue, and the Catholicity of the Church," *America* 178, no. 3, January 31, 1998, 28.

6. Ann Carey. "Confused About Changes in the Liturgy? Join the Club," *Our Sunday Visitor* 84, no. 21 (September 24, 1995).

7. David R. Carlin, "Breaking the Gridlock in the Church," *Our Sunday Visitor*, 84, no. 39 (January 28, 1996): 15.

GLOSSARY

altar   table on which the Eucharist is celebrated and the bread and wine are consecrated.

apparition   a miraculous vision of a supernatural figure, e.g., Mary appearing at Lourdes, France.

archdiocese   the principal diocese, led by an archbishop, in a regional group of dioceses.

Ash Wednesday   the first day of the penitential season of Lent marked by the distribution of blessed ashes in the shape of a cross on the foreheads of the faithful.

baptism   one of the sacraments of initiation (with confirmation and Eucharist), in which water is poured over the candidate's head and the words "I baptize you in the name of the Father, and of the Son, and of the Holy Spirit" are recited in order for the candidate to become a Christian.

bishop   a priest who is consecrated as a successor to the apostles for a role of leadership, usually in a diocese.

brothers   male members of clerical orders or congregations who take vows but do not receive ordination to the priesthood.

cardinal   title of a member of the College of Cardinals who is appointed by the pope to act in an advisory capacity in governing the church. Upon the death of a pope, those cardinals under the age of 80 elect one of their own to succeed him. Currently the College has approximately 120 members representing six continents, with Europe having the largest number. The United States normally has 10 to 12 cardinals at any given time. American archdioceses, usually headed by a cardinal, are: Baltimore, Boston, Chicago, Detroit, Philadelphia, Los Angeles, New York, St. Louis, and Washington, D.C.

Catechism   a compendium of Catholic teachings. Many pre-Vatican II Catholics learned the question-and-answer edition known as the *Baltimore Catechism*. Today, the universal *Catechism of the Catholic Church* issued by the Vatican in 1992 is the best-known version.

Catholic   from the Greek meaning "universal," it means a member of the Catholic Church.

celibacy   the vowed state of remaining single in order to serve the church and work toward the fullness of the reign of God.

chrism   oil made from olives and perfume blessed by the bishop on Holy Thursday and used in the rituals for some sacraments.

communion   the reception of the consecrated bread and wine either within the context of Eucharistic liturgy or using previously consecrated bread in other settings (e.g., for the sick or at a Eucharist service not presided over by a priest).

confirmation   a sacrament of Christian initiation usually received during the teen years, after one has been baptized and received communion, calling upon the Holy Spirit for guidance and signaling one's acceptance of the faith.

consecrate   meaning to bless or make holy, this term applies in a particular way to the words the priest says ("This is my body, this is my blood") during the celebration of the Eucharist by which the bread and wine become the body and blood of Christ.

convent   communal residence for nuns.

council   official gathering of bishops with the pope to establish beliefs and practices for the entire church; a gathering of national or local officials to guide the church in that region.

creed   an authorized code of beliefs.

cross   the wooden structure on which Jesus was crucified; the chief symbol of Christianity.

Curia   the personnel and offices by which the pope (Roman Curia) or a local bishop (Diocesan Curia) governs the church.

deacon   the order just below that of priest; those who are becoming priests receive this as a transitional order; others receive it as permanent order; women are not permitted to become deacons.

diocese   the region over which a bishop has jurisdiction.

doctrine   an official teaching of the church.

dogma   an official teaching that is held infallibly by the church.

Easter the commemoration of Jesus's resurrection from the dead.

Easter Vigil the liturgical celebration of Easter that takes place on the night of Holy Saturday, the night before Easter.

ecclesiology literally the study of the church, it signifies a way of understanding and interpreting the church.

encyclical a papal document addressing the entire church.

Eucharist mass, literally "thanksgiving"; it is one of the seven sacraments; also the bread and wine consecrated by the priest at mass.

excommunication the process of excluding a Catholic from participating in the activity of the church.

Good Friday the day on which Christians commemorate the death of Jesus on the cross.

Gospel(s) literally "the good news," they are four accounts of Jesus's activities and his significance to believers written in the first century by Mark, Matthew, Luke, and John.

hierarchy the ranks of clergy (bishops, priests, deacons), it usually refers to the bishops in their role as administrators and leaders.

Holy Days of Obligation Special feast days on which Catholics in America are obligated by church law to attend mass. They are: The Solemnity of Mary (January 1); Ascension (sixth Thursday after Easter); Assumption (August 15); All Saints (November 1); Immaculate Conception (December 8); Christmas (December 25). These were determined for the church in the United States by the Third Plenary Council of Baltimore in 1884. Other countries may observe different combinations of these days and Epiphany, Corpus Christi, Saint Joseph (March 19) and Saints Peter and Paul (June 29).

Holy Thursday the day on which Christians commemorate Jesus's Last Supper on the day before he died.

homily a reflection on the scriptural readings offered by the priest or deacon during mass.

imprimatur Latin term for "let it be printed," found in books about Catholicism and granted by a bishop signifying that the work is in agreement with church teaching.

Jesus Christ first-century religious figure from whom Christianity takes its name and who Christians believe is the Son of God and the Savior of the World.

John XXIII (Angelo Giuseppe Roncalli) pope from 1958 to 1963, who convened the Second Vatican Council in 1962.

John Paul II (Karol Wojtyla) a Polish cardinal until he became pope in 1978, the first non-Italian pope since 1523.

liturgical calendar   the feasts and celebrations of the church's year.

liturgy   the official public prayers and rites of the church involving clergy and laity.

magisterium   the official teaching authority of the church.

Mary   Jesus's mother, revered in a special way by Catholics and known by many names including the Blessed Virgin, Our Lady, and the Mother of God.

mass   the liturgical celebration of the Eucharist, presided over by a priest and participated in by the laity.

Messiah   the anointed who some Jews still await as God's messenger and redeemer and who Christians identify as Jesus.

monastery   the place where monks, clerics, or nuns live a secluded communal life.

monsignor   an honorary title the pope bestows (on the recommendation of a diocesan bishop) on diocesan priests to recognize their contribution to the church.

National Conference of Catholic Bishops   the official organization of U.S. bishops.

New Testament   twenty-seven books of the Bible that relate the story and significance of Jesus and the early formation of the church.

nihil obstat   literally "nothings stands in the way," the approval of a book by a diocesan theological censor before it receives the bishop's imprimatur.

novena   a nine-day prayer routine offered on consecutive days or in a set sequence (e.g., nine first Fridays of the month) for a special intention.

nun   a woman in religious orders under solemn vows of poverty, chastity, and obedience. The term is used popularly to refer also to a sister.

Old Testament   sacred texts relating the story of God's interaction with humanity from creation to the time of Jesus. The Catholic canon of Old Testament books numbers 46 books, including seven (Judith, Tobit, Baruch, 1 and 2 Maccabees, Ecclesiasticus, and Wisdom) which the Protestant Bible omits.

Opus Dei   a religious group of laity and clergy founded by Monsignor Josemaría Escrivá de Balaguer in Spain in 1928 dedicated to following closely the directives of the pope. Membership lists are not made public.

ordination   a sacrament that confers the office of deacon, priest, or bishop on a candidate.

original sin   the state of moral failure said to be passed down from the transgression of God's law by Adam and Eve and into which all humans are born.

parish   the members of a local church community that worships in a designated church building.

parochial   pertaining to a parish.

Paschal Candle   the Easter Candle lighted at the Easter Vigil symbolizing the light of Christ.

pastor   a priest who is designated by the local bishop to lead a parish; today, some parishes are led by sisters, brothers, or lay persons.

pastoral letter   official document issued by an individual bishop or a group of bishops (e.g., U.S. bishops) addressed to the people in the region which they oversee.

Paul   the disciple of Jesus who founded many of the first-century Gentile (non-Jewish) church communities on his missionary journeys. His letters to these communities are in the New Testament.

Paul VI   Giovanni Montini) pope fom 1963 to 1978 who reconvened the Second Vatican Council after the death of John XXIII and saw it to its conclusion in 1965; issued encyclical Humanae Vitae in 1968.

Pentecost   the commemoration of biblical event when the disciples of Jesus received the Holy Spirit in the form of tongues of fire and began to preach; this event signaled the birth of the church.

pope   the title for the head of the Roman Catholic Church.

priest   a person ordained by a bishop to perform sacraments and other rituals as well as a variety of other ministries among the faithful.

Protestant   a Christian who belongs to a community with roots in the sixteenth-century Reformation when some Christians broke their ties with Rome.

resurrection   Jesus's rising from the dead three days after his crucifixion.

rosary   a devotional prayer honoring Mary for which Catholics use beads on a string to structure the prayer.

sacrament   one of seven central rites that connect the faithful to God, Christ, and the Holy Spirit. They are: Baptism, Eucharist, Confirmation, Reconciliation, Matrimony, Anointing of the Sick, and Holy Orders.

saint   one who is canonized by the church in recognition of his or her extraordinary holiness.

salvation   the process and result of the ultimate fulfillment of humans and all creation to be with God.

sanctuary   in a church building, the space where the altar and lectern are located.

scripture   the texts of the Bible.

Second Vatican Council (Vatican II)   the meeting of all the world's bishops and their advisers convened at the Vatican by Pope John XXIII from 1962 to 1965. It issued sixteen documents of a pastoral nature designed to modernize the thinking and practice of the church.

sin   a transgression of God's will as it is made known in scripture and tradition.

sisters   women taking simple vows who need not live in a cloistered community.

spirituality   the ways to, and the pursuit of, holiness.

theology   the systematic study of divine revelation, tradition, and religious experience.

Vatican   the small city-state within Rome where the pope presides; also used to refer to the pope and/or the church's central administration.

worship   a communal or individual act of praise of God.

SELECTED FURTHER READING

Church and Culture

Carroll, James, *An American Requiem: God, My Father, and the War that Came Between Us* (New York: Houghton Mifflin, 1996)

In this award-winning memoir, Carroll recounts his life growing up in a family that was loyal to the church and the government. His father, a general in the United States Air Force, served as the head of the Joint Chiefs of Staff during part of the Vietnam War. Carroll entered the seminary and became a Paulist priest. The book chronicles young Carroll's shift from proud patriot to antiwar protester and his subsequent struggles with his relationship with his father.

Church Structure and Organization

Deedy, John, *American Catholicism: And Now Where?* (New York and London: Plenum Press, 1987)

Deedy examines the church in the 1970s and early '80s, highlighting the controversies of the period and the challenges facing the church. He explores the tensions between Rome and the American church on a number of issues including sexual ethics, exercise of authority, role of clergy and laity. The author is sympathetic to the liberalization of the church and he covers the personalities behind the reforms.

Reese, S. J., Thomas J., *Archbishop: Inside the Power Structure of the American Catholic Church* (San Francisco: Harper and Row, 1989)

Everyone knows that bishops play a prominent role in Catholic life. Most people, including Catholics, do not know much about the specifics of their work or their lives. This book describes in detail the process by which bishops are chosen, the power that they wield, and the problems that they face. Reese, a Jesuit trained in political science and editor of *America* magazine, covers all aspects of the role of bishop/archbishop, from finances to personnel decisions, including the relationship of bishops to the Vatican, one another, priests, and the people whom they serve. The book chronicles a few cases of bishops' conflicts with Rome. The author, who uses a social science methodology, spent two years researching the issues and interviewing bishops and their staffs throughout the United States. He often uses the words of bishops themselves to describe their work, their ambitions, and their understanding of the role of the bishop within the structure of the church. Written in fluid style, the book includes interviews, commentary, and analysis providing the reader with a comprehensive picture of the episcopacy.

Reese, S.J., Thomas J., *A Flock of Shepherds: The National Conference of Catholic Bishops* (Kansas City: Sheed and Ward, 1992)

American bishops belong to a national organization that coordinates their efforts and allows them to speak in a unified voice to American Catholics and the nation as a whole. It also permits them to interact regularly with one another and to address the Vatican about issues that affect them and their constituencies. This book describes the internal workings of the bishops' administrative body. Reese explains how bishops are elected by their peers to influential positions, offers brief portraits of the presidents of the organization, details the structures, including how the staff operates, who played key roles, and the influence on the American church. This thorough study examines committee work, budgets, pastoral letters, and the relationship of the organization to Rome. Helpful appendices include official documents that govern the internal mechanisms of the conferences of bishops.

Reese, S. J., Thomas J., *Inside the Vatican: The Politics and Organization of the Catholic Church* (Cambridge: Harvard University Press,1996)

This examination of the politics and organization of the central offices of the Roman Catholic Church completes Reese's series. The author researched the book in Rome partly by interviewing cardinals and others who work in the Vatican. The church has the distinction of being among the oldest continuous institutions in the world. The Vatican bureaucracy has survived popes in exile, inept and corrupt managers, intrigue of all sorts, and near bankruptcy. Reese offers balanced and insightful access to Vatican diplomacy, bureaucracy, and leadership.

    A quasi-government, the Vatican has a Secretary of State, posts a diplomatic ambassador with virtually every country on earth, and wields considerable power of moral persuasion. And, as Reese makes clear, it is not only Catholics who are affected by Vatican policies and politics. The Vatican and the pope play significant roles on the world stage. For example, when the pope visited Cuba in 1998, John

Paul II's speeches and Castro's concessions to Roman Catholics, had implications for U.S. policy.

A world cloaked in secrecy, governed by strong personalities, and deeply sectarian, the Vatican is a complex organization that represents all that is good and bad about Catholicism.

Electronic Resources

Fox, Thomas C. Fox, *Catholicism on the Web* (New York: MIS, 1997)

Catholicism has not been left behind in the electronic information explosion. As the editor of the *National Catholic Reporter*, Thomas Fox keeps abreast of information for, by, and about Catholics. Pope John Paul II's 1989 acknowledgment that "In the new 'computer culture' the Church can more readily inform the world of her beliefs and explain the reasons for her stance on any given issue or event" has not gone unheeded by ordinary Catholics, the Vatican, the bishops, and any number of Catholic groups. The proliferation of "Catholic" websites in the past five years is astounding. The difficulty is sorting out what is officially posted, and what is put on the web by well-meaning (and not so well-meaning) organizations and individuals. With no gatekeeper, Catholic websites offer a vast array of information, proselytization, agitation, and propaganda. These range from sites sponsored by the United States Catholic Conference, to sites posted and maintained by dioceses, parishes, organizations, and individuals. Not unlike other sites on the web, the quality of the sites and the reliability of the information they carry depends largely on the technical capabilities and the political agenda of the organization or individual who posts it.

Fox organizes the sites into four categories with subheadings: Catholic Organization (From the Vatican to Local Parish, Religious Orders, Organizations, People); Ideas (History, Teachings, Education, Communications, Information); Activism (Peace/Justice/Environment, Renewal, Pro-Life, Ministry, Information); and Transcendence (Scripture and Theology, Spirituality, Liturgy and Worship, Art and Meditation), and has an appendix with on-line directories. After a brief introduction to each category, he lists the site name and address followed by a short description of its content, some occasional technical critique (e.g., "complicated and difficult to follow") and an assessment of the merits or faults of the site.

Fox includes the 500 sites he found the "most interesting, or useful, or typical, or otherwise significant." Links to all the sites listed can be found at www/mispress.com/catholicism. Lest his list omit some important sites, this website invites readers to make suggestions for inclusion in future editions, which no doubt will be needed since the world of the web changes daily, with deletions, additions, and expansions occurring at the speed of e-mail.

History

Dolan, Jay P., *The American Catholic Experience: A History from Colonial Times to the Present* (Notre Dame, Ind.: Notre Dame University Press, 1992).

A readable, informative, and well-written social history of Catholics, this book details the development of the Catholic community in America from its colonial roots to the 1980s. Dolan chronicles the migration of immigrant communities from Europe to the New World, recounts these immigrant Catholic Communities' struggle to assimilate while creating a rich subculture—a subculture that eventually became a ghetto preventing them from advancing in the larger society.

McGreevy, John T. *Parish Boundaries: The Catholic Encounter with Race in the Twentieth-Century Urban North* (Chicago: University of Chicago Press, 1996)

A social history of the African-American Catholic population's move from the south to the north and the misunderstanding, intolerance, and bigotry they encountered from Catholics. McGreevy has done original historical research and presents it in a narrative that is compelling and informative. It is a story that has not been told before in such rich detail and careful scholarship.

Morris, Charles, *American Catholic: The Saints and Sinners Who Built America's Most Powerful Church* (New York: Times Books, 1997)

With informative and engaging narratives describing the personalities who built and dominated the institution, Morris traces the Irish roots of the American church. The author is quite candid in his assessment of bishops and cardinals who wielded power, sometimes flaunting their ability to influence the direction of the local and national church. Morris traces the development of Catholic culture in America, arguing that in its heyday in the 1950s it became the dominant cultural force in the country. The tentacles of the institutional church reached all aspects of American life including social, cultural, political, educational, and economic dimensions. Its dominance ended in the early 1960s and the American Catholic Church has been struggling with its identity and influence ever since that time. Written in accessible and engaging prose, this book is entertaining as well as informative. It includes extensive notes, the voices of some contemporary Catholics, and a number of black-and-white photos that depict key personalities, trends, and events.

Official Teachings

Catechism of the Catholic Church (New York: Doubleday, 1995). The original English translation for the United States of America, 1994, by the United States Catholic Conference

This *Catechism* is the official compendium of Catholic teaching approved by Pope John Paul II and issued by the Vatican. This is the first universal catechism issued by the church since the time of the Council of Trent (1547–1562). Its comprehensive scope addresses all aspects of belief, from essential doctrines to sacramental practice, morality, and spirituality. Its teachings apply equally to Catholics all over the world and thereby support the universality of the Roman Catholic Church.

Parish Life

Keller, Robert F., *Parish!: The Pulitzer-Winning Story of a Vibrant Catholic Community* (New York: Crossroad, 1997)

This is the book version of Robert Keeler's New York *Newsday* series chronicling the personalities and activities of St. Bridget's Parish in Westbury, Nassau County, New York. Keeler paints a complete picture of this parish's life—including the parish school, youth ministry, sacramental life, social outreach, and other dimensions—demonstrating how a vibrant community of faith functions internally. But St. Bridget's, as Keeler describes it, represents a particular type of parish: large (with over 23,000 members), active, and seemingly harmonious. The pastor gets along with the other priests, the staff, the deacons, and the volunteers, all of whom share a common vision of ministry and work to make it come true. The story lacks the tensions between competing ecclesiologies evident in other parish profiles such as Jim Naughton's *Catholics in Crisis*. However, it gives a complete picture of the variety of activities, personalities, and policies that make up parish life.

Naughton, Jim, *Catholics in Crisis: An American Parish Fights for Its Soul* (New York: Penguin, 1996)

This is the story of Holy Trinity Church, a Jesuit parish in the Georgetown neighborhood of Washington, D.C. Naughton, a journalist with *The Chronicle of Higher Education*, who at the time of the writing was a member of the parish, writes in a compelling manner about the struggles that the pastor, staff, parishioners, and prelates went through in the early 1990s. The story begins with what came to be known as "the standing." Inspired by his daughter, parishioner Ray McGovern quietly stands through the entire Sunday liturgy to protest the church's prohibition against women priests. The controversy affects the entire parish and attracts the attention of the cardinal archbishop of Washington, James Hickey, who investigates the matter and probes the parish to see how the local church is conducting itself. The pastor tries to reconcile the various factions that inevitably develop or deepen, but also has personal issues and questions to resolve.

"The standing" separates the parish into differing camps, disrupts the routine, and forces the people of Holy Trinity to confront charges of injustice within the policies of the larger Roman Catholic Church. The drama includes the voices of many parishioners drawn from public meetings, private conversations, and interviews by the author. It gives an intimate inside look at a parish that does not always follow the rubrics and laws of the church to the letter but attracts a large and loyal community, many of whom travel from other parishes or a neighboring diocese to worship with and/or join it. By one assessment the parish is a stellar success, integrating the young and the old, involving parishioners actively in the life of the church, providing inspiring and prayerful liturgies, educating children and adults with equal attention, ministering to outcasts and Washington insiders, balancing the rule of the institution and the needs of the community. By another assessment it is out of touch with (or deliberately indifferent to) hierarchical authority, renegade, going its own way and doing its own thing with a self-serving hubris that will surely lead to its downfall.

Public Policy

Burns, Gene, *The Frontiers of Catholicism: The Politics of Ideology in a Liberal World* (Berkeley: University of California Press, 1992)

This volume in the "New Directions in Cultural Analysis" series is a comprehensive and detailed study of American Catholicism's relationship to American culture on the one hand and to Rome's authority on the other. Burns, a sociologist, understands the nuanced differences between doctrine, practice, and politics. He explores their interrelations by investigating the change from an immigrant to an established community, Catholic social teaching, change and dissent by constituencies (for example, religious women) within the church, the bishops and the Vatican, the pluralism of the post-Vatican II church, and a comparison of the American church with the Latin American church. A thorough scholarly work, the book includes detailed footnotes and an extensive bibliography.

Byrnes, Timothy A., *Catholic Bishops in American Politics* (Princeton: Princeton University Press, 1991)

Byrnes, a political scientist, examines the political agenda of the American bishops, particularly from 1976 to 1988. After a brief history of the establishment of the American church, the author closely examines the bishops' attempts to influence public policy, particularly on moral issues such as abortion, nuclear war, and the economy. The book chronicles the establishment of the National Conference of Catholic Bishops (NCCB) and acknowledges differences among the bishops on a variety of issues but argues that the NCCB has given the bishops an unprecedented unified voice in American politics and social policy. The book includes an eight-page bibliography.

References Works

Catholic Almanac (Huntington, Ind.: Our Sunday Visitor, published yearly)

The *Catholic Almanac* is a one-volume compendium of information that includes news events for the previous year, encyclicals, statistics, biographies, special reports, and significant church events, to name some of the myriad content. It is a very handy and relatively inexpensive (about $23 for the paperback edition) reference book.

The Encyclopedia of American Catholic History, Michael Glazier and Thomas J. Shelley, editors (Collegeville, Minn.: Liturgical Press, 1997)

A single-volume work of over 1,500 pages, this thorough compilation of topics includes biographies of key figures in American Catholicism, locations, colleges and universities, states, organizations, movements, publications, religious orders, entertainers, and ethnic groups, to name some of the categories covered. The over 400 contributors include both well- and lesser-known scholars who provide bibliographical references with each entry to assist those who wish to pursue any topic further. Hundreds of black-and-white illustrations complement the 1,200 plus articles.

This book stands alone as the first of its kind. It is a useful resource for those who need a thumbnail sketch of almost any aspect of America Catholic history. In keeping with its historical character, living figures (for example, Theodore Hesburgh and Andrew Greeley) are excluded. Women, native and African Americans are accorded the coverage they deserve but have not always received in earlier historical works. Some entries are accompanied by "related documents," that is, important original texts to which the article refers. Informative charts and lists (often taken directly from other acknowledged sources) are also included. These include the necrology of American bishops, a state-by-state breakdown of Catholic populations, and religious orders and congregations of women. Each entry is followed by a brief bibliography.

The HarperCollins Encyclopedia of Catholicism, Richard McBrien, general editor
    (San Francisco: HarperCollins, 1995)

This one-volume compendium is the work of mostly University of Notre Dame scholars under the direction of Richard McBrien, a well-known theologian on the faculty of Notre Dame. Entries are thorough, readable, and of varying lengths. This is an excellent resource for individuals and libraries.

The Modern Catholic Encyclopedia, Monika Hellwig and Michael Glazier, Editors
    (Collegeville, Minn.: Liturgical Press, 1994)

A thorough compendium of Catholic thought, this single-volume encyclopedia includes over 1,300 cross-referenced entries and more than 200 black-and-white illustrations as well as 16 full-color pages of artistic depictions of Jesus. With entries by scholars from the United States and several other English-speaking countries, the work concentrates on contemporary concerns and figures. Compiled under the direction of publisher/scholar Michael Glazier, and Georgetown University theologian Monika Hellwig, the encyclopedia is a valuable resource for scholars, libraries, parishes, and individuals. Entries range in length from a few lines to a few pages, covering the major themes of Catholic thought.

Sociological Portrait

Davidson, James D. et al., *The Search for Common Ground: What Unites and Divides Catholic Americans* (Huntington, Ind.: Our Sunday Visitor, 1997)

Although there are numerous surveys of American Catholics, even sociologists admit that it is difficult to obtain a completely accurate picture of the American Catholic community. Scholars from universities in Indiana, led by Purdue University and funded by the Lilly Endowment, conducted extensive research in Indiana with the cooperation of the Indiana bishops as well as a national sample of American Catholics. In his introduction, sociologist Dean Hoge touts the book for its "reliable picture" in "nonideological terms." One of the important things the researchers discovered is that chronological distinctions separate Catholics by more than years, with younger post-Vatican II Catholics holding significantly different views about the church from pre-Vatican II and Vatican II era Catholics.

Theology

McBrien, Richard, *Catholicism* (San Francisco: Harper, 1994; new edition completely revised and updated)

One of the most complete single-authored compendiums of theology. McBrien, a theologian at the University of Notre Dame, exhibits a liberal bias, often commenting on where the church should be as well as where it stands theologically. This brings a realism to the text, giving the reader the sense that Catholic theology is ongoing and constantly in dialogue with lived expressions of the faith that influences the ways in which teachings find expression. Arranged in sections covering human existence, God, Jesus, the Church, and Christian life, this work exhibits a grasp of a broad range of knowledge including history, theology, and anthropology. Since its initial publication in 1980, it has become a standard reference work, revised after some criticism from the American bishops, who feared that uninformed readers would not be able to distinguish between the author's speculations and official church teaching.

Rausch, Thomas P., *Catholicism at the Dawn of the Third Millennium* (Collegeville, Minn.: Liturgical Press, 1996)

A thorough, careful, and judicious examination of traditions, beliefs, and practices that covers Catholicism in general, but by its examples and descriptions focuses on the American church. Rausch's treatment is generally even-handed and objective. His criticisms, suggestions, and objections are tempered with historical contextualization and loyalty to the church. The comprehensive work includes dogmatic and ethical teachings, spirituality, and challenges facing the church in the next century.

Weaver, Mary Jo and R. Scott Appleby, editors, *Being Right: Conservative Catholics in America* (Bloomington: Indiana University Press, 1995)

One volume of a series chronicling American Catholics, this work speaks from and about conservative Catholics, the so-called Catholic right. The book is a mixture of essays ranging from analysis of the Catholic right by scholars who are not in sympathy, to explanation, arguments, and advocacy by authors who often represent conservative groups as well as themselves. The dividing point for most of them is the interpretation given to the documents of the Second Vatican Council (1962–65), although a minority of ultra-conservatives reject this Council outright.

ELECTRONIC RESOURCES

Catechism of the Catholic Church

www.christusrex.org/www1/CDHN/ccc.html

Presents the first official catechism of the Catholic Church to be published in four hundred years. The catechism covers all the major teachings that the church holds.

Catholic Answers

www.catholic.com/-answers

Designed to attract converts and inform Catholics this website has tracts on Catholicism listed by topic.

Catholic Information Center

www.Catholic.net

Official teachings, news items, links to other Catholic sources. This site provides links to many popular and informative websites.

Catholic Internet Directory

www.catholic-church.org

Includes parish directories, Catholic media, bishops, religious orders, organizations, ecumenical resources, and a list of the most visited Catholic websites.

Catholic Internet Network

www.cin.org

Includes recent church news, frequently asked questions, list of bishops, catechetical tools, and more.

Catholic Online

www.catholic.org

Useful material and connections to other sites. The mission of Catholic Online is to serve as a center for the exchange of information for Catholics and all people of God to help them deepen their understanding of the Catholic faith.

National Conference of Catholic Bishops

www.nccbuscc.org

Official website of the American Bishops.

Papal Encyclicals Online

abbey.apana.org.au/OFFICIAL/PAPAL/-index.htm

Access to official papal documents.

Vatican Home Page

www.vatican.va

Official Vatican home page, including papal audiences in several languages and Vatican Information Service, daily news briefs.

INDEX

Killea, Lucy, 181, 311*n*21
King, Coretta, *74*
Kirkness, Michael, 9, 246
Kissling, Frances, 182
Knights of Columbus, 9, 69, 291; and
    abortion, 185
Know-Nothings, 68
Komonchak, Joseph, 96
Kos, Ralph, 117–18
Krol, John, 100
Kugler, Sharon, 122
Ku Klux Klan, 68
Küng, Hans, 108; *Infallibility?*, 140

Labor movement, Catholics and, 72
Laborem Exercens (On Human Work),
    114
La Dolce Vita (film), 226
Laity, Catholic, 198, 255; and abortion,
    179; canon law and, 214; and
    Catholic schools, 203; and church
    hierarchy, 42; and control of
    parishes, 61–62; and Eucharist,
    149; future influence, 272–73,
    275–78; and Latin mass, 91; loyal-
    ty to America, 68, 69; and parish
    administration, 30; participation in
    mass, 91–92; relationship with
    priests, 116–17; spirituality of,
    128–29, 172–73, 175; theology of,
    128; Vatican II and, 27–28, 90
Lamb, Matthew, 242
"Land O'Lakes Statement: The
    Nature of the Contemporary Uni-
    versity," 263
The Last Priests in America, Unsworth,
    123
Last Rites, 171–72
Last Supper. *See* Eucharist, 174
The Last Temptation of Christ (film),
    228
Latin Mass, 28–29, 90–91

Law, Bernard, 40, 182, 212, 242
Leadership: local, changes in, 272; in
    parish councils, 30; of pope, 2
Leadership Council for Women Reli-
    gious, 98–99, 100
Lead Us Not into Temptation, Berry,
    253
Legion of Decency, 223–26
Leo XIII, pope, 72, 291–92; and
    American church, 65–66; and eco-
    nomic issues, 114
Lex orandi, lex credendi, 147
Liberal Catholics, 30, 34, 36–37;
    Americanist controversy, 43; and
    church hierarchy, 42; and Com-
    mon Ground Project, 41; and
    racism, 82; theologians, 123; and
    Vatican II, 90; women's groups,
    119
"Life Is Worth Living," (TV show),
    229
"Life on the Rock" (TV show), 229
Lifestyle changes for religious orders,
    96–97
Light, symbolic, 13
Limbo, 159
Linkh, Richard, 60
Lipscomb, Oscar, 40
Literary criticism of biblical texts, 134
Literary tradition, Catholic, 235–36
Liturgical calendar, 326
Liturgy, 326: and church commitment,
    45; Eucharistic, 161–62; experi-
    mental, 29; Hispanic population
    and, 81; priestless, 249–51; Vatican
    II changes, 91; women and, 15–16
"Liturgy Renew" program, 276
Local church, Vatican and, 144
Local leadership, changes in, 272
Local nature of Catholicism, 32–33
Loisy, Alfred, 67
Lonergan, Bernard, 31

"On Combating Abortion and
Euthanasia," 184
On Common Ground, 193
Operation Rice Bowl, 216
Opus Dei, Walsh, 31
Opus Dei (organization), 35–36, 292,
326
Ordinary magisterium, 132
Ordination, 326: of priests, 167–68,
168
—of women, 101, 119–20, 305*n*14; and
ecumenism, 192; Protestants and,
191
Ordinatio Sacerdotalis (Priestly Ordi-
nation), 119
Oregon Death with Dignity Act, 190
Oriental Orthodox Church, 192
Original sin, 12, 145, 326
Origins (bishop's publication), 138, 222
Örsy, Ladislas, 213
Our Lady of Guadalupe, feast of,
13–15
"Our Lady's Prayer," 147–48
Our Mother of Africa Chapel, 86, *87*
Our Sunday Visitor (magazine), 222

Pacem in Terris (Peace on Earth), 114
Paintings, religious, 154
Papal authority, Protestants and, 191
Papal bulls, 308*n*11
Papal encyclicals, 132, 138; on American church, 65–66; on Bible, 133;
on bioethics, 259; on birth control,
106–8, 243–44, 293; on capital
punishment, 190; on economic
issues, 114; on ethics, 243; on modernism, 67; on non-Christians,
194; on religious liberty, 66; on
role of papacy, 41; on social justice, 72
Parallel communities, 124–25
Parish Boundaries, McGreevy, 65

Parish councils, 30, 298*n*27
Parishes, 16, 326; city, and population
shifts, 83–84; differences in,
29–33, 60–61; future changes, 272;
and marriage sacrament, 164;
priestless, 248–51, 318*n*13; racially
segregated, 64; and schools,
207–8; women as staff members,
122
Parish schools, 202–3
Parish Boundaries, McGreevy, 332
Parochial, 327
Pascendi Dominici Gregis (On the
Doctrine of the Modernists), 67
Paschal Candle, 327
Pastor, 327
Pastor Aeternus (Dogmatic Constitution on the Church), 139
*Pastoral Constitution on the Church in
the Modern World*, 111
Pastoral Letters, 132, 327; on abortion,
188; on antiwar movement, 106;
on education, 207; on environ-
mental issues, 185; on homosexu-
ality, 177; "Human Life in Our
Day," 108; on motion pictures,
231; on nuclear war, 293; on social
issues, 111–16, 291; on women in
the church, 118–19
Pastoral Plan for Pro-Life Activities,
183
Pastors, and church rules, 30
Patriarchy, Roman Catholic, 239;
Holy Orders and, 167; protest
against, 15
Patrick, Saint, 141, 154
Patriotism, of American Catholics, 68,
69, 114–15; postwar, 77
Paul, Saint, 131, 219, 327
Paulists, 67
Paul VI, pope, 114, 141, 150, 192, 213,
292, 327; and abortion, 187; and

Scorsese, Martin, *The Last Temptation of Christ*, 228

Scott, Judy Restak, 45–46

Scripture, 327; readings, 191

Seamless garment, defense of life as, 187–90

The Search for Common Ground, Davidson, 21, 22, 335–36

Second Council of Nicea (787), 194

Second marriages, 165

Second Vatican Council (Vatican II), 2–3, 5, 26, 86–95, *89*, 125–26, 138, 292, 327; American Catholics and, 272; backlash against, 29; and canon law, 213; and church attendance, 19; and confessions, 169–70; and ecclesiology, 198; and ecumenism, 191–92; and education, 198–99, 207; and Eucharist, 160; and generational differences, 19–20; and infallibility doctrine, 139–40; and Mary, 149, 150; and non-Christians, 193, 195; and social issues, 111; and view of priests, 116

A Secret World: Sexuality and the Search for Celibacy, Sipe, 253–54

Secular ecumenism, 192

Secularism, 238

Secularization of rituals, 266–67

Seed, Richard, 258

Segregation, 82; ethnic, 63; racial, 59, 64, 65

Selected reading, 329–37

Selective Catholics, 23

Self-selection of parishes, 32–33

Seminarians, number of, 256

Seminaries, 257–58

Separation of church and state, academic freedom and, 109

Separatist Catholics, 29

Sermons: by Protestants, 191; post-Vatican II, 87

Serra, Junípero, 49

Service, church and, 218

Service-oriented spirituality, 176

Seton, Saint Elizabeth Ann, 140–41

The Seven Storey Mountain, Merton, 75

Sexual ethics, 36–37, 128, 176–77, 242–45

Sexual misconduct of priests, 116–18; and decline in priesthood, 252–53

Shattered Faith, Shelia Rauch Kennedy, 165

Shea, Thomas, 156

Sheed and Ward books, 222

Sheen, Fulton J., 229

Sheen, Martin, 74, *106*, 288–89

Shelley, Thomas J., *The Encyclopedia of American Catholic History*, 334–35

Shiva, 154

Shrines, 154; instant, 156–57

Sigmund, Barbara, 282

Single-sex education, *209*

Sins, 328: forgiveness, by priests, 168–69; symbolic cleansing by baptism, 12

Sipe, Richard, *A Secret World: Sexuality and the Search for Celibacy*, 253–54

Sister Formation Conference, 101

Sisters, 295n2, 328

Sisters in Arms: Catholic Nuns Through Two Millennia, McNamara, 98

Sisters of Charity, 141

Sisters of Loretto, 58

Sisters of Mercy, 101–2

Sisters of the Blessed Sacrament, 65

Sisters of the Holy Family, 141

Skinner, James, *The Cross and the Cinema*, 224

Skylstad, William, 190, 245

Slaves, 54, 58–59, 64

Smith, Alfred Emanuel, 69, *70*, 292